Management for Professionals

The Springer series *Management for Professionals* comprises high-level business and management books for executives. The authors are experienced business professionals and renowned professors who combine scientific background, best practice, and entrepreneurial vision to provide powerful insights into how to achieve business excellence.

More information about this series at http://www.springer.com/series/10101

Karlheinz Zuerl

Effective Cost Cutting in Asia

Practical Modern Approach for Managers and Engineers in Industry to Achieve Profit Growth

Springer

Karlheinz Zuerl
German Technology and Engineering Cooperation (GTEC)
Schneckenlohe, Germany

ISSN 2192-8096 ISSN 2192-810X (electronic)
Management for Professionals
ISBN 978-3-030-82781-6 ISBN 978-3-030-82782-3 (eBook)
https://doi.org/10.1007/978-3-030-82782-3

This Springer imprint is published by the registered company Springer Nature Switzerland AG.
The registered company address is: Gewerbestrasse 11, 6330 Cham, Switzerland

Strategy, Communication, Calculation, Negotiation and Exercises

Preface

The e-book/book/audio-book here is a summary of my practical preparations and follow-up work for conferences, discussions, negotiations, and lectures during my assignments at various companies between 1983 and 2020, dealing with cost management in general. During my work in Asia, I used several supplier process evaluation methods, which I will introduce to you in detail, and I designed ECOCUT™—the Tool of Effective Cost-Cutting in Asia.

Currently, I work as an executive consultant and interim general manager, COO, or CEO at European automotive, electric motion, and industrial manufacturing companies. I am the person you need if you need working capital, profit, and EBITA growth by business development and cost-reduction activities at your plants in Asia.

To fulfill the requirements of European Headquarters in time, cost, and quality, I need to manage, train, and support your purchasing department to be able to gain profit for your company. To achieve excellent performance, my company GTEC created a lot of new ideas for successful purchasing, which I will introduce to you as well. However, the following is more important:

Every minute of your manager's work should focus on quality, timing, and costs. You are a professional, and you know what to do. First, prepare and create the prerequisites. In other words, you will select and set priorities so as to train and motivate your people accordingly. You need at least a full week with the selection process before you can proceed to anything else. For example, you will have the following considerations:

- Savings in business process cost reduction
- Build up a learning organization with supply-chain-related training and workshops
- Savings in relocations/increase localization content (if possible)
- Savings in purchasing of raw material
- Savings in logistics (bundling, transportation)
- Savings from pooling with your company plants or external partners

- Savings from contracts
- Savings in non-production material
- Cost control

Next step is your target setting. For example, define realistic targets to be met by the end of year 202× (starting year + 2 years):

- Fifteen-percent savings of negotiated items in China
- Twenty percent savings due to localization of parts and modules
- Thirty percent of orders and contracts to be reported, to prevent maverick buying by other departments

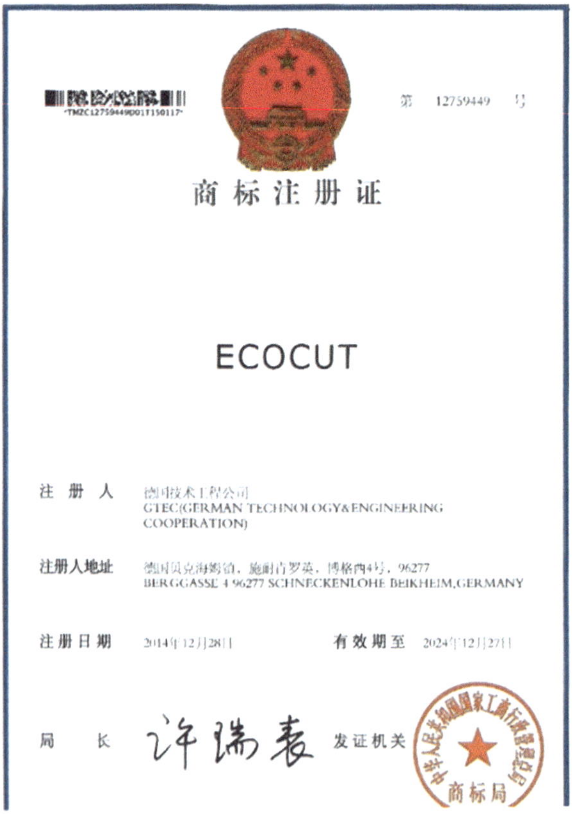

TMZC12759449D01T150117

第 12759449 号

商标注册证

ECOCUT

注册人 德国技术工程公司
GTEC(GERMAN TECHNOLOGY&ENGINEERING COOPERATION)

注册人地址 德国贝克海姆镇，施耐肯罗英，博格西4号，96277
BERGGASSE 4 96277 SCHNECKENLOHE BEIKHEIM,GERMANY

注册日期 2014年12月28日 有效期至 2024年12月27日

局长 许瑞表 发证机关 中华人民共和国国家工商行政管理总局商标局

Trademark ECOCUT. *Source*: GTEC, 2014

Please be patient. You should not overreact if the millions do not tumble, nor should you document every little aspect of your work and forward it to HQ. After all, too much reporting is a waste of time. Let the results speak for you.

Please refer to one of my trademarks, ECOCUT, the software tool for effective cost-cutting. I will describe it so you can see how the tool can support your business in Asia.

Schneckenlohe, Germany Karlheinz Zuerl

About This Book

The days of cheap raw materials and energy sources are gone. Our suppliers in Europe will demand price increases due to the rising costs of energy and materials. Is the relocation of your production facilities and purchasing sources to low-cost countries the alternative? How do you calculate the total costs so as to determine whether procurement in China will actually pay off? How do you determine a fair price for your purchased parts? How do you create transparency in the supply chain between sub-suppliers and OEMs in order to identify optimal costs and ensure performance?

The answer is that the managers and buyers of the companies must intervene in the price calculation of the suppliers in order to make the right decisions. Professional purchasing and supplier development increase the competitiveness of your company.

To ensure that your company stays competitive, purchasing staff need to have a CI (continuous improvement) mindset. It involves relentless evaluation, most important of which is interaction with suppliers so as to improve their processes. This assumes that all have skills to handle the challenges of purchasing.[1]

This book describes:

- How your purchasing department is able to gain (more) profit for your company?
- Excellent performance and new ideas for successful purchasing and supplier development.
- How to reduce costs in non-productive materials (NPMs)?
- How to calculate product and tool costs?
- How to negotiate your results with your suppliers in Asia?
- How to build an effective system of supplier relationship management?

Several templates with proper formulas will support your work to save working time and external consulting costs, as you do not need to invent the wheel twice.

---

[1] *Source*: https://www.industryweek.com/supply-chain/article/22025924/ask-the-expert-lean-leadership-what-are-good-metrics-to-measure-the-performance-of-the-purchasing-department, Author Larry Fast, from July 10, 2018, Access date 11.2.2021

Acknowledgments

I want to thank my dear family in Germany and China, particularly my beloved wife Zheng and my son Adrian, who have given me so much support as I worked to complete this book. Adrian, in fact, supported me in IT-related matters. With his skills and expertise, I have developed a deeper understanding of the outside world. Several proofreaders and editors, too, contributed a great deal to its eventual publication. I thank my proofreaders and editors for reading my texts and advising me professionally.

I thank my father, my sister, and my nieces. You were always there for me, particularly in the most difficult moments, to make sure I had enough time left to complete this book.

My thanks go to the following companies, Siemens, BMW, General Motors, Opel, Saab, Valeo, WEMA, ZF, Continental, Bosch, Schaeffler, and GTEC. Without them, my life would not have been what it is today. I cannot thank you enough.

Please forgive me if I have failed to mention any others. My heart goes out to all of you. Thank you.

Disclaimer

Names in this book, people, companies, and places are all fictitious. Similarities to the living or deceased persons, as well as Chinese or Germany company names, are all purely coincidental but not intended.

Shanghai, in the spring of 2022

Karlheinz Zuerl

Contents

1 GTEC Service, Consulting, and Training 1
1.1 GTEC Cost Management 1
1.2 Reporting 1
1.3 Manufacturing 2
1.4 Cost Calculations 3
1.5 Trainings and Workshops 3
1.6 GTEC Cost Calculation Service with ECOCUT™ 6
1.7 Introduction of Product Costing Tool ECOCUT™ 6
1.7.1 ECOCUT 6
1.7.2 ECOCUT Results for Product Costing 11
1.7.3 How to Define Cost Savings 11
1.7.4 Supplier Facilitation and Development 15
1.8 Profitable Company Restructuring by GTEC 17

2 The Purchasing Manager's Challenges in Asia 19
2.1 Psychology 19
2.1.1 How Do You Bring Buyers into a Comfort Zone Without Fear? 20
2.1.2 Why Does Psychology Play Such an Important Role in Purchasing? 20
2.2 Database 21
2.3 Teardown of Competitor Parts 22
2.4 Preparing to Deal with Buyers 23
2.5 Which KPIs Are Useful? 25
2.6 How to Quickly Eliminate Compliance Issues at PUR Departments? 27
2.7 Low-Hanging Fruit 27
2.8 Low-Hanging Fruits in Logistics 28
2.9 Low-Hanging Fruit in Production 31
2.9.1 How Exactly Do We Harvest These Low-Hanging Fruit? 32
2.9.2 What Do We Do When the Low-Hanging Fruit Is Gone? 34
2.9.3 Can DMAIC Help You? 34

2.10 Where Are the Low-Hanging Fruit of Nonproduction Areas? . . . 34
2.10.1 How Do We Obtain These Savings? 36
2.10.2 How Do We Run an NPM Project? 37
2.10.3 Lead Buyer Concept 37
2.10.4 How Do We Implement Pooling in Each Region? . . . 37
2.10.5 Time and Motion Study 38
2.10.6 Efficiency Review 39
2.10.7 Optimizing Labor Budgets 41
2.11 Kaizen 42
2.12 Example of How to Reduce NPM Costs in China 44
2.12.1 RMO (Repair, Maintenance, and Operations) 47
2.12.2 Energy 47
2.12.3 Professional Services 48
2.12.4 IT 51
2.12.5 Tools 51
2.12.6 Machines 51
2.12.7 Development Service, Test Equipment 52
2.12.8 Development Service, Engineering Material 52
2.12.9 Canteen Food for Lunch and Shift Workers 53
2.12.10 Consumables for Production and Supply 53
2.12.11 Office Supplies 53
2.12.12 Finance 54
2.12.13 Disposal Costs/Waste 54
2.12.14 Environment–Health–Safety: EHS 54
2.13 Lean Process Flow of Nonproduction Material 55
2.14 How Do Chinese Purchasing Managers and Buyers Think? 56
2.15 Are Exhibitions Able to Support Cost Reduction Activities? . . . 58
2.16 What Does Standardization Have to Do with Purchasing? 59
2.17 Is Teamwork Required to Harvest Low-Hanging Fruit? 59
2.18 News from China 60

3 Asian Supplier Productivity Diagnosis 63
3.1 The Toyota Production System TPS 63
3.2 Supplier Diagnosis 67
3.3 Supplier Process Evaluation in the Asia-Pacific 90
3.4 How Much Does a Product Really Cost? 98
3.4.1 Material Costs 98
3.4.2 Manufacturing Costs 100
3.4.3 Overhead (General Analysis) 102
3.5 Economic Analysis: Basic Understanding of Product Costing . . . 103
3.6 Economic Accounting: Basic Understanding of Accounting . . . 104
3.7 Why Is Benchmarking So Dangerous? 108
3.8 Is LPTA Working in Your Favor? 108
3.9 Do You See the Big Picture? 109
3.10 Transformation into a New Organizational Structure 112

3.11 How Do We Reduce Costs? 112
3.12 Cost Breakdown 114
3.13 Easy Supplier Evaluations 116
3.13.1 How Do You Calculate Profit and Overhead in the Cost Breakdown (CBD) Process? 118
3.13.2 What To Do When Overtime Is Needed to Finish Products on a Deadline? 118

4 Supplier Development in Asia in 5 Steps 119
4.1 Service, Consulting, and Training for Cost Reduction and Quality Improvement 119
4.1.1 Lean Management 119
4.1.2 Supplier Development Program in Asia for Professionals 128
4.2 Selecting the Proper Suppliers in Asia 129
4.3 Developing an Approved Supplier Base 130
4.4 How to Audit Suppliers 130
4.5 Measuring Supplier's KPIs 131
4.5.1 What Are the Key Performance Indicators (KPI) for SD Program? 132
4.5.2 How to Achieve Your KPI? 133
4.5.3 Records from Buyer and Supplier 135
4.5.4 EBEI Every Part Every Interval 138
4.5.5 Monthly Operation Costs 139
4.5.6 Fulfillment of Internal Project Agreement 140
4.5.7 Designing Supplier Development Programs 144
4.5.8 Kick-off Week 144
4.5.9 Information for Customers 145
4.5.10 Process and Subprocess Information 148
4.5.11 Raw Materials and Subsupplier's Information 151
4.5.12 Key Performance Indicators and Costs 151
4.5.13 Key Performance Indicators and Continuous Improvement Processes for the Shop Floor 155
4.5.14 Workshops and KPI Amendments 156
4.5.15 KPI Tracking 157
4.5.16 How Do You Create a Benefit Calculator? 157
4.5.17 How Is the Benefit Calculator Used? 162
4.5.18 How Do You Report Benefits? 164
4.6 Supplier Relationship Management (SRM) 164
4.6.1 Systematic Supplier Evaluation with SPECTRA 165
4.6.2 SPECTRA Is SRM and CRM 166
4.6.3 Goals and Tasks of SRM and CRM 167
4.6.4 The SRM/CRM Process and applications 168
4.6.5 SRM Challenges 169
4.6.6 Supplier Relationship Management Asia 170

5 The Purchasing Organization of the Future . . . 173
5.1 How Do You Become the Best Purchasing Department Ever? . . . 174
5.1.1 Sources of Error in Worldwide Shopping . . . 176
5.1.2 Determine the Right Key Figures . . . 176
5.1.3 Audit Your Purchasing Department with the Following Question List . . . 177
5.1.4 New Purchasing Strategies . . . 181
5.1.5 Examples of a Continuous Improvement Process Within the Company . . . 182
5.2 Best in Class in Purchasing . . . 183
5.2.1 What Makes Us a Best-in-Class Company? . . . 184
5.2.2 How Do I Lay the Foundations for Best-in-Class Shopping? . . . 187
5.2.3 Sourcing Strategies . . . 192
5.2.4 The Purchasing Process . . . 194
5.2.5 Do You Need a Supply Chain Manager? . . . 203
5.3 Checklist for Best-in-Class Buyers . . . 212
5.4 The Best Websites for Buyers . . . 214
5.4.1 Websites with Asian Products . . . 214
5.4.2 China . . . 215
5.4.3 Asia . . . 218
5.4.4 East Europe . . . 218
5.4.5 Global . . . 218
5.5 Useful Cost Reduction Tracking Templates . . . 219
5.6 Personnel Development Plan for Supply Chain Staff . . . 220
5.7 Introduction of Digitalization at Purchasing in Asia . . . 222

6 Cost Break Down and Cost Structure Analysis . . . 225
6.1 Overview Cost Calculation (detailed) . . . 226
6.1.1 Net Sales Price . . . 227
6.1.2 Material Costs . . . 227
6.1.3 Manufacturing Costs . . . 227
6.1.4 Manufacturing Step Costs . . . 228
6.1.5 Cost of the Working System . . . 229
6.2 Material Costs . . . 229
6.2.1 Raw Materials . . . 229
6.2.2 Scrap . . . 232
6.2.3 Purchasing of Raw Materials . . . 232
6.3 Asian Price Barometer Compared to the Previous Years . . . 244
6.3.1 Manufacturing Costs . . . 247
6.3.2 Cost of Working System . . . 248
6.3.3 Exercise MHR Calculation . . . 257
6.4 Improvements at Shopfloor and Toolshop . . . 259
6.4.1 How to Improve Total Productive Maintenance (TPM) and Overall Equipment Efficiency (OEE) at the Shop Floor? . . . 259

6.4.2 Toolshops Cost-Check in Low Cost Country: China . . . 261
6.4.3 Tooling and Fixtures . . . 265
6.4.4 Tooling Costs (Direct Payment) . . . 265
6.4.5 Die Casting and Plastic Injection Moulds . . . 266
6.5 Overhead Costs . . . 270
6.5.1 What About Material Overheads? . . . 270
6.5.2 Manufacturing Overheads MOHC? . . . 277
6.5.3 Selling, General and Administration Expenses SG&A . . . 283
6.5.4 Other Overheads . . . 286
6.5.5 Change Management . . . 286
6.5.6 Profit Margin . . . 287
6.5.7 Overheads and Profit . . . 288
6.6 Profit . . . 288
6.7 Terms of Payment . . . 289
6.8 Taxes . . . 290
6.9 Delivery Terms . . . 292
6.10 Warehouse and Inventory Costs . . . 294
6.11 How to Improve Warehouse Management KPIs of Suppliers . . . 294
6.11.1 Carrying Cost of Inventory . . . 295
6.11.2 Inventory Turnover . . . 295
6.11.3 Order Picking Accuracy . . . 295
6.11.4 Inventory to Sales Ratio . . . 295
6.11.5 Units Per Transaction UPI . . . 296
6.11.6 Rate of Return . . . 296
6.11.7 Inventory Accuracy . . . 296
6.11.8 Back Order Rate . . . 297
6.11.9 Perfect Order Rate . . . 297
6.12 Inhouse Transportation with Forklifts in China . . . 297
6.13 Benchmarking Transportation Costs China . . . 298
6.13.1 How to Calculate Savings by Benchmarking? . . . 299
6.13.2 Sea Freight China . . . 303
6.13.3 Railway Service China . . . 303
6.13.4 Parcel Express Service China . . . 305
6.13.5 Domestic Transportation . . . 305
6.13.6 Distributors or Direct Purchasing From Manufacturers? . . . 307
6.13.7 Why Not Ask Your Operators at Your Chinese Warehouse? . . . 307
6.14 How to Build Databases . . . 309
6.14.1 The Personnel-Cost Database . . . 309
6.14.2 The Material Database . . . 311
6.14.3 The Machine Database . . . 312

6.14.4 The Process Database . . . 313
6.14.5 The Tool Database . . . 316
6.14.6 ECOCUT Databases . . . 316

7 Negotiations with Asian Suppliers . . . 317
7.1 Productive Negotiation Between the Buyer and the Supplier . . . 320
7.2 Strategies in Negotiation . . . 320
7.2.1 Project Management with a Systematic Approach . . . 320
7.2.2 Stage 1 Out of 5: Analysis with a Benchmark Calculation . . . 320
7.2.3 Quality Gate 1 . . . 321
7.2.4 Stage 2: Process Validation . . . 323
7.2.5 Stage 3: Benchmarking Market . . . 323
7.2.6 Quality Gate 2 . . . 324
7.2.7 Stage 4: Discussion and Negotiation . . . 325
7.2.8 Stage 5: Realization of Potentials . . . 327
7.3 Handling Difficult Situations . . . 328
7.3.1 Important Behavior Principles . . . 328
7.3.2 Emotions, Mistrust, and Fears Regarding ECOCUT . . . 329
7.3.3 Killer Arguments Against ECOCUT . . . 329
7.3.4 False Cooperation on the Part of the Supplier . . . 330
7.3.5 Categorical Rejection of ECOCUT . . . 330
7.3.6 Discussions in Difficult Situations . . . 330
7.4 Win-Win Negotiation . . . 331
7.4.1 Goals and Basic Principles . . . 331
7.4.2 Negotiation Strategies and Countermeasures . . . 332
7.4.3 Good Guy/Bad Guy Characteristics . . . 332
7.4.4 Insufficient Rights Characteristics . . . 332
7.4.5 Ultimatum/Final Deadline Characteristic . . . 333
7.4.6 Piecemeal Encroachment Characteristic . . . 333
7.4.7 Make a Deceptive Show of Strength/Bravado Characteristic . . . 333
7.4.8 "Showing a Tendency to Be Conciliatory" Characteristic . . . 334
7.4.9 "Look One Way and Row Another" Characteristic . . . 334
7.4.10 A Characteristic of Cherry Picking . . . 334
7.5 Negotiating in Critical Situations . . . 335
7.5.1 Dealing with Objections . . . 336
7.5.2 The Model for Dealing with Objections . . . 337
7.6 Dealing with New Projects . . . 338
7.6.1 New Project Concept for ECOCUT Discussion in AP . . . 338
7.6.2 New Approaches . . . 339
7.6.3 EU Versus AP . . . 339
7.7 General Approach to Yearly Negotiations . . . 340

7.8 36 Stratagems for Negotiation 341
7.8.1 Winning Stratagems 1–6 341
7.8.2 Enemy Dealing Stratagems 7–12 343
7.8.3 Attacking Stratagems 13–18 345
7.8.4 Chaos Stratagems 19–24 348
7.8.5 Proximate Stratagems 25–30 350
7.8.6 Desperate Stratagems 31–36 353

8 Cultural Diversity in Asia-Pacific 357
8.1 Common Attributes in Asia-Pacific 357
8.2 Negotiation Tips for Main Countries in AP 359
8.2.1 China 359
8.2.2 India 363
8.2.3 Japan 364
8.2.4 South Korea 365
8.2.5 Vietnam 367
8.2.6 Malaysia and Singapore 368
8.2.7 Indonesia 369

Glossary 371

Index 375

About the Author

Karlheinz Zuerl A native of Germany, Karlheinz has been a manager in various international projects, with well-known original manufacturers in Europe, America, and Asia. Mr. Zuerl's professional expertise in Japan, Korea, China, Malaysia, Vietnam, and India and his blending with the Asian business culture and the Chinese perception of life have enhanced his overall perspective. Since 2005, Karlheinz has worked as a Purchasing Director and General Manager in Asia, where he gained tremendous experience and thorough knowledge in regard to cost-reduction activities, strategy, business development and operation, blended with Asian business culture. Since 1999, Karlheinz has delivered numerous lectures and successfully published books, audio books, and e-books in German and English.

For more than 20 years, he has worked as an advisor, coach, and supporter of companies in quality assurance, purchasing, and business negotiations in Asia, mainly in the automotive, mechanical engineering, electrical and electronics, and electrification business sectors. His focus is to increase profit and quality with his team from Sales and BD, MFG, TPS, QM, TPM, SC, HR, FIN, and IT and ENG.

Mr. Zuerl holds master's degrees in mechanical and industrial engineering. He has more than 34 years of international working experience in sales, restructuring, industry process engineering, and manufacturing, e.g., BMW, General Motors, Valeo, Bosch, Schaeffler, Zapi, RVT, and ABP. He has worked at companies large and small, and consequently, he understands the methods used to ramp up and develop a business.

He is the person to talk to if you have challenges in business development, change processes and methods, setting up of priorities for team skills, EBITDA, turnover, cost, timing, quality, or/and working atmosphere, and you do not know how to fix it in a short time.

Therefore, all his books and e-books are practical and useful experience for all people, who like to deal with culture, communication, technique, strategies, engineering, management, etc.

He has been living in China since 2005 and, as general manager, has headed various production plants and sales units for European companies since 2013. He is the founder of German Technology & Engineering Cooperation (GTEC) and of the GTEC Profit Growth Academy. He also holds his own trademarks in China with ECOCUT (effective cost-cutting) and SPECTRA (supplier process evaluation and cost transparency).

Contact the author via E-mail: contact@gtec.asia

GTEC Service, Consulting, and Training 1

Following, we split up our service, consultancy, and training activities for our clients. We shall explain how we work and what kinds of tools we use.

1.1 GTEC Cost Management

Your company needs cost management in your supply chain department to calculate and to reduce total costs of purchased parts from your suppliers. Negotiation with suppliers will fail to get the best price, if your purchasing staff does not know the true prime costs.

Or your enterprise needs to calculate sales prices to send offer to your existing and potential customers. Only if you know your true internal costs, you know your bottom line for negotiations of your sales staff with customers to avoid losses.

Due to our comprehensive experience in sales, purchasing, logistics, and general management, our company is able to help you to find the true cost and support you in negotiations with customers and suppliers.

Because of the lack of manpower and knowledge along with other reasons, either you need our service to find the true costs or we will calculate them for you. Or we train your staff to do the work by yourself. Additionally, we can consult you in preparation and negotiation with your international clients and vendors. Our GTEC professionals speak Chinese, English, and German.

1.2 Reporting

Do you as our customer like to have a report to show results of our cost calculations?

Creating a calculation helps customers to understand the interconnected relationships between cost parameters that result in the part price. Analyses are required to effectively achieve cost optimization objectives. From the broad range

K. Zuerl, *Effective Cost Cutting in Asia*, Management for Professionals,
https://doi.org/10.1007/978-3-030-82782-3_1

of reports available, we offer a "Result Report," which is a summary of all of the cost parameters and is an excellent basis for negotiations and similar tasks.

Currencies: ECOCUT© supports the major currencies of the world. Different currency modes can be selected.

1.3 Manufacturing

The cycle time is usually a very sensitive operation. This is why various cycle time calculators can calculate these values themselves on the basis of physical dimensions. The geometric properties of cast and injection molding parts enable us to calculate the machine dimensions (clamping force). The cycle time is then influenced considerably by the solidification time. The cycle time calculators query all of the dimensions that are relevant to and later indicate the cycle time. Machined parts (turning/milling parts) require the most extensive knowledge. Here, they refer to the work sequences are listed step by step and analyzed with processing times due to our experience and knowledge.

We are currently using the following *cycle time calculators* for our cost calculations:

- Die casting
- Plastic injection molding
- Lathing/turning
- Milling
- Assembly
- Stamping

The knowledge domain provides access via the explorer to manufacture steps that have already been calculated and have yielded robust results and allows them to copy these steps. In the process, we can copy entire manufacturing steps and their components and embed them into the calculation to be created.

In the knowledge domain, standardized manufacturing processes are predefined by the users and created as independent modules. The more consistently a knowledge domain is constructed and maintained by us, the faster calculations can be created in the future: and the higher the qualitative value of those calculations.

External (supplier) and internal manufacturing process know-how is stored in the ECOCUT© knowledge domain.

If we switch to the "Manufacturing Details" window, ECOCUT© queries all of the cost-related components within one single manufacturing step.

- Output quantity
- Machine hourly rate
- Setup costs
- Direct labor costs
- Tool costs
- Residual manufacturing overhead cost surcharge

1.4 Cost Calculations

How our calculations performed? The part, assembly, and even the system prices are derived from the three cost pools:

1. Material costs: raw material, subparts, consumables, material overhead costs (MOC).
   We offer a selection of specific material cost calculators that address the unique technical specifications of the various manufacturing processes.
2. Manufacturing costs: production system, setup costs, direct labor, tools, residual manufacturing overhead costs (RMOC).
   The "Manufacturing" spreadsheet initiates all of the manufacturing steps and displays them graphically in an arrow diagram. At the same time, this information is also listed in tabular form directly below the graphical representation and presented with three different "manufacturing arrows" (Fig. 1.1).
3. Overheads: overheads on production costs, profit, payment terms, delivery terms.

1.5 Trainings and Workshops

To train your own purchasing engineers and your suppliers' staff, the following five steps can be recommended (Source: Robert Bosch GmbH):

Step 1: Basics of Cost Structure Analysis

Content Economical basics, use cases of cost structure analysis, basic understanding of cost calculation, common calculation of examples with ECOCUT.

Step 2: Part Calculations with "ECOCUT"

Content Target cost calculations for requested parts by using ECOCUT, verification of parameters and calculations, definition of further steps to realize calculated potential, preparation of supplier cost structure discussion.

Step 3: Supplier Cost Structure Discussions for Beginners

Content Preparation of discussion, behaviors at discussion, specific negotiation training based on ECOCUT.

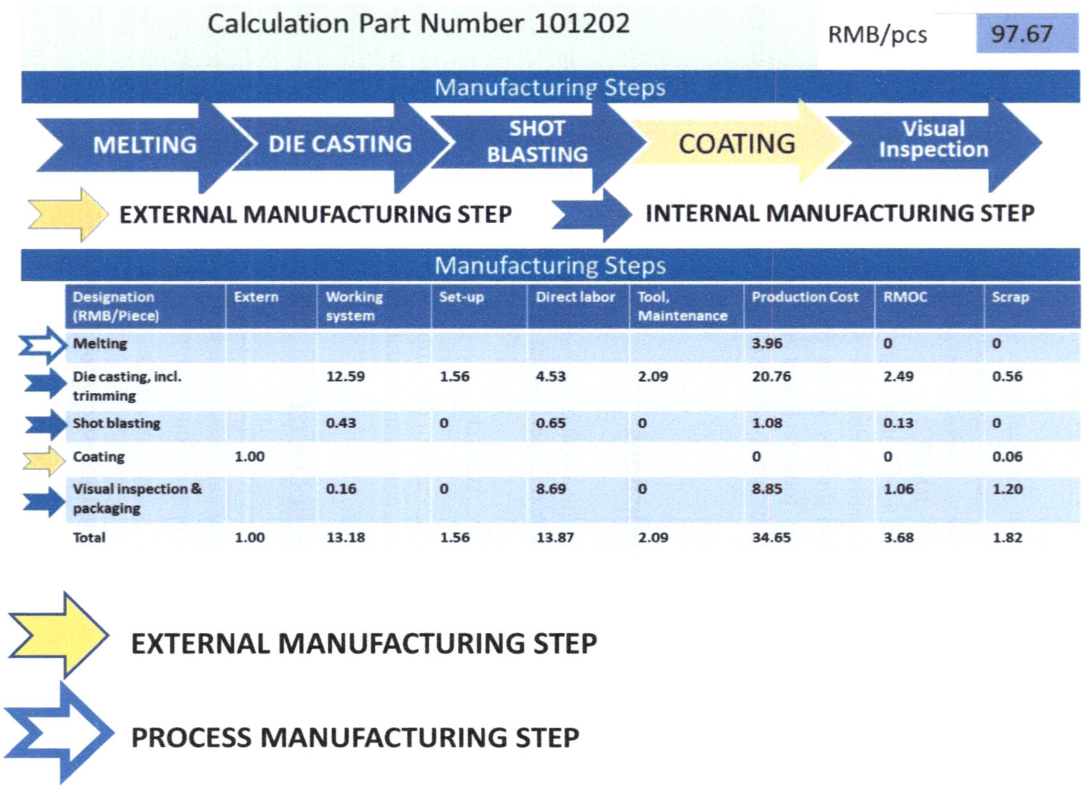

Designation (RMB/Piece)	Extern	Working system	Set-up	Direct labor	Tool, Maintenance	Production Cost	RMOC	Scrap
Melting						3.96	0	0
Die casting, incl. trimming		12.59	1.56	4.53	2.09	20.76	2.49	0.56
Shot blasting		0.43	0	0.65	0	1.08	0.13	0
Coating	1.00					0	0	0.06
Visual inspection & packaging		0.16	0	8.69	0	8.85	1.06	1.20
Total	1.00	13.18	1.56	13.87	2.09	34.65	3.68	1.82

Fig. 1.1 Cost calculation templates of ECOCUT©. Source: Perfect ProCalc, a software and trademark of Perfect Costing Solutions GmbH, which was sold to Siemens in 2012 and named Product Costing

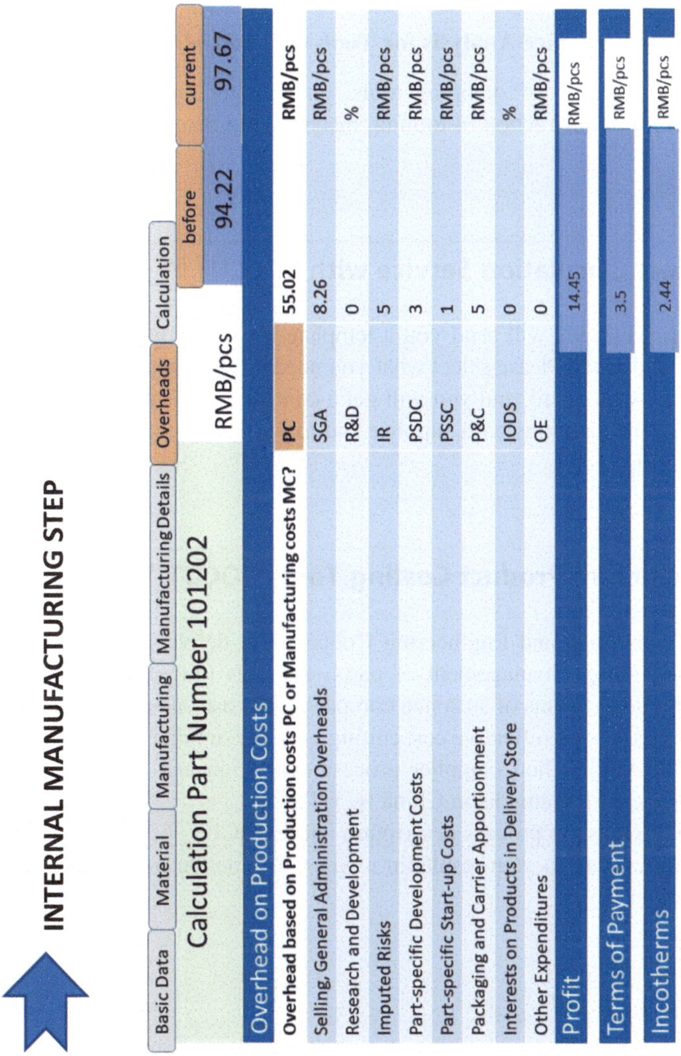

Fig. 1.1 (continued)

Step 4: Train the Trainer: Basics of Cost Structure Analysis

Content Fundamental understanding of standardized Step 1 content, qualification for an independent execution of training Step 1, common calculation of examples with ECOCUT.

Step 5 Basics of Cost Structure Analysis for Tools (Die and Molds)

Content Technical function of stamping tools, plastic injection tools, and die casting tools, construction of tooling, material, and manufacturing costs.

1.6 GTEC Cost Calculation Service with ECOCUT™

According to our process, we will send you a template for your RFQ (request for quotation) of parts and tools. Please select what you need, fill in completely, send it back to our company with email, and you will get a contract proposal and offer for cost calculations and negotiations with supplier and toolmaker, including payment and delivery terms (Fig. 1.2).

1.7 Introduction of Product Costing Tool ECOCUT™

GTEC (German Technology and Engineering Cooperation) delivers service, consulting, and training in cost management of parts and tools (die and molds) for purchasing and sales departments of an Asian company. For cost calculation, we use our own ECOCUT™ software (effective cost cutting), and for supplier development, we use the SPECTRA™ method (supplier process evaluation and cost transparency). Both are registered trademarks in China by GTEC.

However, SPECTRA is the process description and ECOCUT the software tool for product and tool costing to gain results in a win-win situation for all involved parties and stakeholders.

1.7.1 ECOCUT

The process evaluation and cost structure analysis tool ECOCUT™ ("Effective Cost Cutting") evaluates the purchase price of purchased parts and the company's own costs and analyses the cost structure of products, processes, and companies on the basis of recipes, comprehensible for everyone and applicable and transferable to company-specific topics. This analysis results in the following advantages for your company:

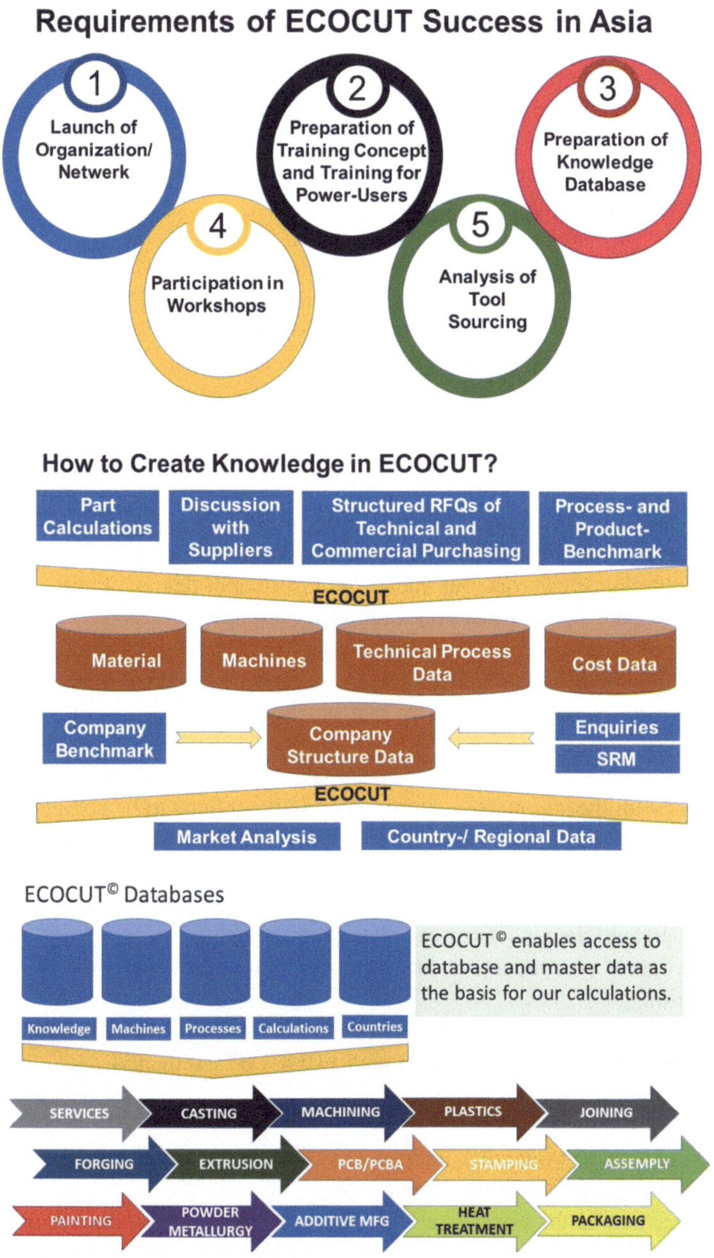

Fig. 1.2 Requirements of ECOCUT *success in* China/Asia: Specific Databases. Source: Perfect Costing Solutions GmbH, Robert Bosch GmbH, 2012

- Price negotiations with customers and suppliers become transparent and thus more emotion-free.
- A faster negotiation result with a win-win situation is possible.
- No one feels pulled over the table when FDF (figures, data, facts) are available.

This process evaluation and cost structure analysis provides you with the answers to the following questions, among others:

- What is the appropriate price for the purchased items? At what price will I be taken for a ride as a buyer and pay far more than I have to?
- What costs does the supplier have, what costs do the subcontractors incur?
- At what price does the supplier pay? If the supplier intentionally does not make a profit to get the order, does he then come later with additional demands or would like to cancel the contract as soon as possible?

Only by the consideration of the total costs of ownership, alternatives can be evaluated in the procurement. Often one finds out that, e.g., a production in China is not worthwhile, and the domestic manufacturer is still the cheapest. This is mostly not due to the logistics costs, but due to the insufficient degree of automation with cheap, uncompetitive machines and their high cycle times.

The use of a tool for cost structure analysis requires experience on the part of employees and management. External consultants learn about the companies in which to "fish" so that the software can be used independently after just a few months.

If you as a buyer have calculated low costs and thereby achieved favorable price agreements with the suppliers, your company will continue to be competitive.

In order to carry out these calculations, you need important prerequisites:

- Knowledge of the manufacturing processes required to manufacture the products and understand the associated calculation structure.
- Knowledge of comparative values of costs with several suppliers or with own production.

The following tasks can be solved with ECOCUT™ (effective cost cutting) and actions can then be taken:

- Determination of your own internal cost structures and cost drivers to derive targeted improvement measures from them;
- Determination of the buyer's internal cost structure for a product in order to be prepared for price negotiations with the customer and to have argumentation aids;
- Benchmarking with reference and competitor products to determine the target costs of your product; and
- Determination of the supplier's cost structures, if necessary, with targeted development measures to reduce costs.

This effective cost cutting method provides the detailing of costs and realizes the financial goals of your company and its SC department.

There are six steps to go through at your company:

1. Create and distribute basic information as foundation of success, e.g., determines how to create a report of cost savings for presentation to HQ.
2. Teach your project and series buyers (SQEs) how to implement SD and how to analyze and calculate the total cost of each product.
3. Create workshops to analyze cost structure of your products to find target costs and true costs.
4. Build a database for manpower costs in your suppliers' region with respect to machines, manufacturing processes, raw material costs and overhead costs, and commodities.
5. Negotiate the results of your workshops with suppliers and convince them to give you a better price and a commitment to work together to even lower prices.
6. Establish supplier development at supplier sites in order to avoid supplier changes and/or bankruptcies.

Discussions with suppliers require that you know and evaluate the manufacturing process at any given supplier. Thus, you need to know the cost and complexity drivers, the technological and qualitative risks. Only then can you formulate the requirements for your supplier and for the purchased part, which ultimately leads to a required target price.

It is no longer sufficient simply to want to set the price from the buyer's position. Political prices or the supplier's mixed calculation prices for the receipt of an order must be recognized. Otherwise, your enterprise will risk serious financial damage, which can be far greater than the alleged favorable savings.

Usually, competencies are missing from the purchase. The specialists usually sit in other departments. The purchasing team must be developed and correctly set up for these future tasks. A buyer determines a high proportion of a company's turnover. This includes at least the A and B parts and technologies, which need to be negotiated with the suppliers at the same level of knowledge in costs and technology.

They must be able to disclose and improve their cost situation. Until your company is ready, be it through training or personnel purchasing, you need to gather cross-departmental teams in order to bundle your company's purchasing know-how.

If the costing structure of the purchased parts can be evaluated, then you can also develop and implement your own procurement market strategies. For this, you need material and process costs of your target procurement markets and A parts. For example, when purchasing welded material, the hourly rates of the welders and the costs of the weld seam/meter and the material must be known in order to estimate the process costs in different countries (procurement markets).

Certain qualities of the material are not necessarily available in every country. The amount of raw material purchased is also a factor. So, the buyer must answer the following questions:

- Does the supplier use the right semi-finished product?
- How much waste does the supplier produce?
- How did the supplier design his tool?
- How high are the logistics costs for internal material transport or for transport to the processing plant?
- How high is the overhead of the company, and how high are the overhead costs?
- Is my company still competitive with the allowed profit margin?

Purchasing now has a tool at its fingertips to put forward real, cost-oriented arguments. The best solution is a database in which all calculations are stored. If every buyer uses this database as a daily tool, it cannot happen that the same products are procured at different conditions.

But first you should examine your procurement portfolio and distribute it in such a way that product groups can be defined and consolidated.

Proceed as follows:

- Define reference parts from the A supplier's delivery program to be used for negotiations with the suppliers. Generally, only the purchase price and the function are known, and the manufacturing process and their cost structure are unknown.
- Disassemble (tear down) your parts, measure, and weigh them.
- Get access to the corresponding drawings and production control plans.
- Determine your target cost level by using ECOCUT™ cost structure analysis.
- Plan a negotiation strategy with your supplier.
- Make an appointment for a visit with the request to view the production of your vendor.
- Check your calculation data in the team from sales, purchasing, development, production, and control.
- Make an appointment with your supplier to negotiate the purchase price and to question improvement measures in material, process, and design. Usually, the "risky" designs are the cost drivers. What should be changed so that production will be less expensive?

How do you successfully ward off the supplier's demands for price increases? Supplier management is one of the most important tasks in a company.

Question the cost bases for machine hour rates and surcharge rates. In most cases, these are no longer up to date. Is the supplier right with his claim? Does he have arguments for increases in material costs, process costs, and surcharge rates? What about logistics services and technology leadership?

Only those who know the cost structures and cost drivers will be successful in purchasing and supplier development.[1]

[1] Source: "Einkaufsmanager"/August and September 2005, www.Pleyma.de, Mr. Jan Scholl, Pleyma GmbH.

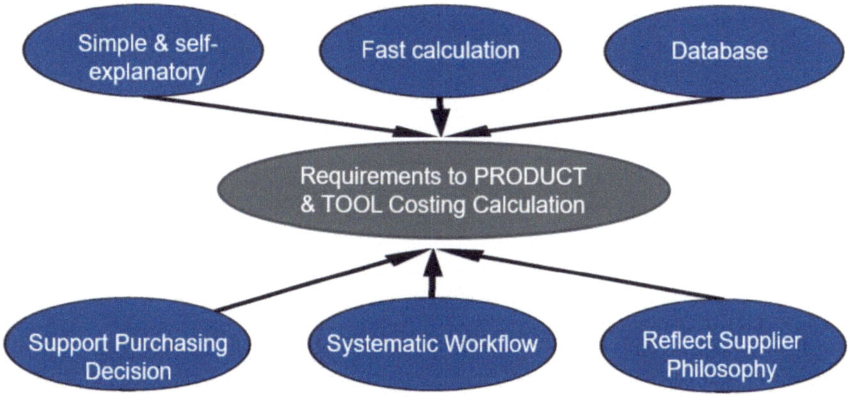

Fig. 1.3 Requirements to product and tool costing calculation. Source: Adapted from Master Thesis of Rolf Meyer, page 57, 24.10.2002 at University of Applied Science Offenburg

1.7.2 ECOCUT Results for Product Costing

Following picture, you see requirements to a product and tool costing calculation tool (Fig. 1.3).

In the following diagrams, you will see a summary report of ECOCUT. There is also an example of how to break down the calculation of a part (e.g., a bracket) for presentations to negotiators and decision makers (Figs. 1.4 and 1.5).

What can be done with products, the same principle will be seen with tool cost calculations at Sect.6.4.2–6.4.5.

1.7.3 How to Define Cost Savings

Following there are several examples, using EURO and Chinese RMB for explanation, how you could define cost savings:

1. Volume is multiplied with lowest piece price. The price negotiation is done, but a saving has not been achieved. The old supplier contract had a cost of RMB 0.08 a piece, and a new 1-year contract with a new supplier with a cost of RMB 0.03 a piece, and reporting of 0.05 RMB savings/piece.
2. Old piece price 77.51*47,4654 (expected life time pieces): new 64.57*474,654 = 6.142 Mio RMB savings = EUR 778,457 (assuming the exchange rate of 7.89). For a maximum of 36 months, cost calculation period = 21,624 Euro/month.
3. Negotiation is done by the operation department due to price verification and reducing content/configuration, and the purchasing department PUR is involved. Old machine price RMB 1,388,000 and new price RMB 500,000, just prove by signed contracts and documents. PUR reports savings of 888,000 RMB.

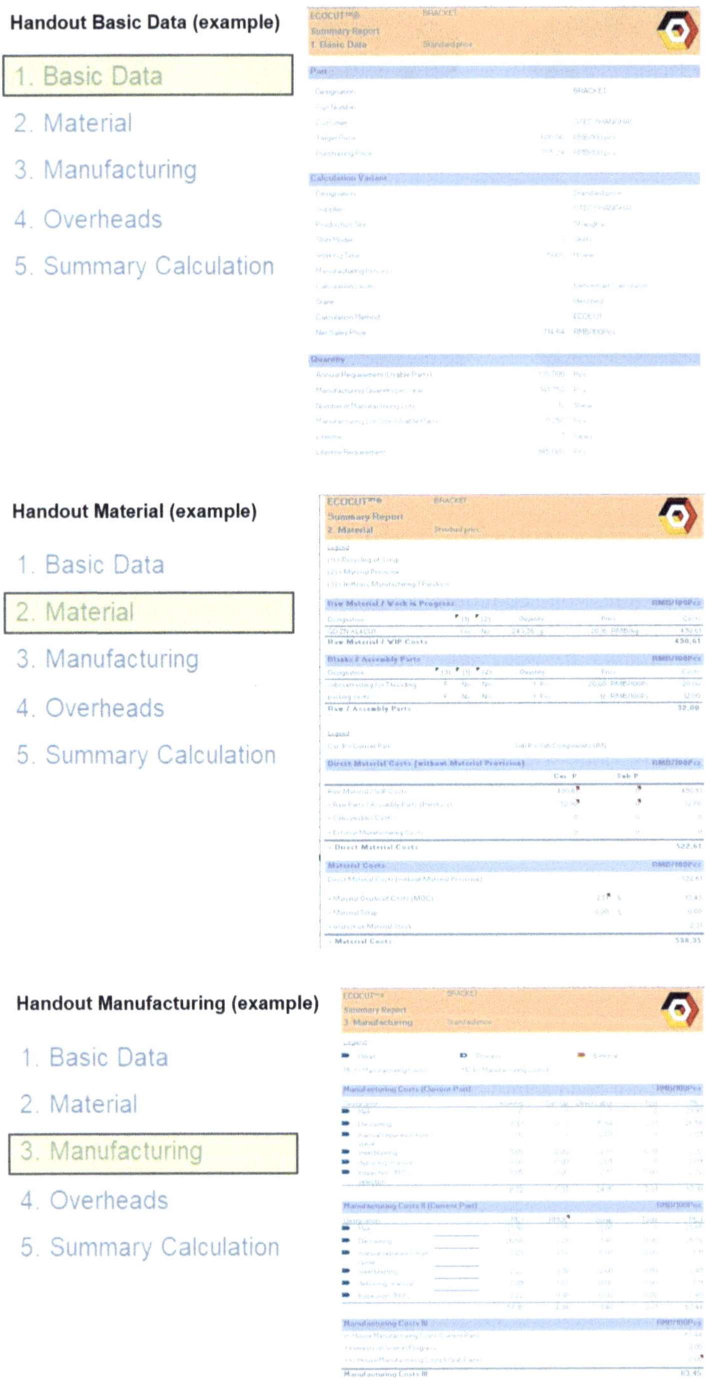

Fig. 1.4 Product costing report for a bracket in five steps. Source: Perfect ProCalc, a software and trademark of Perfect Costing Solutions GmbH, which was sold to Siemens in 2012 and since then named "Product Costing"

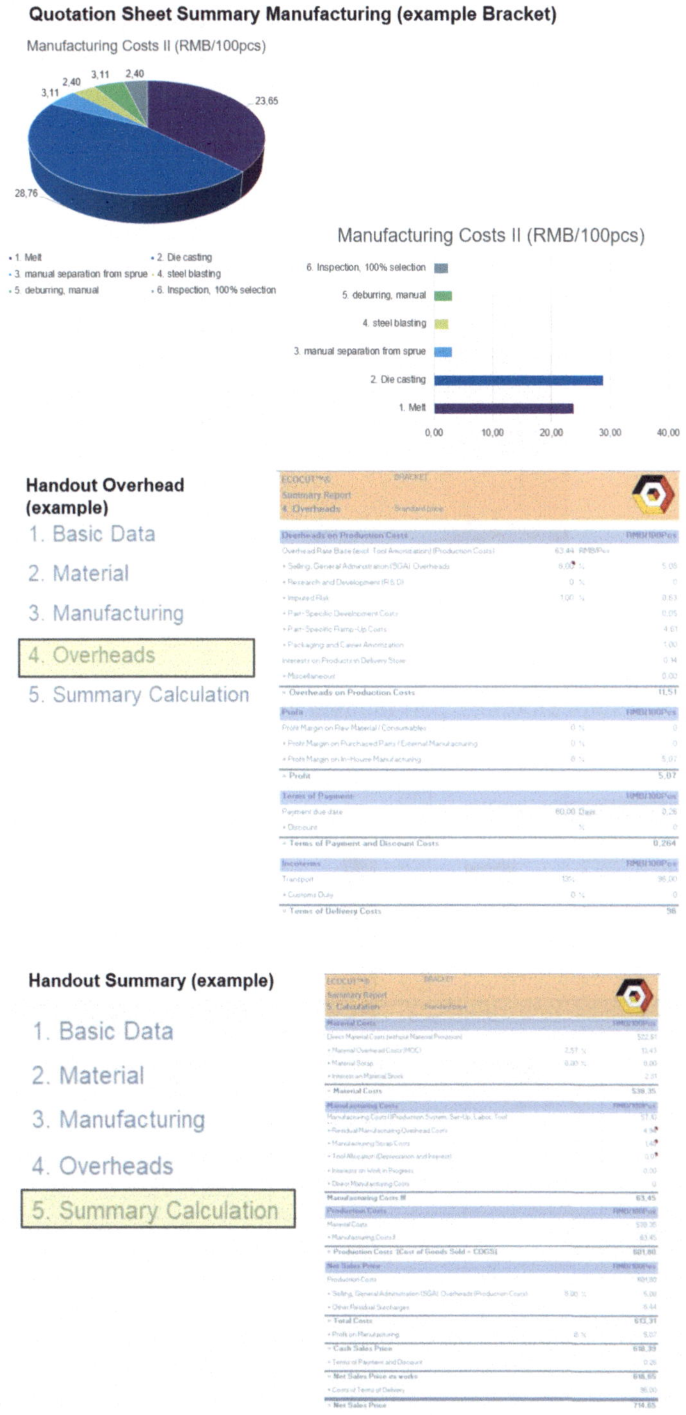

Fig. 1.4 (continued)

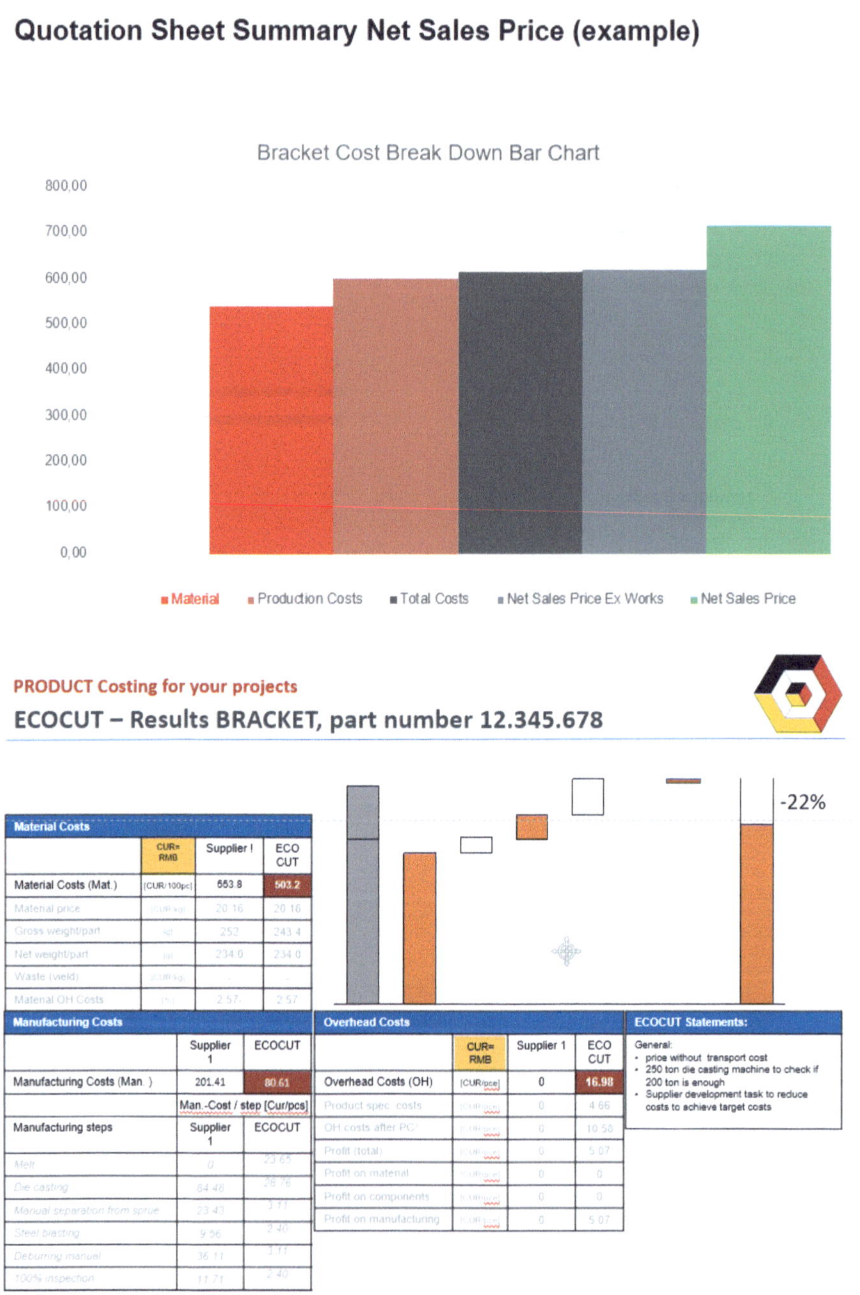

Fig. 1.5 Product costing report for a bracket of ECOCUT vs supplier info. Source: Schaeffler Holding (China) Co., Ltd.—Shanghai, 2013

4. The supplier price of EUR 129,400 was the lowest among three offers. Savings are calculated based on the final offer against the first offer. Negotiations and cost reduction calculation should be done with the same supplier. As in this case, as there is no further price negotiation, there are no savings.
5. Buyers reporting all purchased items running through their hands. This means that some parts have savings but others do not. Calculation result in each buyer monthly saving list could be zero saving. A price increase means a "minus."
6. You need to continue with these listings to show trends in reduction in maverick buying, which is part of your KPI. If you were to consider only financial data, we could not prove what percentage of the purchased items ran through the purchasing department.

1.7.4 Supplier Facilitation and Development

Is supplier development the overall solution to reduce purchasing costs and shorten delivery time while enhancing quality?

For all related plants, I propose you need to roll out the following process:

- Expand Supplier Quality Engineering SQE function with Supplier Development (SD) function.
- Ask suppliers which ideas do they have to reduce costs of our products.
- Discuss these ideas openly with the supplier and write a meeting minute.
- Introduce idea by idea at your company for decision making (investment, benefit sharing between supplier and plant).
- If necessary, introduce idea by idea to customers for decision making (investment, benefit sharing between your plant and your customers).
- If necessary, invite suppliers to present and discuss their ideas with the decision makers.
- Follow up on the processes or modify them for dealing with cost savings.

I am sure, this is not new. How should one proceed? How to roll out a lean process for cost savings?

There are some pitfalls in trainings and workshops, either on supplier or on your plant site.

It seems like a very good way to increase common efficiency. However, to discuss how to carry out this training program you should define a way to fit this strategy to all other locations as well:

- Centralize the skill requirements for all plants.
- Make organizational changes to bring SQE and SD under one roof.
- Get budget approval in advance for special in-house or outside trainings.
- No training certificate is available in Asia. Otherwise, staff will be trained only for their next career step outside your company.

- Identify the individuals and groups that must be trained. Otherwise, you will waste time that could otherwise be productive.
- The training of auditing suppliers should be organized in commodities if your personnel need to focus on technologies or organized by suppliers if several people will deal with them.
- To get support by whole company, and to use this knowledge-based training efficiently, other parties must support R&D, for example, to approve changes or other design concepts.
- To simplify procedure to implement this strategy, you should also consider priorities by defining a timeline with which commodity/material groups and with which suppliers you want to start to get highest effort right at the beginning.
- Unfortunately to train only "SQEs" to frequently visit suppliers: Due to lack of technical background on this level, the technical maturity level is not as high to discuss or find cost improvements.
- You need to set up first targets and structural visions and afterward to convince and to motivate your teams.

It is then necessary to define the current situation in regard to your plants. For example, it could look like following:

- No training plan for PUR staff is available.
- Target cost calculation and cost structure analysis is asked from the product costing department, and no own knowledge in cost structure analysis at PUR is available.
- No tool costing department is in place to control the costs of dies and molds.
- TPS training is available for operation, not for SQEs and suppliers. SQEs need knowledge of supplier development for the sake of improved supplier efficiency.

What Is Your Vision?

We can consider an example from the automotive industry. The customer uses OEM, as with BMW, GM, and SVW, auditing its tier 1 and tier 2 suppliers and checking key figures in the sales quotations if it is reasonable to do so. However, some buyers do not do this job at their supplier sites, only request price reduction at yearly price negotiations. Subsuppliers ask for price increase due to rising prices of raw material, energy, labor costs, etc. Without auditing, these suppliers find themselves in a tight spot. They need to do the same in regard to supplier process evaluation to make costs transparent and create a win-win situation with subsuppliers, because everyone is in the same boat. In the intermediate term, supplier development (paid by suppliers) will benefit both parties.

What Is Your Target?

It is an idea to use SQEs and train them for SD work, instead of hiring and build up a new group. After training, you will see who is able to learn and willing to adapt for their new role. You can sell it as job enrichment.

- SD should be done for preferred suppliers at first step. It must be determined which members of the SD staff should be trained in commodities to understand supplier processes.
- To establish workshops to create cost calculations as reference for others, to be stored in your company's database.
- Each SQE is selected and will be trained for his commodity. He or she knows already suppliers and contacts, and therefore, it is an easy step forward for job enrichment and satisfaction.

GTEC is using this software tool ECOCUT for service, consultancy, and training for our customers for effective cost reduction and profit growth within your own company. Please write an email to contact@gtec.asia, if interested in. I am sure you will welcome this approach as a way to reduce costs in-house and for your suppliers. A win-win relationship will be yours.

1.8 Profitable Company Restructuring by GTEC

Do you want to go ahead in China and Asia-Pacific?

My company and my team would be happy to support you as a system doctor and problem solver in getting financially healthy, in restructuring, and in increasing profits.

What are your advantages of booking us?

Just one of my success stories as an example for you:

Our engagement for a customer who is the market leader in products for electric vehicles. Here, we were able to achieve the following measurable results:

- Increase in sales by 30% while reducing the internal error rate by 86% and consequently as well the customer complaints from 56 units to 0.
- The number of workers has been reduced by 18%, and the absence and layoff rates have been significantly lower.
- As a result, the operating profit rose from 56,000 to 2.6 Mio RMB/month.

How is that possible in such a short time? What is behind this success?

All our previous customers from Germany, USA, France, and Italy had the following advantages through our work:

- 100% loyal to the client
- Innovative thinking and quick actions.
- 24–7 high-performance culture
- Structured approach, reporting, and coordination.

Why is that so important for you in Asia?

From my experience, you need a business partner:

- One with an effective cost reduction methodology.
- One who can build a learning organization for you.
- Someone with years of multicultural experience in east and west.
- Tight communication and proactive motivation.
- Experience in project management, negotiation technique, and control.

Now, simply write an email to contact@gtec.asia and arrange a conversation with us.

Don't wait, Asia is fast! An efficient preparation and ramp-up phase must be well planned, so that you can achieve measurable success even faster.

2 The Purchasing Manager's Challenges in Asia

2.1 Psychology

Assuming, in our WFOE Company, Purchasing Asia is an established organization, but Mr. Wang, the Purchasing Director for Asia, has been dismissed. So, our team in China and Asia is without leadership. Evidentially, Mr. Wang and his team missed the mark with potential direct and indirect cost reductions. Perhaps he had different goals and priorities in mind.

As you may know, in China, purchasing work is highly sought after by employees because they can earn additional income through commissions from suppliers. Usually, companies rotate jobs as early as possible, to prevent any deep relationships between suppliers and buyers. However, this may be counterproductive because without a good relationship between the supplier and the company, the supplier could deliver inferior products in an untimely manner for a less than ideal price.

Our company faces another challenge: We are a foreign company, but our employees are Chinese. They are brainwashed by their government to support their own people. Of course, they do what is required to get their salary at the end of every month. But they are not engaged in the pursuit of reducing costs with other Chinese companies to increase the profits of a Western company. Even when Chinese employees are shown the full financial picture with low profit margins or even losses, they are indifferent. In fact, they often request higher salaries, bonuses, holiday fees, and severance pay to provide for their families and buy properties, cars, etc. This is, of course, similar to most employees in the Western world. However, at least in Germany, there is a small difference. On average, employees stay in companies much longer and are less likely to change jobs so frequently. As a result, employees are usually more loyal to the company.

Therefore, our first vital task as an executive is to bring our purchasing team and suppliers away from fear and into a comfort zone of mutual respect and support.

K. Zuerl, *Effective Cost Cutting in Asia*, Management for Professionals,
https://doi.org/10.1007/978-3-030-82782-3_2

2.1.1 How Do You Bring Buyers into a Comfort Zone Without Fear?

There are several concepts and ideas from my experience which I would like to discuss and share with you. I hold a trademark in China for a concept called ECOCUT. The name ECOCUT was derived from "effective cost cutting," but it is actually a supplier process evaluation to maximize cost transparency. This concept was also used during my time at GM, Valeo, and Bosch. At GM, we developed sophisticated Excel sheets, whereas at Valeo, Schaeffler, and Bosch we used Perfect ProCalc, a trademark of Perfect Costing Solutions GmbH, which was sold to Siemens in 2012 and named product costing. The same process can be done with the calculation of tooling costs with Perfect CalCard, later named tooling costing. I provocatively named my product as well "Easy Cost Cutting ECOCUT," even though it is actually somewhat sophisticated. However, with my structured guidance in this book, it will become easy to utilize.

In most Western companies in China, buyers have a bachelor's or master's degree in economics, but only a few have degrees in mechanical or electrical engineering. However, to discuss technical or quality issues with suppliers on the same level, you need to be willing to go to the shop floor. Most buyers stay in meeting rooms and want to reduce costs purely by requesting a small percentage of cost reduction. Most of them do not even know what the supplier's factory costs are for their specific product.

Therefore, there is a lot of training and preparation to be done in advance before buyers can be successful in getting expected costs down. Training for buyers and suppliers is essential. In China, most suppliers are not afraid of losing customers, especially low-volume customers. Most suppliers like to have Western customers because of their reputation and to gain small advantages in the market through advertising with their valuable names. Western companies know that and react by organizing a second source, even when volume is low. On the other hand, one target of purchasing managers is to reduce the number of suppliers, so that administration costs can be reduced as well.

So, there is not just one solution for each specific scenario. There is no "silver bullet" of purchasing success. However, when buyers or suppliers explain their current situation and current conflicts to me, I can help them with a resolution plan. Together, we can make the right decisions and the right steps to reach a mutually agreeable solution.

2.1.2 Why Does Psychology Play Such an Important Role in Purchasing?

I would like to share a concept with you about the supply chain in Asia, which has been well proven during my 20 years in management: All members of the supply chain are connected and need to support each other to survive.

As mentioned previously, psychology plays an important role here. As a purchasing manager in your new role, first you need to sit together with each of your staff members and ask about their strengths, weaknesses, and concerns. You need to think in advance about what kind of answers your staff may give and prepare direct answers to foster open communication. Maybe they are motivated to support you but have different bonus agreements or their own opinions about cost reduction activities, and therefore find excuses to go to suppliers and initiate deals.

The same will happen if you go to the general managers of your suppliers and ask for support. They will tell you about the rising costs of raw materials, labor, energy, supplies, rent, maintenance, etc. They will refuse to give you any price reduction explaining that soon their small profit margin will be gone, and they will need to shut down the plant or cancel your contract.

Supplier development departments can be a great source of support. Suppliers need an on-site team to focus on process improvements to avoid any profit margin reduction. If you do not have a supplier development department, look for external help at the supplier's location. This is often a more cost-efficient option than having a staff member sitting in an office and regularly spending an exorbitant amount of money on traveling and accommodations at the supplier's site.

The most important thing is for suppliers to understand that they are in the same boat as the customers. If you as a customer will fail to reduce your costs in comparison with competitors or need to increase them, your customers will not give you any orders. Therefore, all members of the supply chain are connected and need to support each other to survive and to squeeze money out of manufacturing or trading.

2.2 Database

Why does the purchasing department need to have a database for cost structure analysis?

You need to have your facts and figures together before negotiating with your suppliers. If you are not prepared for such dialogues, you will be at the mercy of your suppliers and what they present. If you are not well prepared for negotiations, you may lose the supplier's respect and they will not view you as a credible customer. Therefore, your confidence and success are based on your preparation before going to the supplier for negotiations.

To maximize your negotiating power, you need to build up a database of suppliers' processes, machines, and worker salaries to calculate part price based on the supplier's location. As you know, at each location in China or anywhere in the world, square meter, energy, and labor costs vary. Machine costs also vary greatly, based on brand name, size, and cycle time. Therefore, it is vital to get such figures before going to negotiations.

To get the most accurate data from your suppliers, you need to visit their site personally. Of course, this can be time-consuming, but the information gained by being on-site will prove to be profitable in the long run. Do not make the mistake of asking them to send you the information to avoid traveling. You will either get nothing, because they will anticipate what you want the data for, or you will get the wrong data, which will lead you in the wrong direction and to wrong decisions.

2.3 Teardown of Competitor Parts

At General Motors and Valeo, I learned an efficient teardown process in engineering, using competitor parts, which I would like to introduce to you as well. If for any reason, you do not have access to the material bill of complex supplier parts and the process data, you can use a teardown process.

Single components or assemblies can be torn down and investigated in terms of materials, quantity, and the manufacturing process. From these data, part price can be calculated and used in negotiation with the supplier.

For the piece price calculation, you always need material, cycle time, and machine data. So, you need to ask the right questions in a plant tour on the supplier's shop floor. If you ask too directly, your guide will not tell you. So, you need to find a strategy to ask indirect questions.

To get a plant tour, you need to find a reason why you want to see your parts in production, and you need to be 100% sure that your parts will be in the manufacturing process when you arrive.

You also need to have a good understanding of the manufacturing process so you can ask the right questions without making your guide suspicious. Usually, appearing inexperienced and asking "innocent" questions are a good strategy. But there is a fine line here. If you play it too dumb, you will not be taken seriously, and your guide may think it is a waste of time to give you accurate answers.

So, which one of your suppliers are you going to start with? Sure, look at your ABC analysis first and then add a column. When was the last cost reduction agreement made, with which part number, and how much did you get in terms of percentages and money last year?

This activity can be done with direct purchasing, as well as with indirect material and forwarders.

Why Does PUR Need to Have Lead Buyers?

While working with tier 1 suppliers, I learned a helpful technique that I have found to be both useful for the company itself and motivating buyers: Take top people with strategic thinking out of your pool and promote them to lead buyers. Ideally, you need one lead buyer for each commodity, or at least one for every few commodities.

When performing cost analysis on the Internet, it may be impossible to find proper materials or it will at least be very time-consuming, especially if you are not sure exactly what you are looking for. Sometimes, inexperienced buyers do not even understand how parts should be manufactured and assembled, which machines should be used, or how much time will be needed during production. To shorten this process and increase the reliability and level of trust in your quality investigation, you need to create a stable of experts from your company, and you need to list their name, telephone number, and commodity in a table. These experts could also be used as trainers for others, as long as they are willing to support the big picture and their bosses will allow them to work for other departments from time to time.

After a while, suppliers may come up with good ideas, but will be afraid to tell you. I learned at General Motors that, if suppliers share their ideas to reduce costs, improve quality, or speed up delivery times, they will get a financial benefit out of it, so they have a natural incentive to tell you.

RFQs are useful for benchmarking prices, for example, of fasteners, but when ordering small volumes, you will pay a very high price, and your suppliers may not always deliver on time. If you have solid numbers, then check against the previous year's statistics and see how which raw materials you needed and how much of them, and do not order project by project, but put some on stock. Your supplier will give you a nice price if you order their minimum order quantity (MOQ), and you would not have to worry about delivery time or price increases in raw materials.

2.4 Preparing to Deal with Buyers

My approach is to prepare for dealing with buyers through the following points:

- Introduce my background, experience, and core values to the buyer organization in person and within a one-page statement
- Bring buyers into their comfort zone via a face-to-face meeting, or if they do not want to work together, stop dealing with them immediately.
- Prepare Excel part calculation spreadsheets
- Prepare Excel tooling calculation spreadsheets
- Train buyers in their commodities so they have a financial understanding of their technical processes. This should be practical training where they immediately see a benefit for their daily work
- Practical role-play negotiations to learn arguments and what approaches to use to reach a successful result during negotiations and workshops with suppliers.
- Use the Harvard principle to always find a win-win solution in any negotiation, otherwise there will eventually be some unpleasant surprises when one party loses control and or tries to take advantage of someone.

In plant and purchasing organizations, there are a number of possible and advisable actions to reduce costs.

- Introduce external consulting and interim managers
- Introduce our cost management strategies and approaches
- Prepare templates and standardized letters to be sent to suppliers' general managers to inform them and to get their support
- Calculate part price and organize cost management workshops with selected suppliers that offer the greatest potentials for cost reduction
- Lead buyer matrix
- Trainer table matrix

- Organizational structure with logistics, transportation, and warehouses, and supplier quality control in PUR
- Reporting of results
- Supplier days
  - with presentations of supplier cost reduction ideas to share with other suppliers
  - present concepts and summaries to every supplier, instead of time- and cost-consuming trips
  - announce a Supplier of the Year each year
- Create an ABC Supplier pyramid with best-in-class lead suppliers
- Create an annual order frame contract with each supplier instead of sending RFQs
- Bundle groups of similar parts and give orders to a single supplier

How to Prepare a Supplier Visit?
Every step starts with an ABC analysis!

1. ABC *analysis*
   (a) Sorted by turnover
   (b) Sorted by low hanging fruits
   (c) Sorted by last cost reduction activities
2. *Cost structure analysis*
   (a) own cost calculation, update
   (b) compare with supplier costs
   (c) Prepare decision making for supplier Visit
3. *Supplier visit*
   (a) Send email to supplier to inform about our ECOCUT
   (b) Workshop with supplier
   (c) New contract with yearly ×% cost reduction
   (d) Put savings into SAP system

Example for 3a:

"With this email, I hope to be able to start a successful partnership and teamwork, and will reduce costs for your company and thereby increase your profit. Your opinions, ideas, and suggestions are very welcome."

Example for 3b:

At a supplier site, together with the support of the site's general manager, the following tasks must be performed:

1. Check the status and improvement of productivity and efficiency. The goal of this process is to reduce throughput time and production costs per hour. The measures are to be implemented on our production lines. The output per day and times for each workpiece must both be measured.
2. Identify cost-saving potentials which must be implemented by year 202x (with or without investment costs), e.g., reduction in material costs, reduction in process throughput time, reduction in warehouse space, and reduction in inventory.

Possible improvements in the process flow of all production lines need to be analyzed and shown.

The implementation of the two projects must then be advanced. Until then, I suggest using the remaining time in a meaningful way and taking the following procedures:

- Task 1: Inventory lead times/production costs per hour of production lines. Feedback of the results.
- Task 2: Preparation of an Asaichi board. For a concept overview, see https://www.linkedin.com/in/glenknight/detail/recent-activity/posts/, access date 11.02.2021

Following see two pictures/tables of our Asaichi pinboard (Fig. 2.1), which does not cost any money, but is very effective. Please print both sheets in A3-format and apply them to a pinboard, preferably by the next day. For example, we recommend starting every morning with a factory tour, overviewing the pinboard, and list suggestions for improvement, responsibilities, and deadlines. No ideas can be lost, and each must be followed up on daily, until the proposal is implemented.

2.5 Which KPIs Are Useful?

Tasks for Head of Global Cost Analysis for Tools and Processes at Purchasing Knorr Bremse Munich[1]:

- Further develop operational procurement processes and supply models of purchasing and global roll-out of standards and reporting
- Control and implement processes based on defined key figures such as 3P turn rate, lead time, in supply quota, and derivation and discussion of measures
- Support and extend existing standard reports and KPIs in close cooperation with the central IT department
- Prepare data analyses and evaluations as well as implementation of improvement projects
- Training and education of purchasers on-site

Personal profile: Successfully completed a degree in business administration or comparable qualification—possess at least 3 years of professional experience in

[1] Source: https://jobs.bild.de/stellenangebote%2D%2DHead-of-Global-Cost-Analysis-m-f-d-Muenchen-Knorr-Bremse-Systeme-fuer-Nutzfahrzeuge-GmbH%2D%2D6925120-inline.html?suid=455dd3fa-ae1f-45f2-b857-6f5d4af197ed&rltr=14_14_25_dynrl_m_0_0_0, from February 4, 2021. Access date 10.2.2021.

ASAICHI Meeting--Plant tour findings Follow Up																		
	White=ongoing, green = closed, red = overdue																	
Item serial No	Actions	Department	Responsibility	May														
				1	2	3	4	5	6	7	8	9	10	11	12	13	14	15
10-4	cleaning lady need to clean shop floor and empty dust pins every morning. Warehouse staff need to clean warehouse area inside and outside of plant every evening. Operators need to clean their workplace and machines every Friday evening. Operators need to place tools and measuring instruments on dedicated places any time (5S). Need to collect and sell rest material 清洁女工每天早上需要打扫车间和空灰尘刷计，仓库工作人员每天晚上都需要清理工厂内外的仓库区域，操作员需要在每个星期五晚上清洁他们的工作场所和机器，操作人员需要随时将工具和测量仪器放置在专用位置 (5S)，需要收集和销售休息材料	HSE	ZHOU Tony															
10-7	empty wooden pallets need to be collected inside and outside and put on a dedicated warehouse area (marked area) 空的木托盘需要收集内外，并把一个专门的仓库区 (标记区)	MFG	LU James															
10-9	train and instruct new plastic welders to keep on time delivery in upcoming projects; preparation of work instruction to keep quality requirements (e.g. cleaniness) 培训和指导新的塑料焊接机在即将到来的项目中保持按时交货;准备工作指导书以保持质量要求 (如清洁)	MFG	LU James															
10-10	put all machines on proper place; all machines need a maintenance plan (e.g. including cleaniness, painting to prevent rust, greasing mechanical parts) 把所有的机器放在适当的地方;所有机器都需要维修计划 (例如，包括清洁、油漆以防止生锈、润滑机械部件)	MFG	LU James															
12-01	reorganize plastic welding area for better process flow, e.g. put sawing machine at beginning of process. "重新组织塑料焊接区域，以获得更好的工艺流程， 例如在工艺开始时放置锯床.	MFG	LU James															
12-02	use racks for storage in rest material warehouse 使用机架存放在物料仓库中	HSE	ZHOU Tony															
12-04	name place at finish good warehouse for dedicated projects 在完成良好的仓库的名称位置为专门的项目	HSE	ZHOU Tony															
01-02	Build manufacturing flow of customer to save buffer stock (floor space and throughput time) 构建 客户的制造流程，以节省缓冲库存 (占地面积和吞吐量时间)	MFG	LU James															
01-03	machine for cleaning plastic parts 塑料部件清洗机	MFG	LU James															
04-02	customer label on finish products and take pictures 成品上的 客户标签和拍照	SC	YUAN Zheng															
05-01																		
05-02																		
05-03																		

Asaichi meeting attendance list							
Date	Names						
	GM	SC	HSE	MFG	QM	ENG	PM
01.04.2021	Roger	Zheng	Tony	James	Alan	Noah	Anna
02.04.2021	Roger	Zheng	Tony	James	Alan	Noah	Anna
03.04.2021							
04.04.2021							
05.04.2021	Roger	Zheng	Tony	James	Alan	Noah	Anna
06.04.2021	Roger	Zheng	Tony	James	Alan	Noah	Anna
07.04.2021	Roger	Zheng	Tony	James	Alan	Noah	Anna
08.04.2021	Roger	Zheng	Tony	James	Alan	Noah	Anna
09.04.2021	Roger	Zheng	Tony	James	Alan	Noah	Anna

Fig. 2.1 Two Asaichi templates for plant tour findings and follow up. Source: GTEC, Schneckenlohe, Author Karlheinz Zuerl, 9.4.2021

purchasing, procurement, or logistics—have a sound knowledge of ERP consulting—be highly skilled in MS Office, SAP R/3, SAP BW, and SAP MM–fluent in German and English (written and spoken)—strong communication and teamworking skills in cooperating with locations worldwide.

2.6 How to Quickly Eliminate Compliance Issues at PUR Departments?

As a new manager, you need to trust everyone, instead of constantly micromanaging all activities. If you do so, you will ultimately do all of your buyers' work, and they will just relax and point the finger at you for the tiniest mistakes in your Excel spreadsheet calculations.

But there is a quick way to check your buyer to see if they are deeply connected with your suppliers and see if they have become unable to select the best supplier for your company's business.

First, take some standard parts in the buyer's portfolio and check their price changes, review their benchmarking activities, and run your own calculations of their cost structure analysis.

If there is a notable difference between the current purchasing price and your "true cost," and your buyer is not willing to cooperate in finding a supplier offering something closer to your "true costs," you need to immediately either let them go or transfer them to another department more suitable to their own experience and education.

2.7 Low-Hanging Fruit

How Do We Find and Obtain Low-Hanging Fruit?

We have Mother Nature to thank for the expression "*low-hanging fruit*." Fruit-bearing trees often have a few branches low enough for humans and animals to reach without much effort. The fruit growing on these lower branches may not be as ripe or attractive as the fruit on higher limbs, but are usually more abundant and easier to harvest. From this, we obtain the popular expression, which refers to easy rewards able to be reaped with minimal effort.

In business, the term "*low-hanging fruit*" is often associated with the sale of consumer products or services. Sales professionals, especially those who are just entering the field, are encouraged to seek out the easiest customers first. Competitors may spend more of their time seeking out the higher commission sales of customers on "higher branches," more challenging and competitive to obtain, leaving the low-hanging fruit behind for others to claim. Parents seeking low-cost insurance for their school-age children, for example, may be considered low-hanging fruit by insurance companies.

Another use of the expression can be found in the political arena. A politician may set a number of easily attainable goals and accomplish them with minimal effort. Voters may perceive the politician's actions as proof of their strong work ethic, but in reality, they simply wanted the political rewards of reaping this low-hanging fruit. Critics often use the expression to describe someone who chooses a sure thing over a more difficult but more rewarding pursuit.

We follow the same approach here at purchasing, choosing a secure goal to start with.[2]

An important fact in life is that, over time, hard roads become easier to walk, and the easy road becomes a costly think to walk. *If you do not make steps forward in life, you are going backward. If you do not improve, you are regressing.* By putting in extra effort and stepping out of your comfort zone, you hone your skills and become more competent.

It is also true that, to achieve your maximum potential in life, you must have a long-term perspective and the will to curb your desires for instant gratification.

To stay motivated, you need to see the results of your hard work as soon as possible.[3]

That is why business respects the concept of "low-hanging fruit." *Low-hanging fruit is simply targets and goals that are easily achievable.* It is a concept used very often in sales, referring to the desire to first try to sell your products to customers that are the easiest to sell to.

It is obvious that *low-hanging fruit is scarce*. Sooner or later, it runs out and you must start putting in more and more effort to meet your goals. Thus, only going after low-hanging fruit is a completely misguided strategy. Nevertheless, it makes a lot of sense to go after the low-hanging fruit first, and then intensify your effort with a long-term view in mind, and this is often a winning combination.

2.8 Low-Hanging Fruits in Logistics[4]

These simple tips will help you better understand how to reduce your distribution costs.

If you have never put your distribution "under the microscope" before, you could potentially save up to 16% in total distribution costs! This can be very low-hanging

[2] Sources: https://www.wisegeek.com/what-is-low-hanging-fruit.htm and https://agileleanlife.com/first-go-low-hanging-fruit/. Access date 11.2.2021.

[3] Source: https://agileleanlife.com/first-go-low-hanging-fruit/, proverb by Blaz Kos, Access date 11.2.2021.

[4] Source: https://www.logisticsbureau.com/reducing-distribution-costs-the-low-hanging-fruit/, Author Rob O'Byrne, dated February 17, 2015. Access date 11.2.2021.

fruit indeed. We are talking about the transport element of distribution, so whether you have an in-house or contracted delivery fleet, you will find these following tips very useful.

OK, so what does it mean to "optimize" distribution transport? For our purposes here, I will define it as minimizing the cost of distribution transport to customers, while meeting required service standards.

There are five main areas to focus on:

1. *Your customers*

   The things to consider here are the service levels your customers expect, the delivery time "windows" they require, their typical order size, and their delivery frequency.

   Have you ever been involved in a fleet optimization project?

   This is where you load up all of your customers, orders, products, and vehicle characteristics into a "smart" piece of software. You then typically replicate what your fleet does and then let the model have a go at optimizing the fleet operation.

   Do you know the single biggest thing that impacts the optimization process? It is delivery time windows. Stretching delivery time windows is a massive opportunity.

   For example, let us say your customers all have very strict requirements around what time they are willing to accept your delivery. Maybe this is a 1-h "time window," like between 9:00 AM and 10:00 AM (Fig. 2.2).

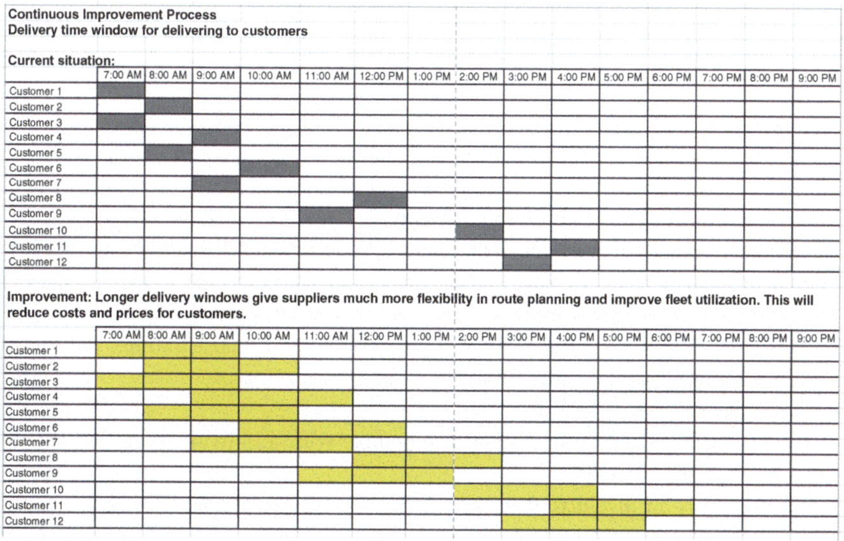

Fig. 2.2 Stretching delivery time windows. Source: https://www.logisticsbureau.com/reducing-distribution-costs-the-low-hanging-fruit/. Author Rob O'Byrne, February 17, 2015. Access date 11 February 2021

If you can work with customers to open that time window a bit more, maybe 9:00 to 11:00 AM or even midday, this has a massive impact on your ability to better utilize your delivery fleet. And I do mean massive, because it opens up a vast range of alternatives in terms of delivery route design and vehicle utilization, in terms of both capacity and time. I have seen 12% cost reductions just from this alone!

2. *Your service offer*
   The same then holds true for *order size* and *delivery frequency*.
   Whatever you can do to encourage customers to order less frequently but in larger orders makes your delivery fleet more efficient (from less stopping and starting).
   Moreover, this will also make your warehouse operations more cost-effective per unit.
   And if you can better understand your customer's service requirements and tailor those a little better to meet their needs, you will gain another slice of cost savings.
   This is because you will find there will be a sizeable part of your customer base that will accept a slower service for greater economy.
3. *Your products*
   Do all your products require the same type of delivery service? Could some be delivered by alternative, slower, or cheaper means? Maybe they need to be delivered together? Are some products constrained by handling requirements? Maybe they are fragile, or need temperature control? Are you using "expensive" delivery means for all products, when in fact some do not need it? Something worth thinking about.
4. *Your supply points*
   Very often, these tend to be "set in concrete." By that, I mean you have no control over the supply points from which you distribute your products. Or is there another way?
   If your distribution area is vast, it can make sense to transport your products in bulk to a distribution "area" and then use the delivery fleet from that later point.
   Quite simply, you get a double benefit.
   Firstly, your delivery fleet is operating closer to your customers, and so it is better utilized in terms of time and distance, and secondly, the transport cost per unit to get your products into the delivery "area" can be much cheaper.
   Of course, there is a trade-off in transport cost and dual handling, but this is often something well worth looking into.
5. *Your delivery fleet*
   This of course is where it all comes together, with a delivery fleet that should match your exact needs!
   Either: it is an *in-house fleet*, which is not really configured for your current needs, because it was put in place a while ago under different conditions or without much understanding of what the right fleet size and mix should be.
   Or: it is an *outsourced fleet*, which in theory should give you greater flexibility and utilization, but the way you are paying for the service is just not working for you.

Finding that right balance of fleet configuration and/or pricing model is a bit of a balancing act.[5]

2.9 Low-Hanging Fruit in Production (Fig. 2.3)

Do you want to reduce your operating costs?

Purchasing managers and purchasing teams are able to help companies realize an average 5% of operating cost opportunities.

By analyzing your current processes and systems, they can provide a detailed roadmap of exactly where improvements can be made.

This could be by investing more in your business priorities, helping your bottom line, or in keeping you agile and able to better respond to ever-changing customer expectations and challenges to your business models.

Executives gain insight into where they are really investing their time and effort, as well as levels of waste and variance across the operation and how these metrics stack up versus competitors.

Fig. 2.3 From ground fruits to difficult-to-reach fruits. Source: https://i-mie.com/how-to-introduce-six-sigma/. Author Business Excellence, dated October 14, 2015. Access date 11 February 2021

[5] Source: https://www.logisticsbureau.com/reducing-distribution-costs-the-low-hanging-fruit/, Author Rob O'Byrne, dated February 17, 2015. Access date 11.2.2021.

2.9.1 How Exactly Do We Harvest These Low-Hanging Fruit?

1. *Bundle purchasing centers to get higher purchasing volumes*
   At the management and company development level, executives also review GPO (global purchasing organization) contracts to ensure all centers are included.
   "At our clients, we looked at our materials management GPO contracting and did a review," interviewee CEO Mr. Zuerl from GTEC said, "and we found that we needed to restructure our contracts so that instead of having our centres buy individually, we could participate in company contracts for our centres. We also previously assumed all our centres were covered, but they weren't, so we had to add a few and then got better pricing. We have to continuously review the GPO contract to make sure we get universal pricing."
2. *Use inventory management tools*
   What do you have in warehouse already? How often inventory is physically checked?
   Purchasing an electronic inventory management system may be worth the investment, by letting you eliminate human error and control materials purchasing. A software allows materials managers to input information and generate case costing reports.
   "We saw on the case costing reports some managers were doing procedures with significantly more expensive devices than others," said Mr. Zuerl. "We were then able to standardize more and improve our spending. This was made possible by our inventory management software."
3. *Participate in a freight management program*
   While shipping for individual deliveries is not very expensive, a company sends and receives packages on a daily basis and those costs add up. Participation in freight management saved one center, that Mr. Zuerl worked with, more than 320,000 RMB in 1 year.
   "There are a lot of companies that offer freight management," he said. "Always review and audit the freight that is sent out and coming in; they are usually supply chain materials. After we realized a huge cost-savings with one of our centres, all of our centres joined the freight management program."
4. *Purchase of alternatives*
   Do you really need to be paying through the nose for high quality? If quality is premium, do you have alternative suppliers on the market which are able to deliver for reasonable prices?
   Name brand machines are expensive, but there are several lower-cost alternatives available that allow to achieve the same quality outcomes. There are several companies offering non-name brand alternatives made with the same materials as the leading products at a fraction of the cost, and most keep overhead low by not having representatives everywhere.
   "By focusing on spending, we are able to have good quality machines at a lower cost," said Mr. Zuerl. "Some technicians at ME department are too close with their representatives or loyal to their device company. See if they are willing to consider alternative solutions. We consider this our biggest opportunity to reduce spending in the future."

5. *Begin reprocessing disposables*
   Did you check with the plant about how to reuse any waste material?
   Some companies will reprocess disposable goods, so centers can reuse them instead of throwing them out after a single use.
   "We have saved a ton of money by reprocessing disposables and that's a program we are really excited about," said Mr. Zuerl. "Most of our centres use major distributors. We found out which companies had programs and connected them with our centres."
6. *Look for lower-cost controlled supplies*
   Some centers use a electronic program to order controlled supplies. The online platform allows materials managers to input which products they want to order and lets them purchase them directly, reducing the chance for error when compared with manual orders.
   The program also suggests generic alternatives for the substances to purchase at a lower cost. "The program brings the generic equivalent to our attention when we order a more expensive name-brand product," said Mr. Zuerl. "We can choose to order the generic equivalent instead and that saves a lot of money. The online program is also a way to track controlled supply purchases."
7. *Forecast product utilization and order accordingly*
   Are you able to predict your yearly expenses in advance? Then you can bundle and purchase goods more cheaply.
   Develop a program to forecast product utilization based on previous months and years to ensure that your center has enough materials to operate, but not so many that they are wasting away on the shelf.
   "We want a clear picture of what the centres are using week-by-week and order our materials on a monthly basis," said Mr. Zuerl. "We update this information every 2 weeks, so there's a week's lead time if we need to order more of something. This gives us a very disciplined review of what stock we have at hand and minimizes the ordering of extra products."
8. *Plan for customers' volume changes*
   Where in a year is there a peak?
   There are certain times of the year, such as the beginning of the year, when order volume dips because people have not yet made their decisions. More cases are then scheduled toward the end of the year, or during vacation times, and purchasing based on those projections could prevent expensive, rushed deliveries.
   "You have higher-volume months in the plant, if tied directly to customers' concerns for their needs," said Mr. Zuerl. "Because we purchase monthly, we can track and adjust to those trends as needed."[6]

[6]Source: https://www.skipprichard.com/pick-the-low-hanging-fruit-to-improve-productivity/. *Author* Skip Prichard, May 4, 2014, access: 11.02.2021.

2.9.2 What Do We Do When the Low-Hanging Fruit Is Gone?[7] (Fig. 2.4)

Fig. 2.4 Then you need to climb one step higher until you will reach sweet fruits[8]

2.9.3 Can DMAIC Help You?

The primary methodology of Six Sigma functions in what is known as the DMAIC, the define, measure, analyze, improve, and control process. The figure below identifies this process and the functions that occur in each phase (Fig. 2.5).

2.10 Where Are the Low-Hanging Fruit of Nonproduction Areas?

In the automotive industry, every change in manufacturing processes needs to be approved by the customer. If a part goes to several customers, and only a single one refuses to approve of your improvements, the whole idea must be scrapped. Therefore, this is not a low-hanging fruit, as approval process takes long time and the outcome is very uncertain. What is better is to focus on nonproduction products, like

[7] Source: https://www.isixsigma.com/new-to-six-sigma/dmaic/what-do-when-low-hanging-fruit-gone/. *Author* Tom Long. from September 11, 2014; Access date 11.2.2021.

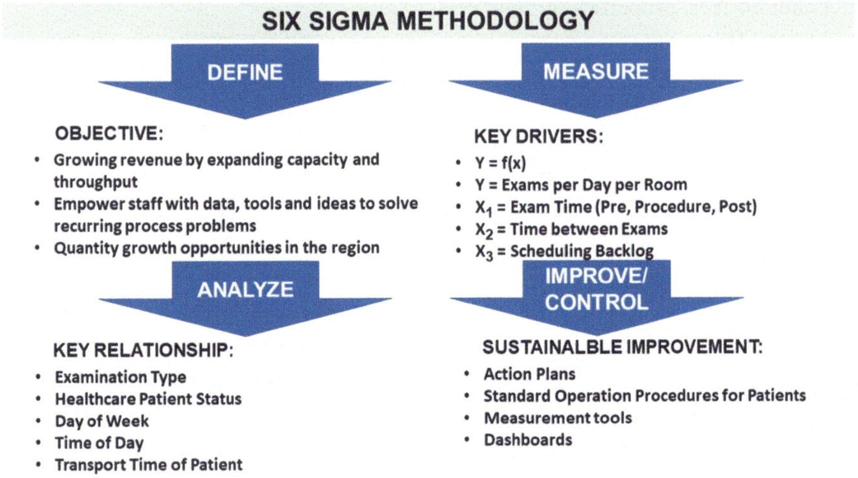

Fig. 2.5 DMAIC cycle. Source: https://www.isixsigma.com/industries/healthcare/what-do-when-low-hanging-fruit-gone//. Author Tom Long, access time 11.2.2021

the following areas (you can pick, choose, and add at will based on what your company needs):

- Advertisements
- Banks, loans, fees, and saving plans
- Batching instead of individual purchasing for each project
- Canteen food for lunch and shifts
- Cleaning and housekeeping/catering services for household and food, external or internal
- Cleaning and toilet paper
- Customs
- Development services
- Driver and cars, rental instead of hiring/buying, or vice versa
- Energy
- Entertainment
- Exhibitions/marketing
- External interpreter and translation services
- Facility management
- Flights, e.g., negotiating and buying business-class contingents in advance
- Gas, water, electricity, and lights, e.g., change to LED bulbs
- Gifts or presents
- Health, safety, and environment (internal or external)
- HR efficiency, e.g., goal agreement forms, MAG, performance reviews, and competency assessments
- Insurance
- Interns instead of full-time staff
- IT and web pages

- Landlord fees, properties, ground costs
- Lawyer fees
- Logistics networks, e.g., bundling and milk runs
- Machine investment, make or buy calculations
- Marketing
- Parking fees, petrol cost checks
- Patents
- Phone and mobile phone costs
- Post and express service
- Printing/external offsets
- Professional services
- Project management costs
- Prototypes
- Purchasing efficiency, e.g., terms and conditions, and OTD (remaining backlog)
- Office equipment, computer tools, e.g., nuance power pdf standard, or any software "where do I find meeting rooms?"
- Online shops instead of catalogs or suppliers
- Outings
- Security guards, security service for plants
- Shuttle buses
- Spare parts, fasteners, service workshops
- Sport activities
- Renting and leasing
- Repair and maintenance for office and shop floors, renovation, watering plants
- Retail outlets
- Telecommunication
- Testing center costs, e.g., certificate costs for raw material or fasteners
- Tooling (dies and molds)
- Training, workshop costs, vocational schools
- Traveling (cars, buses, trains, taxis, undergrounds, hotels, or private accommodations)

2.10.1 How Do We Obtain These Savings?

1. Define a lean process for nonproduction material, first on a regional level, then a global one
2. Make processes transparent to avoid maverick buying
3. Perform pooling (internal/external)
4. Identify the right service provider for each commodity group
5. Perform standardization and reduce variables, e.g., select only one forklift manufacturer to reduce lifetime repair and maintenance costs
6. Benchmark consumption, e.g., gloves for shop floor use
7. Reduce time consumption and process costs through e-procurement/outsourcing instead of traditional procurement

8. After issuing purchase orders and before placing orders, eliminate process steps such as budget checks, approval, and quotation comparisons
9. Look for supporting of service providers such as generalists or specialists in each single commodity group, e.g., energy, logistics, insurance, travel, repair and maintenance, services, IT, facility management, patents, customs, rent and leasing, travel, prototypes, telecommunication, and marketing
10. Prepare a table of commodity groups, the purchasing volume of each, and sources of generalists and specialists of service providers to estimate potential savings
11. Prepare a bar chart of each commodity to see a full-year forecast of expected expenses. You need to break down result by legal entities, if there are very many of them.
12. Open a project for cost reduction of nonproduction material

2.10.2 How Do We Run an NPM Project?

1. Quickly assess initial data and validate the framework conditions
2. Design a project incl. assumption of cost reduction
3. Conduct structured interviews to perform analysis, and determine the degree of maturity of their potentials
4. Prioritize concrete initiatives and release an action plan
5. Implement a roadmap of how to implement operational purchasing processes
6. Obtain low-hanging fruit by implementing initiatives
7. Adapt to processes and organizations
8. Improve processes and organizations

2.10.3 Lead Buyer Concept

If you choose a proposed commodity group strategy, using a global approach whenever possible, otherwise choose a regional or local approach. Lead buyers of each commodity should be nominated to give support in RASIC charts, e.g., to define subcommodities and strategies.

2.10.4 How Do We Implement Pooling in Each Region?

- Globally use only one global logistics provider (e.g., M&M), telecommunication provider (e.g., Vodafone), and insurance provider (e.g., Allianz)
- Approach all JV partners, global suppliers, and tier 1 and 2 suppliers
- Get help from freelance commodity experts, if not available in-house, e.g., logistics, repair and maintenance, and IT
- Differentiate pooling partners for each commodity group, e.g., insurance and telco for cars, and energy for energy-intensive suppliers

2.10.5 Time and Motion Study[8]

The time study is a method used to establish exactly how long it takes your team to complete certain tasks. You can use these task times to underpin your budgeting and resource planning, and we can benchmark your processes versus similar business to understand where time and cost-saving opportunities can be accessed.

How Do We Do It?

- Observe and time your processes
- Create times for your tasks (labor standards)
- Process and analyze your measurements and present the results in a clear and easy-to-use way
- Use industry benchmarks to provide comparisons for your data and to highlight opportunities for improvement
- Identify and quantify time and cost-saving opportunities
- Guide the practical application of labor standards for your business (Fig. 2.6)

Without knowing precisely how long every step in your customer journey takes—and you should probably know the duration each behind-the-scenes task, between final customer interaction, including restocking, refunding, mark-downs,

The Lean Toolbox

1. 5S/ Visual Controls
2. 5 Why's
3. 7 Management & Planning Tools
4. 7 Quality Control Tools
5. Bottlenecks
6. Brainstorming
7. Chaku-Chaku / Load-Load
8. Change Management
9. Control Charting
10. Critical Chain Project Management
11. DFMA
12. Education
13. Employee Involvement
14. Flow Cells
15. Heijunka / Load Levelling
16. Histograms
17. Hypothesis Testing
18. Metrics and Alignment
19. Nominal Group Techniques

20. Pareto Analysis
21. Point-of-Use Delivery
22. Poka-Yoke / Mistake Proofing
23. Pull/Kanban Systems
24. Prioritization
25. Rapid Improvement Events (Kaizen)
26. Production Process Preparation (3P)
27. Root Cause Analysis
28. Set-up Reduction
29. Six Sigma
30. Spaghetti Chart
31. Standard Work
    - *Capacity Analysis*
    - *Takt Time / Cycle Time*
    - *Standard Ops Worksheet*
    - *Production Control Board*
32. Supply Chain Management
33. Total Productive Maintenance
34. Value Stream Maps

Fig. 2.6 Lean Toolbox with 34 items. Source: https://www.slideshare.net/JoyTy/lean-10704083, Lean, page 31. Published on Dec 27, 2011. Author Joy Ty. Access date: 12.2.2021

[8] Source: https://rethinkproductivity.co.uk/case-study/activity-time-studies-paying-attention-to-detail/. Author ReThink company; Access date 11.2.2021

and clean-up—you cannot accurately judge how many employees you might need on a shift, not just to get the job done, but to meet your sales targets. You would be relying on an estimate, a ballpark figure that is not as accurate as it could be.

So, why does accuracy matter? Say you are a retailer employing five persons to cover an 8-h shift, providing 40 h of working time between them. But in reality, it only takes 33 h to serve your target number of customers and carry out every task that needs to be completed. Seven extra hours a day adds up to more than 2500 h per year. If each hour costs you 140 RMB in staff wages, that is a whopping 350,000 RMB, you might not need to be spending, just in one shop.

And, if it turns out you are not employing enough people per shift, that can be just as damaging. Customer service can suffer—and so can sales.

How Our Studies Work[9]

First, we send in a specialist team of work–study analysts to a selection of your stores or sites, with the locations ranging in size and setting. They will spend between 5 and 10 days in each, meticulously timing every task carried out by your people, many times over. We use that data to produce averages across your sites and compare variance between them.

The next step is to build a budget model using average activity times, so you can accurately calculate how much to spend per site, per week—based on the minimum number of staff hours needed—to meet forecasted sales.

We go beyond the data, too. Our analysts use knowledge and experience gained across different industries to spot tasks that are taking longer than they should, and suggest practical steps to shave off valuable seconds. That might be something as simple as moving a counter card reader so it is on a customer's right-hand side—where most of them expect to find it—or upgrading equipment. For Costa Coffee, it was investing in a new, faster panini press in their drive-through stores, cutting down waiting times on food, and preventing a bottleneck (even left-handed people exist).

And these changes provide a very practical, immediate benefit: In the former case, they were able to use tangible facts and figures to reinforce performance discussions with their teams. This can make a real difference on the shop floor; if employees understand how long they are supposed to spend on a task, then it is easier for them to feel motivated and work more efficiently.

2.10.6 Efficiency Review[10]

Efficiency reviews capture how your teams spend time compared to your priorities and how they are benchmarked versus your competitors.

---

[9] Source: https://rethinkproductivity.co.uk/case-study/activity-time-studies-paying-attention-to-detail/ Author ReThink company; Access date 11.2.2021.

[10] Source: https://rethinkproductivity.co.uk/case-study/efficiency-studies-making-every-minute-count/, Author ReThink company; Access date 11.2.2021.

Improving productivity should be at the heart of every business, but this is easier said than done. By spending time with your team, we can conduct efficiency studies to quantify how time is spent by your teams along with quantification of how effectively they work. We create quantified process improvement reports to identify exactly where processes and working methods can be changed to improve efficiency.

Sure, there are back-of-house tasks or essential processes that indirectly support sales, but typically, you do not want them to eat up any more minutes than is strictly necessary. Every second spent on things does not add any value, that is time—and money—down the drain.

So, what is the reality for your business? Do you have a clear picture of how your team splits their time? And perhaps most importantly—how would you use that information?

Knowing that you spend 10% of your total time on replenishing stock, for example, is not particularly useful on its own. Maybe that is a standard percentage in your industry, maybe it is not and you should try to cut it down, but you need to know where and how to focus your efforts, and what the payoff of doing so might be.

Our efficiency studies are not just data finding missions, they are diagnostic tools. And they can make a big difference, often identifying thousands of hours for our clients to trim off their processes or activities that do not add value. They use those savings to tighten up their salary budgets, or reinvest them to increase customer time.

We showed them that a disproportionate chunk of time was spent refilling shelves; they were using customer trolleys to move items from the stock room, and although this was a method that had not posed too much of a problem in the past, it was starting to cost them in terms of employee hours as stores became busier.

Along with other tweaks to manual systems they would begin to outgrow, we recommended introducing new, more efficient stocking equipment, plus options for pricing and ticketing technology, and showed them just how many hours it could save them.

Dealing with Downtime[11]

HQ was surprised by the amount of downtime their current approaches caused, and although there was no quick fix—our recommendations were to either cross-train employees or introduce more digital kiosks—the quantifiable data we have given them will help inform decisions regarding their long-term strategy.

As part of a study for a client, we found that admin tasks were blocking managers from spending time on the shop floor, and recognized that introducing tablets and technology could prevent them from being tied to the back office. We also uncovered data that indicated more time spent on sales meetings and updates did not necessarily translate to better performance.

Our insights helped them take a new approach to staff planning, reducing back-office time by around 12.5%. We identified 14 m RMB worth of savings for a single

[11] Source: https://rethinkproductivity.co.uk/case-study/efficiency-studies-making-every-minute-count/Author ReThink company; Access date 11.2.2021.

plant, mostly through tightening up their processes, reducing noneffective time, and updating technology and equipment.

2.10.7 Optimizing Labor Budgets[12]

We build budget models that reflect client's unique operating model and ensure that salary investment matches his priorities.

Work–study analysts need to keep performance rating up to a certain standard, and annual assessments help prevent drift so ratings do not become too loose or too tight.

Managers, deputies, supervisors, assistants, and team structures can be complex, and if there is any overlap or imbalance, it can make a big dent in client's overall efficiency and profits. We have helped clients to put different roles under the microscope and identify ways that they can become more effective.

Whatever your business, it is likely that a big chunk of your budget goes into team salaries, so it is important to be confident that you are spending it wisely. You can make sure you have the most effective layout, the slickest equipment, a thorough understanding of exactly how long it takes to run every aspect of your business, but if your team structure is not right or there are hazy boundaries of employee responsibilities, you can end up with employees spending a disproportionate amount of their day on back-of-house tasks or killing time instead of dealing with customers and otherwise adding value.

The highest stakes are in leadership roles, where salaries are greatest and opportunities for gain and loss are greatest. How different are managers and assistant managers, in reality? Enough to justify the extra investment? Do you have the right number of people at each level? And, if it is important for them to be interacting with customers and suppliers, how much time are they spending at their desks? A clear picture of how responsibilities are split—in practice and not just on paper—is a vital resource for improving efficiency.

Our expert analysts will head to each location and discreetly shadow your employees for the entirety of their shift. They will measure and observe exactly how they are spending their time, whether they are serving at a till or sending emails, and allocate their work to one of three categories: directly supporting customers, carrying out essential tasks that indirectly support customers, or not adding any value—the latter of which might be downtime, break time, or walking empty-handed between floors.

The data we collect show you how each role measures up, how individuals compare against each other, and how they vary across different sites. We can also benchmark persons in leadership roles as well.

[12] Source: https://rethinkproductivity.co.uk/case-study/role-efficiency-studies-fine-tuning-your-workforce/ Author ReThink company; *Access date 11.2.2021.*

But it is not enough to know whether roles are efficient or not. Our clients want the full story: What is standing in the way of greater productivity—whether that is a lack of guidance, too much crossover, or a mismatch of resource to customer demand—and how to overcome obstacles. Therefore, our analysts add context such as anecdotal observations and use their experience to spot opportunities.

They will also have conversations with the people they are following, uncovering first-hand experiences and useful information that might not otherwise be brought to HQ's attention. Seemingly small, everyday issues can have significant consequences and aftereffects; at a client, for example, a lack of water coolers meant people were traveling from one side of the building to the other just to get a drink, taking up valuable time.

2.11 Kaizen

Kaizen is a Japanese term invented by Masaaki Imai (1986) to describe continuous improvement. The goal of the principle is to achieve continuous improvement in costs, quality, flexibility, and productivity. One of the characteristics of kaizen is that improvements result in lower costs; these costs are certainly much lower than those obtained with other techniques, such as process reengineering or similar methods.

We have been able to observe that suppliers are still not convinced of the profitability of lean systems, despite the favorable opinions of the concept expressed in scientific publications. One of the main reasons for this skepticism is that suppliers lack information and clear examples related to their own activities and savings that Kaizen offers. For the supplier companies' managers, the fact that lean production is a success with automobile manufacturers does not guarantee from the outset that they will also find this success.

Moreover, for the supplier companies, there is no question that the move toward lean production requires investments not just in facilities, but also in worker training, and the time to develop improvements. They are also aware that this method is not free of risks, such as the loss of the buffer provided by stocks, or the greater pressure on workers, among other issues.

The success of improvement proposals shall be measured on the basis of the variation of specific production indicators, with the aim of isolating the effects that could be produced by the type of process followed to put lean production into action.

The Kaizen Event teams, as task forces, are teams that do not form a permanent part of the organizational structure, and are involved in a secondary task for their members. Kaizen Events normally last from 4–5 days, while quality circles and similar systems can be active for months or years.

Moreover, Kaizen Event teams are externally managed groups: They only have the responsibility of achieving specific improvements in specific areas and management designs the group task, selects the components, sets out the basic rules to achieve the objectives, etc. Management also guides the group task and supervises group results, as well as designs the organizational context the group is to work in and sets up the reward system, training, or information that the group is to use.

Kaizen Events are also known in the literature as Accelerated Improvement Workshops, Kaizen Project, Process Improvement, or Industry Forum Master Class, Kaizen Blitz, continuous process improvements, or the Supplier Industrial & Productivity Diagnosis.

Lean Office

Not only does production have to be lean, most waste occurs in bureaucracy and slow workflows across the company.

Online Workflow System

For example, in most Chinese companies, there is no online workflow system available. All applications are done by paperwork, and long walking times are necessary to obtain each signature. If the signatory is not available, they will need to wait or walk the same distance later. If it is too hot, raining, or snow is falling outside, the applicant may be delayed from crossing between buildings or locations until conditions are more favorable.

For this urgent and important cost reduction process, an IT workflow must be implemented instead of a manual application and approval handling process, with dedicated email addresses and persons for approval, each set to certain financial limits. To prevent any additional expenses, you can use current ERP system modules used by other plants, then copy and adapt them, and ask for instructions, if they are available and usable.

Your IT department may tell you that, according to management decision and finance rules, you cannot use an automatic electronic approval system. So, this cannot be a bottom-up approach. Top management needs to be convinced, and orders to implement such an online workflow system need to come from the top, otherwise all departments involved will block it and find excuses to avoid the additional workload.

Project Management

It must be clear to everyone from the start which documents need to be prepared by the requester at each project step, before asking or pushing other departments to act.

According to the purchasing department's assessment, about 30% of their time is lost as a result of unclear, unofficial, vague, or varying information. They need to write reminders of their tasks again and again, and this time could be used to perform other tasks, which they have no or limited time to do.

For example, a checklist can be prepared for other departments to be sent to the purchasing department to buy production material:

- Project no./name
- Bill of material (BOM), final or preliminary, to be checked and signed
- Drawings (final or preliminary), to be checked and signed
- Make or buy MOB (final or preliminary), to be checked and signed
- Time schedule for production SOP.

You can arrange meetings with the project management department to get support, as they are interested in developing a smooth and fast workflow that also eliminates many time-consuming loopholes and arguments.

To make progress in this important area, you need to prepare the following:

- List of items which departments *can* deliver to purchasing department, separated by project phases.
- List of items which departments *cannot* deliver to purchasing department, separated by project phases, but needed by the purchasing department

In the next section, you can see an example of that which is agreed between related departments in a Chinese industrial company and which the purchasing department can obtain in time for each project phase. But be aware, this is traditional. The next steps could be agreement for frontloading, to involve purchasing and suppliers in new projects much earlier, to reduce project time and costs.

This agreement should be distributed by the purchasing head via email to all involved parties. For example:

> Dear all,
>
> The purchasing department has received some purchasing requisitions without required attachments. This caused a lot of emails to be sent back and forth, with time spent writing intensive emails instead of buying the required goods, with excessive time delays which have consequences for every project.
>
> For details of which documents we need to be delivered by departments to purchasing your products in time, please see attachment. All marked items need to be delivered with your purchasing requisition.
>
> As you can imagine, without drawings or other information how to buy required things, without what is documented to be delivered from you, we cannot buy. There cannot be any exceptions of this rules. **We need you to be disciplined in following our procedures and specifications.**

There must be clear rules and time lines when project buyers and suppliers are involved in R&D process. As early as possible, then this "frontloading" will reduce overall product, machine, and equipment costs. See Fig. 2.7.

2.12 Example of How to Reduce NPM Costs in China

Following steps are recommended:

1. Delegate commodities to responsibilities and prepare a RASIC chart for approval, support, and control. See Fig. 2.8.
2. Arrange kick-off meetings to collect current info of suppliers and prices and put it on a purchasing list.
3. Arrange brainstorming and interviews to collect ideas how to further reduce costs at each commodity

Phase	Criteria	Project Manager	Criteria	Engineers	Criteria	Product Costing
	Responsibility					
1	• Project is approved and distributed • Project team is released • Master project plan is created • Status of open issues from open point list	☺	• Product requirements are available • Design review carried out and evaluated	☺	• Target costing available	☺
2	• Timing plan status • Status of open issues from open point list	☺	• Detailed design available • Design review carried out and evaluated • Manufacturing feasibility carried out	☺	• Target costing available	☺
3	• Make or Buy decision is carried out	☺	• Design review carried out and evaluated • Design freeze • Planning of purchased parts is carried out	☺	• Target costing available	☺
4	• Approved package is distributed	☺	• PPAP of purchased parts available	☺	• Target costing available	☺

Fig. 2.7 Product development phases in the automotive industry, tasks, and responsibilities. Source: GTEC, 2021

Non-Production Material	Responsible	Approval	Support	Who will be informed	Controlling
Logistics					
RMO Repair, Maintenance, Operations					
Energy					
Professional Services					
IT					
Tools, Die & Molds					
Machines					
Fixtures, Equipment					
Development Service, Engineering, Material					
Health, Safety, Environment HSE					
Disposal costs/ Waste					
Office Materials					
Consumables in Production, Supply					
Office supplies					
Finance					
Marketing, Sales					
HR					

Fig. 2.8 Cost controlling with RASIC chart of sub-items for nonproduction material commodity. Source: GTEC, 2021

The end result could be that you will be very successful in saving costs, as nobody has done such a huge workload before. The disadvantage could be that a lot of people in your organization will hate you, as you deleted their commission with their selected suppliers by changing their orders to other unknown suppliers.

Logistics

I recommend following tasks to see cost-saving potentials:

- Interview with logistics workers to find savings
- Customs clearance, benchmark of agents
- Forklifts, driver, and cars, rental instead of hiring/buying or vice versa
- Logistics networks, e.g., bundling, milk runs
- Parking fees, petrol cost checking
- Post and express service
- Pallets, boxes, wrapping foils, etc.

For example, back in simpler times, the purchasing manager and logistic manager of my client worked together and gave business to a single local forwarder and companies operating consignment stocks. Statistics showed that volume of one local forwarder increased dramatically over the last few years. Forwarders shipped goods with trucks to several places in China and drove back empty. Running a milk run from destination to destination via a single truck would be much cheaper. The customer of my client requested one consignment stock, however the client installed more than ten across China without any reason.

Why do companies buy their parts from distributors, instead of buying them directly from manufacturers? Especially in the automotive industry, where high volumes are needed and transportation costs per piece are very low, you may think that every buyer has his direct contact to sales of his manufacturing supplier. As China is a commission-based country, every buyer gets commission from distributors to bring them into their business and gain some money from each order. One small plant had over 300 distributors. To eliminate such an array of distributors, buyers will work against you to avoid successfully transfers to manufacturers. This is better, as you will do it yourself and gain tremendous cost savings over the service lifetime of your serial parts.

In such a situation, you may think it easy for the purchasing department to give business to competitors and request a quotation, but other forwarder companies refused to give a quote. What is the reason? Interconnected organizations tied through backdoor relationships are everywhere, and a small one will not compete or try and fight against a big one.

To avoid these compliance issues, the general manager is asked to request benchmarking, especially for domestic logistic transportations, follow up on results, and check and approve related expenses, instead of letting orders be run by just two individuals.

In most companies, logistic departments still run on maverick buying and decide by themselves from whom they want to buy, whether it be transportation, warehouses, cleaning services, or forklifts. Even if purchasing is not involved, if you need to implement a new workflow and get finance involved, you need a written agreement; even if you are just transferring money to suppliers, the purchasing department has to see and approve it.

2.12.1 RMO (Repair, Maintenance, and Operations)

I recommend following tasks to see cost-saving potentials:

- Facility management
- Forklift items, maintenance, etc.
- Machines, equipment
- Tools, dies, and molds
- Repair and maintenance for the office and shop floor, renovation, watering plants
- Cleaning tasks

1. For example, several maintenance contracts for forklifts, cars, trucks, elevators, and facilities, lasting for 1–3 years, avoiding specific negotiations under time pressure when needed. One phone call is enough, if there is something that needs to be repaired. For maintenance, there is a plan available, so even that single phone call can be avoided.
2. For example, racks at a paint shop need to be cleaned by an external service supplier after several spraying cycles. There are two possibilities to reduce costs: First, increase the allowed thickness of the paint on the racks before performing the chemical washing; and second, find cheaper service providers who have comparable cleaning licenses and skills.

2.12.2 Energy

I recommend to check following items to see cost-saving potentials:

- Gas,
- Water (cooling, washing),
- Electricity (light, machines), e.g., change to LED

In China, buying energy is mostly done with state-owned grids and the room for negotiation is limited. Therefore, your focus is to avoid and reduce consumption by intelligent solutions. Old buildings and traditional construction techniques could be a trap of costs. In this area, we recommend the use of specialized service companies to analyze your energy consumption and optimize your facilities on the shop floor and in the office. In Germany, you would use www.caverion.de. In China, I recommend www.venco.net.

Up to 60% of your costs can be reduced, with a rapid return on investment. You can also gain the positive image of an environmentally friendly company and related benefits.

However, most energy costs are accumulated by machines. Chinese companies on average use a higher energy level than European companies; big-level statistics are fine, but the goal here is to find ideas to reduce costs. For example:

- Use a centralized air conditioning system instead of several smaller single ones
- Seal windows and doors in wintertime to keep heat inside.
- Control machines remotely, if they are to be switched off when not used
- Install solar panels/water heating tanks on the roof and walls to create your own electricity or warm water
- Check current operating and maintenance procedures
- Determine existing operation conditions of energy-consuming equipment (e.g., lighting, heating, ventilation, air conditioning systems, and motors).
- Estimate occupancy, equipment, and lighting (energy use density and hours in operation)

You can prepare an overview of your action plan, current expenses, future expenses, investments, calculated ROI, and planned achievement dates.

Note that some Chinese companies have only one electricity meter and only one water meter for entire buildings or even corporate compounds, and this is clearly insufficient for performing cost breakdowns.

2.12.3 Professional Services

Please check what items you have in your company and follow up benchmarking contracts:

- Advertisements for marketing; contracts
- External interpreting and translations service
- Consultancies
- Flights, e.g., negotiation and advance purchasing of business-class contingents. International travel ticket booking services are a must, as are contracts detailing what and how to service.
- Lawyer fees
- Marketing
- Patents
- Security guards and security services for plants
- Retailer outlets
- Training and workshop costs; vocational schools
- Travel expenses (car, bus, trains, taxi, underground, hotels, and private accommodation expenses)
- Health insurances
- Shuttle buses
- HRS

1. For example, across China, 5-star hotel rooms can generally be booked for 500 RMB/night, and in Shanghai you can get a comfortable 4-star hotel rooms for 500 RMB/night, including a gym and swimming pool. But someone is telling you that HQ managers need a much better one, for 800 RMB or more. That is a lie and probably because they are taking commission on the side.

Running a hotel in China is a good business, as people are scurrying from place to place constantly. To reduce costs for your visitors from headquarters, you need to benchmark and negotiate.

In one case, an expensive hotel with a new sales manager increased prices by 10%, arguing that their nights stayed by visitors dropped within the last year. Sometimes in such cases, it is useful to change hotels to a cheaper one with less or the same comfort, and the expensive one will recognize their losses. The result in this example was that 1 year later, they came back for negotiation.

2. As another example, traditionally in China, a company needs one lawyer for HR issues and one for legal contracts for purchasing or M&A. To avoid splitting contracts between them, you can find larger law firms, who can cover all kind of difficulties.

   In one case, due to good relationships between legal and HR, one company found it unnecessary to sign any contracts within the last 10 years, but employed two lawyers full time due to the large number of issues at court. Any and all negotiations were done by HR alone, without involving purchasing or finance. You may know that representing a company at court is expensive and is not covered as regular consulting service fee. A better option is to let your purchasing department do the benchmarking and let them sign contracts with fixed yearly hours of service and fixed prices for court work. In Suzhou, lawyers cost 1000 to 1500 RMB/h, with contractual yearly prices for 40 h working time/year of about 40,000 RMB. In Shanghai, they cost 2000 RMB and above, and yearly prices are negotiable. Court prices are mostly calculated based on a percentage of claims, differing between HR and criminal cases, with maximum and minimum payments regulated by law. Lawyers can take risk orders as well, paid by percentage if successful (e.g., 50%), with no payment required if the case is lost.

3. In China, most employees have no car of their own to commute with. Running shuttle buses is cheaper than paying taxi fees, calculating 365 days' minus 104 days for weekends minus 11 days for Chinese holidays. Running shuttle buses in the morning to bring staff to the office and shop floor on time, and at evening to bring staff back home, is a challenge for both companies and drivers. To avoid having staff wake up too early or get home too late, you need to run several buses along different routes, and these are operated at different costs, due to time, fuel, and administration differences. Benchmarking is very useful to see the borderline.

   In Shanghai, you can roughly calculate based on 700 RMB/day for a 35-seater bus, and 800 RMB/day for a 40-seater bus. As a bus becomes depreciated and worn out, you will get an even lower price; therefore, you will need to monitor feedback from employees according to flexibility, timetables, seat comfort, and other issues.

4. Car insurance: Each car insurance policy has a different expiration date, based on the insurance company's quotation and contract. You need an overview, to react and benchmark in advance.

5. Health insurance for family members is very common at WFOEs. As they cover all costs for children, workers and office people with children love it. But this

insurance is very expensive, costing more than 100,000 RMB/year, even for small companies. If you compare the expenses with the costs of reimbursements, the insurance company mostly wins out, not even covering a majority of major illnesses.

6. Social insurance and housing funds: If employees come from other provinces, they will want to keep their insurance and housing funds registered with their hometown. This is because if they change, they will lose their deposit. Agents will help to pay such kind of costs for these employees. One sample agent's fee is 50 RMB/per person/per month (tax excluded). Another one charges a basic fee of 100 RMB and 20 RMB/month for each person. A third one charges 2200 RMB/year for five people each.
7. Health Examinations: Companies need to pay for health examinations for all employees, once a year. Special workers like welders have different requirements than office workers. There are hospitals or private companies available to do this service at different prices and including different content, from 200 to 500 RMB/person, starting from 7 AM, even on weekends. Unfortunately, expat employees tend to get sick frequently while stationed abroad, and will need expensive treatment to cure any severe illnesses. You can ignore such games with the insurance companies, as they are simply games to squeeze money out of your or company's pocket.
8. Relocation service: Company's need to be very generous to pay service to relocate expats to their new posts, or do benchmark work in advance. If you wait until new staff are already on board, you will be under time pressure for visas, working permits, accommodations, etc. For example, housing and city tours can be charged up to 2000 RMB/day, and immigration services can cost up to 1000 RMB/person.
9. High-tech application and tax reduction: If you run an R&D department, or intend to do, why not apply for this prestigious high-tech status? You need to find experts for this task who are able to prepare the proper documents and have good relationships with the high-tech review committee members, the people who determine whether to give their approval. With this high-tech status, you can reduce your taxes tremendously, and therefore, these service companies charge your company a lot. For example, they may require a lump sum consulting fee ranging from 0 to 300,000 RMB, plus a fee for the deduction of R&D expenses starting from 150,000 RMB to 5% of the tax rate of the expenses. But this task gets more difficult, as according to new regulations in China, the experts forming the committee are to be nominated randomly. So, you may never know who will be responsible for your company's case.
10. Headhunters: To benchmark and avoid signing contracts for each search, the best method is to sign a service agreement with your preferred company. They will charge consulting fees (about 20–25% of the candidate's annual income), incidental expenses (about 5% for traveling, telecommunication, and secretarial costs), and tax (3.4% of total payment).

Handicapped people: Due to Chinese government policies, the more handicapped people a company employs, the less tax the company pays. Sometimes these people wish to work remotely, but other times they will require accessible working places, internal pathways, transportation, and the cost of which has to be calculated against your tax savings.

2.12.4 IT

Some tasks:

- Performing IT services and creating web pages
- Handling phones and mobile phones; conference phones
- Managing software and hardware, e.g., desktops, notebooks, screens, printers, flatbed and hand scanners, projectors, digital cameras, and accessories
- Managing telecommunications, fax software, and routers

For example, an IT hardware catalog with pictures, specification, and prices, running for 1 year, avoids specific negotiations under time pressure when products are needed.

2.12.5 Tools

Some tasks:

- Tooling (dies and molds)
- Tools for operations
- Jigs and fixtures

For example, maintenance for tool shop and molds needs time-consuming preparations and price negotiations. If you are under time pressure due to sudden damages to your machines, you will be charged very highly and will lose a lot of money. A better approach is to check the service life of your tooling and inserts and report on their status every month or two, so you will see any production risks at one glance. See a sample Excel table header below; the yellow part is added to calculate the timing for new inserts (Fig. 2.9).

For new dies and molds, you will need to collect addresses of toolmakers to do efficient and quick benchmarking.

2.12.6 Machines

Some tasks:

- Machine investment, make or buy calculations
- Managing equipment
- Managing machinery

Injection Tooling List (Die & Molds)											
No.	Tooling No.	ERP No.	Tooling Name	Part name	Customer OEM	Part No.	Tool maker	SOP Date	Status	Remark	Contract
1											Number of Cavities?
											Lifetime warranty (shots)?
											When inserts need to be repaired? (time)
											Actual shots/year, according to customer requirements
											Spare parts available?

Fig. 2.9 How to build an overview of your tooling lists. Source: GTEC, 2021

- Oversee all manufacturing steps, for example, at injection process, from drying, to the melting of raw material, to painting, assembly, and packing.

1. For example, a paint shop needs to hire an external cleaning service. A new contract for 2020 has been signed with 5% lower price.
2. For example, instead of buying new machines right away, you need to check:
   (a) The occupancy of your current machines.
   (b) Whether using idle machines and modifying them will be cheaper than buying new ones.
   (c) To use line flexibility with the possibility of changing tools instead of fixed lines only for one product, as you never know if volume will drop down.
   (d) To use screwing systems with the best price and performance ratio.
   (e) To consider to use idle manual operating machines instead of buying new automated ones.

2.12.7 Development Service, Test Equipment

Some tasks:

- Manage test center costs, e.g., certificate costs for raw material or fasteners
- Handle tools, fixtures, and jigs,

For example, a test equipment catalog, including a contract for maintenance, avoids specific negotiations under time pressure, when sudden purchasing is needed.

2.12.8 Development Service, Engineering Material

Some items to control:

- Fasteners
- Development services

- Project management costs
- Prototypes
- Spare parts
- Service workshops

2.12.9 Canteen Food for Lunch and Shift Workers

Some tasks:

- Cleaning; replacing toilet paper
- Cleaning and housekeeping/catering services for household and food, external or internal
- Health, safety, and environment (internal or external)

2.12.10 Consumables for Production and Supply

Some items to control:

- Sandpaper
- Grease

Do you have a production supply catalog available? How many of your supply sources are dealers, and how many do you buy from manufacturers? Do you have contacts to service agents who bundle your small volumes with other companies, if the specifications are the same?

Some companies have more than 400 supply sources, an immense task to handle and to take care of every company, with a huge admin and paper workload. Please think about reducing and bundling a few to one supplier, agent, or service company each.

2.12.11 Office Supplies

Some areas to manage:

- Advertisements
- Exhibitions/marketing
- Entertainment
- Gifts, presents
- Outside printing/offsets

For example, with a new office supply catalog, a 1-year contract for 2020 with new prices due to higher volume, delivered only by one supplier, could achieve an average cost reduction of about 20%. Departments can select what they need according to their budget, with no further negotiations required, which saves everybody's time as well.

2.12.12 Finance

Some tasks to handle:

- Banks, loans, fees, saving plans
- Insurance
- Landlord fees, properties, ground costs
- Renting and leasing

2.12.13 Disposal Costs/Waste

Some tasks:

- Yearly contracts

For example, hazardous waste contracts can only be done with qualified, licensed, and registered private or governmental companies. You will find only a few approved for your area, no matter whether they are local or international. For both, you need to benchmark and negotiate the following: paint slag (disposal costs of 4700–6000 RMB/ton), waste solvents (3400–4000), waste cutting fluid (3300–4600), waste activated carbon (7800–10,500), waste oil (3300–4600), waste acid (18,000), waste water (3000–3700), wasted filters (5600–7000), waste laboratory reagents (20,000–23,000), waste glue (8700–14,000), wasted paint containers (2800–4200), and/or waste PCB (5400 RMB/ton). All prices are without VAT and for a 1-year contract. For a mid-size company with about 100 tons/year of paint slag, waste water, and waste solvent, you need budget of about two million RMB. Please make sure that a single company can cover all type of waste, otherwise you need to handle and manage more suppliers, which increases your workload and reduces your efficiency.

2.12.14 Environment–Health–Safety: EHS

For environmental monitoring tests and discharge permit contracts, you must perform benchmarking and negotiation in the same way as the disposal costs described above.

2.13 Lean Process Flow of Nonproduction Material

How do you organize a lean process flow concept for the approval of NPM?

In your organization, is there a process written, for example, what is required of the ISO9001 certification? You may ask your quality department. If not, then prepare a lean process, based on either paper or online. Check if your ERP system is able to integrate such workflows for approval and what needs to be modified to start with a test run. For example:

1. Sign the approval document by the applicant
2. Sign an approval document by supervisor/department head/general manager/COO, depending on approval templates.
3. Send the document to the responsible person defined in the RASIC chart. This person will benchmark it, compare it with the current supplier, and negotiate a yearly contract and prices based on last year's volume. Do not let them buy single items, otherwise the staff workload will be enormous, or else you will gain no cost reductions.
4. If a delivery arrives at the office or warehouse, quality and volume need to be checked before signing your acceptance.
5. The applicant will be informed to pick up and sign for deliveries
6. The document will be put into the ERP system and be forwarded to finance for final payment, if no advance payment was completed (Fig. 2.10)

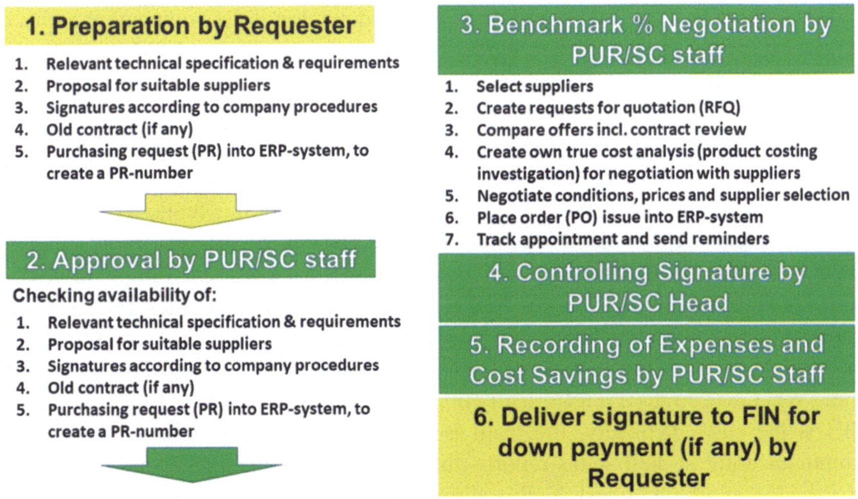

Fig. 2.10 Workflow of NPM from requester to finance department. Red = responsibility of requester. Green = responsibility of purchasing department. Source: GTEC, 2017

How to Calculate Savings?

The chart above shows an example for a plant. According to agreements with HQ, there is a possibility to calculate cost savings for each buyer

- only one time,
- according to contracts for 1 year or more,
  or:
- according to live production times for serial parts, for one to 5 years. In our case, we agreed to 3 years (Fig. 2.11).

You will be surprised how much savings you will reap, but you need to realize these changes and put them into practice and daily routing. Managers need to follow up on issues until topic is closed. The color yellow marks still open projects, whereas green marks items that are already closed and realized.

2.14 How Do Chinese Purchasing Managers and Buyers Think?[13]

I execute projects with discipline. What I have seen with many project managers is that they typically do what is expected of them, and not much more. A purchasing manager (PM) explained to me one time why he did not do status reports. He said, "They've never asked for one, so I've never felt the need to do one." Too many PMs fall into this trap. They know what *needs* to be done, but if the company or project sponsor does not require it, they figure it is not important. A good PM will always produce a status report, always manage issues, always provide meeting minutes, always have a plan for executing a project (with specific dates and assignments), always obtain approval in writing for changes to the project's scope, schedule or budget, and many other things that are never asked for at most companies. A successful PM does what needs to be done, whether or not it is requested.

I use status reports to drive accountability. Status reports are more than a communications tool; a successful PM uses them to drive accountability. An effective status report summarizes the key issues facing the project and reports on the status of major tasks, including the "why" behind any task that is behind schedule, and provides leadership with the information needed to take action. The VP asked me, "What do you do if a team isn't cooperating?" The first step is to identify why this is the case. Typically, the team is tied up working on other priorities. By communicating in their status report—that the project is in jeopardy because team X is tied up working on task Y, this allows the sponsor to take action to reprioritize things. Occasionally, task Y will actually be a higher priority than your project. In that case, you will need to get approval from the sponsor to adjust the deliverable

[13] Sources: (20+) 1141 Group—Posts | Facebook; http://1141group.com/letters-to-mike-what-successful-pms-do/; created 4.1.2019. Author JM Chambers, Playwright, for 1141group.com; Access date 4.1.2019.

Cost saving calculation report template

Financial Data (RMB): green realized, yellow in process

	Names + items	Total	year_month												
PLANT	A		2020_10	2020_11	2020_12	2021_01	2021_02	2021_03	2021_04	2021_05	2021_06	2021_07	2021_08	2021_09	2021_10
	B	47785	47785												
	C	1134132	46753	195517	876004	15858									
	D	57304	15317	19000	13000	9987									
	E			42000											
	F			15500											
	G	1045000		87083	87083	87083	87083	87083	87083	87083	87083	87083	87083	87083	87083
	H	441876					36823	36823	36823	36823	36823	36823	36823	36823	36823
	I	3891300					324275	324275	324275	324275	324275	324275	324275	324275	324275
	J	391200						32600	32600	32600	32600	32600	32600	32600	32600
	Total Reported Savings so far	7008597	109855	359100,3	976087,3	112928,3	448181,3	480781,3	480781,3	480781,3	480781,3	480781,3	480781,3	480781,3	480781,3

Fig. 2.11 Cost-saving template. Green = already finished tasks. Yellow = work in progress, not finished yet. Source: GTEC, 2021

date, engage outside resources to keep the project on track, or adjust the scope of the project (all of which should be documented and approved in whatever format the company uses to approve project changes). Status reports that transparently reflect the state of the project create an environment where teams are held accountable for their progress. Of course, before adding the issue to the status report, you will want to speak with the team's manager and see if you can work out the issue. Let them know that unless you can work something out, the lack of progress will be escalated to leadership via the status report. Make absolutely sure when you include the issue in your status report that you factually state exactly what is going on—facts only, no opinions. For example, "This deliverable will be delayed by 2 weeks because team X is tied up working on project Y."

I create a structure that helps project teams succeed. I often imagine a challenging initiative as a very tall brick wall that the team must get over to successfully complete their project. The team is gathered around the base of the wall, looking up at it, and wondering how they will get over it. The project manager is responsible for building the ladder that helps the team get over the wall, organizing tasks (rungs in the ladder) so that the team can climb.

Every time I finished an event, be it a marathon or a long motorbike ride, I inventory what I have learned about myself, my gear, and, if I am riding, my motorcycle. As lessons learned are a key part of project management, they are also part of being successful in any endurance event. Closing out any project requires that the project manager lead the team through assessing what they have learned, what worked and what did not work, and what would have made the project more successful.

I am not suggesting that you take up endurance sports, but that you gain an understanding what it takes to prepare for and successfully complete such a challenging event can provide a project manager with an interesting perspective on what it takes to successfully run a multiyear project.[14]

You easily can exchange projects via purchasing and this may be very effective, as most tasks in purchasing are like small projects, from sales, to supply chain, to production, to customer satisfaction with OTD, to complaint management, and aftermarket services. Sometimes this is a multiyear project where purchasing is permanently involved with action and expertise.

2.15 Are Exhibitions Able to Support Cost Reduction Activities?

Definitely. You will find new sources of supply and raw materials, and get ideas for the next generations of your current products. For example, exhibitions can show you possibilities to avoid using welding, to substitute it with other, cheaper methods

[14] Sources: (20+) 1141 Group – Posts | Facebook; http://1141group.com/letters-to-mike-endurance/; created 27.12.2018. Author JM Chambers, Playwright, for Author 1141group.com; Access date 4.1.2019.

of assembly, or cheaper methods of reinforcement. Several years ago, a sheet metal supplier offered welded different thicknesses and material, so their customer did not need to do it themselves.

Which exhibitions are worth visiting in Shanghai? See the following links:

https://10times.com/china/logistics-transportation, for example:

The China (Shenzhen) International Logistics and Supply Chain Fair (CILF) is the leading logistics and transport expo in Asia, and is held in Shenzhen, China, to support logistics service, SCM, ports and shipping, transportation, express delivery, e-commerce, IT solutions, mobility, air cargo, material handling, and more. The last was held on 12/10/2019.

https://10times.com/china/automotive/tradeshows

https://10times.com/china/electronics-electricals/tradeshows

https://10times.com/china/technology/tradeshows

2.16 What Does Standardization Have to Do with Purchasing?

I had a meeting with customers who wanted to clean dirty gases, and a German expatriate wanted to standardize his products. His Chinese senior purchaser asked him, "what is standardization is useful for?" For the first few seconds, he did not know what to say, so I jumped in and said "to reduce costs," and everybody agreed by smiling and nodding their heads. The customer's goal was to have the same design in place at towers of different diameters and lengths. But he learned that, the bigger the internal systems, the more reinforcement was needed, so standardization was only partly possible in this case.

However, do be careful, as most of these types of meetings are waste of time for suppliers. They can even be dangerous, if you give them your ideas and your designs. Orders will be given to manufacturers, who will be able to produce your design more cheaply. A clever salesperson will delete the most important and most easily replicable items from an offer, protecting their resources.

2.17 Is Teamwork Required to Harvest Low-Hanging Fruit?

A purchasing manager or external consultant is not able to shoulder all responsibility for every single thing that might deviate them from their course. Instead of removing other people from the process, teams must work to identify root causes and work on improvements together.

Progress and proposed actions should be tracked and reviewed together with HQ on a regular basis. If necessary, workshops can be held with buyers, producers, and suppliers, supported by HQ.

Consultants can only make proposals, hold no managerial roles, and have no influence over whether their proposals will be put into reality. As I said, a team approach is necessary with the support of multiple departments.

For example, as a general manager, my focus here is to reduce costs. Even my buyers have targets to reduce their own costs as well, but few of them are on the shop floor, and they do not discuss their issues with the operators. On the shop floor, I saw a lot of gloves lying in waste paper baskets and took them out to look at them. They were only slightly dirty, with no reason to throw them away. So, I initiated two actions: (1) limiting one pair of gloves per week per operator, with gloves to be changed only if the current pair is truly dirty or damaged beyond use, and (2) hosting a workshop and awareness training regarding 8 types of waste (7 types of waste +1 of creativity) within the company. The result was a 50% cost reduction. We bought thinner and cheaper gloves as well, but this increased the damage rate. So, it is clear that a test period is always necessary to confirm the sustainability of any cost savings.

In addition to reducing wastes on the shop floor, other examples of savings include standardization, maintenance, spare part management, and other related areas. I see tasks to realize cost savings both outside (a) and inside (b) purchasing.

(a) Non-purchasing-based savings requires initiatives to bring the GM and production manager to the table. Currently, I do not know them and do not know what their consensus on their personal goals is, if any. I can only hope that we all on the same page here.
(b) In purchasing measures, even the buyers are motivated and like to support these sort of initiatives, but do they have time for sourcing and benchmarking? What I have seen shows me that most buyers' working time is occupied with tasks related to their purchasing process, and these can generally either be eliminated or be made leaner. For example, you can look at who needs to put which data into the SAP system, or whether internal investigations of lean process flow have already been made.

What I learned in my 15 years at SC is that most low-hanging fruit lies outside purchasing and need a lot of cooperation to be reaped.

2.18 News from China

The southeastern Chinese city of Ningbo is a magnet for buyers. South of Shanghai, Ningbo is home to six million people, the second largest city in Zhejiang Province. Its gross economic product is sixth place among Chinese cities after Guangzhou, Shenzhen, Hangzhou, Chengdu, and Qingdao. Local entrepreneurs in the area are known for their prudence, focus on quality, and customer orientation.

China has a huge variety of manufacturing companies. However, due to the sheer size of the market, a lack of transparency, and quality variations, the supplier landscape of China is not easy to navigate. BME assists buyer companies in finding new potential suppliers, as well as in deepening and improving existing supplier relations. BME Shanghai sourcing services include the following:

- Supplier buyer matchmaking meetings (SBMMs)
- Tailored, prescreened supplier searches
- Demand distribution through a variety of channels (contacts, partnerships, institutions)
- Benchmarking between existing suppliers and new candidates
- Organization and conceptual planning of supplier working days
- Accompanying measures
- Quality controls

As German and European corporations are constantly searching for new potential partners, BME China is also looking for new, high-quality suppliers, who we welcome to join us and find new customers.[15]

https://www.bme.de/index.php?id=9128

https://www.bme.de/en/international-network/bme-in-china/events/

International Sourcing Fair

The International Sourcing Fair (ISF) is the largest reverse sourcing fair in China to support B2B business. Each year, the fair is visited by up to 10,000 suppliers from all provinces in China and several surrounding countries.

SF China is a national-level event organized by China's Ministry of Commerce and the Shanghai Municipal People's Government. ISF Structure: International buyers set up booths, and suppliers come to visit.

We invite quality suppliers from all over China, with the assistance of 30 cooperating provinces and cities (nearly 80% of visiting suppliers come from outside Shanghai).

Website: http://www.sourcing.org.cn/

Shanghai Convention & Exhibition Center of International Sourcing

No.2739 West Guangfu Road, Putuo District, Shanghai, China

Tel: +86-021-60290070

http://en.shcec.com.cn/

2019.11.7-9: https://www.showsbee.com/fairs/ISF-China.html

2022: https://www.showsbee.com/fairs/72491-ISF-China-2022.html

[15] Source: https://www.bme.de/en/international-network/bme-in-china/services/, Author BME.de, created 2021. Access date 13.2.2021.

3 Asian Supplier Productivity Diagnosis

3.1 The Toyota Production System TPS

Before going deeper into diagnosis of industrial suppliers' productivity, following please find some formulas for operating business performance measuring and world-class index as references.

K. Zuerl, *Effective Cost Cutting in Asia*, Management for Professionals,
https://doi.org/10.1007/978-3-030-82782-3_3

Manufacturing performances	Formula/ definition	World class index
Customer Return	$$= \frac{\text{Total quantity of unacceptable products rejected by the customers and acknowledged by the supplier}}{\text{total quantity of components delivered to all customers}} \times 1 \text{ Million}$$	(< 10 ppm)
Cost of waste, scraps, and reworks	$$= \frac{\text{total annual costs of internal waste, scrap and internal rework}}{\text{total annual sales value}} \times 100$$ Remarks: **Internal waste** includes extra material, components, purchased parts and subassemblies... damaged binned or processed without producing parts. **Internal scrap** includes all defective products, resulting from faulty manufacturing or assembly, that do not meet quality requirements after being reworked and reasonably cannot be used for any other purpose. The overall costs including labour, material and overheads must be taken into account. Revenues from selling scrap shall not be deducted. **Internal rework** encompasses the activities aimed at making a non-compliant product meet the quality requirements. Unsuccessful rework usually generate scrap costs in addition to rework costs.	(< 1% of turnover)
Inventory turns	$$= \frac{\text{sales value of all products manufactured within one year}}{\text{appropriate value of total inventory (raw materials, work in-progress and finished goods) within one year}}$$ Remarks: all products owned or controlled should be taken into account even if they are not physically located on-site, e.g. consignment stocks held at customers.	(> 33 in a year)

Dock to dock time (throughput time)	Time elapsed between arrival of 1kg of main raw material (or component) at the receiving dock and same kg of processed material (or component) included in finished product loaded in delivery vehicle at the shipping dock Remarks: the dock to dock time is the physical total duration of manufacturing including all waiting, transfer, handling and processing time from very first receiving to actual shipment.	(< 8 working days)
Overall equipment effectiveness (O.E.E.)	time that the process had to be run for manufacturing good parts at the standard /optimum cycle time speed, output rate, etc. = -- x 100 time the process was planned to run according to the quarterly or yearly budget (opening time) Remarks: O.E.E. is calculated for the bottle neck equipment of the manufacturing process of the big runners.	(> 90% good parts of big runners)
Production Space Utilization/ turnover	sales value of all products produced = -- x 100 total production space including all storages and offices areas, but excluding specialist R&D facilities, etc. Remarks: Areas currently not in use but already owned/constructed in view of future expansion should be included in the calculation	(>4,5 k€/m²)
Change over time (setup time)	Time from the last correct part of one production run to the first correct part of the next (measured in minutes), when production is continuous. Remarks: Set-up time is calculated for the bottle neck equipment of the manufacturing process of the big runners.	< 5 minutes of bottle neck equipment of big runners

Customer delivery achievement	= [total number of "lines of order", supplied against customer schedule (to be defined by each individual site/ company − the quantity shipped early or late + incorrect quantity + subject to customer claim and/or return for incorrect quality or reference number] / [total number of "lines of order" supplied] x 100	(target 100% of customer's schedule)
suggestions per employee per year	= number of employee suggestions implemented or actioned and recorded / average total number of employees, including interim and temporary hired people	(> 20)
Turnover per employee)	= sales value of all products manufactured excluding trading / total number of employees, including interim and temporary hired people	(> 225 k€/ person
Added Value per employee	= sales value of all products manufactured excluding trading, less cost of raw materials, bought out components, sub contracted processing, consumable stores, loose tools, repairs and maintenance of plant and equipment, heat, light and power, transport, packaging, production services and other purchased services / total number of employees, including interim and temporary hired people Remarks: added value is the sum of profit, financial charges and administration overheads	(k€/ person)

3.2 Supplier Diagnosis

The following entire data-obtaining process took place at supplier sites. All companies were observed over a period of 9–12 months, using a four-step observation process.

Step 1
Selection of the line or process to be observed in the plant.

Step 2
Initial diagnosis of the selected line.

This diagnostic period usually lasted 2 days and required the collaboration of a group of four or five managers from different departments. During the visit, measurements were taken of the production indicators published in the lines, and their dates of publication were also noted if available. To deal with specific key issues, the head of quality control or maintenance was consulted to obtain a second opinion in addition to that of the head of the production department.

Step 3
Development of Kaizen Blitz activities and actions.

A 4–5-day workshop model was used under the guidance of consultants. Groups of 5–14 people participated in these workshops, half of whom were workers. The contents of the workshops were selected in line with the needs detected in the diagnosis. The workshops started off by explaining the theory behind the tools that were used in the event and by making sure that everybody understood them. These tools included 5S tools, Visual Factory and Layout Redesigns for less developed plants in lean manufacturing to Kanban, and TPM techniques for those in which these techniques had already been introduced. The workshop participants were responsible for taking samples of the production indicator measurements and for attaching photographs or video\recordings when necessary. These data served to set out the initial values of the indicators, prior to the intervention of the ad hoc group. At the end of the week, the group had implemented the chosen improvements and proposed an immediate action plan for further improvements dependent on management approval. Toward the end, a data were agreed upon for following up on changes in the production efficiency indicators. These data served to establish the final value of the indicators after the group's intervention.

This process was repeated two or three times in each company over a 9-month period until the objectives specified in the initial diagnosis were fulfilled. In total, two or three Kaizen Blitzes were carried out in each company during this period.

Step 4
Drafting a report summarizing the activities and the addition of same to the research database.

All covered companies received the same intervention, summarized in the four steps described above in the data gathering process, with allowances made for the particular circumstances of each company.

To create our dependent variables, we only selected production efficiency indicators gathered by objective measures. We considered that for the proposed research aims, objective performance measures provided a more robust comparison, as they are less prone to short-term fluctuations. As our interest was centered on evaluating the impact on the production process, no financial indicators or human resources-related indicators were registered.

Five operational measures were utilized to assess the efficiency of the productive process, as follows:

1. Quality (Q)–the percentage of the correctly produced pieces, compared to the total number of pieces processed.
2. Overall equipment efficiency (OEE)—the time—ring which the machine is working and producing correct pieces according to specifications, compared with the total net time available.
3. TTP time—throughput time. The throughput time or manufacturing cycle time is made up of process time, inspection time, move time, and queue time.
4. Workforce productivity—units produced per hour.
5. Changeover time—the time that a machine is stopped to make the necessary adjustments so that it can manufacture a different model.

Despite the positive results achieved in this process, we must ultimately consider that the presented measures are not applied independently. For example, improvements in the quality of automated processes will affect the efficiency of the machines. Efficiency is also affected by a reduction in the changeover time, because more machine manufacturing time can be obtained depending on the extent of the time reduction. Nevertheless, this relationship is not direct because the company can take advantage of the increase in changeover speed to make more changes instead of directly increasing the number of production hours. In this case, machine use will not be improved quantitatively, but the TTP indicator would be enhanced, since the work in progress would be smaller when working with smaller batches. As an example, we can see that in the case of Company X, a 6% improvement in OEE results from the improved quality of the products, while the 40% reduction in the changeover time did not improve efficiency, as company policy was to cut the size of the batches. What did improve in this case was the TTP indicator (22%), which meant that on average, the products stayed within the plant for one fewer week (a decrease from 23 to 18 days).

One important aspect for the smooth running of interventions was the support shown by the managers in the ad hoc group meetings, as well as the presence of the CEO at the closing session of each workshop. In addition, the structure of the workshops facilitated communication between the group and management, while the accompanying training acted as a means to reduce resistance to change.

On the other hand, cooperation between external and internal teams was considered highly satisfactory by both sides. One of the fundamental reasons for this good working relationship was the use of standard lean production tools (5S, SMED, TPM, balanced worklines, etc.) whose existence and utility were already well known to all management involved, including even the least experienced personnel.

It should be mentioned here that the client was able to benefit from the obtained results by lowering the prices of the products that benefited from these improvements. This was one of the primary aims of the external consultants, although these changes were met with some resistance on the part of the companies, even if they benefited from the other improvements. This resistance was basically due to the existence of other clients' products that would be negatively affected by these improvements, but the client insisted on partially improving this component and then reducing the price of the related components and products.

In some cases, operations were extended to other departments after the initial cycle of changes was completed. This mostly happened in the case of multinationals who have already experienced this type of practice. Other companies confined themselves to maintaining the implemented improvements and showed limited interest in extending these changes to other areas, despite being aware of the benefits involved. The reasons given in the interviews were the classic "resistance to change" or statements like "right now we haven't time," or that they were more interested in growing than improving, even though they admitted that this attitude was flawed.

At the same time, it must be recognized that without the presence of outside consultants, i.e., without the client being obliged to participate, approximately 80% of the participating companies would not have implemented these sort of improvements, for the same reason that they were not interested in subsequently extending them to other areas. We can say that this experience is replicable, but only with the direct support of management for this type of improvement team. For the reasons cited above, this support is not always forthcoming.

Limitations of this project include the fact that data boxes to be filled in were blank, and this may be significant. The main cause of this issue was the cost to the company of providing the data that enabled us to calculate these indicators, or as in the case of Company Y, policies of confidentiality that prevented our access to the data. Some companies also provided inconsistent data, depending on the source that provided them (the production, quality, or maintenance department). For this reason, during our intervention in the initial workshop, we had to trace the necessary data. This was carried out together with the components of the ad hoc group and under the supervision of the training consultants. These data were then compared with a range of sources or were directly taken from the plants when divergences arose. This process took up almost 2 days of work in each company and required the participation of several managers, usually those occupying key positions in maintenance, quality, or production departments. Therefore, to avoid resistance to change, in each factory, we limited ourselves to obtaining the measures of the indicators that were of immediate practical use, taking into account the needs detected in the initial diagnosis, the implemented training actions, and the changes introduced in the production lines.

An important advantage of our work was our ability to obtain data from multiple sources (through interviews, observations, and documentation analysis), giving a certain degree of confidence in the results. The interviews were formally conducted during diagnostic sessions, and the production managers took part. Line observations were done both during the initial diagnosis and during workshop development. The records of the production, quality, and maintenance departments were also consulted to compare them with the line observations made during the workshops. Due to our selected data-sampling methodology, this task was laborious and demanded great dedication from the researchers. For this reason, adapting to the available resources in our research design, we chose to observe a limited number of cases.

We believed that the use of brief training–intervention dynamics attended by people from different hierarchic levels and different departments, and related to a production line or process, could contribute to improving the production results. These sessions needed to incorporate icebreaker dynamics, to create an atmosphere that encourages problem-solving in groups, as well as the philosophy and methodology of the lean management tools to be implemented. During these sessions, it was also necessary to set aside time to "capture" the necessary data, to analyze them, and to propose alternatives for improvement. It is recommended that these sessions should be guided by experts in the application of these tools and that they should supervise the group's data gathering and other activities.

It is advisable that, at the end of the week, a plan be agreed upon, and if possible, that the participants should make a presentation of the same to the company management, establishing a consensus of acceptance and obtaining a commitment for the dates to be kept by everyone involved.[1]

Operational cost reduction and optimization services. A lot of companies offering this industrial productivity diagnosis service, few examples like

- https://www.gtec.asia
- https://www.facebook.com/ipsipr/
- https://industrialproductivitysolutions.com/

Following practical templates, taken from ICARE Institute[2] with figures from a supplier producing plastic injection parts in China, currency is kept Euro in this case. You will learn how to proceed to do your diagnosis by yourself, saving external

[1] Source: http://www.upv.es/i.grup/repositorio/own/ART_2009Marin%26Garcia-Sabater%26Bonavia_IJATM_Def_impact%20of%20Kaizen%20Events%20on%20improving%20the%20performance.pdf, Authors Marin-Garcia, J.A., Garcia-Sabater, J.J. and Bonavia, T. (2009). Title "The impact of Kaizen Events on improving the performance of automotive components' first-tier suppliers," Int. J. Automotive Technology and Management, Vol. 9, No. 4, pp. 362–376. Source pages 367–374, *Access date 13.02.2021*

[2] SUPPLIER INDUSTRIAL & PRODUCTIVITY DIAGNOSIS TRAINING SESSION, Oct 2005, Paris. Author ICARE Institute, 79, Rue Jean-Jacques Rousseau—92,150 SURESNES, France

consultancy. If any questions or you need support, please contact author at contact@gtec.asia.

1) GENERAL DATA

Year:						
Plant:						
Turnover	15	Mio l		Oversea parts:	2,25	Mio l
Integration Level	48	%				
Total Company People	150					
Added Value	7	Mio l				
Total end year stock value	2	Mio l		% of sales:	14	%
				Inventory returns	7,14	
Total surface	8.500	qm				
reworks and scrap cost	0,28	Mio l				
product quantity delivered/year	200.525.000					
quantity of rejects by customers/year	601.575					
Turnover /person	0,10	Ml/person				
Added value/person	0,48	Ml/person				
Stock/ T.O.	14,00	%				
T.O./qm	1,76	kl/qm				
% of reworks, scraps/ T.O.	1,87	%				
Customer returns	3.000	p.p.m.				

Targets and ambitions of the company in middle term:	**yes**	**no**
Certification		
A rating by customers		
Increase productivity (cost/savings)		
Increase of turnover to .....Mio		

Areas of progress targeted:

co-development with customers for long term win to win relationsship
quality: 50% cutting of customer returns
Equipment effectiveness: 50% cutting of waste

Products

Major product families	Technology used	Batch volumes (in % of T.O.)		
		high volume	core volum	low volume
styling parts	injection	30	20	10
control parts	overmoulding	20	10	
electronic box covers	injection			10

2) COMPANY ENVIRONMENT

The file identifies the contraints, threats and opportunities from outside the company

Customers

total number of customers	200	
number of customers representing 80% of the turnover	5	
Weight of the first customer	30	%
Number of customers in EDI mode	2	
% of variation of the 1st customer program		%
Automotive activity (% of T.O.)	60	%

Suppliers

Number of suppliers:	200
number of suppliers representing 80% of the purchase	22

Competitors:

number of competitors in Asia	?
Leader market share in China	?
Your company market share in China	?

	yes	no
Customers		
Do you participate to the development of new products?	☐	☐
Suppliers		
Do your suppliers get involved in your development?	☐	☐
Product/Process		
Is there any evolution or replacement threat on your current product or process?	☐	☐
Is your process conform with European/Asian regulations?	☐	☐

Competitors

What are your competitive advantages: Technology know-how
flexibility (close to customers)

Reserved for diagnosis:

3) MANAGEMENT

Knowhow of product costing and analysis of the management system

Cost structure	% of turnover (T.O.)		
raw material	36		
components	8		
production consumable and tooling	9		
Labour (incl. Temps)	11		
indirect people, structure people	11		
plant general expenses	6		
production depreciation	8	Product cost	88
R&D costs	1,60		
Selling and Administrative cost	2		
Depreciation	3		
Financial fees	2		
gross results	3,00	Total	100

Management system	**yes**	**no**
Is there an industrial score card board?		
Is there an non productive purchase		
Is there a return of investment follow up?		
cost accounting?		
A MRP (SAP) system?		
Number of items (global part numbers/articles in your MRP) managed?	2000	

Do you calculate often?	**yes**	**no**
your loads vs. Your capacity?		
your supply needs?		
Material needed?		

Reserved for diagnosis:

4) QUALITY

One of the priciples of Lean Manufacturing is the only transfer of a good part between two added value operations, all along the production process from suppliers to the customer Quality Assurance System Analysis

Customers				
Return from customers	3.000	ppm		
Number of customers claims	30	in 12 months		
customer service level				
Suppliers:				
number of claims	22	in 12 months		
level of parts in AQP	0	%		
suppliers service level		%		
rate of return	3.000	ppm		
Internal:				
% of scraps or rework/ T.O.	2	%		
Cost of scraps & reworks, incl. Waste	300	kl		
Number of parameters followed in SPC				
Customers:			**yes**	**no**
Each claim is processed immediately in 100% of cases?			☐	☐
The management team is involved?			☐	☐
if yes how?			☐	☐
Internal:				
What are the 5 products generating the highest level on cost of non-	Box covers			
Have you implemented?			**yes**	**no**
a quality manual			☐	☐
SPC			☐	☐
Product tracking			☐	☐
On-Line self-inspection			☐	☐
problem solving groups			☐	☐
a quality score board			☐	☐
Has the company been audited?			☐	☐
If yes, based on which standard?				
Is there a simpel and visual daily measure of the quality level?			☐	☐
Is there a steady analysis of the scraps and reword analysis?			☐	☐
Reserved for diagnosis:				

5) PURCHASING

The weight of components or raw material is often higher than the labour. It can represent easily more than 50% of the price of the product. The control of this activity is as important as the control of the manufacturing process.

Total Purchasing Volume	8.152	k€		
raw material purchasing value	5.431	k€		
components purchasing value	1.121	k€		
toolings purchasing value	1.220	k€		
other purchasing value (consumable goods, eg. Pencils, gas)	380	k€		
workforce dedicated to purchasing	2			
number of references purchased	450			
number of suppliers	200			
Purchasing department tasks	**name/ group**		**Yes**	**No**
supplier panel management			☐	☐
incoming transportation fees			☐	☐
SQA/ PQA			☐	☐
Ordering			☐	☐
Planning			☐	☐
Purchasing negotiations			☐	☐
purchasing contracts			☐	☐
supplier development			☐	☐
Incoming inspection			☐	☐
warehouse management			☐	☐
% of the supply based on open ordering?				
Is there a supplier evaluation system?			☐	☐
If yes, % of suppliers evaluate?				
Criteria used?				
Is there a purchasing classification by			☐	☐
If yes, what are the families?		raw material components general expenses		
Is there a defined purchasing policy?			☐	☐
Reserved for diagnosis:				

6) PROCESSING

PROCESSING
A performed process has to be under control.
An optimistic use of resources such as materials, labour, machines and energy are key factors of

Designation and monitoring of most used process:

Products	Operation 1 Process 1	Operation 2 Process 2	Operation 3 Process 3	Operation 4 Process 4
Styling parts	moulding	printing		
control system parts	inserts	moulding		
bones & covers	moulding			

NB.: If production process has more than 5 operations, please notify only the most relevant process for your business

Process	No. of parameters under monitoring	Scraps & waste level in %
Moulding	5	2
insers preparation	2	
printing	1	0,05

Material performance	**Yes**		**No**
Do you follow your material usage ratio?			
Are wastes and scraps recycled?			
Are wastes and scraps sold?			

Average material use		%
Losses due to process		KI
Losses due to change overs		KI
Losses due to non-quality		KI

Manufacturing Process	**Yes**		**No**
Do you measure the OEE of equipment?			

	total	
Value of OEE (if measured)?	0,8	
Manufacturing Change Over Time?	4	hours
Number of change overs per day?	10	
Mean time to repair?	2	hours

	Yes		**No**
Do you have technical standards?			
Do you have manufacturing standards?			
Are they reviewed regularly?			
If yes, precise frequency?			

Reserved for diagnosis:

7-1) PROCESS FLOW

The shortening of delivery schedules, the downsizing of batch size and the diversification of items are highlighting the flow control as a key parameter to success. Working in a pull flow mode will help to work on bottlenecks and diminish the throughput time.

s	(please attach a map showing the implementation of the workshop)				
	total surface (offices included)	8.500	m²	100,00	%
	productive surface	4.000	m²	47,06	%
	storage & waiting surfaces	2.500	m²	29,41	%
	Other surfaces	2.000	m²	23,53	%
Stocks	Raw materials	659	k$	28,80	%
	components	198	k$	8,65	%
	work in process	427	k$	18,66	%
	finished goods	1.004	k$	43,88	%
	total value of the stock	2.288	k$	100,00	%

		Product1	Product 2
Summary of process mapping			
	Dock to dock time/ Added value time		
	Distance		

Delivery / Supply

		Supply: Supplier delivery	Delivery to customers	
Number of people dedicated to logistics		3	4	
delivery frequency	daily	0	0	%
	weekly	20	60	%
	monthly	60	20	%
	on request	20	20	%
production stoppages (note the period taken in account)				
customer claim rate				

Data Treatment

Which tool is used to process orders?

With your customers	Fax, EDI
With your suppliers	Fax
Who is in charge of the provisioning?	Planning Departm.

	Yes			No
Is your data base system updated in real time?				
	1	2	3	4
customer forecast liability		x		
the liability of your provisioning forecasts		x		
the liability of manufacturing commitment			x	

1 = weak; 4 = good

Reserved for diagnosis:

7-2) PROCESS CARTOGRAPHY

MANUFACTURING PROCESS ANALYSIS   Date .... From .... To ....

Plant:

Product (Name, Part No.):

Manufacturing frequency:

Daily Quantity:

Δ Miscellaneous → Transport

▽ Storage ○ **Added Value**

□ Control/Checking ® **Waiting**

N°	Description Operation	Batch	Qty	Dist (m)	Time (s)	Surf (m²)	○	Δ	●	→	□	▽	Comments Wastes observed
1	Warehouse Entry of pallets (several rolls)		max. 1900kg each roll		1-2 weeks (ca. 240h)	10 for storage						▽	
2	Check of parts according mat. Spec./ delivery note				few minutes each						□		
3	Transportation to storage place of stamping machine			60						→			
4	storage of one pallet		max. 1900kg each roll			6 (incl. space f.						▽	
5	Worker fills in roll into reverse reel			2	5 /20 min change of rolls/ reels					→			
6a	stamping of material		1 meshed container with 10-15 Tsd. parts		permanent		○						
6b	changing or repairing tools		1 after each lot size	20m	90 min						□		
7	transportation of meshed container to warehouse exit		max. 900kg	60m						→			
8	storage of meshed containers		max. 900kg each		1-2 weeks (ca. 240h)	6 (incl. free space for operating)						▽	
9	Transportation to zinc-coating supplier			500km						→			too long distance. Supplier given by Customer
10	zinc coating process		lot size		240 days		○						
11	Transportation from sub-supplier			500km						→			too long distance. Supplier given by Customer
12	control (spot sample) of coat thickness according procedure				60						□		
13	transportation by forklift to buffer storage yard "automotive"			30						→			10km/h = 2.8m/s, 10sec x 2 distance = 20sec; salary + depreciation = 16000 RMB/month 12,50 Euro/h = 0.0035l/sec; expenses = 0,07l; 280days, 70moves/year= 5l/y
14	storage				1-2 weeks (ca. 240h)	6 for storage						▽	Leasing price = 28RMB/qm/month =
15	transportation to assembly storage yard			20	1-2 weeks (ca. 240h)					→			
16	storage					6 for						▽	
17a	Warehouse Entry of studs (boxes/pallets)				1-2 weeks (ca. 240h)	10 for storage						▽	
17b	Check of parts (lenghts, diameter)				few minutes each						□		
17c	transportation to storage yard "automotive"			60						→			10km/h = 2.8m/s, 20sec x 2 distance = 40sec; salary + depreciation = 16000 RMB/month 12,50 Euro/h = 0.0035l/sec; expenses = 0,14l; 280days, 70moves/year= 10l/y
17d	storage					6 for						▽	Leasing price = 28RMB/qm/month =
17e	transportation to assembly storage yard			20						→			
17f	storage					6 for						▽	
18	Worker (setter) transfers box to assembly place by lifting crane			5	2 minute each box, each 15 min					→			
19	assembly (riveting)		1 piece		12 parts/min		○						
	control (spot sample) of		1								□		missing
20	Worker (setter) transfers box from belt to pallet by lifting crane		150 pieces	5	2 minute each box, each 15 min					→			
21	storage					6 for storage						▽	
22	transportation to warehouse exit		1 pallet	60						→			
23	packaging of parts for transportation		800.000/ year	20m	2 min		○						
24	storage				1-2 weeks (ca. 240h)	6 for storage						▽	
25	transportation to Customer			15 km						→			
	TOTAL		min. 7500 kg motion	362 m internally	storage time 1680 h	68 m²							580 l/year potential saving by eliminating buffer stock

7-3) PROCESS CARTOGRAPHY SUMMARY

	Gross Weight:	Date:			
Product No.: GTEC	0.025kg	xx.xx.xxxx			
Customer requirement:	6.000	per day			
Available production time	16	hours	2,00	shifts	
Total number of operations	25				
Added value	**1**		4,17	%	
Handling	7				
Waiting	7				
Inspection	3				
Storage	2				
Miscellaneous	5				
Total handling distance	320	m			

Raw material stock: In the flow chart, the products are under the raw material form from operation no. 1 to no. 6.
Quantity found: 5250kg (operation no. 5); 60% for the followed reference, 40% for another reference.

Raw material inventory	**21**	days	3.150 kg	126.000 pieces	Position No.	5
Material & components flow =	29.802	Euro/day	(39.73 RMB/part = 4.967 Euro/part)			
Working days per year	220	days/year				
raw material stock in Euro/year	6.556.000	Euro				

Work in process (WIP) stock (to move from warehouse to machine; operation 7 to 17 included):
Raw material = 300+35=335kg
raw material stocks = 335kg/part weight/0.025 = 13.400
customer consumption equivalent in days = 19.100/6000= 5

Parts in stock =	5500+400+9000+800=15.700 parts					
number of pieces =	15.700+13.400 = 29.100					
Work In process inventory	**5**	days	335 kg	13.400 pieces	Position No.	8;9
Material & components flow in Euro/year	2.928.543	Euro	(2680pcs/day=589600pcs/y*4.967= 2928543Euro)			

Finished goods stocks = 1200 + 96000 = 97.200 (operations 18 to 24)
Customer sonsumption equivalent in days = 97200/6000 = 16 days

Finished product inventory	**16**	days	97.200 pieces	Position No.	20
			process inventory 1320000 parts/year = 6556000Euro.		
Sales	15.000.000	Euro	Sales price = 90.91RMB/pcs=11.36 Euro/pcs		
shipment flow (evaluated at the selling price)	68.182	Euro/day	6000pcs/day * 11.36 Euro/pcs		

Dock to Dock Time	**42**	days (21+5+16) =	2422080 sec		
Added Value Time	20	sec		Position No.	10
Total Internal Transfer Time (Dock to Dock Time)/ Added Value Time	121.104				

Wrap-up:

Comments	Too many steps vs. Value Added Time (VAT)	
	42 days of stocks = 1.9 rotation/year	inventory turnover = COGS/ (start inventory + end inventory)/2
Suggestions:	lean tools on floor	= 15000000/ ((6556000+2928543+6556000)/2) =1.9
Potential savings:	min. 2 days in raw material	

8) RESOURCES MANAGEMENT

Operators are those who want to create finally the value. The real problems are seen in the field and solved there. The whole organization should support a unique target: help operational people to create added value with smallest energy expense possible.

Staff (please attach a detailed organizational chart)

number of hierarchic levels	4,00		
number of people/supervisor?	20,00		
Absenteeism	9,00	%	
Accident level	55,00	frequency	0,8 seriousness
Workhood rotation	4,00	%	
Number of suggestions/ people/ year	0,00		
population average age	30,00	years	
Training/ Salaries Ratio	2,00	%	

Distribution of training hours by category of:

	operators	technicians	supervisors:	management	
Resources ratio in %	30	35	20	15	%
Part dedicated to quality:					

Manufacturing department

Human Resources Distribution

	operators	staff	management	total
permanent people	80	8	1	89
temporary people	7	0	0	7
total	87	8	1	96

Support Functions

Human Resources Distribution

	operators	staff	management	total
Design	0	1	1	2
Engineering	0	4	1	5
Incoming Inspection	4	2	0	6
Warehouse	2	0	0	2
Logistics	3	1	0	4
Tooling	3	2	1	6
Maintenance	3	2	0	5
Quality	2	5	1	8
General Services	0	2	1	3
total	17	19	5	41

Other Functions

Human Resources Distribution

	staff	management	total
Purchase	2	0	2
Sales	3	1	4
Data processing	1	0	1
Human Resources	2	1	3
Finance	0	1	1
Top Management	0	1	1
total	8	4	12

Reserved for diagnosis:

9) DESIGN DEVELOPMENT			
More than 70% of the price of a product cost is determined at the design stage. Does your company has a way of capitalizing experiences for the design of new products and process?			
Organization:	**Yes**		**No**
Is there a project board of Directors?			
% of projects managed by a project manager designed by the PBD?			
Are there standards to guide project managers?			
How many projects a year?			
Tools used:	**Yes**		**No**
Formalized Quality Assurance Plan?			
Interactive Questionaire?			
Number of "Product FMEA" per year?			
Number of "Process FMEA" per year?			
Do you have files on critical points?			
Do you have files for a risk review?			
Do you have best design know-how standards?			
Average project review per year?		5	
Schedules:	**Yes**		**No**
Do you use steady planning with milestones?			
% of initial samples presented good at first time?		80	
% of initial samples presented on time?		80	
Profitability:			
% of T.O. dedicated to R&D?		2	%
Number of licences & patents generated each year?		0	
Do you have specific standards for your suppliers?			
products?			
How many projects were stopped for lack of profitability?		0	
% of projects transformed from offer to real orders?		60	%
Reserved for diagnosis:			

10) CHANCE OVER TIME

Date:	Machine: Press No. 16	Info: Change-over already
Operator:	Start: 3.00 p.m	in process when beginning
	Finish: 3.50 p.m	watching the process

Operation	Comments	Distance (m)	Duration (min)	Internal	External	To be deleted	Proposed Improvements
Setting up accessory	walks for getting special tool	10	4,00				
Looking for suitable screw	Too long screw (variable thickness of bed-plates; walks to the tool storage	65	2				
installing fasteners (machine side)			2				
installing fasteners (opposite side)	walks around the machine; climbs over a box	10	5,50				
changing the place of the hook		5	1				
mold operation			1				
plugging the water hoses on the mold			5				
looking for two hoses		50	4				
Installing the hoses			1				
getting the thermal controller; getting wires for the controller		100	5				
looking for wires and for a table		75	2				
helping the operator on machine 15	operator asked for help	45	1				
Looking for a nozzle		40	2				
still looking for wires and for a table		100	4				
looking for a meter		60	3				
Entering the process parameters			1				
moving the table		10	1				
plugging the thermal controller			0,5				
moving the crane		40	2				
looking for a table		50	2				
decision: stop the change over operation							
Total:		660	48,5				

Change-Over Status at the time the operation is stopped:

still missing:

- 2 power wires for the thermal controller
- output conveyor
- parts meter (the bulit-in-meter is considered as a non-reliable one)
- no parts produced

Comments:

- Nobody knows what is the next step (What/who/when/how?
- No instructions provided to the operator

Wrap-up:

Comments

- working instruction missing
- tools are missing/ not at the right place

Suggestions:

- workshop to be prepared for maintenance to reduce lead time.
- 4h to 2.30 h for 1 operator for change over
- What do you do with the time saved? Lot size reduction => calculation of savings

Potential savings:

- savings on machine 2h + operator 2h + stock 2h (labour cost + machine hours)

11) OVERALL EQUIPMENT EFFECTIVENESS (O.E.E.)

Date: Machine: Press No. 32 (200 tons); dedicated to box covers; range to 10 preference			
Period:	20	working days	
Workshop Opening time: 2 shifts, 16 hours per day:	320	hours	
machine time = sum (quantity x cadence) * sum cadence	111	injection s/h	
maximum possible number of parts = machine time * hour * number of mould-prints* opening time	71040	parts	320h*2*111injection s/h

Quantity of good parts = sum (Quantity/Reference) =

REF (part no.)	Produced good Parts	produced bad parts	
520-31	10.138	2.534	(80% good parts of 12672 pieces)
520-32	6.907	767	(90% good parts of 7674 pieces)
520-35	4.001	82	(98% good parts of 4083 pieces)
530-10	3.722	115	(97% good parts of 3837 pieces)
540-21	9.572	1.305	(88% good parts of 10877 pieces)
number of good parts:	34.339	4.804	

Useful time (no. of good parts * no. of batches *machine cycle/h * no. of cavities)

REF (part no.)	Produced good Parts	Number of batches	Number of starts/ changes	% of scraps	Wrong parts	Machine Cycle /h	Number of parts (x cavity moulds)	Useful Time (for good parts) in h
520-31	10.138	1	3,00	20	2.534	120	2	42,24
520-32	6.907	2	2,00	10	767	109	2	63,36
520-35	4.001	1	1,00	2	82	116	2	17,25
530-10	3.722	1	1,00	3	77	109	2	17,07
540-21	9.572	2	4,00	12	1.305	103	2	92,93
no. Of change over (planned stoppage)			11,00					
Production time; Total useful time (to produce good parts):								**232,85**

O.E.E in % =	quantity of good parts over a period/ maximum parts possible over the same period	48
O.E.E in % =	Useful Time/ Opening Time	72,77

Non-O.E.E. Analysis:

Change Over occurred during the period. Average duration:	4	h	
break down occurred:	6		
number of tools break down:	3		
Time of break down of tools:	20	h	mould breakdown
Time of break down of machines:	15	h	
Time of break down of thermal controller:	5	h	
Non Operator available:	20	h	
total unplanned stoppage	**60**	h	
change over (number of changes; planned stoppage):	**44**	h	

ÚNEXPLAINED STOPPAGES			
Miscellaneous:	29	h	unexplained stoppage Working time (155) - stoppages (60) - non quality (44) - miscellaneous (29h)
Micro stoppage and slow downs	11	h	
unexplained stoppages	**40**	h	

Non-Quality:

Scrap REF (part no.)	Produced Parts	Number of parts (x cavity moulds)	% of scraps	Number of injections	Machine Cycle /h	Number of hours of non quality	
520-31	12.672	2	20	1267,2	120	10,56	(= number of injection
520-32	7.674	2	10	383,7	109	3,52	= good parts/cavities;
520-35	4.083	2	2	40,83	116	0,35	non quality =
530-10	3.837	2	3	57,555	109	0,53	injections/machine
540-21	10.877	2	12	652,62	103	6,34	cycle)

total h non-quality, scrap	**21,30 h**

Suggestions:	avoid stoppage	
Potential savings:	total 42h	
	20h to 0h	>10% increase effectiveness
	22h (30%)	
	c.o.t.	55% in one year

MACHINE #32

opening time 320h	break downs 44h	
What to do?		install tool preventive maintenance
		reduce change over time
		check setting time
requested time (gross running time) 276h	unplanned stops (60h)	
break down reasons:		mould break downs 20h
		machine break downs 15h
		miscellanous break downs 5h
		lack of people 20h
		lack of material
Working time (net running time) 212 h	non-quality 21h (scraps and rework 21h)	
Performing time 191h	unexplained stops 40h	
break down reasons:		micro break downs and slow downs 11h
		miscellaneous 29h

Production 151h (212-21-40h)

12-1) SHOP FLOOR QUALITY

Date:

The analysis was focused on the following:
- raw material waste
- scraps and reworks

The considered sample was made of 2 series of references (worth for 25% of sales), using 2 types of raw material and 5 dedicated machines

Raw material waste

period:	20 working days	
recorded quantities:	9610 kg	for 500-21
	7050 kg	for 500-32

Actual production

Machine 500-21 / **Machine 500-32**

REF (part no.)	good parts	net weight (kg)	net requirement (kg)	REF (part no.)	good parts	net weight (kg)	net requirement (kg)
521-01	75.000	0,05	3.750,00	510-20	25000	0,06	1500
522-03	20.000	0,06	1.200,00	511-21	12000	0,06	720
521-03	18.000	0,04	720,00	511-02	60000	0,05	3000
521-05	50.000	0,05	2.500,00	505-10	28000	0,04	1120

Scrap & reworks:

The 5 dedicated machines may be stopped if operators are missing. Production schedule is frequently changed according to short term priorities: actual number of production starts is twice the number of originally planned batches

No recycling material is included in the injection material. Actual average weight of parts is 3% higher than the nominal

Only defectives parts rejected at the final sorting out are recorded as scraps be the Quality department. Sorting out requires 3 permanent people

Some bad trends happen with respect to the quality of raw material

The company has no in house equipment for proceeding with rheology tests

Wrap-up:

Comments	No monitoring of bad parts scrap: level too high	
Suggestions:	weight of the parts has to be lowered / under control reduce raw material of scrap; check fire wall with customer (convincing customer, depends on ppm)	
Potential savings:	reducing scrap	10,2% to 6%
	selling scrap	10,2% to 6%
	recycling scrap	10,2% to 6%

12-2) QUALITY

Customer Claims: 3000 ppm	Customer Quality: 0.3% of Sales
Finished goods, scraps and rework	
rejected parts at final control:	2% of sales
non managed material losses (outlets, tuning, trials, non conform in process)	
Labour cost:	
3 persons sorting yearly:	60000 RMB/person
3x7.5=22.5 k€. 22.500€/15000000€=	sorting cost: 0.15% of sales
Raw material losses:	
Machine 500-21	Machine 500-32

REF (part no.)	good parts	net weight (kg)	net requirement (kg)	REF (part no.)	good parts	net weight (kg)	net requirement (kg)
521-01	75.000	0,05	3.750	510-20	25000	0,06	1500
522-03	20.000	0,06	1.200	511-21	12000	0,06	720
521-03	18.000	0,04	720	511-02	60000	0,05	3000
521-05	50.000	0,05	2.500	505-10	28000	0,04	1120
Total kg good parts			8.170	Total kg good parts			6340

addition of technical losses (carrots, ..):	3%	8.415,10	addition of technical losses (carrots, ..):	3%	6.530,20
To build parts quantity used:	9610kg of raw material		To build parts quantity used:	7050kg of raw material	
Raw material losses:	14,20 %	=(9610-8415)/ 8415*100	Raw material losses:	7,96 %	
average raw material losses	11,08 %				
The raw material represents:	35% of sales				
material losses =	11% of raw material = 3,6% of sales				
Components losses					
manufacturing scraps =	21 hours / 320 hours	6,6	=6.6% of total volume		
component purchase =	7,5	7.5% of sales			
component losses =	0,49	0,5 % of sales (6.6%*7.5%)			

Machine usage to build bad parts (see 11. O.E.E.)

	21 hours / 320 hours	6,6	=6.6% of V.A. (50% of sales)	in process
Machine usage to build bad parts (see O.E.E.)			=0.1% of sales	9900 Euro machine costs (165h losses *60Euro/hour MHR)

Summary Cost or Scraps and Reworks

Customer claims	0,3 % of sales
scraps and rework	2% of sales
sorting cost	sorting cost: 0.15% of sales
material losses	3,6 % of sales
component losses	0,5 % of sales
machine usage	=0.1% of sales
total:	**6.65% of sales**

The Improvement Program

Operating Business Performance Measures:		Year N -> Year N+1			
Deliveries less than 1 months after order:	0,76	M€		> 1	M€
late deliveries:		M€	devided by 3	> 1	M€
year)	44	%		67	%
Inventory turns/sales:	16	%		12	%
waste + scraps + reworks / manufacturing costs	10	%		8,6	%
Set-up time	70	min		< 10	min
Economical results:		Year N -> Year N+1			
labour efficiency		%	7%		%
operational result:		%	+1,4 Mio€ (= 1,3 points)		%
cost of Diagnosis & Training workshops:	76000	€			
		Year N -> Year N+1			
turnover	54	M€		62	M€
employees (direct labour)	140	p		170	p
actual timing of improvement program:					
	Industrial diagnosis:		January	Year N	
	writing the plan:		April + May	Year N	
	training workshops (SMED, TMP, ..)		June	Year N	
	Project mgt.		Dec	Year N+1	
Market		Year N -> Year N+1			
market price trend	minus 3	%	per year		
new customers:	40	%	new car makers		
parts of new products in sales:			+ 25 points		

Diagnosis Report Presentation

Diagnosis Objectives:	To achieve operating business performance measures To point out major potential ways of performance improvement
Involved departments:	Production Sales Purchasing Quality Human Resources Industrial Engineering
Not Involved departments:	Finances (we thougth, it was not necessary)
Achievment done during the on the spot diagnosis:	Cartographies Evaluation of O.E.E. Watching a one change-over analysis Shop Floor Quality Analysis Interviews

Operating Business Performance Synthesis

Indicators for Plastic Injection SMEs	Units	Your current performance	Automotive Suppliers Industry Performances			if you start improving right now, potential in 2 years ahead
			weak	good	excellent	
Customers Return	ppm	3000	5000	50	10	500
Cost of waste, scraps, and reworks	% T.O.	10	5	2	1	4%, then 2%
Inventory Turns	No.	6,7	7	20	33	10, then 12,5
Dock to Dock Time	Days	42	50	15	8	<15
OEE	%	48	50	85	90	65, then 70
Sales per Square Meter (integration rate = 50%)	€/m²	1,6	1,5	3	4,5	>2,12
Change Over Time	Min.	240	60	15	5	< 60
Customer Delivery Achievement	%	60	95	98	100	> 95
Realized suggestions/employee/yea	No.	0	0,1	10	20	formal system to be set up
Turnover per Employee	k€	100	75	150	225	120

Following, at next pages in yellow marked fields, you will find a summary of mayor ways of improvements and recommended action items.[3]

[3] SUPPLIER INDUSTRIAL & PRODUCTIVITY DIAGNOSIS TRAINING SESSION, Oct 2005, Paris. Author ICARE Institute, 79, Rue Jean-Jacques Rousseau—92,150 SURESNES, France

Positive / Strengths:

up to date technology and newly installed process machinery and equipment (some new machines)

young and dynamic team

efficient business approach

Fair profitability

Major Improvement ways:

External quality level (customer returns) of ...ppm can be achieved in less than 1 year

Internal quality doesn't comply with ...

Recommendations:

Reconsider quality department missions: suppress 3 people minimum

Train operators to self inspection

implement and extend SPC principle throughout shop floor

Identify process steps ...

Implement action plans

set up a 5S Pilot work shop..

Major Improvement ways:

The effectiveness of machinery ..

An improvement of 20 OEE points can be achieved in less than 1 year

10 additional OEE points accessible in less than 2 years

Recommendations:

Set up SMED workshop with the help of ..

Set up a 5S and TPM workshop aimed to increase...

Set up a tooling preventive maintenance system (e.g. mould problem should be seen before the machine stops)

List miscellaneous and unknown causes...

allocate to production people, transferred from non productive quality tasks (e.g. sorting, control); not added value operations should be deleted

Major Improvement ways:

The inventory turns are out of limits...

Recommendations:

Reconsider the lay-out and the planning of the shop floor by:

- putting to practise
- opimizing the equipment

Reengineer the supply chain from procurement to shipment by:

- setting up ..
- organizing Kanban systems with ...

Major Improvement ways:
Management and employees involvement are lower than automotive standards
Recommendations:
issue a 2 years improvement plan, the content of which will:
- prioritize improvement ways
- assess steering people
- assess proper information channels...

present and explain this plan to all employees

Major Improvement ways:
Provide the amount of purchased material and components in the Turnover, reconsider position, tools, and methods of the purchasing department as a compulsory side-action plan within the company improvement plan.
Recommendations:
Create a dedicated purchased function in charge of:
- setting up ..
- manage the suppliers panel:
- place quotation requests based on ..

Major Improvement ways:
Provide the production volume increase forecasts...
Recommendations:
Define sales strategy
Reconsider product/customer portfolio
benchmark competitors
adjust development/industrialization potential

Proper Links Between Corporate Strategy and Supply Chain Design
A healthy company strategy always starts with customer needs. Those needs transform into a broad spectrum of customer purchasing behavior. Whereas one customer makes price-driven purchasing decisions, another is motivated by convenience. A successful company has clearly formulated its mission or driving force—its right to exist and the ways it wants to add value for its customers.[4]

3.3 Supplier Process Evaluation in the Asia-Pacific

Performing supplier process evaluations in the Asia-Pacific, through a process I refer to as ECOCUT, is a method to strengthen relationships with one's suppliers.

[4]Source: issued 30 November 2016, taken from article "A strategy compass for companies," author *Martijn Lofvers. Access date: 14.02.2021.*

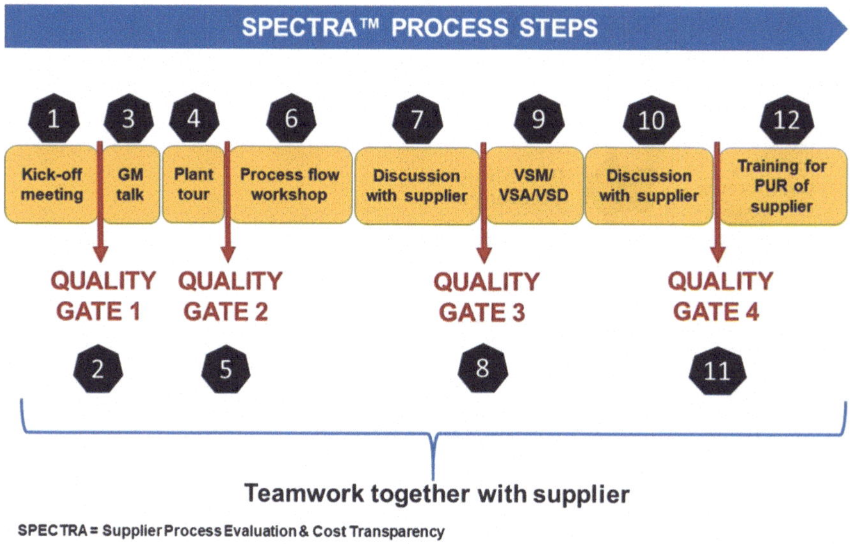

Fig. 3.1 Process steps for cost reduction and negotiation with suppliers. Source: Schaeffler Holding (China) Co., Ltd.—Shanghai, 2013

Don't worry, we'll skip the high-minded details, and focus on the exciting, espionage-like processes of information gathering and subtle relationship building involved.

First, we conduct a process summary covering how to treat suppliers fairly, with a proven process for value stream analysis at supplier sites. Targets should be clearly set for all persons involved: cost reductions conducted for one investigated product with new contracts/parts/assembly prices at the end of process.

To ensure the process runs in the proper direction, you need to install several quality gates through the course of your project. You also need a dedicated team with a leader who is able to control this process (Fig. 3.1).

For cost calculations of manufacturing processes, we first need to define whether we are dealing with internal or external accounting. In our cases, we use internal statistics, financial planning, and cost accounting to define and control costs.

Here, we perform a fundamental understanding of the process's economics, and the advantages and disadvantages of overhead calculations (Fig. 3.2).

In the fundamental economic and cost accounting overhead calculation structure for product costing, it is necessary to focus on both direct and indirect costs to perform cost reductions and stronger negotiations (Figs. 3.3 and 3.4).

Take care of the constant risk of "double counting" the costs of machines, labor, and tools.

What Are Direct and Indirect Costs?

Costs directly accumulated during production count as *direct costs*:

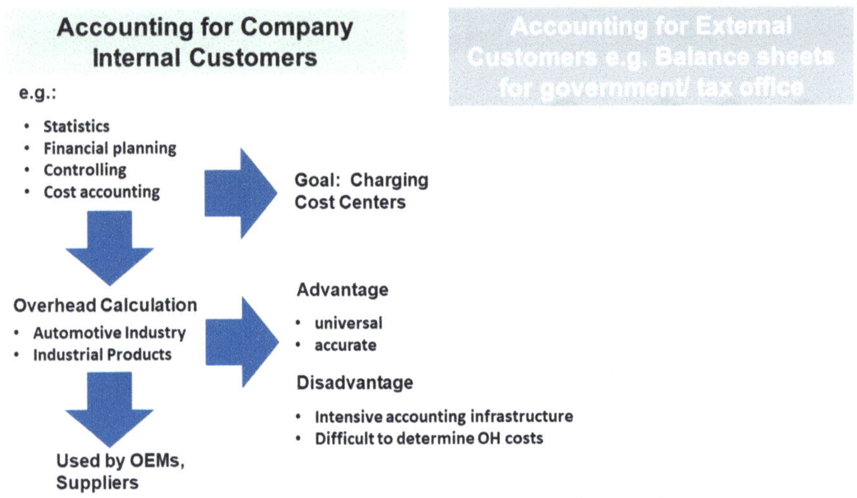

Fig. 3.2 Accounting for internal vs. external customers. Source: Training Course "Basics of Product Cost Calculation," 2009, Page 3. Author: Tsetinis+Partner

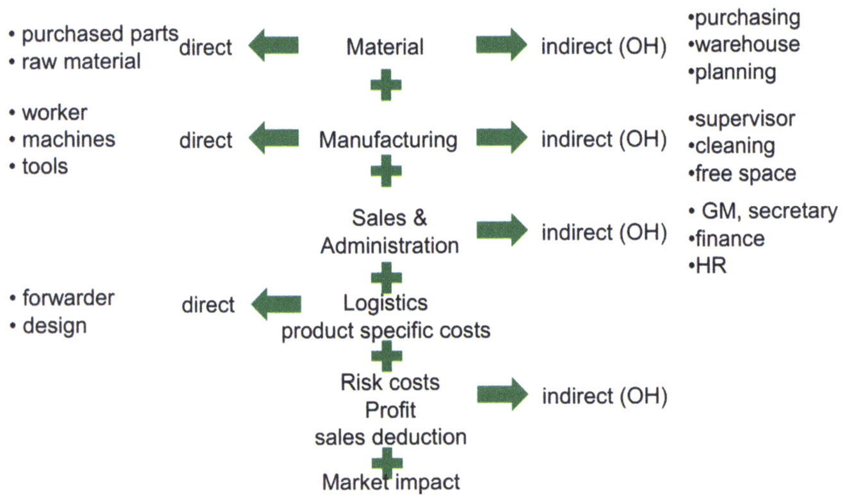

Fig. 3.3 Every step along the manufacturing process has overhead costs, which ultimately have to be allocated in product costs. Source: GTEC, 22.5.2014

- Materials*
- Machine/working systems
- *Machine operators*
- Assessment tools

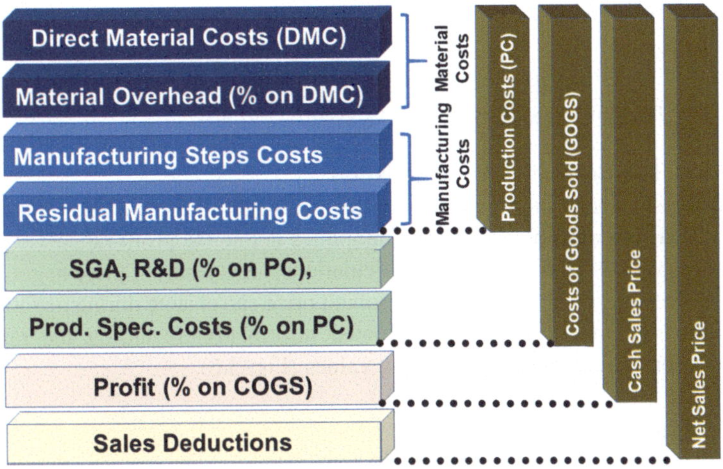

Fig. 3.4 Schematic of cost structure and designations. Source: Training Course "Basics of Product Cost Calculation," 2009, Page 35. Author: Tsetinis+Partner

Costs of maintaining the productivity of the department:

- Indirect labor
- Resources,
- Facilities
- Production spaces

These are residual manufacturing costs (*indirect costs*).

Costs and expenses of the company for administration and sales are calculated in the

- SGA (selling, generalized, and administrative expenses)

Or *indirect costs*. SGA costs do not include the cost of collecting the material, and these costs are charged in the material overhead rate.

Product-Specific Costs

These so-called one-time costs are allocated to the total product costs and must only be related to this product.

For example: *One-time cost of an embossed plate design is 120.000 RMB.*

These so-called one-time costs may be paid in part or be directly apportioned.

The cost of the design should be allocated to 1,500,000 pcs. 25,000 RMB will be paid directly (immediately). The balance, 95,000 RMB, will be allocated to the part price.

Assumption: The production of the embossed plate continues and exceeds the production volume of 1,500,000 units.

After reaching the levy amount of 1.5 million units, 95,000 RMB are taken out of the calculation.

95.000 EUR/1.5 mil units = 0.06 EUR/part

After 1.5 mil units = cost reduction of 0.06 EUR/part.

Base Price: The Basis of Price Negotiation

A product cost calculation is generally performed without taking market impact into consideration. For example, supplier monopolies define the profit range.

These, as well as corrections to the calculations, are a result of price negotiations, and define the margin by which the component price can change during negotiations. The calculation quality gives an estimated information regarding the range of negotiation or correction of the resulting values (Fig. 3.5).

Six Cost Types

There are six cost types which need to be considered in your cost calculation, and I will explain them in detail.

1. Material costs (indirect and direct)
2. Machines/fixed assets (direct depreciation)
3. Personnel costs (indirect and direct)
4. Capital costs (interest rates of investment)
5. External services
6. Statistical risks

Material Costs

Following, please find all cost items which belong to indirect material as overhead costs and direct material cost steps in two pictures (Fig. 3.6).

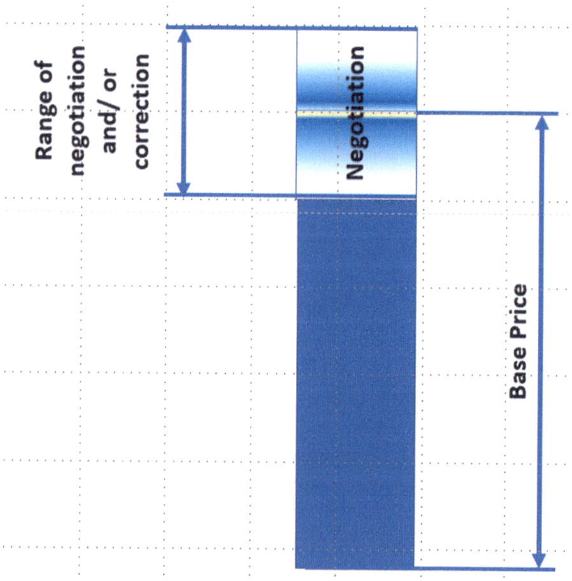

Fig. 3.5 Negotiation and/or correction range. Source: GTEC, 22.5.2014

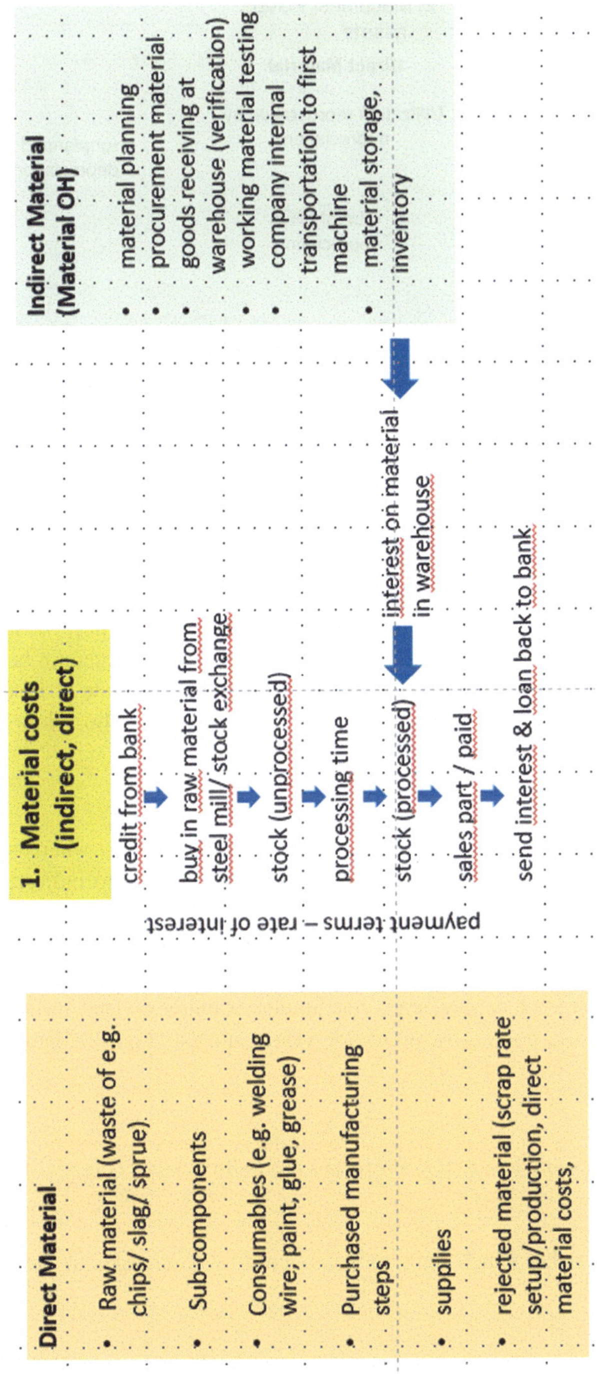

Fig. 3.6 Material costs (indirect, direct). (1) Workflow of material overhead (OH) and payment terms. (2) Direct material items. Source: GTEC, 22.5.2014

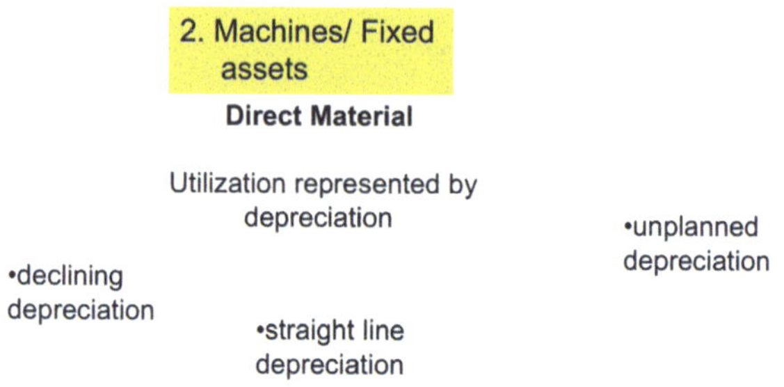

Fig. 3.7 Three different depreciation types of fixed assets. Source: GTEC, 22.5.2014

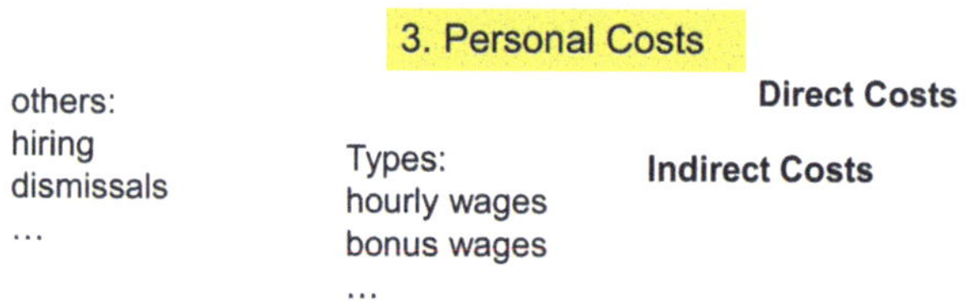

Fig. 3.8 Direct and indirect personnel costs. Source: GTEC, 22.5.2014

Machine/Fixed Asset Costs

Machine and other fixed assets costs are depreciated by three different types. Most used in practice is straight line depreciation. If machine breaks down and cannot be repaired, then it will be depreciated unplanned. If you decide to depreciate at first years with higher percentage than later, due to practical experience at shop floor, then finance will use declining depreciation (Fig. 3.7).

Personnel Costs

Workers' salary and their personnel expenses belong to direct costs, whereas overhead staff salary and bonus, and hiring and dismissal costs belong to indirect costs (Fig. 3.8).

Capital Costs

For cost calculation of operating capital, e.g., machinery, warehouse, and buffer stock of raw material and finish goods, always divide yearly interest rate from banks or other external sources by two (Fig. 3.9).

Service Costs

All kind of costs for services and external labor forces are indirect costs (Fig. 3.10).

Risk Costs

There are certain business risks, which have to be covered by surcharges to your calculated costs (Fig. 3.11).

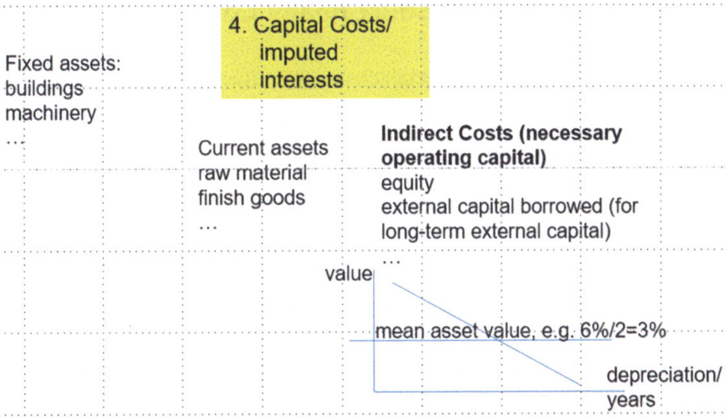

Fig. 3.9 Calculation formula of interest rate at capital costs. Source: Training Course "Basics of Product Cost Calculation," 2009, Page 17. Author: Tsetinis+Partner

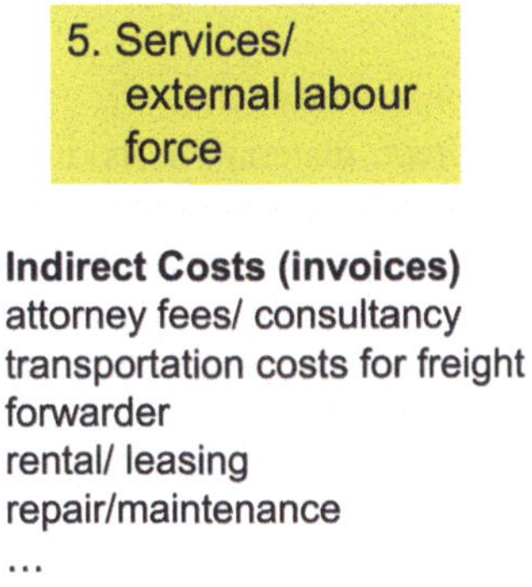

Fig. 3.10 Summary of external labor forces. Source: GTEC, 22.5.2014

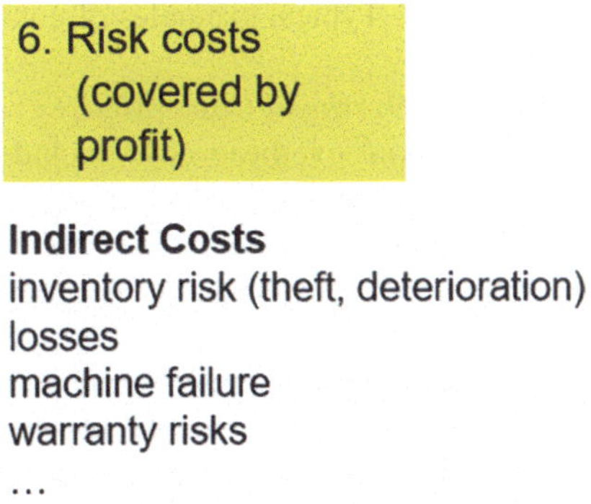

Fig. 3.11 Summary of different type of risk costs. Source: GTEC, 22.5.2014

3.4 How Much Does a Product Really Cost?

Net sales price is spitted into material costs, manufacturing costs, and overhead costs.[5]

3.4.1 Material Costs

Material costs can be divided into:

1. Direct material costs
2. Material overhead costs
3. Costs of rejected material
4. Interest on material in the warehouse

The material costs cover all expenses and costs of the company from warehouse entry until material is delivered in front of the first machine.

1. *Direct Material Costs*
   Direct material costs include raw material, purchased subcomponents and consumables, and purchased manufacturing steps.
   Attention: *Waste≠Rejects*
   What is the difference between waste and a reject?
   The cost of the raw material includes the costs of material usages, as well as income and expenses for waste. Typical examples of waste include chips, clippings, slag, and sprue (from gating systems).
   Rejected parts are strictly divided according to material and manufacturing processes and are allocated accordingly.
   Unlike used supplies (e.g., oil, water, paper), consumables can be sold to customers. Typical examples of consumables are welding wire, paint, glue, and grease.
2. *Material Overhead Costs (MOC)*
   The material overhead costs include all expenses for the company to provide material in the first production step.
   Material overhead covers the expenses for purchasing, planning, income testing, and transporting all needed resources to the first working system (e.g., machine).
   Accounting department staff will take the MOC out of the SAP system or calculate them alone, simply adding the central cost figures.
   In MOC calculations, usually the MOC are charged using a % of material costs (numbers defined based on experience).

[5]Source: ppt-Training "Basics for Cost Calculation and Negotiation." Author Christian Andersch, Herzogenaurach. 14.12.2012, Schaeffler AG. pp. 3–27. Source material costs, manufacturing costs and overhead costs, page 3–5.

The percentage value (material overhead) can vary between 1.5 and 5% and can be considered as one of the company's performance indicators.

3. *Cost of Rejected Material*
   The cost of rejected material is calculated as follows:
   - Direct material costs
   - Scrap rate
   - Manufacturing lot size

   The costs of rejects are divided into those of material and manufacturing.
   An initial example of calculating the cost of rejected material is as follows:
   - Production lot size: 100 parts
   - Scrap rate: 1%
   - Direct material costs: 10 RMB/part

   Solution: 10 RMB/part × 100 parts = 1000 RMB/lot in material costs = rejected material costs of 10 RMB/lot (1%).

   The material costs are constant along the production chain. Added value only increases the manufacturing costs.

   Calculating the cost of rejects:
   - Used material multiplied by the volume of rejects.

   However, the scrap rate refers to the production lot size of each production step.

   Example:
   - 100 tons of used material
   - Number of rejects: 10% rejects; scrap = 10 tons
   - 1 part = 1 kg
   - Solution: scrap of 10 tons/1 kg = 10,000 parts
4. *Interest on material in the warehouse entry (inbound)*
   Cost of interest on material in warehouse entry = interest rate of incoming material for time of the stay until processing begins on the first production step.

$$\text{Cost of Interest}_{\text{material income}} = \text{Material value} \times \text{average wait time}_{(\text{of incoming supplies})} \times \text{interest rate}$$

   Exercise:

   How much money will you spend if the material value is 1 million RMB, and the average waiting time at the warehouse is 6 months at an interest rate of 10%/year?

   Solution: 1 mil RMB × 6 months (0.5 years) × 10% interest = 50,000 RMB.
5. *Cost of Interest on Finished Products in Warehouse*
   Calculation using the following parameters:
   - Average duration at warehouse
   - Value of finished product

$$\text{Cost of Interest}_{\text{Finished products' time at warehouse}} = \text{Value}_{\text{Finished products}} \times \text{Duration}_{\text{Warehousing time}} \times \text{Interest rate}$$

- Interest rate
  Exercise:
- Value of finished parts = 1,000,000 RMB
- Stay in warehouse = 6 months
- Interest rate = 6%/year
- *Wanted*: Cost of interest at finished warehouse
  Solution: 30000 RMB = 1,000,000 RMB × 6 months (0.5 years) × 6%/year

3.4.2 Manufacturing Costs

The production costs are divided into:

1. Cost of manufacturing from step 1 to final step
2. Costs of rejects during manufacturing
3. Interest on material during process

The production costs incorporate all product-specific costs in the production chain.

The scrap costs are added from all production steps and are split into manufacturing and material scrap costs.

The return on the bounded capital is compound. It accounts for each added value per production step.

1. *Cost of manufacturing step*
   The cost of a manufacturing step is calculated based on:
   - Hourly rate of working system
   - Hourly rate of direct labor
   - Tool costs
     Allocated based on output quantity. Added with residual manufacturing costs (Fig. 3.12).
2. *Cost of rejects in manufacturing*
   The cost of rejects produced during manufacturing is calculated by using the added value from production and the number of discovered rejects.
   The production chain features an accumulative value increase from each manufacturing step to the next. For example:

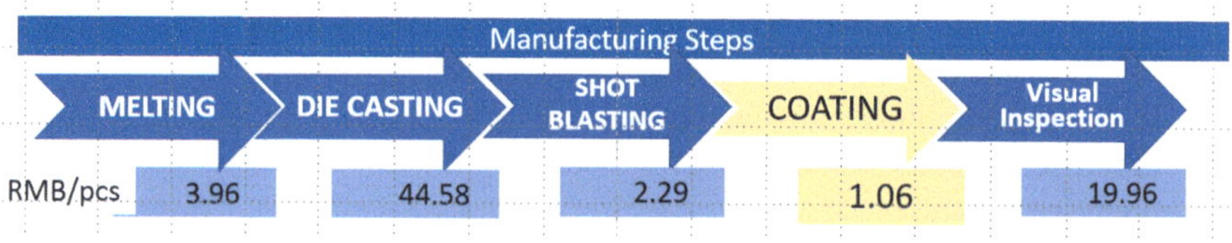

Fig. 3.12 Example of die casting manufacturing process steps and cost/pcs of each step. Source: GTEC, 2020

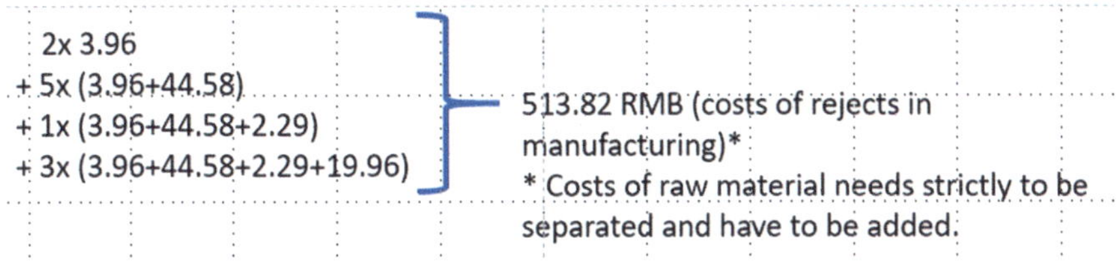

Fig. 3.13 Adding cost of rejects, for example, 3.96 RMB/rejected part for first in-house step, 44.58 RMB for second in-house step, 2.29 RMB for third in-house step, and 19.96 RMB for fourth in-house step. Source: Schaeffler Holding (China) Co., Ltd.—Shanghai, 2013

The following quantities of rejects are detected during each MS (manufacturing step) (Fig. 3.13).

(a) MS, 2 parts; 2. MS, 5 parts; 3. MS, 1 part; 4 MS, 3 parts.

What are total costs of rejects in manufacturing, if quality checks are performed at each MS?

3. *Interest on material during manufacturing process*

   Interest costs on WIP (work in progress) calculated from the total sum:

   - Interest on material in front of the machine
   - Interest on material behind the machine
   - Interest on material in an intermediate storage

   The calculation of interest charged during any warehousing depends on the quantity (production lot), the average length of stay of the material in the warehouse, and the value of the material being stored.

   While the material before the first working system has only material value, after each production step, the costs of the step are added.

   In permanent production, the result is distorted by inserting the annual quantity. Instead, production lot size is used, which is easier to use than the delivery lot size.

   In a permanent production by inserting the annual quantity, the result would be distorted. Instead of taking production lot size into calculation, it is easier to use the delivery lot size.

Example

Yearly volume = One million parts; permanent production, delivery once a week to customer:

1. Production lot size of one million parts, part price 10 RMB/part due to high warehouse storage costs
2. Instead of using delivery lot size of 1 million parts/50 weeks = 20,000 parts/week, use part price = 5 RMB/part.

3.4.3 Overhead (General Analysis)

Overhead can be divided into:

- One-time costs
- Overhead after production costs.
- Profit
- Terms of payment
- Terms of delivery

All expenses/costs not "material" and "production" are assigned and must be included in the overhead.

Most surcharges to production cost (PC) and profit on COGS are added to the percentage. The surcharge bases can be set individually.

One-time costs, for example, design costs, are calculated out of the following items:

- Total design costs, etc.
- Allocable share (100% = 1 customer, 50% = 2 customers).
- Allocable period (e.g., 3-month design phase).
- Interest rate of investment (e.g., 6% of total costs).

For example, 100,000 RMB total design costs × 100% × 6%/12 × 3-month design phase. One-time costs are 1500 RMB.

Here is a question to be answered by your department: Who is responsible for monitoring the allocation period?

In determining the special costs that must be taken that these may be properly distributed, one-time costs (e.g., design) benefiting other clients must be adjusted so they are calculated "pro rata." If the allocation period has expired, they are no longer part of the net sales price.

When calculating the special direct costs, you must ensure that they are distributed correctly. If other customers also take advantage of so-called special direct costs (e.g., from construction), these are "pro-rated" or discounted proportionately.

Surcharges on Product Costs
These are calculated based on the following items:

- SGA (sales and general administration)
- R&D (research and development).
- Venture (risk costs)
- Interest on finished parts stored in warehouse

Usually, these types of expenses are charged as percentage surcharge within the calculation. SGA and R&D expenses can be split into personnel and material (indirect materials). Venture expenses cover expenses such as reserves for bad debt (loss of receivables), insurance fees, and general reserves.

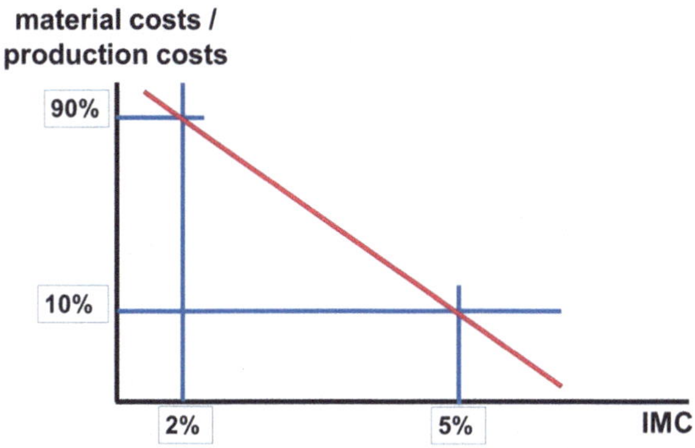

Fig. 3.14 Solution for cause justified allocation of indirect material costs. [Source: ppt-Training "Basics for Cost Calculation and Negotiation." Author Christian Andersch, Herzogenaurach. 14.12.2012, Schaeffler AG. pp. 3–27. Source page 19.] Detailed table see Fig. 6.41

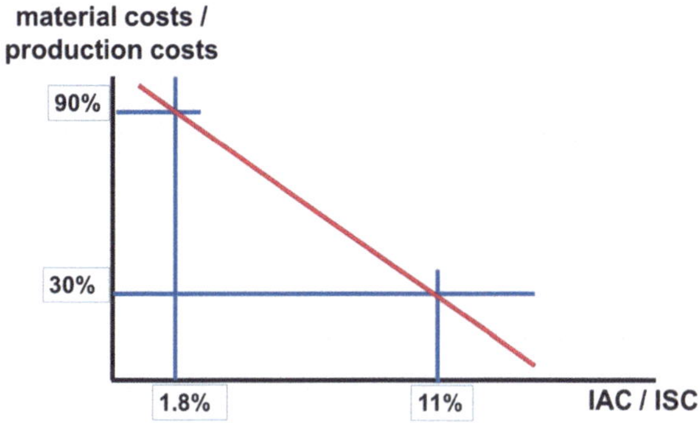

Fig. 3.15 Solution for cause justified allocation of indirect admin IAC and sales costs ISC. [Source: ppt-Training "Basics for Cost Calculation and Negotiation." Author Christian Andersch, Herzogenaurach. 14.12.2012, Schaeffler AG. pp. 3–27. Source page 21]. Detailed table see Fig. 6.44

Practical Overhead Cost Calculations

1. High material costs = high IMC (indirect material costs), which in reality is not justified (Fig. 3.14).
2. High production costs = high IAC/ISC (indirect admin/sales costs), which is not realistic (Fig. 3.15).
3. Industrial standard is that high rate of purchased material means high profit. Our customer-oriented solution: No dealers = 0% profit on purchased material.
4. Standard in industry: High waste cost means high profit. Our solution: no profit on waste material.

To calculate costs of each cost type, see formulas below (Fig. 3.16).

3.5 Economic Analysis: Basic Understanding of Product Costing

The task is to break down a enterprise into accounting areas. There are four different types of accounting areas, where indirect costs are distributed.

IMC (%) = indirect material costs/ direct material costs x 100%
MC (%) = indirect manufacturing costs/ direct manufacturing costs x 100%
IAC (%) = indirect overhead costs OHC/ production costs x 100%
ISC (%) = indirect sales costs/ production costs x 100%

Fig. 3.16 How to calculate costs of each cost center. Source: Schaeffler Holding (China) Co., Ltd.—Shanghai, 2013

cost centers / cost types	A	B	C	
material OH				
...				

Fig. 3.17 Table of cost types and cost centers. Source: ppt-Training "Basics for Cost Calculation and Negotiation," pages 9–10, from 14.12.2012. Author Schaeffler AG Herzogenaurach

1. allocation subsidiaries and main cost centers
2. responsibilities, e.g., sales department
3. place, e.g., central storage and admin building
4. function (e.g., production, procurement)

Companies using expense distribution sheets to allocate costs to each cost center (Fig. 3.17).

The goal of using cost centers is to distribute indirect costs into original areas, to control profitability of each cost center, and apportionment of indirect costs into fixed and variable costs.

Economic: Basic Understanding of Cost Center Accounting
Following picture (Fig. 3.18), you will find relationship between direct, indirect, variable and fixed costs and cost breakdown into different items.

3.6 Economic Accounting: Basic Understanding of Accounting

Direct Costing/Marginal Costing[6]
1. advantage: results independent on used capacity
2. fixed and variable costs

[6]In German, it is called "Grenzkostenrechnung, Teilkostenrechnung, Deckungsbeitragsrechnung."

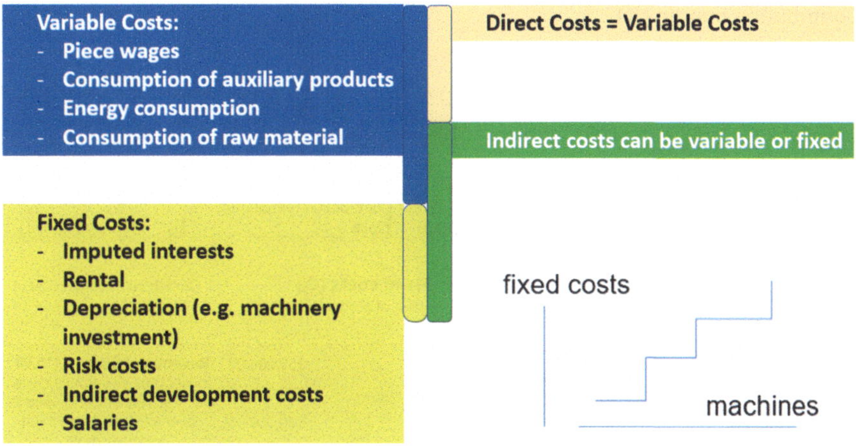

Fig. 3.18 Graph above shows that the more machines you have, the higher fixed costs you get. Source: ppt-Training "Basics for Cost Calculation and Negotiation," pages 9–10, from 14.12.2012. Author Schaeffler AG Herzogenaurach

Direct/marginal costing takes the market price of a product into consideration. The market price must at least cover variable costs (lower price limit). The remainder is the contribution margin. Contribution margins of all products carry the costs of operational readiness.

Example Direct costing/marginal costing[7] (Fig. 3.19).

Following please find the solution for direct costing/marginal costing (Fig. 3.20).

Full Cost Accounting/Full Cost Pricing

1. advantage: results dependent on used capacity
2. fixed and variable costs

Full costing determines the end-to-end cost of producing products or services. Also known as "absorption costing," it is required in most common accounting methodologies, including Generally Accepted Accounting Principles (GAAP), International Financial Reporting Standards (IFRS), and reporting standards for income tax purposes. In this costing method, all direct, fixed, and variable overhead costs are assigned to the end product. These various expenses move with the product (or service) through inventory accounts until the product is sold. The income statement will then recognize these as expenses under costs of goods sold (COGS). COGS are synonymous with unit costs. Establishing total **cost per unit** helps businesses to determine suitable pricing for goods and services. Advantages of full costing include greater transparency. Drawbacks include potential skewed profitability in financial statements and difficulties determining variations in costs

[7] Europa-Lehrmittel Verlag, Mechanical and Metal Trades Handbook, Production planning, Direct costing page 286. first edition 2006. Editor U. Fischer, Reutlingen.

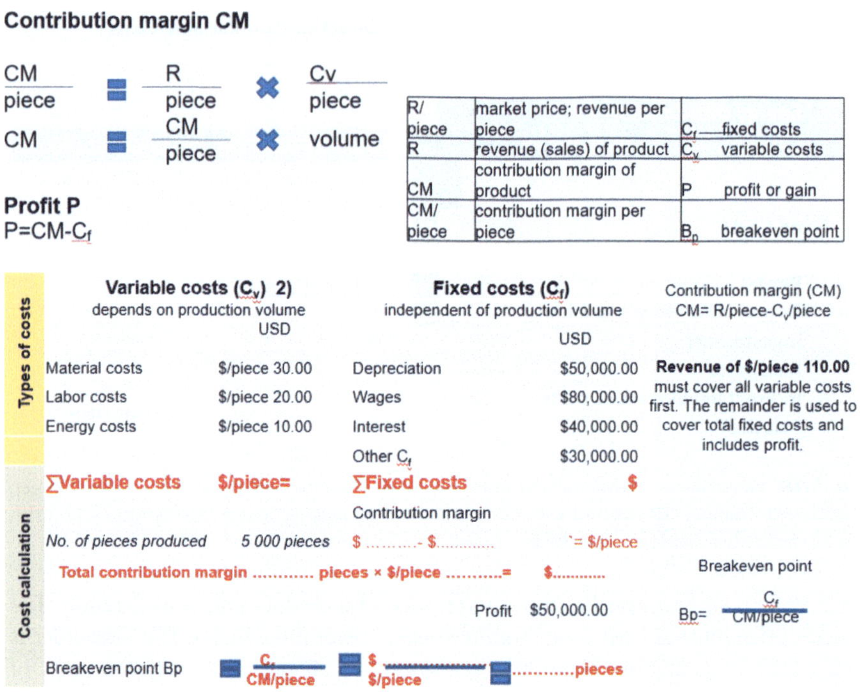

Fig. 3.19 Task is to calculate and fill in red marked gaps. Source: Europa-Lehrmittel Verlag, Mechanical and Metal Trades Handbook, Production planning, Direct costing page 286. first edition 2006. Editor U. Fischer, Reutlingen

at different production levels.[8] Details see https://www.investopedia.com/terms/u/unitcost.asp.

For example, given figures:

- total fixed costs are 400,000 RMB,
- variable costs are 200,000 RMB,
- produced 30,000 units.

What are the total production costs?

Solution: adding 400,000 RMB fixed costs to the 200,000 RMB variable costs for a total production costs of 600,000 RMB.

[8]Source: https://www.investopedia.com/terms/f/full-costing.asp,Article"Fullcosting." Author Investopedia, LLC, New York NY 10018 from January 11, 2021. Access date: 14.2.2021

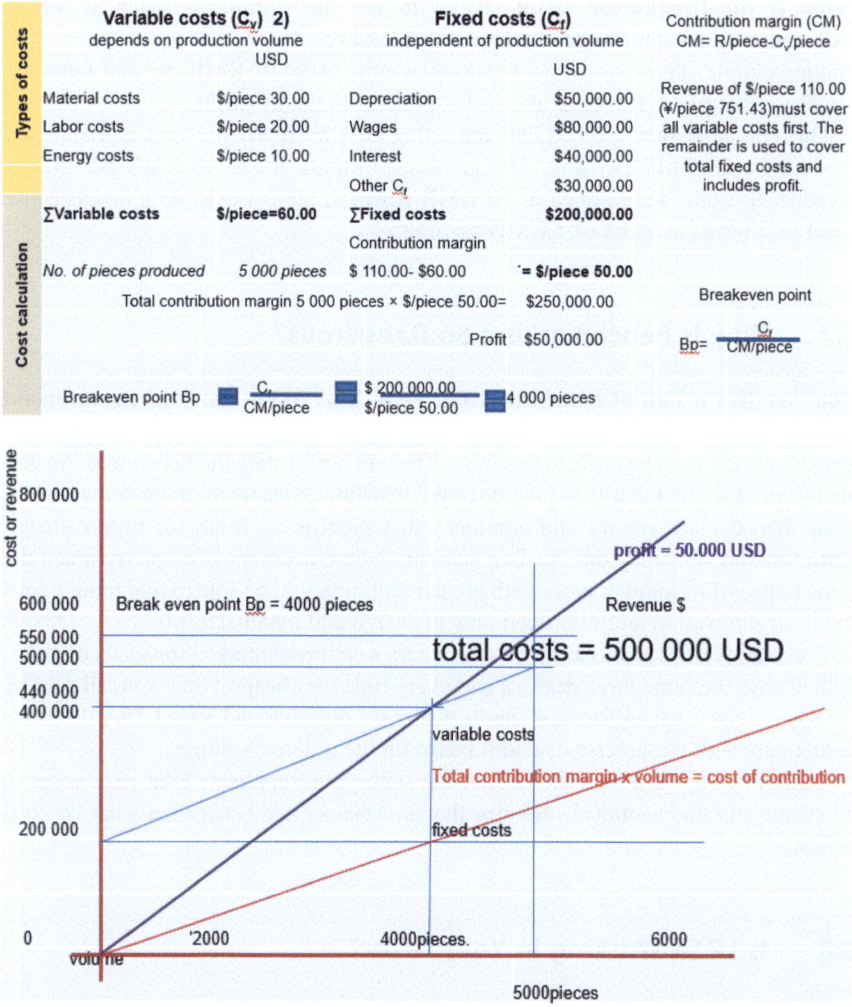

Fig. 3.20 Calculated and graphical of solution for 4000 pieces at break-even point. Source: Europa-Lehrmittel Verlag, Mechanical and Metal Trades Handbook, Production planning, Direct costing page 286. first edition 2006. Editor U. Fischer, Reutlingen

What are the unit costs?

Solution: Divide 600,000 RMB by 30,000 units to get 20 RMB per unit.[9]

[9] Source: https://www.investopedia.com/terms/u/unitcost.asp; Article "Unitcost." Author Investopedia, LLC, New York NY 10018 from October 27, 2020. Access date: 14.2.2021

What is the break-even point (BEP) to get the minimum price at which a company must sell the product to avoid losses?
In our example, a product with a break-even unit cost of 20 RMB per unit must sell for above that price. Revenue above this price is company profit.

Our company produces 30,000 units that cost 20 RMB per unit and sells the product for 50 RMB per unit. The gain is 50 minus 20, or 30 RMB per unit in revenue. If a unit were priced at 10 RMB per unit, there would be a loss because 1 minus 2 (cost) is a loss of 1 RMB per unit.

3.7 Why Is Benchmarking So Dangerous?

You Are Not a Fan of benchmarking. Why Not? What Do You Recommend Instead?
Benchmarking is an obstacle to progress. The unit performing the benchmarking will always proudly find that they are above the benchmark standard along some metric. They then declare victory and announce that there is no room for improvement. Unfortunately, this may only be in a category where everyone does pretty much the same thing, while another party with greater ambition will be able to find tremendous room for innovation and improvements in design and manufacturing.

For example, we had a case where fasteners were benchmarked for spans of years, with always the same three dealers, and every time the cheapest one won, all sold by the same dealer. I then found a fourth dealer on my own and found 15–50% price reductions, with the precise discount based on the ordered volume.

So never stop sourcing and discussing with your suppliers. Find new ways to cooperate and find technical solutions that are cheaper and better than what you had before.[10]

3.8 Is LPTA Working in Your Favor?

I agree that the lowest price technically acceptable (LPTA) method does not work in the acquisition of design, planning, creative, or solution management services. If you try it, LPTA experts tend to haggle replying to architect positions with application development rates for creating apps, using rates typical for architects on initial task order. Technically, this process will be acceptable to buyers, and the rates will be 30% better. But this is very similar to asking a cook, "Can you run a farm?" Technically, the cook probably could, and both are nominally related to food production, but would not you want someone familiar with agricultural economics, planting cycles, key risk, and success factors and someone who knows food and animals to take over that job instead? Such solutions mostly end up costing more

[10] Source: *https://www.skipprichard.com/pick-the-low-hanging-fruit-to-improve-productivity/. Author Skip Prichard, May 4, 2014, access: 15.02.2021*

than planned, the app developer will be replaced, and company pays the cost for missing deadlines and scope creep.

Being "agile" is trending lately. It works great for new transaction systems running on abstracted solutions. It can aid in integration. But, when you have an immovable object, it does not matter how agile you are. In those cases, you need to conduct architecture design, understand alternative operation analysis, perform business case evaluations, define requirements, and register and buy back risk.[11]

3.9 Do You See the Big Picture?

I have been very lucky to have been engaged in several initiatives to identify and remove excess cost and waste in supply chains and operations. My first impression, however, is that you need to be reporting at a higher level than a departmental director. To drive real changes, you need to be reporting to a C-level manager or board of directors, as these changes often cross departments and silos.

For example, I have found the low-hanging fruit of reducing supply chain and operating costs typically lie in inventory—too many of the wrong items, too few of the core stock-keeping units (SKUs). The root cause of this issue is often found in (1) forecasting, (2) procurement, and (3) misdirected cost-saving initiatives.

The results of fixing these items are significant: You need to illustrate that improved forecasting (reducing forecast error), for example, by 6%, will lead to an 8% reduction in inventory (and related purchasing), which results in a 10% net income improvement. Here is a three-step process for doing so:

1. *Forecasting benchmarking* is easy to do—simply extract 3 years of sales data, plug them into one of several PC-based forecasting applications that support multilevel (hierarchical) forecasting and model fitting, and simulate forecasting for prior periods (i.e., forecast for March using actuals through January or February). Then, compare your forecast results against either the company's existing archived forecast for the same period or better yet compare them against the actuals. You can see quickly if you can improve on the company's production forecasts. Based on these results, *update the production forecast system* to better use new models that you have validated from the forecast, or replace the system. Small improvements equal huge savings!
2. You need to audit your *procurement department* as part of your inventory analysis. As part of one assessment, I noted a company ordered several very expensive engines (for sale) worth millions of dollars. They were selling 2 of these engines per year, and they ordered 20 (10 years' worth of engines). The reasoning was that the *minimum order quantity* set in their procurement system was 20 units (to achieve a 10% discount). Procurement did not question the

[11] Source: http://www.xentity.com/top-5-low-hanging-fruit-to-not-bungle-it-procurement-2/, issued Dec. 2013. Author Xenity.com, 14,143 Denver. Access date: 15.2.2021.

default volume–they just triggered the order. Further analysis indicated seemingly arbitrary minimum order quantities for many of their items, which resulted in stock levels that were not in alignment with demand. We extracted the ordering data, ran an economic order quantity (EOQ, calculation see below) and recommended an order quantity analysis, which we were able to load back into their procurement system to override the arbitrary defaults. We also created a *top 25 list of possible procurement issues* (ever changing), which we used to target item purchases that were not in alignment with demand and were causing the biggest problems. Of these, we contacted the suppliers *to validate minimum order quantities and item prices to correct or renegotiate terms that were more appropriate.*

3. *Mid-directed cost-saving initiatives* are by far the most common issues we run across in our operations and supply chain management and are sometimes the hardest to change. These include mass firings without regard for key employees or roles. We have seen companies that decide to "cut orders by 20%," for example. The problem is these arbitrary cuts often affect core SKUs (the ones you need) and do not affect the excess SKU inventory (the ones you do not need). This is the death spiral of a company and is hard to correct. It is very difficult to explain to a company that they *need to INVEST in core items in order to make money* when they are deep in the midst of cost cutting. We have gone so far as to produce a specific order list of core SKU's and quantities for immediate purchase to return the company to safe levels. With margins that can sometimes reach 400%, it can be amusing to tell a CFO in the midst of cost-saving campaigns that it is imperative to *immediately place a $1 million order of (list of core items and order quantities) and show that he will make $4 million from the sale* of those items by the end of the month.[12]

Economic Order Quantity[13]

One important item at PUR is economic order quantity (EOQ).

We define EOQ according to the following formulas:

Total EOQ cost = procurement cost/year + inventory carrying costs/year.

Whereas

Procurement cost/year = A*P/Q
A = total items consumed per year
P = procurement cost per order
Q = economic order quantity

[12] Sources: (20+)1141 Group—Posts | Facebook; created 4.1.2019. Author JM Chambers, Playwright, for 1141group.com; *Access date 4.1.2019*

[13] Source: Mechanical Estimating and Costing, page 172 to 174, by Khanna Publishers, Delhi, 2006. Authors T.R. Banga & S.C. Sharma.

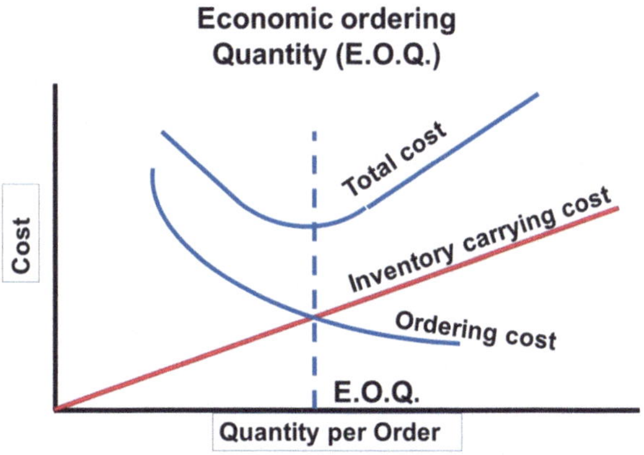

Fig. 3.21 Economic ordering quantity

Inventory carrying costs/year = Q/2 * C

C = annual inventory carrying cost per item

Total cost = A*P/Q + Q/2 * C

Total cost will be minimum, when A*P/Q = Q/2 * C

Then, economic order quantity Q = $(2AP/C)^{1/2}$

Since total cost curve is flat at the bottom, deviation of 25% on both sides is possible. For example, where is quantity discount, we can enhance orders by 25% over the EOQ (Fig. 3.21).

Example 1

Given data:

- Supplier can deliver 750 pieces per months into warehouse.
- The warehouse ships 3000 pieces per year (A) with purchasing price from supplier of 250 RMB/piece (S).
- *Setup and plant ordering costs of 300 RMB (P).* What is behind this procurement cost? This cost includes expenses made on calling and processing quotations, placing orders, receiving goods and incoming inspection costs, and verifying and paying bills, not including any transportation/forwarder costs and custom clearance costs.
- *Inventory carrying cost rate (R) of 20%.* What is behind this cost? This cost includes insurance, storage and handling, deterioration, obsolescence, depreciation, taxes, and interest of inventory. Costs do not include warehouse costs.

What quantities should the warehouse order from the supplier plant?

Solution:

C = annual inventory carrying cost per item = total inventory carrying costs/total no. of item consumed (A)

C = A * S * R/A = 3000 *250 * 20/3000 *100 = 50 RMB

E.O.Q = $(2AP/C)^{1/2}$

Q = (2*3000 * 300/50) ^{½} = 190 units. Ordering 750 pieces would cause financial losses.

Example 2
Given data:

- Production needs 20 pieces raw material per year (A).
- Setup and plant ordering costs of 40 RMB (P).
- The cost of each unit is 100 RMB (S).
- Inventory carrying cost rate of average stock (R) is 16%.

What economic quantities should ordered from supplier plant?

If the lead time (LT) is 3 months (it is the time, which takes the stock to reach from reorder point to minimum stock level), what is the order point?

Solution:

C = annual inventory carrying cost per item = total inventory carrying costs (A)/ total no. of item consumed

C = A * S * R/A = 20 *100 * 16/20 *100 = 16 RMB

E.O.Q = $(2AP/C)^{1/2}$

Q = (2*20 * 40/16)^{½} = 10 units. Only 10 pieces should be ordered, not 20 pieces.

Stock level at reorder point Q_0 = consumption rate a * lead time LT

Consumption rate a = 20 pieces/12 months

Q_0 = 20/12*3 = 5 units. When stock level reaches 5 pieces, warehouse should send orders again.

3.10 Transformation into a New Organizational Structure

The goal of a transformation process is to support cost reduction activities within a new organizational chart, for example, to incorporate principles of logistics and quality in a new supply chain.

You may have following advantages: synergy, cost reduction, and responsibility to lower levels. But quality is not the most important criteria if a decision is made at purchasing department; decisions here are a balance between costs, timing, and quality.

Solution: Compare the company's own cost structure analysis with benchmarks. The decision of which supplier will receive the company's business will not be done by a buyer alone, but within a team composed of purchasing, quality, and finance. These meetings need to be standardized to enable quick decision making.

3.11 How Do We Reduce Costs?

Here is a 9-step gradual approach to successful cost reduction:

1. Know the element to be economized (i.e., the measure, process, specification, or assembly line)
2. Classify elements into families (elemental structure)
3. Perform strategic integration (form creative teams, conduct long-term contracts, benchmarking, global sourcing, set rules, and perform cost breakdowns)
4. Evaluate piece prices (true costs)
5. Identify cost drivers (e.g., material, technique, engineers, labor costs)
6. Internal benchmarking
7. External benchmarking
8. Value management
9. Value analysis workshop

For example, VA workshop for benchmarking ISUZU Diesel Engine Control Module by teardown process. We made following observations:

- 30 sq./in.062" FR4 printed circuit board with additional copper added to improve thermal transfer.
- Housing contains engine cooling passages.
- Topside SMT reflow and bottom side SMT wave solder.
- Passive component count—322
- Active component count—20
- Mechanical part count—12
- Sealed aluminum housing but printed circuit board is not conformally coated.
- 121 pin connector interface.
- 144 pin quad flat pack microprocessor (Fig. 3.22)

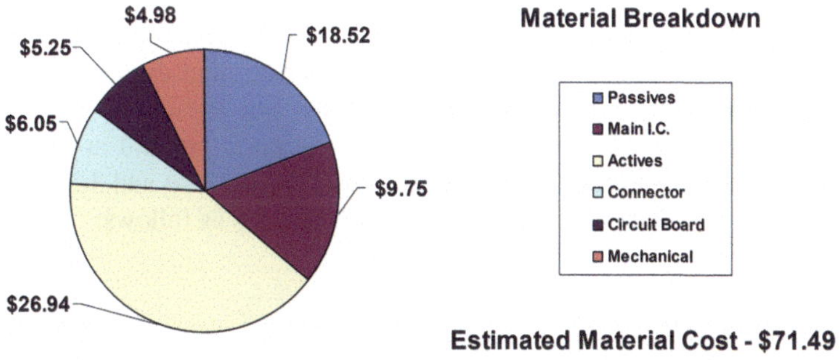

Fig. 3.22 Material breakdown of ISUZU Diesel Engine Control Module. Estimated module cost—$110–$115. Source: General Motors, Detroit, 2004

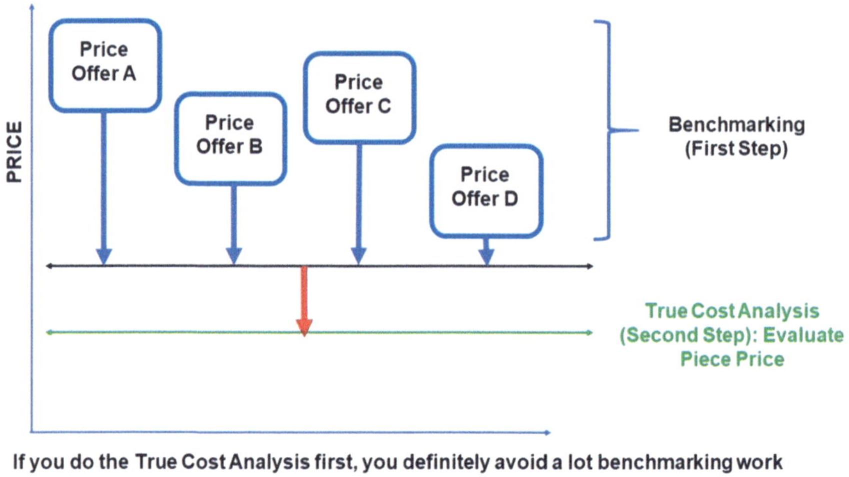

Fig. 3.23 What purchaser normally do in daily business could be improved: First do true cost analysis first, to avoid complete benchmarking work. Source: Robert Bosch GmbH, 2012

3.12 Cost Breakdown

Above, please see standard purchasing activity and a way to make improvements (Fig. 3.23).

Cost breakdowns do not mean anything if they are just talked about. A buyer has to buy into it, and learn to believe it.

Buyers sometimes would not accept the result of cost breakdowns, because they are forced to find a way to negotiate and reduce their prices.

Where is the gold standard for how you want to compete with your strongest rivals worldwide? You need to find the answer yourself, and discuss it with your purchasing department. You know the prices, but not the costs. You have to understand the process of suppliers. Where do the costs lie, and at what level? Where are the cost function-related allowable costs? (Figs. 3.24 and 3.25).

For example, the total cost of an Opel Corsa (100%) is as follows:

- 72% material
- 16% manufacturing
- 7% product engineering
- 3% freight
- 2% commercial
- 0.01% duties

Changes increase the price (cost creep). Try to avoid changes, or find better solutions. It is easy to solve a problem with money; for example, to put money into

Fig. 3.24 Tear down of your parts in value analysis workshops to evaluate single piece prices. Teamwork of some experts is necessary. Source: Robert Bosch GmbH, 2012

better material or to pass tests and certifications like ABS into ABS-PC (high performance). Open your minds to new directions and strategies.

Just spending money to get better material and pass tests is a mistaken approach to solve your problems. Think, for example, of ways to save money by finding better design solutions in agreement with your customer (Fig. 3.25).

If you are not satisfied with your suppliers, change them. Visit your competitors; compare yourself to the competition. Who is the best of best in terms of processes? Man power? Overhead? For example, how many shifts are there, and how many workers are working on that part? How much output does the supplier have per shift? After receiving the answers to this, you will be able to calculate cycle time and compare them with your competitors.

As stated previously, the first step of finding true costs is collecting and updating information (data) and centralizing it into a database. The advantage of a central database is that SQ engineers, SD engineers, and buyers all have access to it and are able to discuss it in open Q&A at workshops while evaluating the content. If you find gaps in the data (price differences), you have to develop a strategy of how to negotiate with the suppliers. For example, SQ engineers will modify processes while doing run and rates with suppliers. SD engineers will use this database for cost breakdowns and for negotiations with suppliers.

For example, at supplier site, we calculate a sum of 25% for overhead and profit, with 20% overhead and 5% profit. If R&D is falling behind, you will certainly have overhead of more than 20%.

If your price is 10 euros, you will have to pay2 euros in R&D per part. At 100,000 parts per year, total R&D expenses are 200,000 euros. If the development costs of this part are 10,000 euros per employee, the company must have 20 employees.

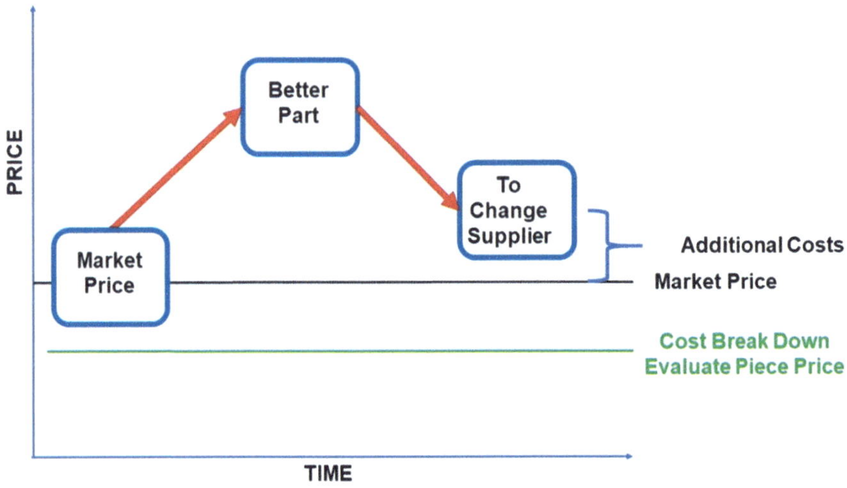

Fig. 3.25 Cost Creep. Source: Robert Bosch GmbH, 2012

Check the number of employees in R&D, and you will be able to check the overhead costs against your supplier.

What about your machines, are they old or new? New machines make less scrap than old ones. 2–3% scrap in manufacturing is generally good enough; cast parts will have 5–15% scrap, plastic parts 1–10%, fabrics 3–5%, and stamped parts 1–3%. If an assembly of one part has 2% scrap, there will be 6% scrap in total (including 1% material losses + 3% manufacturing scrap), which means 106 parts are needed to be delivered to obtain 100 acceptable parts (Fig. 3.26).

3.13 Easy Supplier Evaluations

A high-quality supplier evaluation documents all of a supplier's strengths and weaknesses and provides answers to the following questions:

- What quality level has been delivered?
- Has the order quantity and price been adhered to?
- How does the price compare to the other suppliers? Is the price value verifiable?

The supplier will undergo monthly evaluations of quality, adherence to delivery dates, quantity, price, audit results, and services, with quality indicators and final grades. In addition, the evaluation will also examine the supplier's response to complaints in terms of action, reaction time, and processing, and any assistance with problems and suggestions for solutions, and the state of the partnership are evaluated.

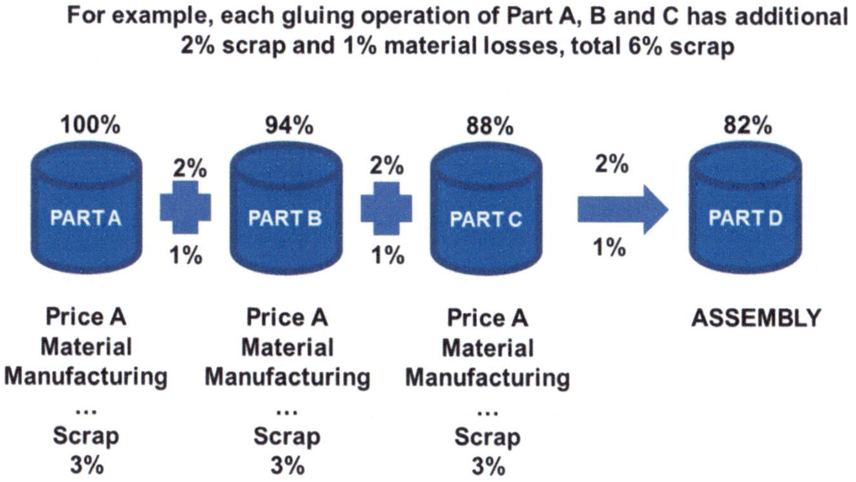

Fig. 3.26 Example of total scrap calculation. Assuming 1% material scrap + 3% manufacturing scrap + 2% assembly gluing scrap = 6% scrap of each part. For 3 parts to be assembled without gluing and with 0% losses in end of line testing, losses are in total 18%. Source: Robert Bosch GmbH, 2012

After 1 year, the collected data will be reset to zero. Thus, the results shall remain up to date and not run together.

The average quality indicator is calculated from the sum of the quality indicators of the individual deliveries, divided by the number of deliveries in the evaluation period, supplemented by the evaluations of audits and services.

To implement the valuation, the posting program of the goods received will be extended by the criteria quality, date, quantity, price, audits, and services. At the end of the month, the program shall determine the corresponding Quality KPI.

The worse the evaluation, the more important it is to investigate the causes for these flaws. Together with the supplier, a catalog of measures for eliminating the weak points will be defined. These corresponding actions have a high priority.[14]

Based on the general results of past supplier evaluations, it can be said that family-run companies are more dynamic than listed companies. They are less strongly controlled and regulated, grow faster, and increase their value more strongly than comparable companies that have gone public. The reason for this lies in the interdependence of the entrepreneur with their company and in the unity of ownership, management, liabilities, and risks. A family stands behind its business much longer than an external investor. In addition, they do not have to look at quarterly financial statements in the short term.

[14]Source: "Purchasing Manager"/August 2005, page 9, Author Jürgen Rehfeld, Medicine Arzneimittel.

If they are not forced by law to publish annual financial statements, family-run businesses will not do so. Where statements are available, high growth rates are frequently published.

3.13.1 How Do You Calculate Profit and Overhead in the Cost Breakdown (CBD) Process?

For example:

Material	100 euros
Manufacturing	200 euros
Overhead	60 euros
Profit	40 euros
Total	400 euros

Profit and overhead are 33% of material and manufacturing costs, but 25% of total costs. We assume that overhead is constant, but it is not if material prices are changing. Be aware of this counterintuitive procedure during CBD calculations.

3.13.2 What To Do When Overtime Is Needed to Finish Products on a Deadline?

First, check the contractual volume and capacity. If additional extra time is needed (e.g., Saturday overtime), the machine will run for free! For example, it may be necessary to produce 450,000 parts a year instead of 400,000. If you make a calculation according to CBD, you will see that the price will decrease, and if you work overtime, the volume will increase.

If the volume drops, check the first contract. Is the price dependent on volume, or is volume only provided for reference? If a price is fixed for 1 year, new prices will be based on IPC rate (Internet Pricing and Configurator (SAP)), material, and other factors. Standard practice at negotiations is changes without price increase and a reduction of 2–3% every year.

4 Supplier Development in Asia in 5 Steps

For sourcing components, it is the same sourcing process and not much difference to sourcing of tools (see Sect. 6.4.2–6.4.5) in China: Supplier needs to provide references so you can check his experience and business partners in toolmaking, service, and maintenance of machines, testing and measuring of parts, lean manufacturing principles and quality management at workshop, and purchasing of single parts and raw materials from their subsuppliers. You also may check the financial situation of the company and turnover rate of employees and blue collar workers.

Additionally at assembly lines in supplier's shop floor, you may check poka yoke stations to avoid high ppm rate, especially if supplier parts will arrive via your warehouse to your CNC measuring room. An efficient qualification of operators is also useful to avoid damage or incorrect installation of components at the assembly line.

For further details and practical experiences to several supplier development service programs with examples out of industries, see Sect. 4.2–4.5.

Only if a company improves their skills, processes, and products continuously, they will stay profitable and earn money. The prerequisite is to generate enough sales volume to cover your expenses.

4.1 Service, Consulting, and Training for Cost Reduction and Quality Improvement

Like few others, the company GTEC as an example is professionals and able to help you in Asia in quality management, quality assurance, supplier quality engineering, supplier development, supply chain, lean production, and shop floor management.

4.1.1 Lean Management

Following tools and methods are in their focus:

K. Zuerl, *Effective Cost Cutting in Asia*, Management for Professionals,
https://doi.org/10.1007/978-3-030-82782-3_4

QM/QA/SQE/SC/Lean/ SFM /SD Tool categories	Well-known tools to put money back into your pocket
Auto quality basics	Quality System Basics (QSB) training teaches all important basic principles, such as[1]: • Fast response and structured problem-solving • Risk reduction • Standardized operator training • Standardized work instructions • Layered audits • Error proofing verification
Autoquality matrix	Ensuring that a defect is detected at the workstation where it was created. Use following tools: • Work instructions • Self-inspection • Stop production at the first reject • Poka yoke • Capable machines and processes • Autonomous machines
CIP & Ideas	SMED (single-minute exchange of die; quick change over, rapid tool changes <10 min): It is used to reduce the time required for changing items. Of course, it can be used to improve the TRS, but in this case we change nothing in the number of product changes, and therefore, nothing changes in the way we respond to customer demands. With a very short product change (2 minutes for example), we can reduce batch sizes and in parallel the overall stock level, and change with each customer demand. The less time we use to change over, the more the machines are available to produce.
	TRS: It masters the overall yield rate application in the management of the company (planning, cost, effectiveness, objective, start-up curve for a new product, etc.) and quantifies the losses of your machines and your organization.[2]
	ANDON: It displays board showing deviations from the norm.
	ASAICHI: It is Japanese weekday morning talk program.[3]
	KAIZEN: Kaizen is a concept referring to business activities that continuously improve all functions and involve all employees from the CEO to the assembly line workers.[4]

(continued)

[1] *Source*: https://www.gpqmbvba.com/en/training-coaching/quality-system-basics, author: G&P QUALITY MANAGEMENT, Training Quality System Basics. Access date: 16.2.2021

[2] *Source*: Lean Training. Author Mind Change Technologies LLC, 2019. Access date: 16.2.2021

[3] *Source*: https://en.wikipedia.org/wiki/Asaichi, article Asaichi, issued February 10, 2021, Access date: 16.2.2021

[4] *Source*: https://en.wikipedia.org/wiki/Kaizen, article Kaizen, issued February 12, 2021, Access date: 16.2.2021

QM/QA/SQE/SC/Lean/ SFM /SD Tool categories	Well-known tools to put money back into your pocket
Cost management	Engineering and change management: It manages the changes a design goes through its lifetime during the engineering change requests stage. The proposals are analyzed and formally approved.
	Document management: It ensures that the right people get the right information at the right time.
	Six Sigma: Variation reducing; quantitative capability assessment DFSS (design for Six Sigma): Frontloading of Six Sigma in Technical Engineering Centres.
Just In Time	Small containers: Smaller containers for frontal loading of lines in-house
	Reusable containers: Use of reusable containers in order to eliminate cardboard.
	Dynamic floor storage systems can increase productivity and reduce labor requirements.[5]
	Kanban (card): Upstream ordering system based on actual downstream consumption. Pull system: Method for maintaining an orderly flow of material; information carrier between internal customer und supplier, e.g., final assembly and pre-assembly: • producing what is consumed • avoid shortage • stop producing when not necessary • having alert levels • materialization needs by cards Pull flow: Used to organize part and information exchanges between processes, control stocks, and highlight material shortages.
	SIOP: To run a business well, demand and supply must be in balance at both the volume and mix levels. In reality, this balance does not exist. Management must step up to understand this relationship. SIOP is a set of tools to balance demand and supply. SIOP operates at the volume level; it deals with rates of sales and production, and aggregates inventories and backlog.[6]
	The MPS (master production schedule) translates the customer demand (sales orders, PIRs), into a build plan using planned orders in a true component scheduling environment. Using MPS helps avoid shortages, costly expediting, last minute scheduling, and inefficient allocation of resources. Working with MPS allows businesses to consolidate planned parts, produces master

(continued)

[5] *Source*: https://www.mfgnewsweb.com/archives/4/43224/Energy-Mfg-sep15/Oil-and-Gas-Companies-Reduce-Floor-Space-with-Dynamic-Storage.aspx; issued 1.9.2015, author Gross Publications, Inc., Texas, USA. Access date: 16.2.2021

[6] *Source*: http://thirdparty.biz/siop.pdf, Author Third Party International Ocala, Florida. Access date: 16.2.2021

QM/QA/SQE/SC/Lean/ SFM /SD Tool categories	Well-known tools to put money back into your pocket
	schedules, and forecasts for any level of the bill of material (BOM) for any type of part.[7]
Kaizen (improvement)	Training follow-up: Successful training and employee development efforts provide a real-time connection between the classroom and the workplace.[8,9]
	Material flow analysis (MFA) is based on two fundamental and well-established scientific principles, the systems approach, and mass balance.[10]
	Manager's role: Regardless of the management structure, it is vital that businesses adopt a means of organizing employees to ensure effective communication.[11,12]
	Action plan follow-up: Action plans prevent contacts from slipping through the cracks and keep your schedule on track.[13]
	Lean design process: That is because most of the costs and much of the quality in a construction project are locked in long before production launch, and therefore, the design process will be crucial not only to "do things right" but also, more importantly, to "do the right things." The lean philosophy, with its focus on minimizing waste and maximizing value, is therefore recommended to be applied as early as possible in a building process.[14]
	CIP (continuous improvement process): Gathering ideas, supplementing the best ones as soon as possible, and awarding individuals, install PDCA as a permanent progress tool.
	PDCA: Method for following up action plans. Plan (improvement actions), do (implement action on a pilot

(continued)

[7] *Source*: https://en.wikipedia.org/wiki/Master_production_schedule#:~:text = A%20master%20production%20schedule%20(MPS,each%20product%20will%20be%20demanded.; article Master production schedule; issued December 17, 2019; Access date: 16.2.2021

[8] *Source*: https://www.thebalancecareers.com/tips-for-training-transfer-1919307 , article Strategies After Employee Training; Author thebalance.com, SUSAN M. HEATHFIELD, issued October 29, 2019, New York. Access date: 16.2.2021.

[9] *Source*: https://www.businesstrainingworks.com/training-resource/five-fantastic-ways-to-follow-up-after-training/. Author Business Training Works Inc., Port Tobacco, issued 2020. Access date: 16.2.2021.

[10] *Source*: https://en.wikipedia.org/wiki/Material_flow_analysis; article Material Flow Analysis, issued December 24, 2020, access date 16.2.2021

[11] *Source*: https://jobs.telegraph.co.uk/article/what-are-the-main-responsibilities-of-managers/; author Telegraph Media Group Limited, published: November5 07, 2017, access date 16.2.2021

[12] *Source*: https://techmoran.com/2013/03/26/why-it-pays-to-learn-from-the-seven-ms-of-management/, author Milcah Lukhanyu, published 26.3.2013, access date 16.2.2021

[13] *Source*: https://help.followupboss.com/360002584134-Setup/360014655953-Action-Plans-Overview; article Action Plan Overview, written by Erik Wantland; published at: December 9, 2020. Access date 16.2.2021

[14] *Source*: https://leanconstructionblog.com/Applying-Lean-Thinking-to-the-Design-Process.html; written by Nawras Skhmot, published at July 17, 2015. Access date 16.2.2021

QM/QA/SQE/SC/Lean/ SFM /SD Tool categories	Well-known tools to put money back into your pocket
	workshop), check (finalize the pilot workshop in respect of the initial target), act (deploy the actions to all equivalent areas).
	Kaizen costing and cost analysis (focusing on continuous cost reduction rather than simply meeting the standard: Set a cost target, calculate cost gaps, and plan activities to reduce costs).
Lean MFG	Value stream analysis, flow analysis (PDA, process depth analysis): Analysis of flows to identify problem areas, e.g., stocks, unnecessary movements, and waiting time. The aim of flow analysis is to reduce lead times of our products by reducing work in progress and nonproductive operations. We cannot take on all problems at the same time, so we carry out a process flow to analyze problems and prioritize the use of the VPS tools. So, it is necessary to stand back and analyze the different problems confronting us. Flow analysis consists of going back up the flow and qualitatively and quantitatively observing the problems and then deciding on the sites to treat them. In each operation, we measure the stock, the progression distance, technical time, and tuning time. The summary of all give the ratio of value-added time over the dock to dock time (throughput time)
	Leveling: Daily production schedule to achieve even utilization of production capacity.
	Green triangle: Triangles always highlight some form of waste on a value stream map. Use a green triangle for inventory, or a yellow triangle for any other form of delay.[15]
	Lean process design: Here are five process design principles of LEAN[16]: • Specify *value* from the standpoint of the customer • Map the *value* chain or *value* stream • Create *flow* • Let customers *pull value* from upstream processes • Seek perfection
	Pull principle (production produce and logistics delivers only as much as the customer requires). The pull flow system is used to organize part and information exchanges between the cells. Among the tools, we find the Kanban, small containers, flat storage at the foot of the line, the train, and milk run.
Logistics	Chaku Chaku line (transfers parts to the next process, provides flexibility to cope with volume fluctuations).
	Milk run (providing material for production at set time intervals); circuit for collecting products at several suppliers.

(continued)

[15] *Source*: https://www.systems2win.com/c/vs_inv_symbols.htm; article Lean Tools, Training, and Systems. Author Systems2win . Access date 16.2.2021

[16] *Source*: https://medium.com/designrover/what-is-lean-process-improvement-d723ee5826a8; Author Prateek Vasisht, published May 12, 2019; Access date 16.2.2021.

QM/QA/SQE/SC/Lean/ SFM /SD Tool categories	Well-known tools to put money back into your pocket
	Demand planning (delivery schedules to create forecasts at a variety of levels).
	EDI (electronic data interchange): Forecasting, delivery schedules, billing.
	Vendor-managed inventory: Instead of sending Kanban signals to suppliers, you can give them responsibility for replenish goods.
MUDA	MUDA: Within just in time, any activity that, from the customer's point of view, does not add value to the product or the service: e.g., scraps, overproduction, waiting time, stocks, and transportation.
Prevention tools	Poka yoke (error proofing; physical devices within the product on the process to avoid the transfer to the next station).
	FMEA (failure mode effect analysis; for managing risks in a design and manufacturing process) to identify potential failure cause, the effects and the detection mode, define risk evaluation by prioritizing of risks by the risk index (RI), work on to reduce RI as corrective plan, and validate the efficiency of the corrective actions by measurement and follow-up.
Problem-solving; root cause analysis (RCA)	5 Ws: According to the principle of the five Ws, a problem-solving report can only be considered complete if it answers these questions starting with who, what, when, where, and why.[17] 5 Ms&E: Abbreviation stands for *"Manpower, Machine, Measurement, Material, Methods and Environment,"* and it is a technique where you ask questions about the 5Ms & E till you find the root cause of the problem.[18] The Shainin System™ (SS) is defined as a problem-solving system designed for medium- to high-volume processes where data are cheaply available, statistical methods are widely used, and intervention into the *process* is difficult. It has been mostly applied in parts and assembly operation facilities.[19]
Process control	SPC (statistical process control), monitoring of process deviations, to keep a process under control by: • manufacturing histogram • technical process of analysis • design of experiment (DOE) • capability measurement • control card

(continued)

[17] *Source*: https://en.wikipedia.org/wiki/Five_Ws, article Five Ws. Published January 5, 2021; Access date 16.2.2021.

[18] *Source*: https://www.linkedin.com/pulse/how-conduct-effective-root-cause-analysis-5ms-e-nashwa-saad-mba/, published on November 23, 2017, Author Nashwa Saad, MIBA, access date 21.2.2021

[19] *Source*: https://asq.org/quality-resources/shainin-system; Article WHAT IS THE SHAININ SYSTEM™? published on January 2008, Author American Society for Quality ASQ, access date 21.2.2021

QM/QA/SQE/SC/Lean/ SFM /SD Tool categories	Well-known tools to put money back into your pocket
	Operators are more responsible, involved and willing to communicate
	SQA (supplier quality assurance): General and specific standards for the product, process, and organization.
	Visual management (systems clearly show what is produced where and when).
	RCA (root cause analysis (RCA) is a step-by-step method that leads to the discovery of a fault's first or root cause). Every equipment failure happens for a number of reasons. There is a definite progression of actions and consequences that lead to a failure. An RCA investigation traces the cause and effect trail from the end failure back to the root cause. Much like a detective solving a crime.
Production System Foundations	Respect for the product, e.g., detailed view of your product's journey, from the origin of its raw materials, to its production, transport, and distribution.[20]
	QCDM follow-up (quality, cost, delivery management).[21]
	Working standards: A machine shop will have physical working standards (gauge blocks for example) that are used for checking its measuring instruments.[22] Standard that is used routinely to calibrate or check material measures, measuring instruments or reference materials. A working standard is usually calibrated against a reference standard.[23]
	5S: Improving workplace order and cleanliness by sort out, set in order, shine, standardized work, sustain, or sort, step by step, sweep away, spotless, standardize to have a clean, organized, clear, performing, and secure work environment, to make people proud of their workstation and make them more involved.
	Zoning: Past standards and codes for floor marking,[24] as part of 5S.
	Lean production (interaction of all business sectors in an optimally coordinated process chain): Benefits of operational, administrative, and strategic improvements.

(continued)

[20] *Source*: https://www.respect-code.org/, Text "Make a Difference" published 2021, Author Product DNA, Lausanne, Switzerland. Access date 21.2.2021

[21] *Source*: https://en.wikipedia.org/wiki/Quality,_cost,_delivery. Last edited on January 11, 2021, Access date 21.2.2021

[22] *Source*: https://en.wikipedia.org/wiki/, Working standard. Last edited on February 8, 2021, Access date 21.2.2021

[23] *Source*: https://elsmar.com/elsmarqualityforum/threads/reference-standard-vs-working-standard-differences.26489/#:~:text=Standard%20that%20is%20used%20routinely, calibrated%20against %20a%20reference%20standard. Author Raffy, last edited on July 16, 2008. Access date 21.2.2021

[24] *Source*: https://www.plantservices.com/articles/2010/09floormarking/, Article "5S floor marking tape color standards," published on September 20, 2010, author Chris Rutter, Brady Worldwide, Inc.; access date 21.2.2021.

QM/QA/SQE/SC/Lean/ SFM /SD Tool categories	Well-known tools to put money back into your pocket
	5 principles: • rely on people • produce the just requested quantity • reduce internal transfer time • build quality at the very origin during process • improve continuously 3 tools: • overall operating business performances • flow analysis • company structure and organization
	Operating Business Performances Measures Examples of an automotive industry KPI standard: (1) Customer return (< 10 ppm) (2) Cost of waste, scraps, and reworks (< 1% of turnover) (3) Inventory turns (> 33 in a year) (4) Dock to dock time (< 8 working days) (5) Overall equipment effectiveness (> 90% good parts of big runners) (6) Production space utilization/turnover (>4,5 k€/m^2) (7) Change over time (setup time, < 5 minutes of bottle neck equipment of big runners) (8) Customer delivery achievement (target 100% of customer's schedule) (9) Suggestions per employee per year (> 20) (10) Turnover per employee (> 225 k€/person) (11) Added value per employee (k€/person)
Quality management	ISO/TS 16949:2002 auditor
	ISO 9001:2000 auditor
	EFQM, ISO 9004:2002 auditor, VDA
	QS 9000
	8D report
	TQM: Total quality management is used to continuously improve all areas of a company's operation.
Shop floor management:	Shop floor management is an activity of planning, designing, operating, and maintaining the shop floor of a manufacturing facility.[25]
	Autonomous team (one team, one system, one target) manage • its KPI (quality, productivity, 5S, absenteeism, OEE, suggestions) • manufacturing • machine tuning • maintenance level • self-inspection quality • to ask for help from support functions

(continued)

[25] *Source*: https://www.tutorialspoint.com/shop_floor_management/shop_floor_management_tutorial.pdf; published in 2017, author Tutorials Point (I) Pvt. Ltd, access date 21.2.2021.

QM/QA/SQE/SC/Lean/ SFM /SD Tool categories	Well-known tools to put money back into your pocket
	Yamazumi: Line balancing. A Yamazumi chart is a stacked bar chart that shows the balance of cycle time workloads between a number of operators typically in an assembly line or work cell.[26]
	Cellular manufacturing: A U-shaped production line; product flows smoothly from one operation to the next.
TPM	TPM (total productive maintenance): Identifying and eliminating the causes of machine stoppages. First concentrate on machines which generate bottlenecks, and monitor the performance of the machines, then • improve the reliability and availability of equipment • reduce the time lost due to breakdowns and micro stoppages by using the role of the operators and maintenance team, which spend 8 h with the equipment every day. Capitalizes on proactive and progressive maintenance methodologies, calls on the cooperation of operators, and supports personnel to optimize machine performance and is used to reduce breakdowns and micro stops, increase responsibility, and create cross-functional teams: It helps to improve the OEE of your equipment. Treatment methodology of breakdown and micro stoppages, mean time between failure. OEE (overall equipment effectiveness): Status of an equipment: Utilization, TRS (%) = number of good parts * cycle time × 100/opening time Reliability, MTBF = actual running time/number of stoppages
Waste reduction	Hoshin Kanri/Hoshin: Identifying and eliminating waste in a process: Stocks, lost time, transport. Policy deployment is used to remove waste in a process that is both manual and automatic by process analysis: • adjust the manufacturing rhythm to the customer consumption rhythm • decrease dock to dock time • increase team work spirit
	Non-value-added activity are as follows: • excess (or early) production • delays • transportation (to/from processes) • inventory • processing • defects • movement Techniques for reducing or eliminating waste: • value stream analysis • total quality management • total productive maintenance • Kaizen costing and cost analysis • engineering and change management • document management

[26] *Source*: https://www.acsco.com/yamazumi?gclid=Cj0KCQiA2af-BRDzARIsAIVQUOfus0hRdcbgAfVdXpTdeCXkIy6Qu_r7jekBaFmI4Caur9QjqO0D608aApaOEALw_wcB. Author Applied Computer Services, Inc, published 2021. Access date 21.2.2021

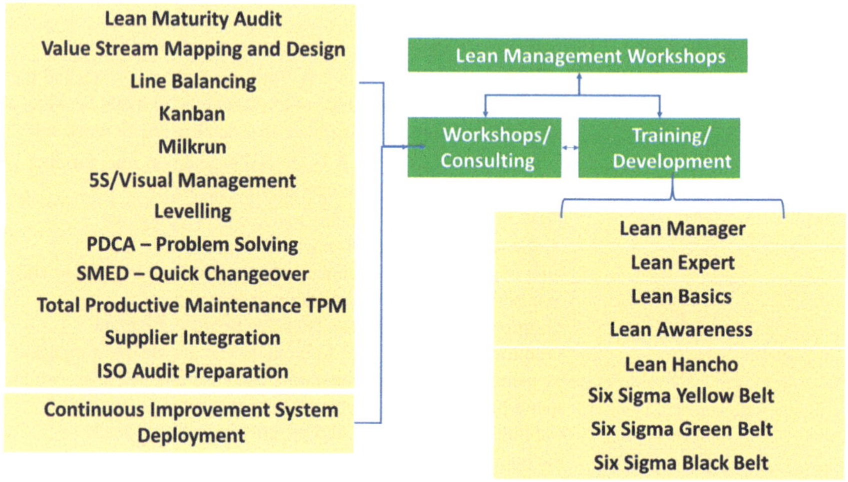

Fig. 4.1 Some methodologies that support lean thinking. *Source*: https://la-asia.sg/service-range. Service Range—Lean Associates Singapore (la-asia.sg); Author Lean Associates Singapore Pte. Ltd., published 2021. Access date 21.2.2021

4.1.2 Supplier Development Program in Asia for Professionals[27]

Suppliers are an important factor in the success of any company. Suppliers have a direct impact on quality of product or service. Suppliers are an essential key to your success. And the ones you choose to work with can either make or break you and your company (Fig. 4.1).

Where confidence levels are high, and the quality and delivery of products and services from your suppliers exceed your expectations, then you can trust them.

Or they become a burden for purchasing, logistics, and production, swallow up precious resources in QM and SD staff, and cost thousands of Euros in managing costs, OTD, and quality.

Changing a supplier is definitely the last solution you should take, due to high risks and costs. Better is always to invest in developing great supplier skills, performance, and relationships.

Therefore, sourcing to find the right suppliers is one of the most important functions of purchasing department. Firefighting later in the process is costly and wasteful, and finally will lead to loss of revenue.

Following, please find a step-by-step approach to reaping the rewards. You will start by choosing the suppliers that best match your criteria, then compile your suppliers into a categorized pool, and audit each of them.

[27] *Source*: https://www.intouch-quality.com/blog/6-steps-to-supplier-quality-development , Author: **Graham Young**, published February 12, 2019;

By auditing and working with your suppliers, you will measure the predefined KPIs of your suppliers and evaluate each objectively. This means you need to invest your time in your suppliers, maintain good lines of communication, speak to the right people, and avoid confusion. By taking all of the following five steps, you can make decisions how to go on in managing relationship, quality, and cost improvements.

4.2 Selecting the Proper Suppliers in Asia

In order to avoid bad suppliers, the selection process is very crucial to your business. Before starting in sourcing and selecting, you need to categorize your supply base into a pyramid shape. On top, there are your preferred suppliers which need to fulfill certain requirements, other categories could be suppliers in phase-out process, strategic ones, or defined by customers. This is vital in decision making where to spend your available resources when managing those suppliers. And, please do not forget, handling suppliers cost money; therefore, number of suppliers always need to be minimized. However, taking risks in consideration, a second source supply is a very clever and cautious purchasing strategy.

You would ideally want all of your suppliers to perform at a high level.

But in reality, after evaluation of your current suppliers, even best ones will have sometimes bad performance in ppm, getting too expensive for you and your customers or cannot deliver in time anymore. According to my experience, this can have several reasons, from management change, critical business finance situation to prioritizing production for other, more important customers.

Therefore, selection with a proper audit and good prepared questions to management, finance, R&D, QM, and other related department should be the first priority for active supplier development management. For example, following criteria could be considered as important when searching, based on which quality standard you have chosen, as well as the objectives and policies of your company:

- **MOQ** (minimum order quantity): Based on suppliers' cost calculation and optimized batch volume, the minimum order size is a challenge for smaller purchasers or those with a limited budget.
- Payment terms: Especially if you need to pay in advance for oversea suppliers, importers consider payment terms as an important factor in choosing a supplier.
- Certifications: Common certifications like ISO 9001 and ISO 14001 are always required by customers. Therefore, in Asia all extended workforces make advertisement with it to get orders. But remember, here those certifications may not always be legitimate. I strongly recommend to visit suppliers by yourself or by a verified third party at an on-site audit, to be able to ask proper questions and see supplier's conditions, especially in production and health, safety, and environment.

- Production capabilities and capacity: You can verify by requesting and approving a preproduction sample and performing an on-site audit by yourself or by a third party.

4.3 Developing an Approved Supplier Base

As mentioned above, you need to balance your number of suppliers according to your business needs. Therefore, you need to **review your supply base.** Listing your suppliers by category and measure their performance in cost, quality, and delivery is an efficient and value-added initiative.

Following minimum categories and its criteria are recommended:

- **What supplier type do you have?**—critical, tooling, office supplies, maintenance, and training
- **What is the spending capacity of your supplier?**—high, medium, low
- **What spending behavior does your supplier have?**—high, medium, low
- **How which frequency is your supplier used?**—often, occasionally, rarely
- **Is this your second source supplier?**—yes or no

Out of these classifications of your suppliers, you can filter following information to find:

- The top 10 critical suppliers in terms of quality, costs, and OTD (alarm)
- Marking of critical suppliers with no second source (alarm)
- The top five suppliers with highest spending of your company
- Infrequently used suppliers with low spending of your company

If you prepare your audit questions accordingly, the categorized supplier base becomes a powerful tool for making the most of your resources to get the best added value from your supply chain.

4.4 How to Audit Suppliers

Auditing suppliers is a mandatory requirement for most QM systems. However, it is only a snapshot in time. Therefore, need to be repeated from time to time. There are two main types of supplier audits: audits by phone calls based on a questionnaire, or audits on supplier sites. However, asking questions on phone is an initial step that often saves time by helping you evaluating your new unknown suppliers quickly. To be honest, most answers you can get as well from a supplier presentation, if asking facts and figures.

If you need to get an answer how effective and efficient their processes are, you need to go on-site. An on-site supplier audit is the best way to get more in-depth and reliable information. If you go there and spend time and money, you should combine asking not only quality and finance-related questions, but also investigate their cost structure for your products you have in mind:

- The organizational structure of your supplier's QMS
- Performance data of your supplier (e.g., OEE, throughput time, output per operator, quality ppm rate, scrap rate, OTD in %)
- Product and process management (e.g., documentation, transparency, KPIs, RASICs, VSM/VSA, MES)
- Results of supplier internal audits and certification audits
- Personal interaction and communication with key members of the supplier's staff

While asking for a plant tour to look around in manufacturing and warehouse, you will get a feeling of how the company operates and the atmosphere on shop floor and offices. Finally, you will see if the supplier can manufacture or assemble the products you hope to purchase, or they have not the required machines or skills and will use their supplier base to deliver what you need.

You do not need to be a professional black belt at first step to notice when a plant is dirty, raw material is dusty, disorganized, many buffer stocks between manufacturing steps, workers in unsafe working conditions not wearing required cloth, shoes, helmet, gloves, glasses, etc., and no maintenance of rusty equipment, machines, and tooling. And last but not least, if you go in a toilet at shop floor, the cleanliness reflects the attitude of management how to deal with their staff.

You need to be aware, that your potential suppliers will control what you are allowed to see and what will be hidden during your visit, how to answer your questions. If the plant tour is not covering the areas or machines you want to see, you need to focus and ask.

As mentioned above, an audit is only a snapshot in time. Therefore, the most effective audit technique is a sustained process, means you need to visit your suppliers more often and each time, for whatever reasons, some kind of audit need to take place.

An alternative solution is to hire a professional auditor, e.g., an accredited auditor, who is able to give you far more details than those from a amateur, especially if your company requests a C-TPAT validation or compliance. A C-TPAT compliance is an independent verification for an exporting company in Asia to see its compliance against C-TPAT security criteria or guidelines, whereas a SEDEX (supplier ethical data exchange) audit is designed to help businesses improve ethical performance of their supply chain.

Finally, after an audit and with your collected information, you will be able to analyze the required key performance indicators (KPIs) data for your products.

4.5 Measuring Supplier's KPIs

KPIs will become a very powerful tool for customers to measure overall supplier performance, if used correctly. For example:

- Right first time
- OTD (on-time delivery)
- Response time of quotes and inquiries
- Out of box or other defect rates in ppm
- Evaluation of inspection and auditing (to reach a minimum limit result in %)

If your company is big enough, you might have own resources in auditing suppliers, input, and track KPIs at your own ERP (enterprise resource planning) software, in China either SAP or Kingdee.

Alternatively, you can hire independent inspection and auditing firms. They are very useful, if your suppliers are far away from purchasing office. They offer cloud-based access to ongoing reporting of product quality and supplier performance results. Reports show for each supplier an analytics dashboard, including a charted breakdown of quality defects by severity, and stock-keeping units (SKUs) of each part number.

For example, using company SupplyOn AG as a third party, who has customers from **A**irbus, **B**osch, to **Z**F. For details, see https://www.supplyon.com/en/solutions/supplier-management/. They consolidate supplier performance data for your own digital ERP system, which can greatly enable supplier selection and continuous quality improvement.

4.5.1 What Are the Key Performance Indicators (KPI) for SD Program?

KPIs evaluate the success of an organization or of a particular activity (such as projects, programs, products, and other initiatives) in which it engages.

Value Contribution

We understand our KPIs as those for direct impact of main business targets quality, costs, and deliveries and those, who measure the penetration, adoption, and development of lean production system principles.

All KPIs need to have a value for a company and contribute to success. We measure value contribution as economic benefit results out of CIP (continuous improvement process) activities, which is the success of a SD program.

By analyzing the economic impact of each indicator, we can see that savings are the direct benefit of actions. For example, to improve the output rate, supplier focuses on reducing operating time, which saves machine operation costs and labor costs.

KPI Tree

Our KPIs for value contribution are divided into three different levels. Quality, costs, and deliveries are measured directly as “Value” level, while the “Monitoring” level tracks the variables that compose the value level. The “Improvement” level defines points that must be refined in shop floor operations. The continuous improvement

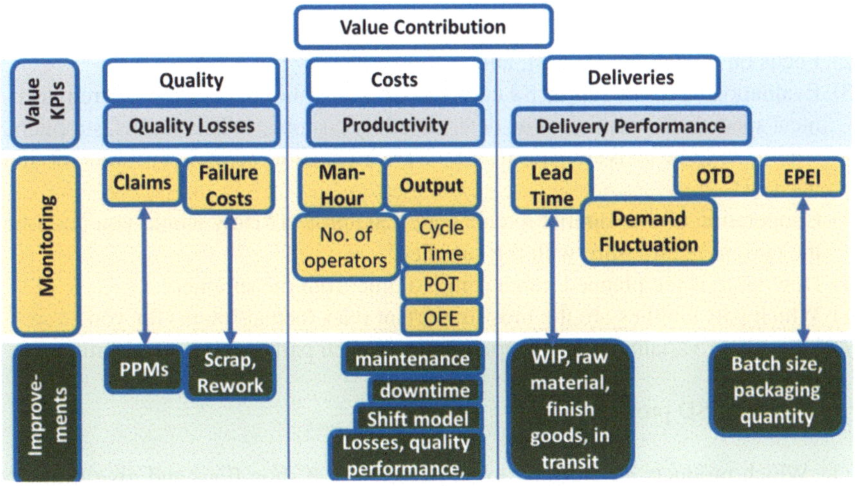

Fig. 4.2 KPI Tree. *Source*: Robert Bosch GmbH, 2012, see as well https://yourflow-2015-eng.blogspot.com/2020/01/blog-post.html

strategy is supported and facilitated by the relationship between these three levels (Fig. 4.2).

4.5.2 How to Achieve Your KPI?

During a first supplier development visit (FSDV), the monitoring level KPIs will be established and measured by SDE. The SD engineer searches for the necessary information and in fixing targets for each improvement-level indicator. Then, an internal project agreement (IPA) with a first draft of potential benefits to be settled on with the buyer recommended to be signed by his/her PUR head.

This process forms an agreement to the target KPIs of the SD program with the supplier.

The supplier development program needs a strong and reliable data set. Therefore, the SD engineer requires certain information to support this process. Here, one kind of information sources is collected from the buyer and others from supplier. Each information is provided in two separate documents.

SD Information Sheet/SD Checklist

To prepare a draft version of potential benefits, SD checklist or supplier development information sheet will be divided into supplier profile, SD project preparation, and logistics.

Supplier Profile

(1) Supplier name, address, contact persons at supplier site?
(2) Focus on quality and/or cost, and/or delivery?
(3) Evaluation status of supplier's competence at supplier pyramid: preferred, technical specialist, essential, new, determined by customer). This means, suppliers, who need to be actively eliminated, or are blocked to get new business, do not need SD.
(4) Cooperation of the supplier to carry out a SD project? How would you describe the current relationship with the supplier?
(5) How large is the planned purchasing volume from the supplier?
(6) Which part families are the most important ones (actual/future) for you?
(7) How many variants do the supplier have in each part family (actual/future)?

Preparation of SD projects:

(1) Which products are planned to be phased out at shop floor and give it to the supplier?
(2) What are the reasons to choose this supplier for this project?
(3) Is there then a new line needed or new products could be produced on an existing line?
(4) How to classify suppliers for value stream mapping VSM? For example, high runners, process complexity, and ppm/KPI troubles?
(5) Is the current process not mastered or it is new for the supplier? Do you see technical or supplier's management issues, cost/exchange rate issues? What actions are taken to overcome these issues?
(6) Are cost breakdown and cost structure analysis done? Where are they stored? What percentage of piece price is raw material, value added? or not value added?
(7) Which quality figures of your supplier can you get for the last six months (e.g., ppm, KPI, scrap rate)?
(8) Did your company sign a quality ppm/KPI (goal) agreement with your supplier? What is the contracted scrap rate at which sales price?
(9) What are the main problems which are caused by your supplier on your in-house production line?
(10) To create a lean value stream, which part family should be connected?
(11) What are the requirements/goals from our own production system or according to TPS for your supplier?

Logistics:

(1) What are the main problems caused by your supplier to your logistic department?
(2) What are the main problems caused by our logistic department to supplier's logistic department?

(3) Which actions are taken to overcome these challenges?
(4) In which areas do you see the main opportunities?
(5) What are supplier's logistic KPIs within last six months (e.g., OTD?
(6) What are the actual/target number of stock points which are to be delivered from supplier to us?
(7) What is your current/target way of managing inventory? For example, do you follow the market trend before deciding the right stock?
(8) What are current/target agreements of frequency and minimum/maximum shipping lot size of JIT/JIS delivery?
(9) What is current/target of Incoterms?
(10) What type of packaging (current/target) is necessary?
(11) Is supplier's line leveled? Are there any plans to level them?
(12) Which time is needed at supplier to realize your forecast?
(13) How do you send current forecasts and how will you send your forecast planning?

4.5.3 Records from Buyer and Supplier

Records for Buyer

Before an FSDV, the SDE prepares a document with an overview of the reasons, and why the supplier was chosen for a SD program. It also contains some information required from the personnel of your plant, for example, such as information of classification, labeling and packaging (CLP), and quality monitoring and management (QMM) system.

Previous Records from Supplier

The first supplier development visit is aimed to introduce the scope and objective of the program to the supplier, while also giving the SD engineer the opportunity to validate and confirm the information which he/she provided to the responsible PUR.

Long time before this visit, the SD engineer provided the management team of the suppliers with an information form (called "cost sheet") of prior data records and explain how to fill in any remaining gaps. The target of this cost sheet is to provide the SDE with an overview of the supplier's value stream and initial state of the diagnosis process. If the SDE considers the supplier to be unable or insufficiently well-developed to provide reliable information, it will be necessary to ask the supplier to collect the data at least one month before the FSDV.

This cost sheet includes a general information section, used for contracting and documentation purposes, and fields/cells for the lean drivers quality, costs, and deliveries. Others are designed for comments, remarks, or information that the supplier considers relevant.

The supplier must send the information back to the SDE at least 1 week before the FSDV. At the time, this cost sheet is fully completed, and the diagnosis process starts. Based on the checklist of required cost data, future benefits calculations by the buyer are possible. This checklist must be sent to the buyer, who must return it at least a month before project closure.

For example, the cost sheet is divided into four sections, general information, quality performance, manufacturing, and logistic information.

General information

Demand fluctuation	Date	Demand (planned)	Demand (real)
Fluctuator = (forecast—real orders)/forecast × 100%			
Average variation of demand within last three months			

Shift model	Record data	
(1) Number of shifts		Shifts/day
(2) Duration per shift		Hours/shift
(3) Working days		Days/month
(4) Lunch break time		Hours/month
(5) Organizational downtime, e.g., meetings		Hours/month
(6) Percentage of supplier time dedicated to our parts		%
Total shift model	$((1 \times 2 \times 3) - (4 + 5))*6$	Hours/month

Quality performance information

Data from one month prior project start	Record data	
(1) Internal scrap rate		Pieces/month
(2) Customer reported scrap rate		Pieces/month
(3) ppm of finished goods		ppms/month
(4) PLKZ[a] of finished goods		PLKZs/month

[a]**PLKZ** (problem supplier quality indicator) evaluates the number of complaints. A distinction could be made as to whether the complaint contains a notice (HW), a service complaint (RS), a product complaint (RP), or a complaint by the customer (FR)[28]

[28] *Source*: https://www.schweizer.ag/tl_files/7-Kontakt/downloads/agb/Guideline_for_supplier_evaluation_Rev3.pdf . Author Jochen Keidel, published 23.04.2018 by Schweizer Electronic AG. Access date 21.2.2021

Manufacturing information

Manufacturing process and cycle time	Record data	
(1) Parallel processes		
(2) Only single process		
(3) Serial processes		
(4) Bottleneck or core process (1)		Sec/piece
(5) Manufacturing process step 2		Sec/piece
(6) Manufacturing process step 3...		Sec/piece
(7) Skilled operators		No. of operators/process
(8) Unskilled operators		No. of operators/process
(9) Total number of operators		No. of operators/value stream

Carry over time (C/O time) of each process step	Record data	From last good part of A to first good part of B
(1) Bottleneck or core process (1)		Hours/month
(2) Manufacturing process step 2		Hours/month
(3) Manufacturing process step 3...		Hours/month

Breaks downtime, one month prior to VSP	Record data	
(1) Bottleneck or core process (1)		Hours/month
(2) Manufacturing process step 2		Hours/month
(3) Manufacturing process step 3...		Hours/month

Unplanned maintenance time, one month prior to VSP	Record data	
(1) Bottleneck or core process (1)		Hours/month
(2) Manufacturing process step 2		Hours/month
(3) Manufacturing process step 3		Hours/month

Lead time	Record data	
(1) Work in progress (WIP)[29]		Days
(2) Finished goods		Days
(3) Raw materials		Days

[29] *Source*: http://www.leanmanufacture.net/leanterms/wip.aspx; Article "Work in Progress WIP," Author leanmanufacture.net, published 2019. Access date 21.2.2021

EPEI (Every Part Every Interval) Calculation

Given: $T_{a\Delta}$ (min) = available time, typically minutes, for changeovers per day or shift, for a given machine or manufacturing step

$T_{\Delta i}$ (min) = internal changeover time in minutes of each part on a given machine or manufacturing step

PART #	$T_{\Delta i}$ (min)/ day
A	33
B	34
C	33
D	33
E	32

Total $T_{\Delta i}$ (min)/day: 165 minutes per day of internal changeover time of all parts in all manufacturing steps

$$EPEI = \frac{\Sigma T_{\Delta i}\text{ (min)/day}}{T_{a\Delta}\text{ (min)/day}}$$

$T_{a\Delta}$ (min)/day = 75 minutes

Wanted: EPEI

$$EPEI = \frac{165\text{ (min)/day}}{75\text{ (min)/day}} = 2.2\text{ days}$$

Fig. 4.3 EPEI calculation. *Source*: Lean Math, page 206 and 207, ISBN 9780872638815, Author Mark R. Hamel, published 2017 by Society of Manufacturing Engineers SME. Access date 18.3.2021

Logistic information

Deliveries, one month prior to VSP	Record data	
(1) On-time delivery OTD		%
(2) EPEI (every part every interval)		
Number of changeovers in our production line		Number/month
Working day per month		Days/month

4.5.4 EBEI Every Part Every Interval

Let me introduce you this KPI to you. EPEI aims to reduce excess inventory, shelf time, and order fulfillment time for on-demand production. It gives your company the ability to keep up with existing orders while as well making room for often unusual orders. Load leveling can get you there. This efficiency in the production stage means less idle time for stock, quicker order times, and happier customers.[30]

How to calculate EPEI? (Fig. 4.3)

[30] *Source*: https://blog.flexis.com/what-is-every-part-every-interval#, What is Every Part Every Interval? Posted by Jesse Kelber on July 23, 2019, by flexis AG, "Access date 18.4.2021

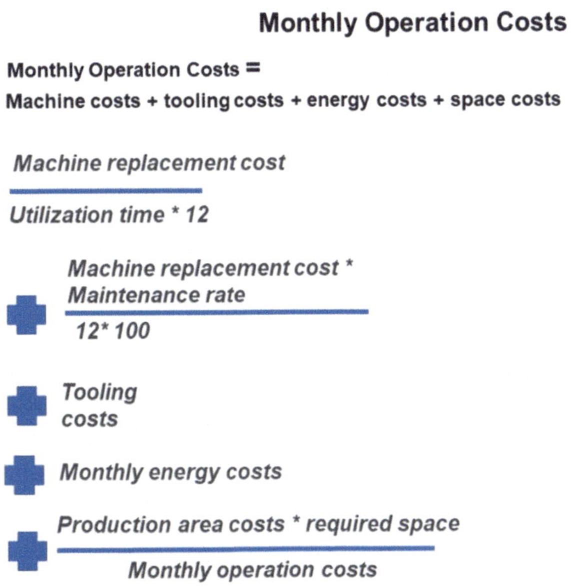

Fig. 4.4 Formula of monthly operation costs (machine +tooling+energy+space)

Second example:

The extended daily run time is 440 minutes (170 + 150 + 120). With a working time of 500 minutes, we have 60 minutes per day of time available for changeovers (500–440). However, all of the changeovers add up to 180 minutes (45 + 60 + 75). Therefore, our EPEI for this process is 3 days (180/60).

EPEI is a length of time. Thinking about it another way, it is how long it takes to accumulate enough available time to allow for all of the changeovers needed to produce every member of the product family. EPEI is an excellent indicator of capacity utilization for a value stream.[31]

4.5.5 Monthly Operation Costs

Most costs can be directly obtained directly from an ECOCUT calculation or RFQ; however, "monthly operation costs" are not always available or easy to obtain. If the exact cost is known, it is entered in the respective cell, in USD/month. In cases where these costs are unavailable, the buyer must provide the list of costs required below, after which this "monthly operation cost" will be filled in automatically. The formula used for this calculation is as follows above (Fig. 4.4).

[31] *Source*: https://blog.mcaconnect.com/epei-part-1-every-part-every-interval2. Article EPEI by Author Phil Coy, published 3.03.2014 by MCA connect, Denver/CO. Access date 21.2.2021

Template to collect data from supplier's or own production:

Required costs	Value	Units	*Source*
Cost of ppm		RMB/ppm	
Cost of PLKZ		RMB/PLKZ	
Cost of piece (RM)		RMB/pc.	CBD/RFQ
Cost of piece (FG)		RMB/pc.	CBD/RFQ
Cost of piece (WIP)		RMB/pc.	CBD/RFQ

If monthly operation cost is available, please fill in following template:

Skilled labor costs		RMB/hour	ECOCUT
No skilled labor costs		RMB/hour	ECOCUT
Indirect labor costs (logistics, quality, maintenance, etc.)		RMB/hour	ECOCUT
Space cost RM warehouse		RMB/m2	ECOCUT
Space cost FG warehouse		RMB/m2	ECOCUT
Space cost WIP		RMB/m2	ECOCUT

If monthly operation cost is **not** available, please fill in next template:
Fixed costs:

Machine replacement cost		RMB/unit	Supplier
Utilization time		Years	Supplier
Tooling cost		RMB/month	Supplier

Variable costs:

Energy cost		RMB/month	ECOCUT
Production area cost		RMB/m^2/month	ECOCUT
Maintenance rate (% of machine cost)		%	ECOCUT
Required space		Qm	ECOCUT

4.5.6 Fulfillment of Internal Project Agreement

With the previous information collected and a plant tour conducted along the defined line or cell, the SD engineer will conduct a value stream mapping during the FSDV period and will provide a detailed explanation to the supplier team how to measure each one at the monitoring level, e.g., OEE.

The first step after gathering and analyzing the received information is to set a target state for the supplier's value stream, based on the observations of the SD engineer.

This information is established and contracted in an IPA (Internal Project Agreement). In this agreement, all responsible parties agree to the targets set for this project and agree to the benefits.

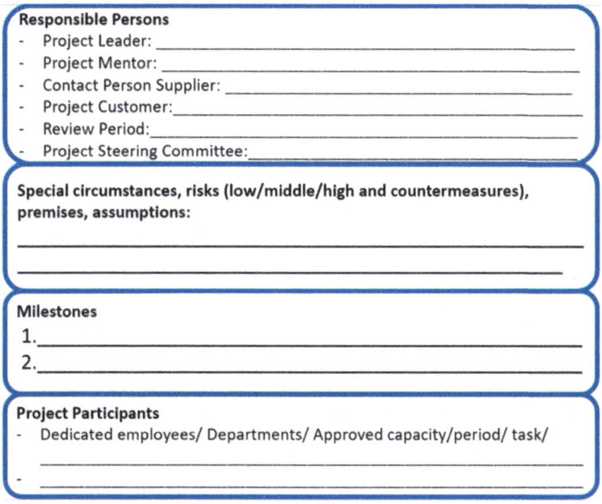

Fig. 4.5 Milestones, responsibilities, and project team members. *Source*: Robert Bosch GmbH

This IPA contract could have different sections. For example, the first part includes general information about the supplier and the type of project to be conducted with them.

- Project name
- Supplier name/location/commodity
- Scope of project (part no./part family/quantity, e.g., planning two years in advance)
- Project category (enabling phase, build fundamentals, roll-out of SD, mentoring, multiplicator, task force, supplier learning group, shop floor management SFM)
- SD maturity grade (actual and target)

The purpose of the second sections is to outline the responsibilities that each party agrees to undertake, to establish consensus on project milestones (Fig. 4.5).

The third section is related to the KPIs at monitoring level, which are aligned to every aspect of the value stream. We define starting base at project start, realistic but challenging targets and expected minimum achievable KPIs.

Quality:	Starting base	KPI targets	KPI real
PPMs/month			
PLKZs (problem supplier index number)/month			
Scrap rate customer (pieces/month)			
Internal scrap rate (PLKZs/month)			

Logistics	Starting base	KPI targets	KPI real
OTD (%)			
Lead time (days)			
EPEI (days)			
Demand fluctuation (%)			

Production	Starting base	KPI targets	KPI real
Man-hours (number of skilled operators)			
Man-hours (number of unskilled operators)			
Output (pieces/hour)			
OEE (%)			

After elaboration and presentation of a lean roll-out concept to top management and their mentoring by conducted reviews, sustainability in process will be achieved.

The columns are meant to be completed using data obtained from the prior information forms, which are filled according to what SD engineer observes during the FSDV. He and the buyer can also set targets for the suppliers, and once these targets have been set, the SDE will be able to run the first drafts of targets and minimum achievable figures.

It is very important that, at this point, SD engineer and buyer have agreed which benefits are considered manufacturing cost reductions (MCRs) and which are not (no MCR). Using this tool, the SDE obtains an initial understanding of what the economic benefits could be, and he/she has evidence for making the decision whether go on with different projects or not.

Example	% of MCR of KPI Targets
Scrap rate customer	2.0
Internal scrap rate	1.0
Output	3.5
OEE	1.5
MCR potential benefit (total)	8

In this case, it means that supplier agreed to reduce 8% in total of their manufacturing costs, if KPI targets are achieved.

If it is decided to continue with the project, this table provides a very useful tool to design the SD strategy for dealing with the supplier. This column represents the contribution of each indicator to the overall MCR savings, in addition to identifying the indicators with the highest contribution. This way, SDE is able to design a strategy mainly focused on these indicators, and ensures that the savings goal can be achieved.

In handling the MCR and no MCR savings, the SD engineer can calculate "Potential Benefits," providing a very general overview of the potential savings obtained with each KPI improvement.

Example:

With monthly demand of 50,000 pieces, monthly operation costs of 69 RMB/piece, and piece sale price of 138 RMB, there is a turnover of 6.9 Mio RMB/month.

Quality:

Example	Target Delta	Unit	Potential Benefit	Unit	MCR
PPMs	100	PPMs/month	0	RMB/ month	No
PLKZs	0	PLKZs/ month	0	RMB/ month	Yes
Scrap rate customer	200	Pieces/month	27,600	RMB/ month	Yes
Internal scrap rate	100	PLKZs/ month	6900	RMB/ month	yes

Potential benefit of scrap rate at customer: 200pcs/month*138RMB/pcs

Internal scrap rate: 100 pcs/month * 69 RMB/pcs

Quality loss total: 34500 RMB/month

Production:

Output delta	30	Pieces/hour	331,200	RMB/month	yes
OEE delta	10	%	690,000	RMB/month	yes
Manpower	0	Operators	0	RMB/month	yes

Potential benefit of more output: 30pcs/hour*160 h/month*69RMB/pcs

OEE delta benefit: 10%*6,900,000 pcs/month

Total potential benefit of 1,021,200 RMB/month.

Assuming shop floor has 10 workers, productivity increase is calculated 30pieces/hour+50000pieces*10% OEE/160 hours = 61 pieces/hour/10 workers = 6 pieces/workhour

Logistics:

Lead time	10	Days	3,450,000	RMB/month	yes

Lead time: 50000pcs/month/20 days/month*10 days*138RMB/pcs

Total potential savings: 34500 + 1,021,200 + 3,450,000 = 4,505,700 RMB/month.

Total potential savings are 4,505,700/6900000 = 65.3%.

4.5.7 Designing Supplier Development Programs

After first supplier visit and collecting first data, you decided to go on with a SD program with this supplier and agreed target figures. Now, it is the moment to specify a custom-designed program, based on bilateral needs and requirements.

You definitely need to take a deeper look into your supplier's value stream to obtain a deeper understanding of the supplier's conditions. To support this, the SD engineer needs to carry out a kick-off week, which focuses on information verification (Value Stream Planning workshop).

VSP information is the primary source of information for analyzing the initial situation and for reporting purposes. During this workshop, information about the supplier's value stream will be directly gathered by shop floor observation and compared with the previously obtained information from the buyer and the supplier. However, all acquired data must be linked to a key performance indicator (KPI) and put in following forms

- Customer information
- Processes and subprocesses
- Material and supplier information

4.5.8 Kick-off Week[32]

As already said, this workshop sets the initial situation for the supplier development program, establishes a strong linkage to the shop floor CIP, and begins the tracking of the key performance indicators. As well, this information will be used to complement the value stream mapping and will be the base for defining projections of value stream designs.

This kick-off week consists of 4 days of activities, including value stream planning, Asaichi tools, and instructing supplier personnel.

The first day is used to familiarize your SD engineer with supplier's value stream and join the supplier's team in facilitating the workshop. The SDE also will separately interview the key people involved in order to collect their opinions on the processes and value stream, and to confirm or update the information previously obtained from the supplier.

The second day begins with a general introduction to the supplier development program, and includes the basics of value stream planning (VSP), an introduction to the used metrics and key relevant concepts, and finally, gathering information with drawing the value stream mapping, which will reflect the actual condition of the supplier. The SD engineer works together with the whole VSM team of supplier. The VSM team includes engineers from the quality, logistics, maintenance, production, and management departments.

[32] *Source*: Robert Bosch Mexico GmbH, 2010

Then next, in the morning on day three, there is a brief explanation of your selected key performance indicators (KPIs). This includes their purpose and usefulness, and how to calculate them. After having reflected the actual situation with an VSM, next step is to outline the supplier's future conditions through the elaboration of a value stream design (VSD). Based on the VSD, the supplier's team must develop an open point list in which all defined improvements must be noticed, including due dates and responsible parties involved.

The fourth and last day of activities includes the Asaichi workshop and complements the methodologies and improvement activities covered in previous days. Along with your SD engineer, the VSM team will learn the basics of Asaichi and will develop activities that reinforce the knowledge gained in this program. Company's core competence is mastering the continuous improvement process with establishing a learning organization. Successfully installed improvements result by involving all employees in distinctive problem-solving activities. You have to make sure the management of your supplier understands this and lead their company accordingly.

4.5.9 Information for Customers

For the customer loop, the following form is provided to the VSM team to gather information. This is divided according to the lean drivers and contains the required indicators and a brief description of each (Fig. 4.6).

The form contains a space to fill in the respective values, and includes indicators that need to be calculated. The formulas for calculating these are provided on the form, as well as space for the user to make these calculations.

(1) Quality scrap **percentage** (percentage of produced parts that become scrap)

Data	Value	Units
Parts produced per day (average 1 month)		Number
Scrap pieces per day (average 1 month)		Number

$$\text{Scrap Percentage} = \frac{\text{Scrap pieces per day}}{\text{Parts produced per day}} \times 100\ [\%]$$

(2) Quality **rework percentage**

Percentage of produced parts that have to be reworked:

$$\text{Rework percentage} = \frac{\text{Rework pieces per day}}{\text{Parts produced per day}} \times 100\ [\%]$$

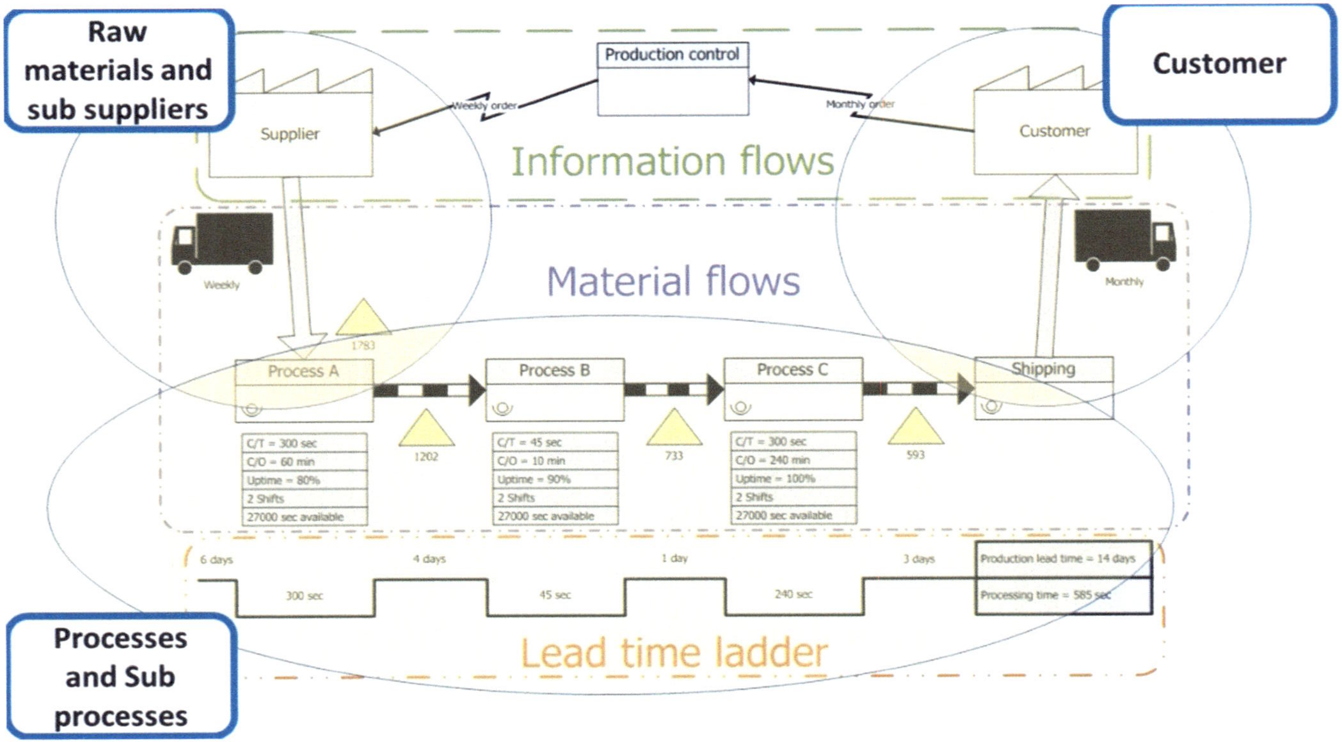

Fig. 4.6 There are three forms, each one corresponding to one of the loops defined in the value stream: Customer Information, Processes & Sub-Processes, and Materials & Supplier Information. *Source*: https://en.wikipedia.org/wiki/Value-stream_mapping. Last updated January 28, 2021; access date 22.2.2021

(3) Inventory **levels**
Please fill in your information into value column.

Inventory	Concept	Value	Units
In transit inventory	Time elapsed since the material leaves the subsupplier's plant until it arrives at the raw material warehouse		Days
Finished goods inventory	Time finished goods remain in warehouse		Days
	Designated space		m^2
Lead time	Time it takes for parts to pass through the entire value stream. This is the sum of all the inventories		days

(4) Demand fluctuation

Please fill in your information into value column:

Data	Value	Units
Forecast for × months		Pieces
Real order for × month		Pieces

$$\text{Demand fluctuation} = \frac{\text{Real order - Forecast}}{\text{Forecast}} \times 100\%$$

(5) Takt time
Takt time = Speed at which the client requires product.

Data	Value	Units
No. of shifts per day		Number
Duration of shift		Minutes
Planned downtime (e.g., lunch, breaks)		Minutes
Daily demand		Pieces

Available work time per day =
[(No. of shifts per day × duration of shift))—downtime] × 60 [seconds]

$$\text{Takt time} = \frac{\text{Available work time per day}}{\text{Daily demand}} \text{ [seconds/piece]}$$

(6) Plan for every part
Shipment data:

Data	Value	Units
On-time delivery		%
Frequency of shipments to client		# deliveries/day
Means of sending customer orders		Email, fax, etc.
Forecasts		Weeks
Batch size		Pieces/container
Area in charge of planning		
Means of planning (SAP, etc.)		
EPEI		

4.5.10 Process and Subprocess Information

The process and subprocess loop form have a similar layout to the previous form, but to help the user understand certain concepts, such as OEE or Changeover time, it also contains explanatory diagrams.

The indicators corresponding to the process and subprocess loop are as follows:

(1) **Quality** scrap and
(2) **Rework** percentage, see information for customer, as formulas are identical.
(3) Changeover time (C/O)

C/O is the time from last good piece of the current product run (A) to first good piece of the next different product run (B).

C/O is calculated as

- Preparation, after-process adjustment, checking, return to storage of parts, tools, fixtures
- Removing parts, blades, jigs, etc.; mounting same for next lot
- Machine settings, measurements
- Making trial pieces and adjusting

For example, if you need to change tooling for one customer A to next customer B, to serve OTD for both parties. See Fig. 4.7.

Data	Value	Units
External setup time		Minutes
Internal setup time		Minutes

- External setup time: duration of activities to be performed while machine is working [minutes]
- Internal setup time: duration of activities performed while machine is not working [minutes]
- C/O = External Setup Time + Internal Setup Time [minutes]

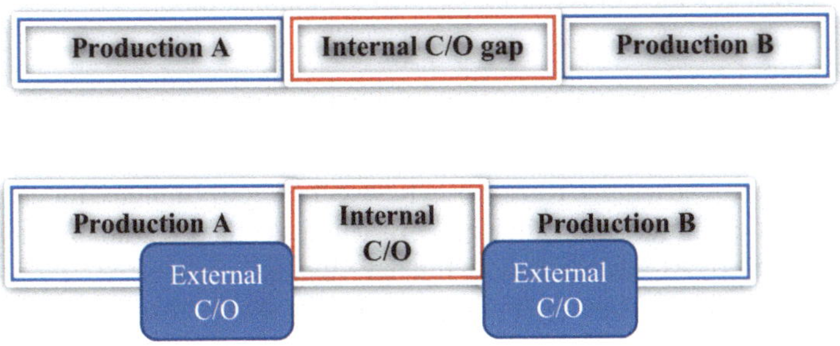

Fig. 4.7 Using external setup time is an opportunity to reduce internal C/O gap. Source: GTEC, Schneckenlohe, Author Karlheinz Zuerl, 2021

This task can be done with following activities:

- Develop and implement changeover checklists
- Perform function checks on parts and tools before changeover
- Isolate transportation of tools, parts, and materials
- Prepare operating conditions in advance
- Standardize functions
- Use intermediary jigs

(4) **OEE (overall equipment effectiveness)**

OEE (overall equipment effectiveness) is the gold standard for measuring manufacturing productivity.[33]

Please fill in your information into value column:

Data	Value	Units
Available work time per day		Minutes/month
Cycle time		Seconds/piece
Planned maintenance time		Minutes/month
Corrective maintenance time		Minutes/month
Changeover time (setup time)		Minutes/month
Downtime		Minutes/month
Rework		Pieces/month
Scrap		Pieces/month
Produced good parts		Pieces/month

[33] *Source*: https://www.oee.com/, last edit 2019; published by Vorne Industries Inc., access date 22.2.2021

OEE[34] efficiency measures during planned operational time

- Availability Losses = Changeover time + Corrective Maintenance duration [minutes/month]
- Performance Losses= Downtime [minutes/month]
- Quality Losses = (Scrap + Rework) × [Cycle Time/60] [minutes/month]
- Net Production Time = Available Work Time Per Day–Availability Losses–Performance Losses-Quality Losses [minutes/month]
- Planned Operational Time = Available Work Time per Day—Planned Maintenance [minutes/month]

Net Production Time
OEE =

× 100 [%]
Planned Operational Time
No. of good pieces/day * Cycle time
OEE =
-- × 100 [%]
Planned Operational Time
Output
OEE =
---------------------------- × 100 [%]
No. of Operators

Alternatively, OEE = Availability × Performance × Quality

Availability: If, in a 8 h*60 min =480-minute shift, a machine stops during a 30 + 15 + 15 = 60-minute break and has up to 30 minutes of unscheduled downtime and setups, then the planner can count of 480–60-30 = 390 minutes in which to schedule work, which yields a ratio of availability = 390/480 = 87%.

Performance: This factor is meant to account for micro stoppages and reduced speeds, and it is a relevant and important equipment metric in its own right. If the machine actually takes two minutes to process a part when it is supposed to take only one, its *performance* is 50%.

Quality: In the OEE, this factor is just the yield of the operation, meaning the ratio of good parts to total parts produced. It is not the *first-pass yield*, because reworked parts are still counted as good.[35]

---

[34] *Source*: https://www.oee.com/calculating-oee.html#preferred-calculation; last edit 2019; published by Vorne Industries Inc., access date 22.2.2021

[35] *Source*: https://michelbaudin.com/2012/04/15/metrics-in-lean-part-3-equipment/; published 15.4.2012; author Michael Baudin; access date 22.2.2021

4.5.11 Raw Materials and Subsupplier's Information

And finally, the raw materials and subsupplier's information loop gather all information regarding the company's subsuppliers. It operates along the same lines of the mentioned forms, including the units in which the data must be recorded.

(1) **Quality** scrap,
(2) **Rework** percentage and
(3) Inventory **levels** see information for customer, as formulas are identical.
(4) Plan for every part

Shipment data:

Data	Value	Units
On-time delivery		%
Frequency of shipments		# deliveries/day
Means of ordering		Email, fax, etc.
Batch size		Pieces/container

4.5.12 Key Performance Indicators and Costs

Once information has been confirmed on the shop floor, the next step is to concentrate all information on a single form, and this should allow the user to visualize the state of the entire value stream. For that purpose, the SD engineer should use the KPI database.

These worksheets are intended to gather all KPI data from both the beginning and the end of the project. Both worksheets have the same layout.

The rows are separated according to their respective lean drivers: **quality**, **costs,** and **deliveries**. These columns also divide the different value contribution levels: the **improvement, monitoring,** and **value** levels.

Quality

Improvement level indicators					
ppm's	Plkz's	Scrap FG	Scrap RM	Rework FG	Rework RM
3056	12	11	0	0	0
ppm's/ month	Plkz's/ month	Pieces/ month	Pieces/ month	Pieces/ month	Pieces/ month

Let us start with lean driver quality. Just an example with some figures:

Monitoring level indicators			
ppm's	Plkz's	Scrap	Rework
0	0	56	0
RMB/ month	RMB/ month	RMB/month	RMB/month

Value level indicator
Quality losses
56
RMB/month

Costs

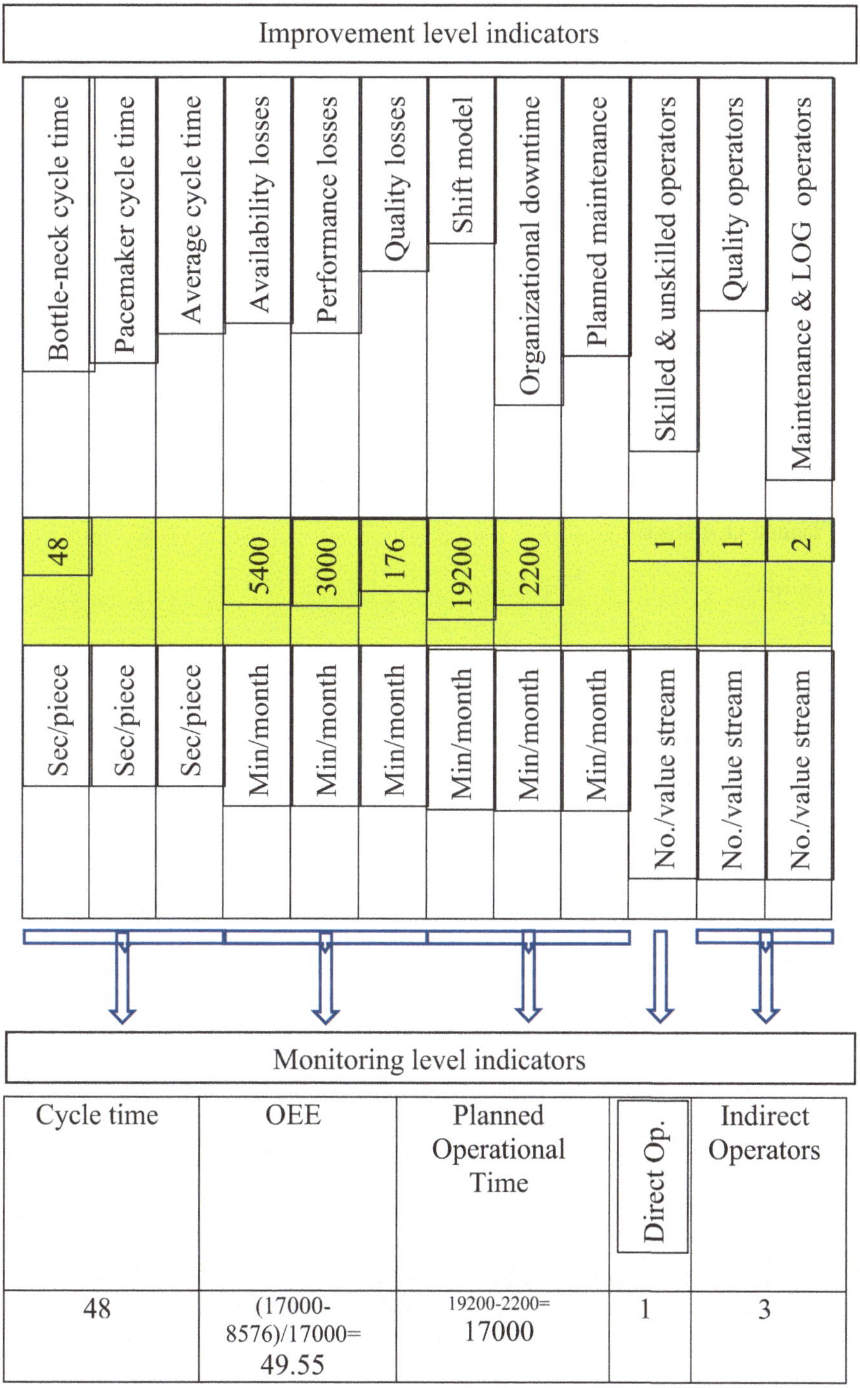
Improvement level indicators
Bottle-neck cycle time
Pacemaker cycle time
Average cycle time
Availability losses
Performance losses
Quality losses
Shift model
Organizational downtime
Planned maintenance
Skilled & unskilled operators
Quality operators
Maintenance & LOG operators
48
5400
3000
176
19200
2200
1
1
2
Sec/piece
Sec/piece
Sec/piece
Min/month
Min/month
Min/month
Min/month
Min/month
Min/month
No./value stream
No./value stream
No./value stream
Monitoring level indicators
Cycle time
OEE
Planned Operational Time
Direct Op.
Indirect Operators
48
(17000-8576)/17000=
49.55
19200-2200=
17000
1
3

Just an example of a serial process with some figures:

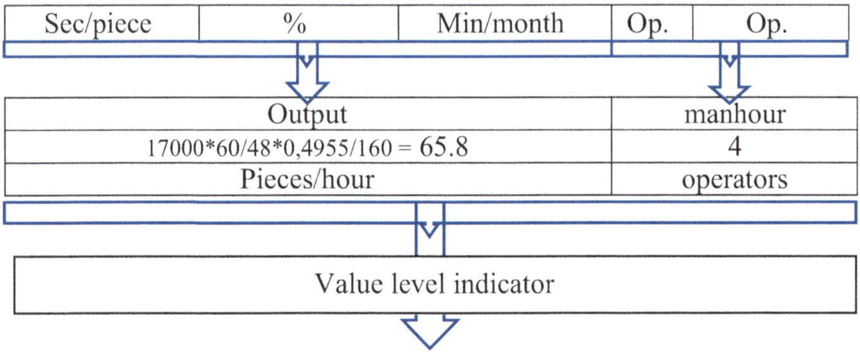

How to calculate productivity[36]?
Quantity of parts produced by operator
No. of good pieces per day × cycle time
Productivity = −--------------------------------------- [Pieces/Man-hours]
Planned Operators

Productivity
16.45
Pieces/man-hour

[36] *Source*: https://www.smartsheet.com/blog/how-calculate-productivity-all-levels-organization-employee-and-software#:~:text=You%20can%20measure%20employee%20productivity,by%201%2C500%2C%20which%20equals%2053; published 2021; author Smartsheet Inc. Access date 22.2.2021

Delivery

Last but not least just an example for delivery. Assuming output = 1000 pieces/day

Improvement level indicators

Raw mat.	In Transit (FG)	In Transit (RM)	Finish goods	WIP	RM space	FG space	WIP space
4	5	5	5	6			
days	days	days	days	days	qm	qm	qm

Monitoring level indicator

OTD	Lead time
80	25
%	days

Lead time
25000
Pieces (in 25 days)

Value level indicator

Delivery performance	
25/80*100 = 31.25	25000/80*100= 31250
days	pieces

4.5.13 Key Performance Indicators and Continuous Improvement Processes for the Shop Floor

Shop floor CIP at improvement level (Fig. 4.8)

- Plan: Identify/plan for change
- Do: Implement change on small scale
- Check: Analyze results of the change
- Act: If change succeeded, increase scale; if not, begin cycle again

Continuous Improvement Process

The continuous improvement process (CIP) is closely related to KPI, as these provide us with the ability to visualize the shop floor's current state, and to enable the

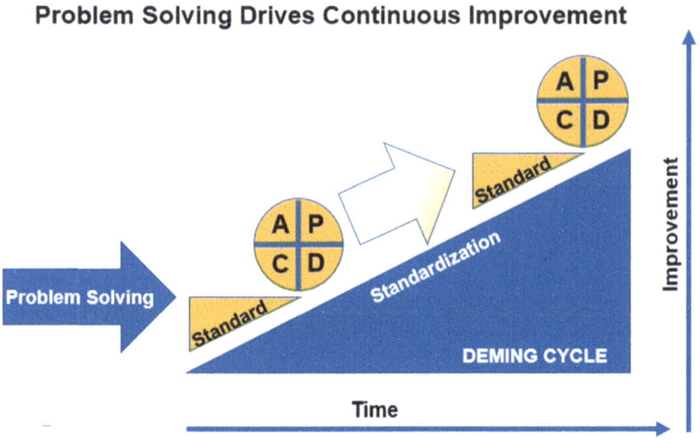

Fig. 4.8 Using the self-propelling plan–do–check–act (PDCA) cycle is one tool to implement CI. *Source*: https://www.proactiongroup.com/metrics-culture-of-continuous-improvement/; published 2019; author The ProAction Group. Access date 22.2.2021

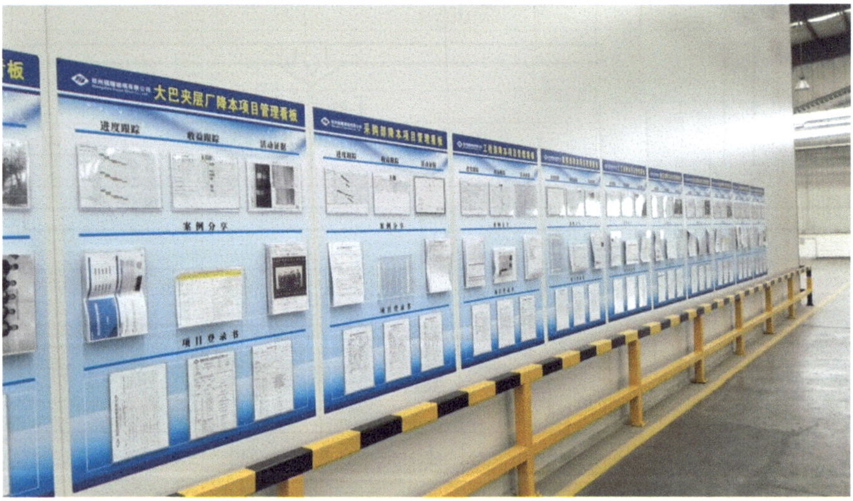

Fig. 4.9 Example of an Asaichi board at Zhengzhou Fuyao Glass Co. Ltd. *Source*: Six Sigma Black Belt Jonah Kou, China; published June 18, 2021

visualization of the gap between the desired state and the actual one, as well as the ability to make any necessary adjustments to reach these targets in time. The Asaichi and shop floor CIP are focused around the KPI, and are based on the improvement or monitoring level to identify the problems or issues that prevent targets from being reached (Fig. 4.9).

4.5.14 Workshops and KPI Amendments

What is an amendment? An amendment is a formal document used to extend or to clarify agreements or important tasks in a project agreement.

How to use amendments? The results of the workshops' KPI could be noticed in an amendment. Along with the supplier, it could be signed as potential impact of the indicators. The action plan defined during the workshop event could cover as well all necessary tasks to meet these targets.

Amendment example:

- Date of the workshop, participants, project part number
- Updated indicators: quality losses, productivity, delivery performance
- Supplier manager signature
- SD engineer signature

4.5.15 KPI Tracking

Through the Asaichi workshop at supplier, the SD engineer together with supplier must able to track the performance, stability, and success of each of the defined indicators. It could be done with a standardized format to be fulfilled by the supplier in a defined period of time, and to visualize this behavior.

For this purpose, the supplier will report the status of their value stream activities to your SD engineer. This process could be standardized with a formula, Excel, or ppt charts, or commonly used databases (Figs. 4.10–4.12).

4.5.16 How Do You Create a Benefit Calculator?

The Excel "Costs" worksheet contains a list of all the costs required to calculate the benefits (yellow marked fields) of the SD program. You need to calculate delta and benefits in RMB/month at deliveries, costs, and quality.

		Delta	Unit	Benefit	Unit	MCR
Quality	PPMs		PPMs/month		PPMs/month	No
Quality	PLKZs		RMB/month		RMB/month	No
	Scrap		RMB/month		RMB/month	Yes
	Rework		RMB/month		RMB/month	Yes
	Quality losses		**RMB/month**		**RMB/month**	
Costs	Cycle time		Sec/piece		RMB/month	Yes
	OEE		%		RMB/month	Yes
	Output		**Pieces/hour**		**RMB/month**	Yes
	Direct operator		Operators		RMB/month	
	Indirect operator		Operators		RMB/month	
	Man-hour		Operators		**RMB/month**	Yes
	Productivity		**Pcs/man-hour**		**RMB/month**	
Delivery	Lead time		Days		RMB	Yes
	Inventory space		Qm		RMB	No
	OTD		%			
	Delivery		**Pieces**		**RMB**	

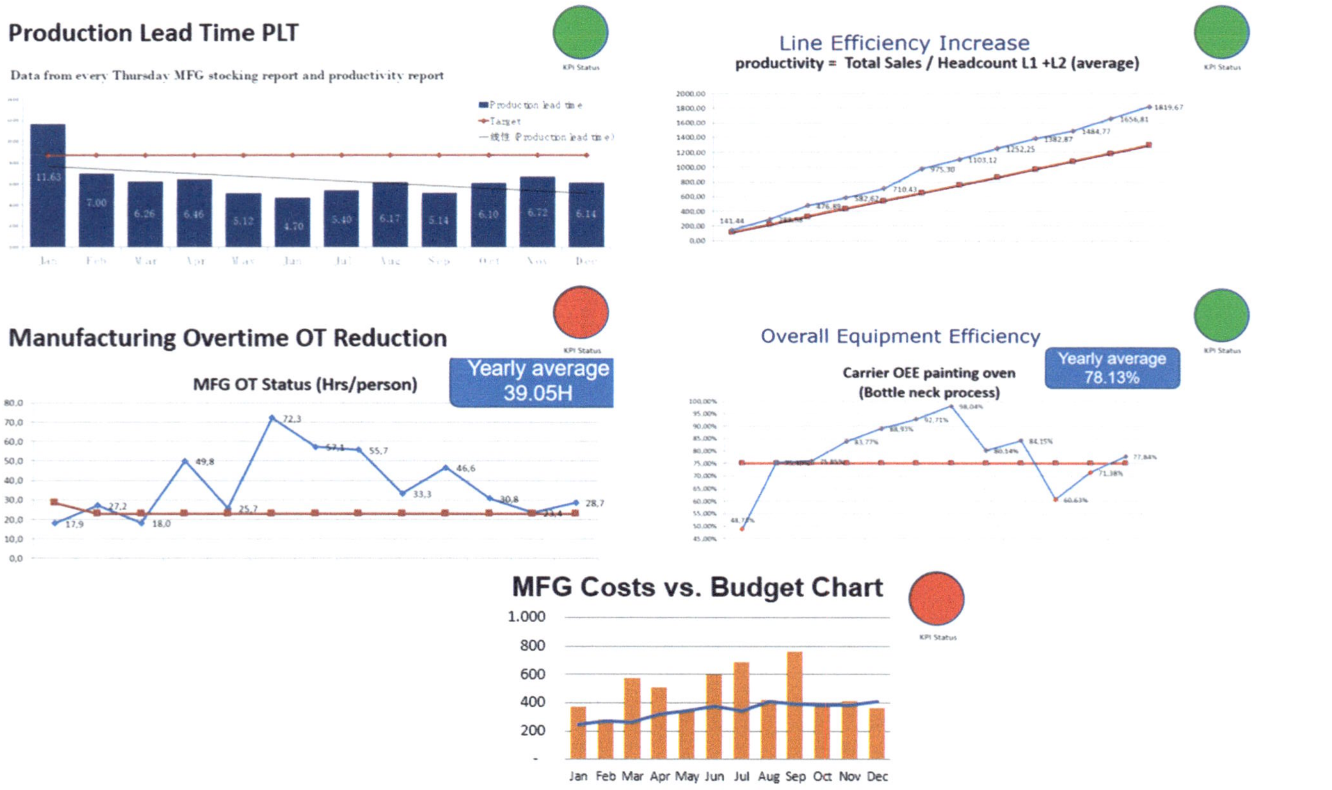

Fig. 4.10 Example of Manufacturing Cockpit Chart for follow-up with KPI-figures given by supplier. Other KPIs are Output and Man-hour. *Source: GTEC, 2021*

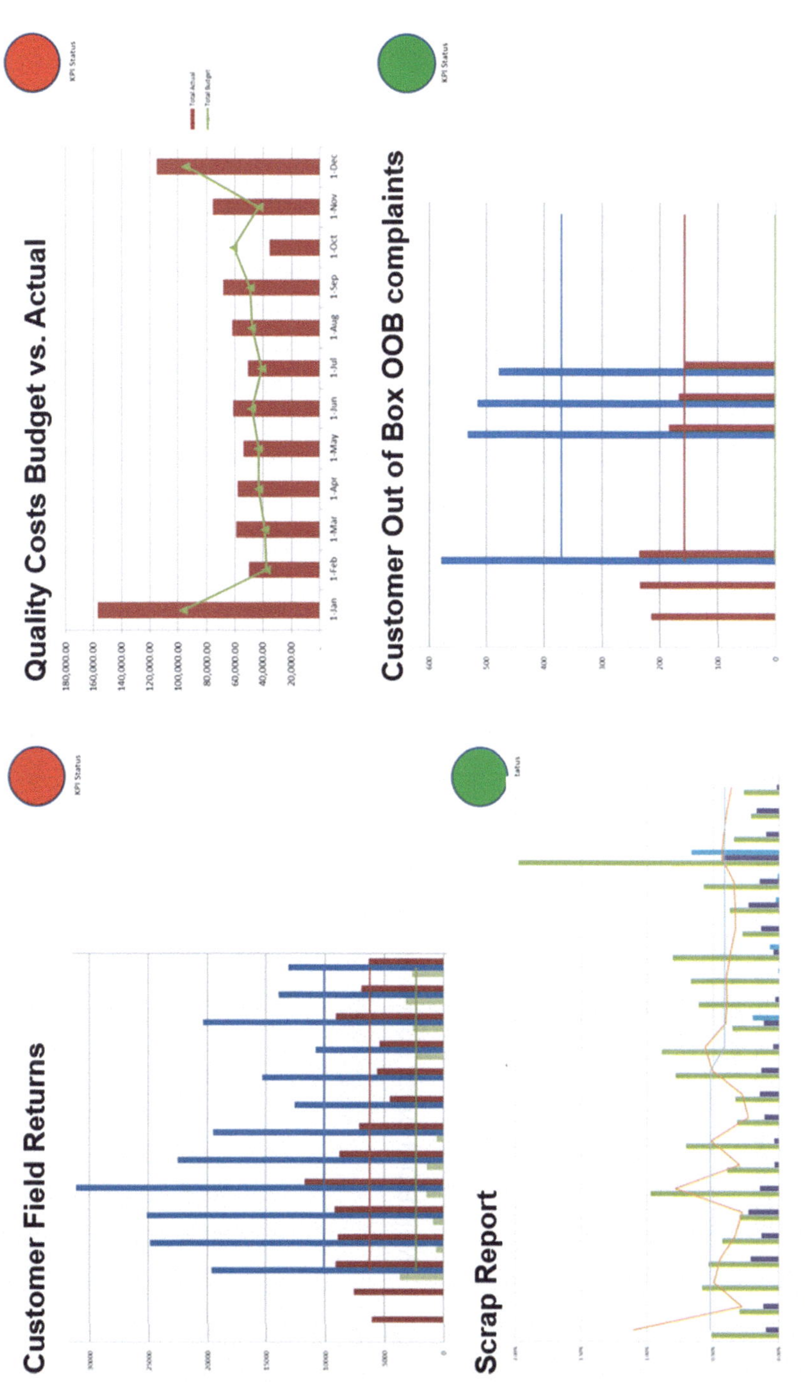

Fig. 4.11 Example of Quality Cockpit Chart for follow-up with figures given by supplier. *Source: GTEC, 2021*

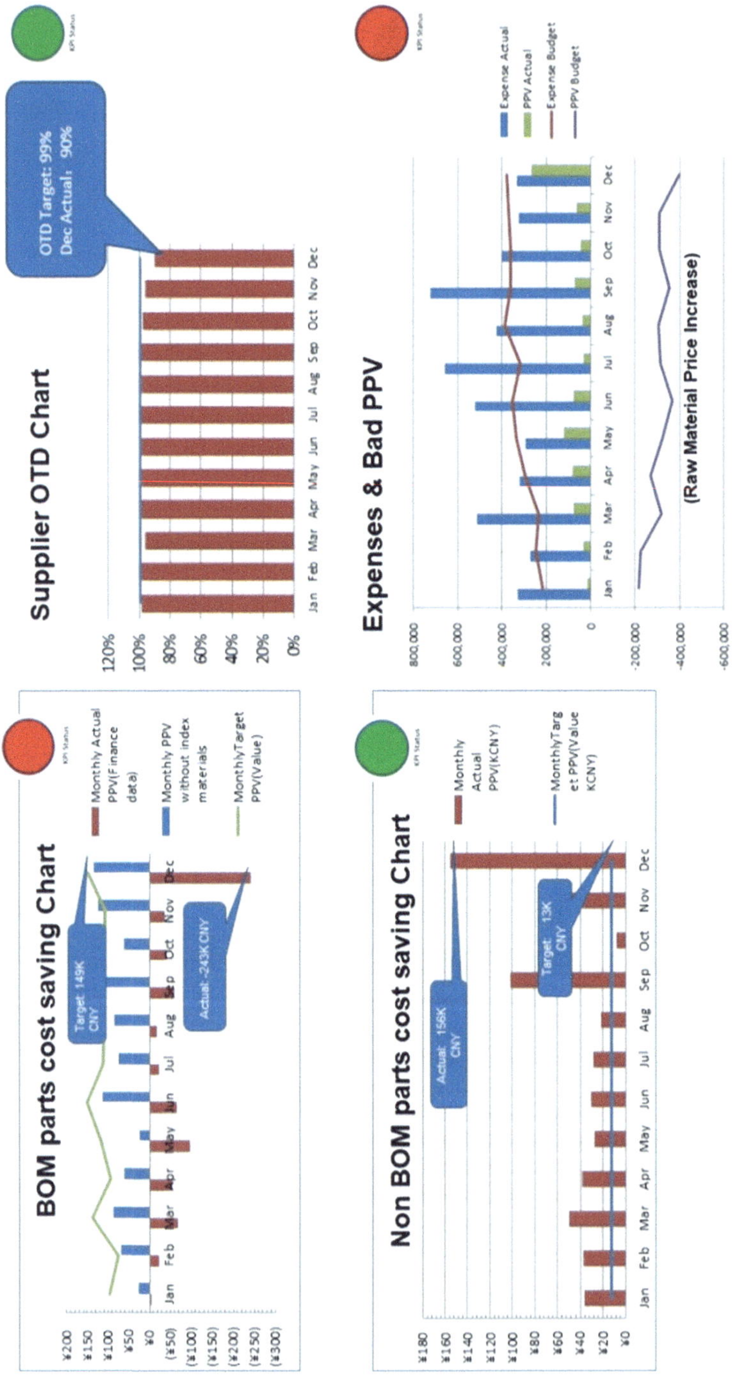

Fig. 4.12 Example of a Supply Chain Cockpit Chart for follow-up of Cost Savings and OTD. *Source*: GTEC, 2021

MCR (manufacturing cost reduction) savings =		RMB	
No MCR savings =		RMB	
Special benefits		RMB/month	
Monthly demand		Pieces	RMB/month

All benefits are divided according to the lean drivers and allow to visualize the savings it represents on a monthly basis.

Starting from the top, it is important to highlight that the calculation follows the logic of the KPI tree. Therefore, the quality loss savings are the sum of savings in PLKZs, scrap, and rework.

The output savings include the savings in cycle time and OEE. And the OEE savings are the result of obtained benefits in availability, performance, and quality losses. Based on that, the productivity savings are given by those obtained in man-hours and output.

As for the delivery driver, the savings are obtained through a reduction in lead time and inventory space.

At the bottom, the total MCR savings can be viewed.

Finally, the "Special Benefits" worksheet allows to calculate extraordinary savings obtained during specific projects, such as the pull system or total productive maintenance. These savings will be listed in the total savings of the "Benefits" worksheet (see blue marked fields).

For proper calculations, following indicators and its units are listed for deliveries and costs. Also note that it is crucial to maintain the units specified to avoid miscalculations.

Deliveries:

Indicators	Units
Quantity of packaging material	Container/month
Forklift, carts, and other equipment	Number
Quantity of boxes for internal logistics	Number
LOG-problem supplier classification number reduction	PLKZ/month
Expenses with premium freights	RMB/month
Supply problems	Number/month

Costs:

Indicators	Units
Machine capacity used	Percentage
Monthly depreciation of machines	RMB/month
Hours of maintenance or repair	Hours/month
Work time of maintenance team	Hours/month
Repair and maintenance costs	RMB/month
Special monthly repairing costs	RMB/month

Quality: Your complaints for bad quality from suppliers can be considered and calculated accordingly.

4.5.17 How Is the Benefit Calculator Used?

The benefit calculator worksheet provides a way of tracking the status, and the SDE calculates the benefits by using the VSP loop information from workshops.

It is recommended to protect cells with formulas and to avoid accidental data modification Also, note that it is crucial to maintain the units specified in the file to avoid miscalculations.

Once both worksheets (benefit and special benefit calculator) are fully completed, the file can calculate the changes between the initial and the future state levels.

The next step is to calculate the benefits that these changes represent. For this purpose, it is necessary to update the "Cost sheet." See an example below, as already described in Sect. 4.5.6.

Quality:	Starting base	KPI targets	KPI real
PPMs/month	141	0	9
PLKZs/month	0	0	0
Scrap rate customer (pieces/month)	1184	1000	1030
Internal scrap rate (PLKZs/month)	406	190	185

Logistics	Starting base	KPI targets	KPI real
OTD (%)	100	100	100
Lead time (days)	66	52	51
EPEI (days)	6	6	6
Demand fluctuation (%)	10	5	5

Production	Starting base	KPI targets	KPI real
Man-hours (number of skilled operators)	5	5	4
Man-hours (number of unskilled operators)	5	5	4
Output (pieces/hour)	220	300	262
OEE (%)	74.5	80	80.5

For further inquiries, the source from which the information is obtained can also be specified (Fig. 4.13).

Once the validation is completed, the SD engineer compares these results with the targets, thereby ensuring that the project goals will be achieved.

It is also important to compare the obtained benefits with the improvement-level indicators (the KPI database) and monitoring level indicators (internal contracting).

The SD engineer is not supposed to gather all cost information themselves, but instead to provide this list to the responsible buyer, and to ask for cooperation.

Quality:	Starting base	KPI targets	KPI real
PPM's/month	141	0	9
PLKZ's/month	0	0	0
Scrap rate customer (pieces/month)	1184	1000	1030
Internal scrap rate (plkz's/month)	406	190	185

Logistics	Starting base	KPI targets	KPI real
OTD (%)	100	100	100
Lead time (days)	66	52	51
EPEI (days)	6	6	6

Demand fluctuation (%)	10	5	5

Production	Starting base	KPI targets	KPI real
Man hours (number of skilled operators)	5	5	4
Man hours (number of unskilled operators)	5	5	4
Output (pieces/hour)	220	300	262
OEE (%)	74.5	80	80.5

Fig. 4.13 Example of Cost Sheet for follow-up with figures given by supplier. *Source*: Robert Bosch GmbH

For example, with monthly demand of 50,000 pieces, monthly operation costs of 69 RMB/piece, and piece sales price of 138 RMB, there is a turnover of 6.9 Mio RMB/month. See example at Sect. 4.5.6.

Example	Delta	Unit	Realized savings	Unit	MCR
PPMs	132	PPMs/month	0	RMB/month	No
PLKZs	0	PLKZs/month	0	RMB/month	No
Scrap rate customer	154	Pieces/month	21,252	RMB/month	Yes
Internal scrap rate	221	PLKZs/month	15,249	RMB/month	Yes

Scrap rate customer = 154 pieces/month * 138 RMB/pcs sales price
Internal scrap rate = 221pieces/month * 69 RMB/pcs
Realized quality losses total: 36501 RMB/month

Output delta	42	Pieces/hour	463,680	RMB/month	yes
OEE delta	6	%	414,000	RMB/month	Yes
Manpower delta	2	Operators	12,000	RMB/month	Yes

Output delta = 42 pcs/h * 160 h/month * 69 RMB/pcs
OEE delta = 6%*6.9 Mio RMB/month
Manpower delta = 1*8000RMB/month +1*4000RMB/month.
Realized benefit at shop floor of 889,680 RMB/month.

Assuming shop floor has realized reduction of 2 workers, realized productivity is calculated 42pieces/hour+50000pieces*6% OEE/160 hours = 60.75 pieces/hour/ 8 workers = 7.6 pieces/workhour

Lead time delta	15	days	5,175,000	RMB/month	yes

Lead time: 50000pcs/month/20 days/month*15 days*138RMB/pcs

Total potential savings: 36501 + 889,680 + 5,175,000 = 6,101,181 RMB/month.

Total realized savings are 6,101,181/6900000 = 88.4%. Expected savings were 65.3% (see Sect. 4.5.6).

4.5.18 How Do You Report Benefits?

With the results obtained from the benefit calculator, the SD engineer elaborates a report for your organization in which he/she specifies the percentage of savings obtained through the program.

In addition, if the SD engineer includes information regarding future purchasing volumes, they can produce a long-term projection of gained benefits. This report is added to the internal contract as a means of validating and concluding the program.

4.6 Supplier Relationship Management (SRM)

In order to build up a good connection, communication, and relationship with your suppliers, which is important in China to get your parts within required KPIs, you need to visit them.

According to my experience, in some large companies with well-known names, purchasing staff expect that suppliers will visit them in their office and talk about open issues. If these so-called supplier quality engineers (SQEs) are not forced to visit suppliers' facilities, the purpose of supplier quality engineering is not reached. Only with presence there**, by reviewing the organizations' requirements and clearly defining your company's deliverables and expectations, t**hey have an impact and influence on first-pass yield[37,38] (FPY) and other KPIs (see above) of supplier's performance. To help supplier to develop themself is crucial for your company's and supplier's financial success. Therefore, the value of personal visit of SQEs at suppliers is very high.

However, SQEs focus only on quality-related items and often require suppliers to invest in a stable manufacturing process, e.g., automatic counting parts or automatic visual inspection. In order to balance price increase with requested cost down year by year, commercial buyers need to be involved, but mostly these buyers visiting

[37] Further information see https://de.wikipedia.org/wiki/Erstausbeute

[38] Further information see https://en.wikipedia.org/wiki/First_pass_yield

suppliers at one single visit in November or December for yearly price negotiations. You can image how the results will look like.

Better is to plan visits over the whole year, by developing an agenda in advance, to give supplier a chance to prepare your visit. If this is one of your key suppliers, you may stay a few days and go through the whole process with them, starting from design, manufacturing, to inspection, packaging, delivery, etc. After asking well-prepared questions at a plant tour, you can update your cost structure analysis and start a negotiation at same knowledge level as supplier staff. Your supplier's management will get a good feeling that they clearly understand of what you have required from them. Nothing beats spending more time up-front with your suppliers to avoid problems later. Required corrective actions need time, communication, and technical and commercial discussions.

Once the communication stage has matured to an acceptable level, it is time for your company to go to the next level, to tailor a continuous improvement plan to the needs of your supplier.

Therefore, some companies have installed a SDE (supplier development engineer), who takes over both tasks and knowledge in one, quality improvement, and cost reduction activities. This kind of engineer needs to be well trained in lean production and supply chain to support supplier to find root causes and proper sustainable solutions.

For example, disruptions in shipments due to seasonal fluctuations in production capacity need historical OTD statistics and find appropriate actions to avoid disruptions at your facility. For example, discuss installation of warehouse, consignment stock, JIT/JIS implementation, seasonal increase shift model, training of employees, etc. This transparency of supplier's status, financial and technical possibilities, will lend to better supplier management strategies.

4.6.1 Systematic Supplier Evaluation with SPECTRA

For supplier development, the company GTEC uses the method called SPECTRA (supplier process evaluation and cost transparency). ECOCUT and SPECTRA are registered trademarks in China by GTEC. Company Robert Bosch GmbH is using SPECTRA internally worldwide in its purchasing departments at all divisions to evaluate suppliers' manufacturing processes and makes the costs at suppliers transparent for more effective negotiations.

Figure 3.1 shows how to manage this item step by step, in total eight steps to do teamwork with suppliers. However, Fig. 4.14 shows five steps with a different approach.

We use this systematic approach for preparation and negotiation with suppliers as the basis for a win-win solution. We cover the true costs and find a way to the realize cost reduction activities and **as a result to reduce purchasing price in agreement with the supplier.**

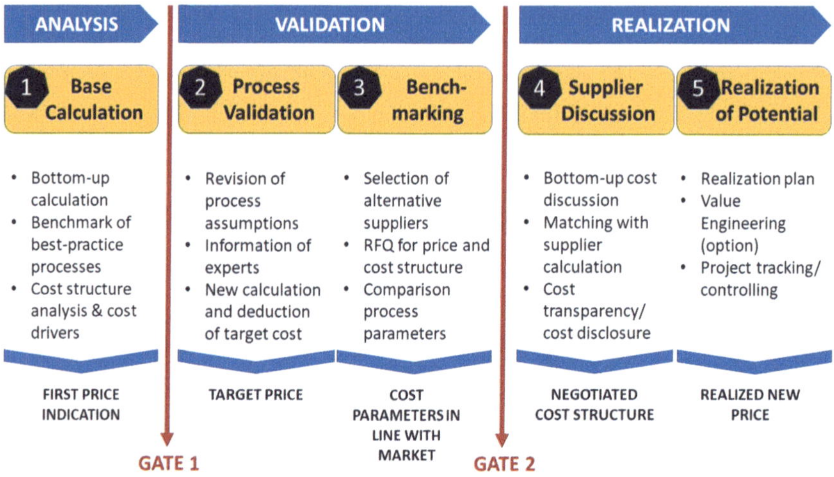

Fig. 4.14 Teamwork with suppliers in five steps. *Source: Robert Bosch GmbH, Shanghai, 2012*

4.6.2 SPECTRA Is SRM and CRM[39]

SRM is the systematic approach of your company to evaluating suppliers that supply goods, materials, and services to you, and then developing strategies to improve their performance.

Customer relationship management (CRM) intends to streamline and improve the processes between a company and its customers.

The discipline to go step by step helps to determine costs close to the truth, but sees the value and performance which each supplier provides. It also enables managers and staff to cultivate better relationships with selected suppliers in order to improve each supplier's performance.

Supplier relationship management is used by supply chain professionals who regularly deal with suppliers in areas such as procurement, project management, and operations, however, also could be expand to the IT, and finance and marketing departments if necessary. Refer to Fig. 4.15.

SRM is one of the many disciplines of supply chain management. It includes cost management and procurement processes. Cost management generally focuses on the establishment of costs and service-level agreements between the organization and its suppliers while procurement focuses on the administration (i.e., ordering, contracting, invoicing, and paying).

[39] https://searcherp.techtarget.com/definition/supplier-relationship-management-SRM, TechTarget, Authors Diann Daniel, Mary K. Pratt, Access date 11.2.2021

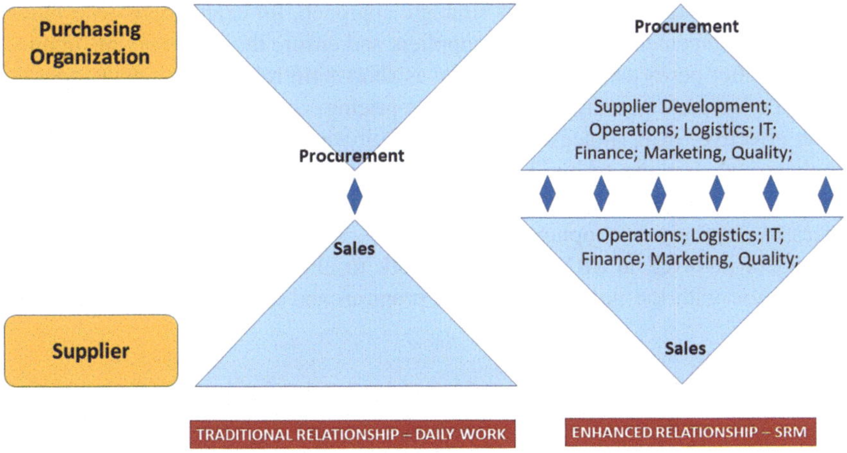

Fig. 4.15 Traditional vs. enhanced relationship. *Source: Schaeffler Holding* (China) *Co., Ltd.—Shanghai, 2013*

4.6.3 Goals and Tasks of SRM and CRM[40]

The overall goal of SRM in all industries remains the same: to improve the processes that take place between the organization as the buyer of products and services (i.e., the purchasing department) and the businesses that supply them (suppliers).

The purpose of SRM is to develop quality, efficiency, and innovation between both parties. A successful SRM/CRM discipline seeks not just cost savings but also to maximize the value of suppliers/your company to gain a competitive advantage in the marketplace.

Supplier relationship management has become increasingly important as buyer supplier networks become more global and interdependent and companies are more reliant upon strategic and preferred suppliers. SRM identifies preferred supply partners and organizes the relationship life cycle, which includes effective communication between an enterprise and its suppliers as well as the measurement of supplier performance.

Certain suppliers are particularly critical to business continuity in the automotive sector and others. For example, a supplier of PCBAs (printed circuit board assemblies) has a huge impact, and therefore, it is a key strategic partner. Any risk to the electronics maker's operations will be a major risk to the customer. Therefore, to achieve its goals, an organization's SRM/CRM program must be strategic in approach, from the articulation of objectives to planning, before it can react in firefighting mode.

[40] https://searcherp.techtarget.com/definition/supplier-relationship-management-SRM, TechTarget, Authors Diann Daniel, Mary K. Pratt, Access date 11.2.2021

Enterprise leaders who take this strategic approach, for example, to determine a long-term engagement with specific suppliers and ensure the continuity of supplies, will run better performance at long term, as short-term relationships with suppliers can best ensure business agility and flexible pricing.

An effective SRM strategy also requires cultivating personal relationships with suppliers and working to build trust and mutually beneficial partnerships, which means involving suppliers in planning for key initiatives, frontloading in early R&D processes or jointly developing innovations.

Leaders involved in SRM must also work to align other departments in their organization with the goals of the SRM program and ensure compliance with its objectives.

4.6.4 The SRM/CRM Process and applications[41]

The processes of strategic sourcing related to SRM can vary from one organization to the next. However, SRM generally involves three steps:

Segmentation of suppliers: In this first step, the company identifies all of its suppliers and categorizes them by their importance to the business, ensuring that the suppliers most critical to OTD (on-time-delivery), cost, and quality get the right amount of attention.

Development of a supplier strategy: In this second step, the organization develops a tactical plan for how it will work with each supplier or category of suppliers to ensure the relationships are successful and mutually beneficial (win-win situation).

Execution of the supplier strategy: The purchasing executive who owns the SRM discipline in the organization needs to ensure that the strategy is put into action. He/she needs to delegate to managers to take on day-to-day tasks to operationalize the SRM plans. They should also devise ways to monitor and measure SRM success as well as identify deficiencies and points of failure in the SRM strategy or its execution.

Organizations have reported numerous application cases for implementing SRM to improve performance:

- Take better advantage of supplier capabilities
- Reduce costs
- Ensure the continuity of the supply chain
- Limit risks in the supply chain
- Increase responsiveness of suppliers
- Gain the ability to project future prices and hedge against price volatility

[41] https://searcherp.techtarget.com/definition/supplier-relationship-management-SRM, TechTarget, Authors Diann Daniel, Mary K. Pratt, Access date 11.2.2021

4.6.5 SRM Challenges[42]

A 2020 survey found that 70% of respondents experienced disruptions due to the COVID-19 pandemic, while 44% indicated supply constraints and 35% faced global trade and tariff issues. Moreover, 95% of respondents said their company was affected by component shortages. Such findings speak to the importance of having a solid SRM program, but other research also points out the challenges inherent to the achievement of that objective:

- Overemphasis on its use for cost reduction as opposed to the means to cultivate value and strategic ties;
- Lack of visibility into suppliers, their importance to the organization, and the value they can deliver; and
- Insufficient commitment to the development of clear program objectives, the assignment and training of supervisory staff, and the alignment of other business units with respect to the objectives.

We applied SPECTRA to all industrial processes as a revolutionary approach that would transition from traditional behavior to modern supplier relationship management (SRM/CRM). The relationship between suppliers and customers will change dramatically, resulting in multiple advantages for both sides, particularly given that they are in the same boat.

Basic trainings will start for cost structure analysis and cost transparency for top suppliers at each commodity. After the training, SQEs are able to perform these tasks. SQEs should be trained in SD tasks first, before confrontation with suppliers (as part of skill training for purchasing personnel).

- Data collection: Process mapping to collect data for cost structure analysis and to write an analysis afterward is easily accomplished by current SQE staff at their supplier sites.
- Negotiation training is necessary as the means to deal with suppliers.
- Technical training in commodities so as to become a leading expert in one pillar is more difficult, and engineering background is required:
  1. Die casting
  2. Plastic injection
  3. Stamping
  4. Machining
  5. PCBA (printed circuit board assembly)

[42] https://searcherp.techtarget.com/definition/supplier-relationship-management-SRM, TechTarget, Authors Diann Daniel, Mary K. Pratt, Access date 11.2.2021

4.6.6 Supplier Relationship Management Asia

Most customers in the realm of industry complain about their Chinese and Asian suppliers, saying they are not willing to work together anymore. Their sales departments simply refuse to give an offer or will make their offers excessively high so as to be sure not to receive the order but still have the privilege of continued contact. What is going wrong in customer–supplier relationship? (Fig. 4.16).

Suppliers are fed up with the constant pressure from their customers, requests for cost reductions, quality-related complaints, and the inability to deliver the required quantities in a timely manner. Consequently, the suppliers are not able to solve their problems by their own, due to lack of knowledge, people, or money. They need support and partnership, but they get neither.

It is much better for both parties to work together in all departments instead of having a business relationship only between sales and procurement departments. With an enhanced relationship, your sales and purchasing departments will be informed instead of being responsible for everything. The RASIC chart looks very different. The project managers on both sides need to indicate the department personnel who will be responsible for specific tasks and follow-up (Fig. 4.17).

Do not try to solve relationship problems between departments. First step is always top management of both parties sit together and agree how to move ahead, to define the steps and timeline. Both parties also need to define the budget for visits, investments in new projects, process, technologies, product and service optimization, and continuous overall improvement (Fig. 4.18).

Whereas the total cost of ownership is needed in order to see the whole picture, to achieve success, you need to break down your objectives into several steps. In project management, these steps are called quality gates or milestones. For example, as a team comprising the supplier and customer, start with a kick-off meeting or

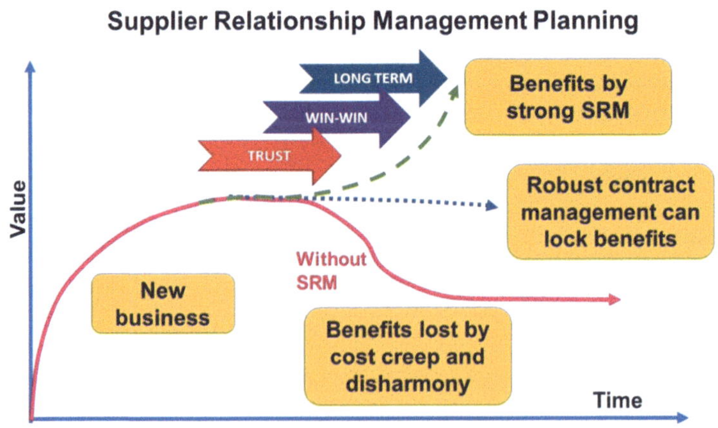

Fig. 4.16 The purchasing department's best approach is to build strong relationships with suppliers (*source*: Schaeffler)

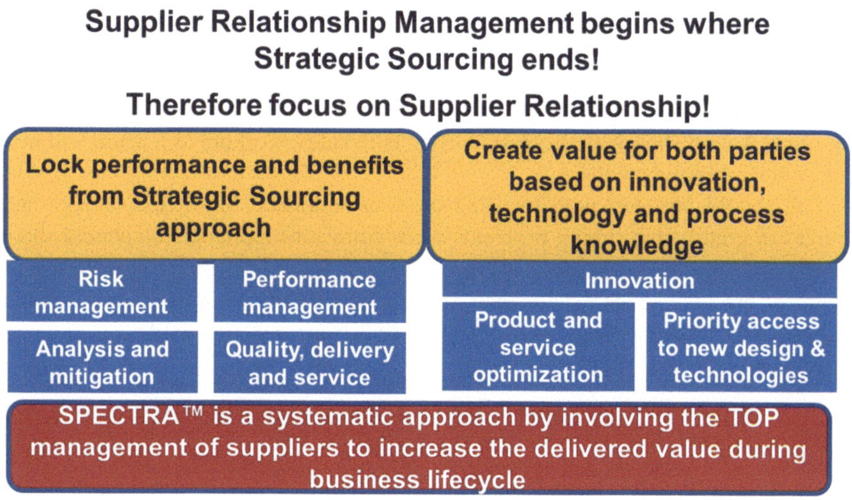

Fig. 4.17 Involving top management in the supplier relationship (*source*: Robert Bosch GmbH)

Fig. 4.18 What is expected from suppliers (*source*: Valeo)

written agreement to confirm working together to achieve certain targets in quality improvements, delivery performance, and cost reduction. There are many possibilities.

Based on trust and long-term partnership, the supplier shows process from warehouse entry to exit, including all manufacturing steps. The customer shows its assembly process, in which supplier parts are involved, so as to educate suppliers in the technical requirements.

The next step, once the status is documented, could be to analyze the value stream in detail (VSA). It would include determining the number of staff people and the cycle time, costs and waste of idle time, and buffer stocks. What can be improved and modified to achieve better results and a better value stream with better throughput time? A workshop with professionals on both sides, working as a team, will find tremendous improvements.

You should not stop with focusing on your suppliers. Most cost savings and sources of quality and timing problems come from subsuppliers. You should share your knowledge with the customer's purchasing department, emphasizing that staff members are able to deal with their subsuppliers in the same way as has been experienced in practice from quality gates 1 to 4 (shown in Fig. 4.14).

5 The Purchasing Organization of the Future

If you are creative, you will have a lot of ideas how to improve your organization, for example, bundling. Sure, someone will ask, why do we need bundling?

One advantage is that bundling usually requires prior standardization, and results in a better, lean supplier structure.

What are the risks for buyers?

A total cost of ownership approach cannot be neglected. Logistics costs, service levels, and delivery times must also be taken into account, and supplier potentials are correctly assessed. Can the supplier handle the bundled volume alone? Is the dependence of the supplier on the customer wanted?[1]

What is better, central or decentral procurement?

Switching from pure central procurement to decentralized purchasing and forming cross-functional purchasing teams allows you to form a material group management system. For example, department secretaries can create office supplies (C article supply) based on an internal catalog and order them directly through the supplier's ERP system. This process can also be used for the "technical purchasing" of technical supplies, for the marketing department with regard to advertising materials, or for laboratories that want to purchase laboratory supplies.

The purchasing department continues to manage (control, monitor, coordinate) the general conditions and the contracts.

Thanks to material group management (MGM), a company with a turnover of four billion can manage with 25 purchasers. However, 70 employees buy individually.

Why do we need a supplier day?

At a supplier day, your target is to impart important information to all suppliers at one time, in order to save time and to get feedback at Q&A sessions. For example, you present new projects and give an overview of the current purchasing situation, especially if you have capacity problems and are looking for support. You might ask

[1] Text from "Purchasing Manager"/August 2005, page 6, Holger Thrun, Schüco Internat. KG.

K. Zuerl, *Effective Cost Cutting in Asia*, Management for Professionals,
https://doi.org/10.1007/978-3-030-82782-3_5

for early involvement of suppliers in some R&D projects to reduce risks in terms of quality, timing, and costs, for example, by asking for PFMEA. Some OEM companies call it a frontloading process with parallel running tasks to reduce lead time. Furthermore, you will nominate and honor your supplier of the year and motivate others to follow them.

5.1 How Do You Become the Best Purchasing Department Ever?

What is best practice in industry to reduce costs for your company?

Leadership should expect material pricing to be adjusted consistently with the true costs, but be sure to share the year-end savings on all projects with your supplier partners. I have decided not to do, this is a huge disincentive for suppliers, and you will run into difficulties when you approach them next time to help you. Keep in mind that these projects consume their scarce resources just as it does for your company. It must be a win-win. As leaders, it is important that you do the right thing. It is a basic part of seeking a long-term, trusting relationship with your suppliers. The mutual objective with key suppliers should be to have a long-term strategic partnership that benefits both companies. Improvement ideas should seamlessly flow from both sides of the table into practice.

Purchasing professionals are expected to push for price reductions, which too often is their entire focus. These people are trained to be heavy-handed in negotiations—betting that their business is important enough to the supplier that they will cave on price. This is an old school behavior and will not be rewarded in future. Especially in Asia, rules for business are different, dependent on relationship and cordial behavior.

Retrain your team and expect a more professional approach. Good faith bargaining is always the better path. Over the long haul, creating an antagonistic relationship, or worse, putting your good suppliers out of business or causing them to move your business to a more reasonable company, is a lose–lose proposition. I can guarantee for cash and earnings and improved service that result when the number of suppliers is reduced drastically and the focus is shifted to building strategic relationships.

Culturally, in the case to modify existing materials or developing entirely new material or manufacturing process needs, the purchasing staff must understand the extraordinary level of collaboration that is necessary starting with the design, materials, and manufacturing engineering groups working with the supplier, but always include the manufacturing team of suppliers in this process, as after all they will be the users of the material. Their involvement will provide hands-on insight and get them onboard to help make any changes successful on the machine.

All proposed changes to existing raw material specifications, or any new materials and processes need to be tested in the laboratory and proven with a pilot run in the shop. Purchasing professionals make certain that the "critical to process" characteristics of your company's specs are being fully met. Once all parties have signed off, set the date when specifications are changed, and commence mass production with the new material.

You can see the work of purchasing from two different views:

(a) How are your customers measuring your company's performance? This you have to find out by asking your sales staff and then using these KPIs of your customer to measure your suppliers, for example, delivery, lead time, PPM rates, and cost structure.
(b) Your internal customer is your manufacturing department. What are their expectations? What kind of transparent information they request from you? Do you have all information to represent their needs in discussion with your suppliers?

Out of these, you need to summarize what data you need and what you already have, and then close the gaps, for example, by interviewing your staff and your manufacturing representatives. Following are the some useful activities to become best-in-class purchasing department:

1. Your suppliers are professionals and should be respected as business partners. Do not treat them as a vendor, who just sell ordinary steamed buns on streets.
2. Optimizing the supplier base will provide mutual long-term benefits for all. In most companies, their supplier base is too big and need to be reduced. Seldom, you need to enlarge your qualified base for effective benchmarking.
3. Instead of yearly price negotiations, start sharing ongoing savings with suppliers. For example, if they have ideas for cost reduction in manufacturing process or material change, ask them to share.
4. Piece price focus does not deliver ongoing competitive advantage, nor does it facilitate development of lean supply chain performance. However, it is effective, when suppliers successfully support either forecasts or a level of unforeseen market demand through order fulfillment.
5. Maintain nonpiece price-related structural cost drivers, such as finished goods inventory. This is because suppliers operate under the same strategies as your company does.
6. You only need to look to find internal areas where a change in supply management strategy can significantly impact company financials.[2]
7. An important supply management capability target is built consensus and communication for a supply management policy SMP. In order to get your ordered

[2] Source: https://www.industryweek.com/supply-chain/article/22025924/ask-the-expert-lean-leadership-what-are-good-metrics-to-measure-the-performance-of-the-purchasing-department, published July 10, 2018. Author Larry Fast. Access date 25.2.2021.

parts in time, your requirements to suppliers need to be flexible, adapted to the volatility of market demand and raw material prices.[3]

(a) A firm zone (usually lasting a couple of weeks) where supplier schedules would not change but after which an increase (or a decrease) in shipments would be expected.
(b) A subsequent trade-off zone (usually lasting a month or two), during which suppliers would be expected to ship a certain percentage above what was in the previously issued quarterly forecast.
(c) After this, a forecast zone where suppliers need to be able to support changes in orders up to the consuming OEM's factory capacity.

5.1.1 Sources of Error in Worldwide Shopping

According to A.T. Kearney, the purchasing behavior of companies that source globally needs to be improved:

- Risk assessment for newly found suppliers too low
- Employees do not receive the funds and tools for global purchasing
- Knowledge of the markets and language skills are of little importance to companies.
- Few companies have their own purchasing departments in China or India

5.1.2 Determine the Right Key Figures

- Total turnover
- Number of products and variants
- Personnel structure, distribution, and costs of those departments involved in the processes.
- Inventory levels
- Total procurement costs, quantities, and per material type
- Duration of all processes, and downtimes or break times within the individual process steps
- Use of EDP and E-commerce
- Number of creditors

[3]Source: https://www.industryweek.com/next-generation-supply-management; Supply Management Policies: Consensus Building and Communication|IndustryWeek published November 12, 2014. Author Paul Ericksen. Access date 25.2.2021.

Proceed as follows:

- Ensure the trust and openness of the companies involved
- Perform an accurate process cost analysis of all process steps
- Development of questionnaires
- Definition and presentation of cluster sizes
- Set the key figures to be displayed, for example, warehouse stock and employee numbers in relation to the company's own sales. This is how you recognize their value and quality.
- Determine the reasons for the results using feedback discussions with the analysis team and with participating companies.
- Create a priority list of steps for planning and implementing improvement measures: change processes, initiate actions, and improve strategies
- Benchmark repeatedly to identify improvements

Benchmarking Results

- Successful companies that care more about time and costs have better communication and intensity of purchasing with other departments than less successful ones.
- Performance-oriented remuneration was not recognizable in purchasing.
- The higher the purchasing volume, the lower the unit costs.
- Peak value of discount granted at 0.46%/year. Worse companies do not negotiate intensively enough and give money away.
- Capital commitment costs high: stock of 2–11%.
- Number of purchasing employees at 0.84–1.1% in relation to total number of company employees.

5.1.3 Audit Your Purchasing Department with the Following Question List

Have you already implemented the following purchasing tools?

- Does the constant exchange of information with other departments and top management work?
- Are there clear and detailed purchasing goals? Where are they recorded in writing?
- Do you have a detailed purchasing concept?
- Are target and action templates being used?
- Do all purchasers know their purchasing targets?
- Are checklists used for all purchasing tasks?
- Are there binding purchasing principles and rules?
- Are the purchasing rules displayed in the purchasing department?
- Is there a written requirement profile for suppliers?
- Is there a standard set of guidelines distributed to suppliers?

Is a systematic, timely purchasing controlling system in place?

- Is purchasing solely responsible for the procurement of all required products and services?
- Is the purchasing volume of your company known?
- Are the material costs known exactly?
- Is the purchasing program classified into A, B, and C groups?
- Are the A suppliers known?
- Is XYZ analysis used?
- Are the results of the ABC and XYZ analysis combined?
- Is the purchasing department continuously examined for weak points?
- Is there a meaningful purchasing key performance indication system (KPI)?
- Does management regularly receive a purchasing report?

Is there a plan for improving purchasing conditions?

- Do you respond to any price increase requests from suppliers with an effective standard letter?
- Do you send a price reduction request once a year to your A and B suppliers?
- Do you know the structure of a sales calculation?
- Do you have argumentation guidelines for price discussions?
- Do you have precise reasons for supplier price increases?
- Do you have different negotiation strategies for A, B, and C suppliers?
- Do you demand additional services from your suppliers?
- Do you ask your main suppliers for suggestions to reduce purchasing costs?
- Do you monitor product price developments using federal statistics?
- Do you regularly launch enquiry campaigns to monitor the market price levels?

Do you constantly explore purchasing markets?

- Do you have a detailed understanding of all of your important purchasing markets?
- Do you specifically select candidates for purchasing market research?
- Do you precisely define the information requirements in advance?
- Do you visit trade fairs in Germany/Europe/China which are important for your purchasing requirements?
- Do you have an overview of those international trade fairs which are relevant and important for you?
- Do you got catalogs sent to you from trade fairs that you cannot attend?
- Do you have many contacts to other buyers?
- Do you use industry organizations to find suppliers?
- Do you find new sources of supply in an efficient way with the help of modern online databases?
- Do you consistently include world markets in your research?

Are your import transactions worthwhile?

- Are the processes within your company focused on the import business?
- Are eligible products selected?
- Does your purchasing department speak English?
- Do you know the most profitable purchasing countries for your company?
- Do you have an address list with the most important information spots for international business contacts?
- Are you familiar with international trade practices?
- Are you familiar with the steps of import processing?
- Can you carry out an import calculation?
- Is there any product that is suitable for a test import?
- Do you know any importers who can assist you in handling import transactions?

Is there a systematic supplier management system for evaluating and controlling suppliers?

- Are your suppliers classified according to their level of profit margin and purchasing risk?
- Have you defined evaluation criteria on the basis of a supplier requirement profile?
- Do you evaluate your suppliers regularly and systematically using a template or EDP software?
- Have new suppliers been tested in the last 12 months?
- Have any suppliers been eliminated in the last few months?
- Do you use the evaluation results specifically for purchasing negotiations?
- Is there a target and drive for a systematic concentration of suppliers?
- Are your contacts to important and influential suppliers maintained and further developed?
- Do you visit new and important suppliers?
- Do you organize a supplier day on a regular basis?

Have you set up a joint purchasing department with other companies?

- Do you know how much money you can save by reducing your annual purchasing costs by 1%?
- Are there specific products that could be used?
- Is there a clear target catalog?
- Have you drawn up an individual roadmap for implementing the project?
- Are you sure that you cannot join an existing purchasing association?
- Do you know the legal requirements for a purchasing association?
- Have you defined those purchasing tasks that are to be handled jointly?
- Should a contract regulate the cooperation with your cooperation partners?
- Have you selected the right search paths for purchasing partners?

- Do you have clear and convincing arguments ready for contact discussions with new purchasing partners?

Do you use regular professional external purchasing service providers?

- Do you know the advantages of professional external purchasing service providers in detail?
- Do you spend less than 50% of your time on routine administrative tasks?
- Do you have a sample contract ensuring the legal protection of purchasing services?
- Do you use external purchasing services to find suppliers?
- Are you familiar with information services for purchasing?
- Do you work together with database providers?
- Do you have price detectives working for you?
- Do you delegate complete purchasing processes to purchasing agencies and import aides?
- Do you regularly use the services of competent purchasing training institutes?
- Can you accurately determine the potential savings from purchasing service providers?

Do you deal intensively with e-purchasing (eSourcing)?

- Does your company have Internet access?
- Can you access the Internet at your workplace at any time?
- Does your company have a homepage? Is the purchasing department represented on this homepage?
- Does your purchasing department have its own homepage?
- Have you already informed yourself comprehensively at seminars or conferences on the subject of "virtual purchasing"?
- Have you already found new potential suppliers with the help of the internet?
- Do you use emails regularly and with an increasing tendency for communication with suppliers?
- Have you talked to your most important suppliers about email communication and "virtual purchasing"?
- Do you know any "virtual marketplaces" for buyers?

Is purchasing up to date when dealing with purchasing steel and raw materials? The following questions have to be answered:

- How high is the share of raw materials and metals as a part of purchasing volume?
- Are the global markets being observed?
- Does purchasing have sufficient basic and specialist knowledge of the steel and raw materials markets?
- Are personnel capacities sufficient for professional raw material purchasing?
- What market information does purchasing have, and what is still missing?

- Can purchasing gain any benefits from mergers?
- Are there other manufacturing processes that save on raw materials?
- Are there alternative materials, raw materials, and input materials?
- Are there cost-effective production processes available for these substitute materials?
- Are there several locations for purchasing and production available?
- How do these alternatives affect customer satisfaction?
- What is the potential for price increases on the sales side?

The average material cost reduction in German medium-sized companies is 4%, but top companies achieve 12% (20% more purchases than average, clearly limited supplier base, lower number of active articles, fewer but larger tenders, more long-term purchasing contracts, higher reporting level of purchasing to top management).[4]

5.1.4 New Purchasing Strategies

The formation of lean corporate structures, the rapidly changing market, competitive environment, and changes in the structure of the value chain create new requirements for procurement departments. Purchasing is mutating from an order processing function to a cross-divisional subcompany. The buyer must be familiar with all processes throughout the entire supply chain. In addition, unlike in the past, he or she must treat the supplier as a partner, cultivate the relationships, and contribute his specialist knowledge to solving product-specific problems.

Suggestions for Reducing Costs in Processes and Products

- The cost reduction potential is biggest for electronic commodities.
- Reducing the number of suppliers for C items.
- The import quota will continue to rise. Sharing of international work is important. The potential for this has not yet been exhausted.
- If they do not form joint purchasing co-operations with other companies and ensure significant demand quantities, smaller companies will have their purchase prices dictated by suppliers.
- Millions of RMBs can be saved by managing overhead materials (nonproductive materials). Has a specific manager been appointed to handle this?
- Since 80% of the total costs of a product are determined in the development stage, purchasing must be integrated into the process right from the start. An advance shift of purchasing activities (frontloading) involves the supplier becoming involved in the product development process at an early stage (advanced purchasing) and helps to save costs.

[4]Text from "Einkaufsmanager"/August/October 2005, Fachverlag für Einkaufswissen, Verlag der Deutschen Wirtschaft AG.

- Introduction of electronic control and standardization of procurement processes and automation of operational processes, e.g., IT-supported annual marketing planning, determination of quantity structures for production in order to meet annual targets, transfer of material requirements to procurement, electronically formulated purchase orders forwarded to the supplier, electronically monitored deliveries from the supplier, and automatic reminders for missing deliveries.
- Reduce supplier invoices and related process costs with electronic support for invoice generation, credit memo processes, invoice receipts, and invoice verification, release, and payment.
- Redesign of delivery and payment terms:
  - Conversion to direct debit including 4% cash discount agreements with reliable suppliers.
  - Comparison of shipping costs between "ex-works" deliveries with own shipping companies and DDP/DDU regulations. Self-collection may reduce shipping costs. In which case, your suppliers should be given the name of your contracted freight forwarder.
- Supplier evaluations help to reduce costs by creating transparency, so that regulatory intervention and countermeasures can be taken. The prerequisite is the definition and maintenance of key supplier figures (KPIs).

5.1.5 Examples of a Continuous Improvement Process Within the Company

Who else in the company, other than purchasing, has an overview and examines overall cost structures? This exercise is no less important than taking actions (restructuring programs) to improve the profit situation and regain competitiveness in the fight for new orders. This means that more costs can actually be saved through questions and answers on restructuring than through the measures described so far. As a purchasing manager, put this topic on the management agenda and ask for support. Teamwork is the only way to get accurate results quickly.

Which products with a high share of labor costs are currently in production? You have to find out and relocate to another LCC plant (e.g., from Poland to China or vice versa) and produce there. If you have intention to relocate your sourcing of parts and tools to low-cost countries, please consider following: Small parts have a high impact on manpower costs. It is mandatory to move these to low-cost countries. Big parts, however, require higher transportation costs, so they have to stay close to the assembly plant.

Example 1: Valeo wiper systems: relocation of the Neuses site (Northern Bavaria) to the Polnish wiper plant in Skawina. This affected 22 employees as a result of production relocation for manual wiper bearings and wiper systems for buses and trucks, specifically affected the lines for Iveco, Liebherr, MAN, Jaguar, and the spare part business.

Which production parts are not part of the core manufacturing know-how? In the future, these parts will no longer be produced in-house but purchased from suppliers.

Example 2: Valeo wiper systems: Neuses site. Relocation of prefabrication areas of the stamping shop and the injection molding shop to suppliers. 27 employees were affected.

Are the offers competitive? Which positions are not competitive with customers in the bid analyses? Which cost blocks in the quotation calculation are above those of the competition? Organizational measures and changes are necessary to reduce "indirect costs."

Example 3: Organizational change in Valeo wiper systems. The Neuses site was integrated into the Wiper Systems Northern Europe Division as an APU (autonomous production unit). This eliminated location-related indirect functions and eliminated the need for in-house reporting and the monthly closing required for Neuses.

Example 4: The relocation of parts of the production (see Example 1) also relieves the indirect structure, so that a personnel adjustment in the nonproduction area was planned.

Are handling processes optimized? Are parts fed on a technology adapted to the machining process? Is the plugging process quick and easy?

Example 5: Coated wiper arms must be attached (plugged on) to painting racks adapted for the painting process. The equipped painting frames are transported to the painting plant via a conveyor system. The fast and simple plug-on process relieves the workers and minimizes production costs. Workshops with participants from the areas of maintenance and process development develop a new painting rack that meets the requirements for high volumes ("direct loading"). Previously "non-value-adding" activities could be eliminated and the cycle time for plugging on was reduced, thus making a significant contribution to securing the location of the site.

Have all possible manufacturing processes and production sites been investigated for the manufacture of the parts?

Example 6: Instead of machining, the same parts can be made more cheaply by cold forming. This is particularly true if production is simultaneously relocated from Western Europe to LCC. You need to take this chance.

5.2 Best in Class in Purchasing[5]

Our goal is to significantly increase the professionalism and efficiency of the purchasing department in the company. Through KPI analyses, purchasing gains transparency about its cost structures and processes, with the desired result that the most important key figures have developed positively. Our goal is to create a

[5] Source: TOP-Kennzahlen im Einkauf, published 2016 by BMEnet GmbH, Bundesverband Materialwirtschaft, Einkauf und Logistik e.V.

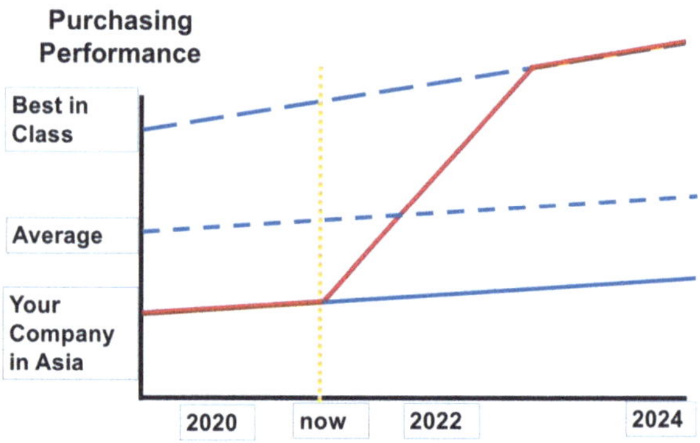

Fig. 5.1 Purchasing performance vs. time. Source: "TOP-Kennzahlen im Einkauf", publisher "Bundesverbandes Materialwirtschaft, Einkauf und Logistik e.V. (BME)", page 5, 2016, author BMEnet GmbH

standard for measuring the efficiency and effectiveness of processes and organization in purchasing, to compare it with other companies, and to report the results.

To do this, we proceed in five steps:

1. We determine the measurement parameters and the comparison partners
2. We know where we are
3. We assess our potential
4. What do the best-in-class buyers do better?
5. Continuous controlling and benchmarking (Fig. 5.1)

5.2.1 What Makes Us a Best-in-Class Company?[6]

Purchasing as a Value Creation Manager High hierarchical integration of purchasing and active internal purchasing marketing means that purchasing assumes responsibility for more than 90% of the total procurement volume.

Purchasing also works closely with consumers in indirect purchasing and in so-called nontraditional procurement fields such as travel, consulting, or marketing services. Strategies are jointly defined for almost all procurement categories as to how costs can be reduced.

Purchasing Organization The hybrid form of organization in connection with project purchasing and product group management has been introduced. We rely on flexible, adaptable structures. We use just a third of our human resources for day-to-day operations.

[6]Source: TOP-Kennzahlen im Einkauf, published 2016 by BMEnet GmbH, Bundesverband Materialwirtschaft, Einkauf und Logistik e.V.

High Process Effectiveness and Efficiency The automation of the ordering and billing process in connection with the standardization of requirements is continuing. As the best in class, we not only write more orders than the other buyers on average but also manage a 30–50% higher purchasing volume per FTE[7] p.a. Our number of articles and suppliers is also only half as high as the average. This enables us to reduce costs by 30–50%.

Supplier Management We regularly conduct supplier evaluations. In recent years, this has enabled the supplier base to be optimized. We operate on the principle of "one article, one supplier" and manage the risk through a good supplier relationship.

Regular Controlling/External Benchmarking We regularly participate in analyses and statistical market evaluations and thus gain a clear lead over the competition. The most important principle of an analysis is the comparison with similar companies. Thus, the selection of suitable comparison partners is critically important to us.

Following our best-in-class KPIs.[8]

The mean values of five selected best-in-class companies were shown as best-in-class values.

Overall KPI: Purchasing costs as a percentage of the purchasing volume. The average of all companies of all commodities is 1.56.[9]

	Best-in-Class	Average
Metal, electrical, and plastic industry, mechanical engineering:	0.65	2.14
Energy, care:	0.98	1.36
Service provider:	0.87	1.13
Chemical, organic and pharmaceutical industry:	0.57	1.12
Automotive:	0.90	1.16

[7] Full-Time Equivalent.

[8] More details, see https://www.apqc.org/resource-library/resource-listing/implement-formal-supplier-approval-process

[9] Source: TOP-Kennzahlen im Einkauf, published 2016 by BMEnet GmbH, Bundesverband Materialwirtschaft, Einkauf und Logistik e.V.

Purchasing Organization[10]

	Low performers (25th percentile)	Median	High performers (75th percentile)
Number of purchase orders per buyer[11]	200	635	2258
Number of FTEs that procure material and services per I billion USD revenue[12]	68 (14.7 Mio USD/FTE)	33.5 (29.8 Mio USD/FTE)	14.8 (65.5 Mio USD/FTE)

However, there are a lot of others for purchasing process or procurement structure, which can be benchmarked (arranged alphabetically) according to your needs at current situation and targets:

1. Access quota from framework agreements and catalogs
2. Active suppliers per € million purchasing volume
3. Adherence to delivery dates for all deliveries
4. Average value per order
5. Average payment term
6. Avoidance of costs
7. Change in costs
8. Complaint rate for all deliveries
9. Compliance rate: Understand if suppliers fulfill your requirements
10. Cost of each order process
11. Cost of purchase order: Control the internal costs incurred by each purchase
12. Distribution of the total costs of the purchasing department
13. Emergency purchase ratio: Track the number of your emergency purchases
14. Full costs per buyer
15. Lead time: Understand the total time to fulfill an order
16. Number of items per € million purchase volume
17. Number of orders per buyer
18. Number of order items per order
19. Number of suppliers: Track your level of dependency toward your suppliers
20. Procurement cost avoidance: Avoid potential extra costs in the future
21. Procurement cost reduction: Streamline the tangible costs savings
22. Procurement ROI: Determine the profitability of investments
23. Purchases in time and budget: Monitor purchasing time and budget
24. Purchasing costs based on purchasing volume

[10] Source: https://www.datapine.com/kpi-examples-and-templates/procurement#supplier-defect-rate, published August 3, 2020 by RIB DATAPINE GMBH, access May 9, 2021.

[11] Source: https://www.sdcexec.com/sourcing-procurement/blog/21066745/apqc-number-of-purchase-orders-processed-per-procurement-fte, May 6, 2019, Author APQC; access May 9, 2021.

[12] Source: https://www.sdcexec.com/sourcing-procurement/article/21086878/apqc-benchmarking-the-number-of-employees-in-procurement; published at September 21, 2019, by Marisa Brown from APQC; access May 9, 2021.

25. Purchasing costs from sales
26. Purchasing costs per supplier
27. Purchase order cycle time: Know who to address your urgent orders to
28. Purchase volume via discount
29. Purchasing volume for which purchasing is responsible
30. Purchasing volume from sales
31. Purchasing volume per employee in purchasing
32. Purchasing volume through long-term contracts
33. Share of order items with electronic (automated) invoice processing
34. Spend under management: Track and optimize your expenditures
35. Supplier availability: Measure suppliers' capacity to respond to demand
36. Supplier defect rate: Evaluate your suppliers' individual quality
37. Supplier quality rating: Analyze the quality of your suppliers
38. Training costs per employee in purchasing
39. Vendor rejection rate and costs: Examine your quality management strategies
40. Volume of purchases via Internet tenders and online auctions

5.2.2 How Do I Lay the Foundations for Best-in-Class Shopping?[13]

What is current standard situation in your company in Asia?

- *Savings in direct material (DM) and indirect material (IM) are being documented*
- *Just procurement on behalf of other departments*
- *Low reputation of purchasing due to slow speed in execution*
- *Little professional training in procurement*

Our purchasing department in Asia is currently undergoing a structural change. The reason is the digitization of the economy and Industry 4.0, which have necessitated extensive changes in all industries and areas, for example, the possibility of networking with partners along the supply chain and the real-time availability of internal and external data.

Particularly in the automotive industry and in mechanical and plant engineering, purchasing should enjoy a great reputation, because the low vertical range of manufacture and the quality of the suppliers, their products, and raw materials play an important role in the company. In order to promote purchasing in the long term, as a global player, purchasing should even be on the board.

Against the background of structural change, professional training in procurement is also becoming more and more important. Standstill is a step backward, and here, it is important to prepare all specialists and managers in purchasing for the future and to offer in-depth specialist courses. Regular workshops with the exchange

[13]Source: "Grundlagen des Einkaufs," published 2016 by Judith Richard at BMEnet GmbH, Bundesverband Materialwirtschaft, Einkauf und Logistik e.V.

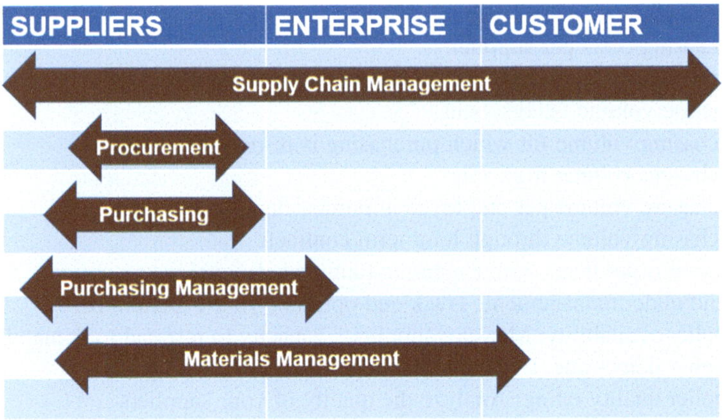

Fig. 5.2 Supply chain management is more comprehensive than purchasing because it looks at the entire value chain. The further development of traditional purchasing as an operational partner goes toward a strategic position in the company. He not only acts as buyer and exporter but is also a value-added partner. The new task is the holistic control of the value chain. Purchasing is also meeting the requirement to shift its activities from the functional view to the process view. Source: "Grundlagen des Einkaufs", publisher "Bundesverbandes Materialwirtschaft, Einkauf und Logistik e.V. (BME)", page 4, 2016, author Judith Richard

of knowledge and experience serve as a supplement, because here buyers from all hierarchical levels can intensively discuss current purchasing topics with their professional colleagues on equal footing.

The current procurement serves to maintain the supply of the factors required for the operating processes that are not available in the company. The term "procurement management," however, encompasses the decisions about the supply of the users in the production facilities with goods and services. These include the procurement of labor, information, capital, rights, and material goods and services.

Successful procurement management can make an outstanding contribution to corporate success. In addition to maintaining security of supply and reducing procurement costs, procurement complexities can also be managed. The tasks of this management include, among other things, product group management, purchasing controlling, and supplier management.

Material management encompasses the entirety of all material-related functions, such as supplying production with materials and controlling the material flow through to delivery.

In contrast to material management, supply chain management goes one step further by encompassing the flow of materials and information across the entire value chain, from the supplier (possibly upstream supplier) to the end customer (Fig. 5.2).

Generally, in order to clarify terminology based on the scope of activity, it is necessary to determine your current stage in Asia:

Supply chain management: Controlling of material and information flow from suppliers to customers.

Procurement: To supply enterprise with raw material, products, and services.

Purchasing: Additional to procurement to determine and assess demands, i.e., deciding whether to make or buy and managing all suppliers.

Purchasing management: Additional to purchasing to manage all commodity groups and to control procurement.

Material management: Additional to procurement to manage material flow up to dispatch and delivery of the shipment.

What could be improved at your department immediately without any expenses?

- Introduction of a few sensible KPIs and the comparison of the services with selected partners.
- Increased value due to the assumption of all operational and strategic activities in the context of the procurement of materials, goods, operating resources, and services.
- The task of purchasing is to work with the supplier to ensure the availability and required properties of the procurement objects for the company, with execution and planning being closely interwoven.
- Regular subject-specific internal training and workshops to share experiences
- Restructuring for future challenges in purchasing management and supply chain

Direct and Indirect Purchasing

What is current standard situation in your company in Asia?

- *In the manufacturing trade and industry, direct materials make up approximately 70–85% of the total purchase volume.*
- *Indirect purchasing is sometimes neglected. Maverick buying in HR, services, IT, and marketing with no focus on cost reduction.*

What could be improved at your department immediately without any expenses?

- Elimination of maverick buying
- And concentration of all important purchasing activities

Strategic Versus Operational Purchasing

What is current standard situation in your company in Asia?

- *DM: Strictly operational procurement. Little to no research for new suppliers, footprint not optimized. Long-term framework agreements and supplier development not installed.*

- *IM: Strictly operational procurement. There is no strategic purchase of machines, devices, logistics, and services. Mostly single sourcing.*

What could be improved at your department immediately without any expenses?

- Installation of strategic, value-added purchasing in DM and IM (including logistics).
- Purchasing is viewed as a success factor with a focus on strategic activities.
- There is also a rethinking toward process orientation, which is supported by the creation of lean and digital processes.

While operational purchasing takes on administrative and executive purchasing activities, strategic purchasing is responsible for long-term tasks.

The tasks of operational purchasing include order processing, complaint processing, appointment coordination, invoice verification, and processing of order confirmations.

Strategic purchasing takes care of procurement market research, supplier management (research, selection, evaluation) negotiating framework agreements, and implementing the purchasing strategy.

Improvement is implemented through the use of electronic procurement tools. These tools take over operational and administrative tasks, and there is more space for strategic tasks.

Relationships with suppliers are becoming more strategic, and consequently, the price is no longer the only criterion for selection. Instead, an assessment of the overall performance of the supplier and the total costs incurred are carried out and partnership-based cooperation is sought.

The "new" purchasing department is therefore quality-oriented, customer-oriented, strategic, innovative, and future-oriented.

Project Purchasing Versus Series Purchasing

What is current standard situation in your company in Asia?

- *The buyer in DM and IM takes on both functions, project, and series purchasing*

In the context of industry, project buyers procure goods that have to be procured for a company before the start of series production. Project purchasing is permanently assigned to a customer or development program and is responsible for all relevant project-specific purchasing activities, for example, helping to design products in the project team and representing purchasing interests within this team.

On the other hand, series buyers procure the volumes that are necessary within series production.

For example, the project buyer is a member of the project team and the contact person for all questions relating to purchasing. He ensures a close coupling and implementation of purchasing and development tasks, and manages communication and purchasing activities.

Due to the necessary integration of suppliers in the product development process (frontloading) so that costs, deadlines, and quality can be adhered to, the project buyer is also responsible for helping to design the product and accompanying the entire process.

What could be improved at your department immediately without any expenses?

- Differentiation through differentiated JD, which increases the qualification in purchasing and ensures more reputation and importance in value creation.

Decentralized Versus Centralized Purchasing Organization

What is current standard situation in your company in Asia?

- *The business unit in DM knows the buyers in the plants by name in Asia, but they have no dotted line, and therefore, central function has no decision-making power.*
- *In IM, the local buyer acts with total freedom without consultation. In the case of joint ventures (JV), cooperation with the central business unit is even rejected.*

In a decentralized purchasing organization, each business unit or each location has its own purchasing department, which operates independently and without coordination with other units. This results in short decision-making paths and shorter delivery times for local procurement. However, no bundling potential can be developed and there is no transparency about the procurement activities of the individual units and no approach and no potential for standardization.

In any given organization (company, group of companies, industry sector, association), several different buyers are often in charge of purchasing the same materials or the same material group independently of each other, and with no coordination.

Purchasing activities across all areas can be bundled in a central organization so as to achieve price advantages. Therefore, there is transparency about all procurement activities and uniform controlling and reporting.

In practice, a hybrid purchasing organization combines the advantages of a central and a decentralized form of organization. The best-known form of implementation is the lead buyer concept. A lead buyer is the person who, as an expert, takes on all strategic tasks for a specific procurement market or product group. This includes the development of a product group strategy and the development of bundling potential across different locations or company units. The lead buyer is often referred to as the material group manager.

In the future, lead buyers will be needed. Lead buyers are responsible for a specific product or material group. By bundling purchasing with the associated improved quantity degression, procurement and process costs can be reduced.

For this, it is necessary to provide the proper prerequisites for implementation. One prerequisite is the software that creates the necessary transparency within the purchasing organization. For example, portal technologies connect ERP systems (e.g., SAP) with external supplier catalogs. Lead buyers should be able to convince others through professional competence, industry knowledge, purchasing tools, language skills, and soft skills.

The lead buyer has the task of negotiating the defined total requirements with suppliers. He or she is also responsible for any supplier errors and negotiates the framework agreements on the basis of which the respective purchasing departments take over the operative processing.

What could be improved at your department immediately without any expenses?

- Establishment of a hybrid purchasing organization
- with a dotted line to business unit buyers and lead buyers
- and with transparency of names and RASICs.

5.2.3 Sourcing Strategies[14]

The sourcing strategy is an important part of the purchasing strategy. There are three types of strategies, the number of suppliers, the complexity of the procurement object, and the procurement location.

What is current standard situation in your company in Asia?

- *The DM buyer avoids global sourcing and buys domestically. However, the footprint is not optimized, and there is still potential to reduce transport costs.*
- *Products that have been developed in Europe or in the USA are imported. Tasks are to localize to save costs and time. However, sourcing staff at business unit does not leave the local buyers free to optimize and develop.*

Single Sourcing, Dual Sourcing Versus Multiple Sourcing

Even if a single supplier as a strategic partner offers price advantages due to possible larger order quantities, there is a high level of dependency on the supplier and there is a high risk if the supplier fails. A forced sudden change in suppliers can result in a

[14] Source: "Grundlagen des Einkaufs," published 2016 by Judith Richard at BMEnet GmbH, Bundesverband Materialwirtschaft, Einkauf und Logistik e.V.

high loss of quality. In the automotive industry, however, a change can usually only be carried out with the consent of the customer and reduces flexibility in the event of unforeseen price increases.

In order to prevent the risk of failure, a second supplier is being developed parallel to a long-term supplier. If one of the two suppliers offers the better price, an unequal distribution of the shares makes sense.

Multiple sourcing is usually used for standard products without much need for explanation due to the low-price advantages due to smaller order volumes and the high logistics effort.

Unit Sourcing Versus Modular Sourcing and System Sourcing

When sourcing individual parts, there is a high coordination effort due to the large number of suppliers. With modular sourcing, few suppliers deliver complete systems or assemblies. This reduces the number of suppliers and enables concentration on core competencies. This results in a unified production process with a low level of vertical integration.

Local Sourcing Versus Global Sourcing

Deliberately local procurement is used in order to avoid logistical risks during delivery. There is a risk of higher prices than on international markets and the risk of limited availability. Contrastingly, with global sourcing, quality risks arise from intercultural differences and language barriers as well as risks from exchange rate fluctuations. Logistics costs, and legal and political risks increase prices. However, new markets can be opened up that enable a price reduction. Ensuring availability is also one of the main goals of global sourcing. With this step, however, companies also hope to gain and secure competitive advantages, open up new markets and sales areas, and gain know-how. This finds not only bottleneck suppliers abroad but also strategic suppliers.

Standardized, low-complexity products that can be manufactured in large quantities are particularly suitable for global sourcing. Target countries must be determined as part of a procurement market research. The points that should be considered when selecting a country include, for example, political stability, available raw materials, existing supplier base, logistical effort, technological status, and total costs. Some companies only procure globally but then produce in their home markets. Others have also relocated production and sales activities abroad.

What could be improved at your department immediately without any expenses?

- Investigation and development of modular sourcing with strategic partners, which must be developed in order to avoid loss of know-how and high dependency.

(continued)

- Procurement market research can also be used to investigate which parts or modules could be purchased cheaply in neighboring countries, starting as a bottleneck supplier.

5.2.4 The Purchasing Process[15]

The entire purchasing process consists of finding a strategy (purchasing strategy and commodity/material group strategy), its core process, and supporting processes. The core processes are different for the purchasing strategy and product group strategy. The support processes of supplier management, purchasing controlling, and risk management accompany the core process permanently (see Fig. 5.3).

Purchasing Strategy Versus Commodity Group Strategy

What is current standard situation in your company in Asia?

- *Both a purchasing strategy and a commodity/material group strategy are not apparent.*

Let us consider the purchasing strategy. It is not derived only from the corporate strategy but derived also from sales targets and discussions with internal customers. Discussions are also held with management and the product area. It includes the delimitation of the areas of activity in purchasing, the market strategies, the sourcing

Definition of Strategies	Purchasing Strategy	Commodity Group Strategy	
Core Processes	Identification of demand and suppliers	Fulfillment of demand	
	Step 1: detection of demand	Step 1: Sourcing, managing offers, negotiations	
	Step 2: research of resourcing market	Step 2: Assignment of suppliers	
	Step 3: pre-selection of suppliers	Step 3: Execution	
Supporting Processes	Supplier management (evaluation, development)	Purchasing controlling (measuring success and reporting)	Risk management (identification, deduction of provisions)

Fig. 5.3 Reference process "purchasing". Source: "Grundlagen des Einkaufs", publisher "Bundesverbandes Materialwirtschaft, Einkauf und Logistik e.V. (BME)", page 14, 2016, author Judith Richard

[15] Source: "Grundlagen des Einkaufs," published 2016 by Judith Richard at BMEnet GmbH, Bundesverband Materialwirtschaft, Einkauf und Logistik e.V.

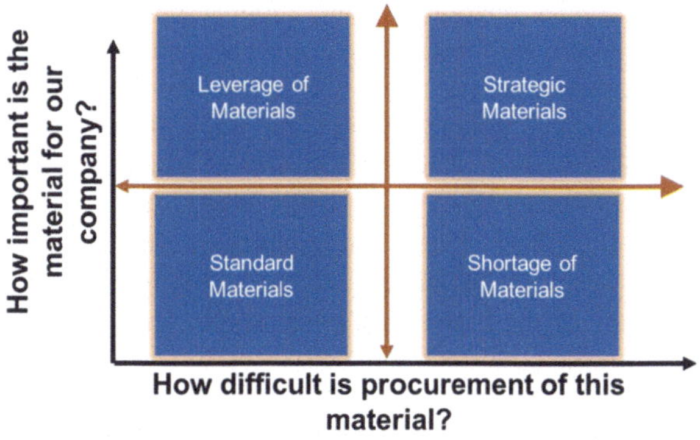

Fig. 5.4 Commodity/material group portfolio. Source: "Grundlagen des Einkaufs", publisher "Bundesverbandes Materialwirtschaft, Einkauf und Logistik e.V. (BME)", page 15, 2016, author Judith Richard

strategies, and the setting up of purchasing in the business model. The size of the company also has an influence on the purchasing strategy (e.g., global versus regional purchasing). When deriving the purchasing strategy, it is important to have a certain flexibility so as to adapt quickly to internal and external changes. If the purchasing strategy is recorded in a purchasing manual, the content can be communicated to the employees.

Contrastingly, with commodity group management (also known as material group management), all items in a company's procurement portfolio are grouped together on the basis of common characteristics. These characteristics should be chosen so that the purchasing department can attain the greatest possible benefit, which will be recognizable within the company and outside.

The aim in product group management is to recognize one's own position and to derive measures from this and to recognize optimization potential. Contents of the product group strategy are, e.g., the importance of the product group for the company, the market structure and market strategy (local/global), the supplier strategy (single/multiple), a price strategy, the risk assessment, and the requirements of internal customers. A so-called product group portfolio can be used to determine the position of the different product groups and to derive a suitable strategy. The following portfolio shows the importance of the four different materials for the company depending on the difficulties in procurement (Fig. 5.4).

Lever materials have a high impact on the operating result, whereby their proportion in terms of value in the procurement volume is high. Lever materials are usually relatively simple individual parts that should be standardized as much as possible in order to ensure the best possible bundling of quantities. In order to reduce costs, it is essential to exploit the market potential, for example, by promoting competition with the selection of suppliers and through product substitution in a global context. What else should be done? Define targeted price and negotiation strategies with current market data and at least medium-term requirements planning with development of part prices and freight rates.

Strategic materials, on the other hand, are difficult to procure, and their share of value in the procurement volume is high. For these materials, a close and long-term partnership with the supplier should be sought and this should be deeply integrated into the processes. The contents of a suitable strategy are the establishment of a long-term supplier relationship and supplier development, intensive observation with detailed demand forecasts, and precise market research.

Standard materials are easy to obtain and do not account for a large proportion of the purchasing volume. The procurement of these products should be as simple as possible or standardized. It can also be checked whether the procurement can be handed over to a service provider who, for example, fills up a company's office supplies or the fasteners and supplies on the shop floor independently. The focus here is on a few suppliers, volume bundling, and inventory optimization. A good overview of the market can cover higher short-term needs. The optimal inventory level for the goods is calculated.

What could be improved at your department immediately without any expenses?

- Discussions with the VP, R&D, sales director, and other internal customers are combined into a purchasing strategy and designed flexibly for adjustments over time.
- All articles are grouped based on common characteristics, which show a benefit for shopping.
- Classification of all purchased goods into the four areas mentioned above. From this, four different product group strategies are developed in cooperation with the suppliers.
- Procurement is handed over to a service provider, who fills up the office materials, fasteners, and supplies on the shop floor independently.

The share of value of bottleneck materials in the purchasing volume is also not high, but they are still difficult to procure because there are either only a few suppliers here or the materials are not often found. If possible, bottleneck materials should be replaced with standard materials. It is also conceivable to work with a service provider who has very good knowledge of the procurement markets so that the supply risk is reduced and the inventory is secured.

Now, we come to the various core processes in purchasing.

Core Process of Identification of Requirements and Suppliers

Step 1: The Identification of Needs

Various sources from the past, from sales planning, and from customer surveys can be used to identify and determine requirements. Regular analyses of customer satisfaction complement the investigations.

Step 2: Procurement Market Research

Here, we look for information and prepare it on current and potential procurement markets. The sources for this are the Internet, economic analyses, associations, networks, market research by the lead buyer in the respective country, and external service providers.

Step 3: (Pre)Selection of Suppliers

The following practical methods can be used to narrow down and select suppliers:

- Request and examination of certificates
- Sending of preliminary questionnaires to suppliers/self-assessment (content: basic data, development capacities, quality)
- Supplier prequalification such as D&B (https://www.dnb.com/business-directory.html). In order to correctly assess the supplier and to identify added value that the inclusion of the new supplier in the supplier base, for example, in addition to the RFQ the following basic information can be requested:
  - Business information (e.g., creditworthiness), planned investments, current legal form
  - Main customers, reference customers, and products
  - Sales
  - Certifications
  - Logistic information (e.g., connection to the nearest airport, seaport)
  - Information on production possibilities and machinery
  - Department information
  - Export licenses, trade permits (for foreign suppliers)
  - Insurance against the risk of failure, fire, destruction
  - Code of conduct
  - IT connection The procedure for selecting a supplier depends on the situation and differs depending on the case, for example, when looking for a replacement supplier in the event of a supplier failure, looking for suppliers for new products and product groups, or relocating locally.

What is current standard situation in your company in Asia?

- *Requirements are passed on from upstream specialist departments to purchasing, thrown over the wall, so to speak. The department then communicates with the buyer by giving him the supplier contact, requirements, and deadlines.*
- *There is often no time for a thorough supplier preselection or a correction loop in the engineering, so the quality of the parts is accordingly.*
- *A procurement market research is not evident.*

What could be improved at your department immediately without any expenses?

- Objective evaluation of all suppliers with a predefined question–answer matrix (similar to an audit) before the conclusion of a contract is absolutely necessary.

Core Process by Which to Meet Requirements

What is current standard situation in your company in Asia?

- *List/overview of all framework supply contracts and quantity contracts or binding forecasts missing.*
- *Processing is disturbed by the lack of understanding of the tasks between supplier quality engineer, plant quality engineer, and customer quality engineer.*

The core process of meeting demand is part of the commodity/material group strategy.

Step 1: Sourcing/Offer Management/Negotiation

The choice of sourcing method depends on the material group. In practice, tenders are most often carried out (particularly for services) or individual queries are sent to the supplier. Auctions can also be carried out using software from service providers. This saves time, but fees apply. It is said to have happened several times that the bottom line was that no savings were made. Thorough preplanning is therefore absolutely essential, and quick action is guaranteed to fail.

As part of offer management, the offers received are assessed, and the offers are compared with the aid of a decision matrix, and the resulting award decision. In Asia, a decision must not only be made on the lowest price, but technical discussions are essential so that the supplier knows what demands are placed on his employees and machines. Preparing for a negotiation is also crucial for success. A SWOT analysis, main and secondary goals, and alternatives should be defined before a negotiation meeting. If other departments (e.g., technology) are also present at the negotiation, the conversation and the procedure should be prepared together. If the buyers have not yet been trained in this, a lot of potential is wasted.

Step 2: Commissioning of Suppliers

When commissioning new suppliers in the industry, samples are often requested first. This step is not necessary for existing suppliers. If a framework delivery contract already exists, it will be expanded, otherwise it will be renegotiated. Framework contracts are usually concluded regardless of the quantity and contain a product list with the planned quantities as an attachment. Alternatively, individual contracts are negotiated. For products with a long lead time, such as PCBs and PCBAs, for which the supplier has to buy primary material himself, it can be helpful to conclude a quantity contract directly, to have a buffer store set up at the supplier or to submit a binding forecast.

Step 3: Settlement

As part of the process, agreements are discussed within the previously negotiated framework agreement (quantities, dates, etc.).

The incoming goods are checked by the incoming goods department. The goods receipt posting is also made there. Purchasing is only used again in the event of a complaint. In the event of a defect, the incoming goods department issues a defect information and forwarded it directly to the operational purchasing department, which then takes over communication with the supplier. If the supplier has major problems, strategic purchasing is involved. It is advisable to work out the process flow and a RASIC chart meticulously in order to avoid internal disputes about responsibility. A document that describes good parts and bad parts, or a limit sample part, serves as a guide for incoming goods inspection. If you think it is all taken for granted and yesterday's news, then why not come and see your buyers and suppliers in Asia.

What could be improved at your department immediately without any expenses?

- Elaboration of schedules for the negotiation of framework supply contracts and RASICs.

Last but not least, we also have the three support processes of supplier management, purchasing controlling, and risk management.

Supplier Management

What is current standard situation in your company in Asia?

- *No active or passive supplier management (self-development) evident.*
- *Strategic decisions regarding the type and intensity of the relationship with a supplier aimed for in the future are not apparent.*

The classic process of supplier management consists of six stages, with the first stage being defined as part of the product group strategy. The second stage takes place in the core process. So, there are still four levels left (Fig. 5.5).

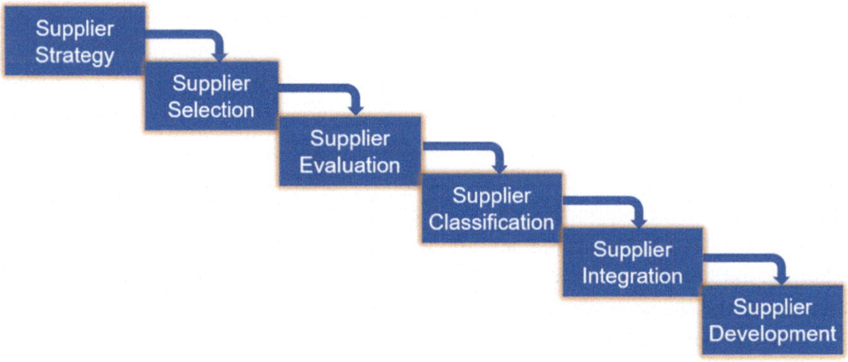

Fig. 5.5 Supplier management process. Source: "Grundlagen des Einkaufs", publisher "Bundesverbandes Materialwirtschaft, Einkauf und Logistik e.V. (BME)", page 19, 2016, author Judith Richard

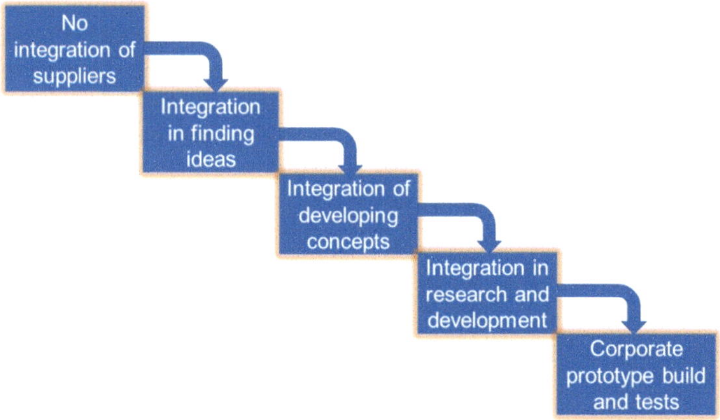

Fig. 5.6 Levels of supplier integration. Source: "Grundlagen des Einkaufs", publisher "Bundesverbandes Materialwirtschaft, Einkauf und Logistik e.V. (BME)", page 20, 2016, author Judith Richard

With the evaluation of the supplier, the performance and strengths and weaknesses of the suppliers are assessed. As a rule, the criteria of price, quality, and delivery date are assessed. Additional criteria can be, for example, management, service, ppm rate of the parts supplied, terms of payment, and the supplier's ability to innovate and potential. It should be specified in a RASIC that the supplier evaluation is not carried out by purchasing alone, but that the specialist department, quality department, and/or development should be involved. It is advisable to carry out the supplier evaluation at regular intervals (at least annually) and to communicate the results to the supplier. This gives him the opportunity to optimize individual criteria and improve his evaluation result.

Some customers have set up a supplier classification and classified each supplier in it. The classification enables the supplier to continuously question his performance, to improve it and accordingly to move up into a higher class. This increases his chances of further business relationships and lucrative orders.

After the classification, there is a 5-stage integration of the supplier into the company processes and procedures. Integrating suppliers into processes earlier is a strategic goal for many companies because, for example, there is insufficient know-how available in their own company or one would like to retain the supplier in the long term. The level of integration of suppliers, however, depends on the product to be procured. Common measures for integration are joint workshops or training courses for suppliers as well as a regular exchange between purchasing, quality assurance, and the supplier. In Asia, however, a deeper integration of the suppliers in the internal processes and procedures is coupled with the risk of loss of know-how and the dependence on the supplier (Fig. 5.6).

In the preparation of supplier development, strategic decisions must be made regarding the type and intensity of the relationship with a supplier that will be sought in the future.

Based on the results of the previous supplier evaluation and supplier classification, precise targets and measures are defined that are intended to improve the performance potential and cooperation with strategically important suppliers.

There are two options for supplier development. The supplier self-development is used as standard, i.e., the supplier is set goals that he has to achieve with self-developed measures. Contrastingly, there is active supplier development, in which measures are developed together with the supplier.

> What could be improved at your department immediately without any expenses?
>
> - Elaboration of a step-by-step plan with specifications and measures for each important supplier.

Purchasing Controlling

What is current standard situation in your company in Asia?

- *The contribution to the company's success is measured solely in terms of cost savings.*

In purchasing controlling, it is important to measure and record the contribution made by purchasing to the company's success. With the help of such a controlling system, measures are derived that serve to control, plan, and analyze purchasing activities. Purchasing controlling tasks include controlling internal and external processes, analyzing procurement potential, uncovering weak points, monitoring costs, or controlling profitability.

KPIs are regularly evaluated and analyzed. A target value should be defined for each key figure so that a target/actual analysis can be carried out and appropriate measures to achieve the target can be derived. The KPIs should be comprehensible and as easy to determine as possible. They should also be consistent to ensure comparability.

Appropriate reporting of the relevant key figures can convince consumers and management of the performance of the purchasing department and can thus also contribute to the self-marketing of the purchasing department.

> What could be improved at your department immediately without any expenses?
>
> - Elaboration and tracking of improvements in purchasing itself, not in Finance.

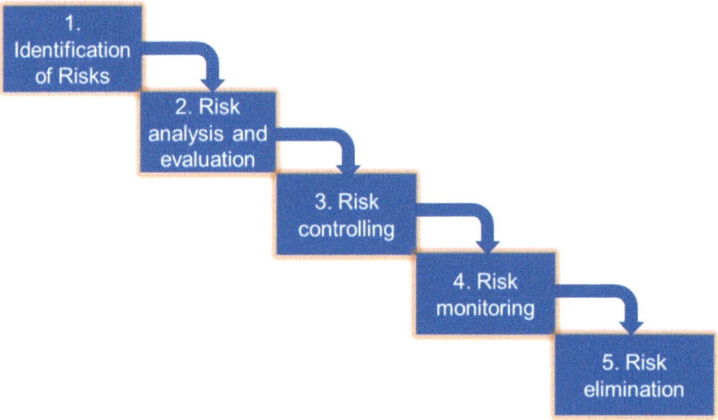

Fig. 5.7 Five steps in risk management. Source: "Grundlagen des Einkaufs", publisher "Bundesverbandes Materialwirtschaft, Einkauf und Logistik e.V. (BME)", page 22, 2016, author Judith Richard

Risk Management

What is current standard situation in your company in Asia?

Risks are discussed, hardly documented but not systematically processed.

Due to global procurement activities, increasing volatility, and complexity, there is an increased risk potential for companies. It is all the more important that purchasing establishes a suitable risk management system. The possible risks in purchasing are price risks, currency risks, quality risks, logistical risks, political risks, legal risks, default risks, financial risks, and environmental risks. One possible approach in risk management is divided into five levels (Fig. 5.7).

It is hardly possible to know all potential risks and to derive appropriate measures. However, in no case does it hurt to grapple with the topic and consider alternative suppliers and materials.

The most critical steps here are the identification and assessment of possible risks. Purchasing can use so-called risk checklists to identify risks, which are usually prepared for each product group and updated regularly. The aim is to identify relevant risks as early as possible. As part of the risk assessment, the probability of occurrence, and the extent of the damage are usually determined.

What could be improved at your department immediately without any expenses?

- Introduction of risk management in purchasing through checklists and the calculation of probabilities and the amount of damage

5.2.5 Do You Need a Supply Chain Manager?[16]

What is current standard situation in your company in Asia?

- *The general manager or president makes the decisions (immediately) if his/her direct reporting managers cannot come to an agreement among themselves.*

Supply chain managers play an important advisory role in the company and have to do a variety of things. They give purchasing, logistics, and sales valuable impulses so as to realize the desired corporate goals. The requirements range from the development of control systems to monitor the supply chain to the use of planning tools and the selection of the right distribution strategy. Supply chain managers are also involved in the strategic planning of all parts of the company so as to weigh up the effects of measures in one area on adjacent departments for the benefit of the company.

In order to be able to act across departments, our specialists should go through several stations along the entire value chain in the company. The manager understands the consequences of a decision for other departments.

Supply chain management (SCM) should include the areas of purchasing, logistics lean (possibly Six Sigma), and, if possible, operations (production). SCM is responsible for managing all of a company's working capital. Working capital includes the component inventory, accounts receivables, and accounts payables.

In order to establish or change existing structures and processes in advance, a dialogue should take place with all managers affected by changes in order to define and determine a route with all these people in a second step.

In order to account for the individual regions and their level of development, regional awards have been introduced, otherwise a less developed business unit would not be able to keep up with the process improvements of established business units, measured in absolute numbers. This regional incentive avoids direct global internal competition and demonstrably increases the motivation of all business units to start projects to improve or save costs.

Change cannot be achieved without trust and communication. Voluntariness and sharing of the best practices could thus be at least as important as savings.

Supply chain management refers to the establishment and administration of integrated logistics chains (material and information flows) over the entire value creation process, starting from the extraction of raw materials through the processing stages to the end consumer. The supply chain management therefore includes the organization and coordination of all tasks from customer acquisition/incoming orders to series production/delivery and coordinates all material, information, and cash flows.

[16]Das Berufsbild des "Supply Chain Managers," 1st edition, published 2013 by BMEnet GmbH, Bundesverband Materialwirtschaft, Einkauf und Logistik e.V.

The supply chain manager is a kind of adviser in the company who advises purchasing, logistics, and sales by showing them the best ways. It is crucial that no one makes a decision alone without knowing the complexity of the process in question. The previous silo thinking is thus broken by the modern supply chain manager. Total costs and effects of processes and decisions on other departments and company areas come to the fore.

Today, in which more and more people are acting in real time and processes have to run and be recorded in parallel globally, the supply chain manager therefore focuses on information technology, which provides exemplary answers to the following questions:

- What resources are available to the company?
- Where and in what quantity are which resources are currently located in storage locations?
- Are there any resources currently in transit?
- What effects does the current resource situation have on the fulfillment of the customer order?
- Can production be ensured?
- Will purchased components be ready for assembly on time?

The following example illustrates the need for timely communication with one another.

The sales department corrects its forecast for the sale of a good upwards due to a planned marketing campaign. What effects does this have on the other processes?

Are there enough materials in stock, or do (partial) components or raw/auxiliary/operating materials (RHB) have to be purchased? Can the machines operate at a higher capacity? Can the additionally produced units be transported away, or have the negotiated freight quantities been exhausted?

It is not primarily about the supply chain manager controlling all processes himself, but rather working together with related areas such as logistics, purchasing, sales, marketing, and production.

Successful SCM is trustworthy, assertive, competent, and capable of working in a team. You negotiate skillfully, have social skills, are creative, have self-confidence, and have a strong will.

New processes and changing competence matrices can either be arranged top-down through the hierarchy or initiated through pilot projects. Successful pilot projects can then be transferred to other and similar processes as a showcase model. Employees should be carried away by success.

First and foremost are the customer and his order. This is followed by planning how the customer order can best be processed. What has to be procured so as to produce and ultimately deliver the desired product? How is it delivered?

In order to be able to manufacture the product desired by the customer or the quantities forecast by sales, a large number of (pre)products and services must be purchased. The responsibility for this still rests with the purchasing department but not with the supply chain manager.

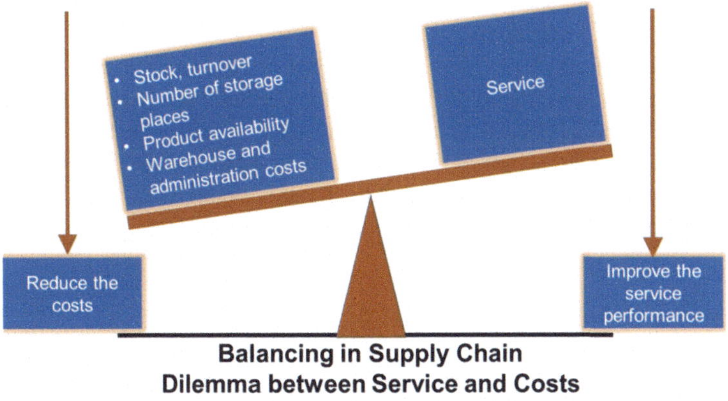

Fig. 5.8 Balancing the supply chain. Source: "Das Berufsbild des Supply Chain Managers", 1. edition, publisher "Bundesverbandes Materialwirtschaft, Einkauf und Logistik e.V. (BME)", page 19, 2013, author Peter Widany, Osram GmbH

For example, should a specific product be purchased that has a higher purchase price in Germany than in China. Where is it cheapest to buy? Aspects such as insurance, packaging, customs, capital commitment due to long transport times and the associated loss of interest, flexibility through fast delivery, product quality, and country risks must be taken into account in the decision in which country the goods are to be procured.

Processes that directly affect day-to-day operations remain in the decision-making power of the relevant specialist department. The logistics department decides on the transport of the goods to the customer with a view to product-specific requirements. Most of the processes associated with delivering the product to the customer are the responsibility of logistics. Purchasing is involved in monitoring. Goods tracking and delivery reliability control are also part of supplier management, which is part of purchasing. However, if purchasing and logistics have conflicts of interest, which the supply chain manager then has to resolve here by observing the overall process. The same applies to production. Production takes over the preparation of the machine allocation plan. However, in inventory management, the supply chain manager should be integrated if changes in inventory in warehouses and in transit to production are discussed.

Supply chain management is included in the strategic planning of all areas in order to consider the effects of measures in a specific area on adjacent areas and to guarantee optimal processes for the company (Fig. 5.8).

Capacity and demand planning is one of the key issues of the supply chain manager. This should be done in close coordination with the sales/marketing managers who carry out the annual planning. On the basis of annual sales planning, the flow of goods is then optimally coordinated in order, for example, to reduce inventory costs.

By streamlining the inventory, the area of "flexibility" is increased. This can be achieved, for example, by discarding products that show little or no movement ("no mover"), parameter maintenance according to replenishment times, sales campaigns for "slow movers" with corresponding volumes ("slow mover"), revising the product range, and reducing complexity.

The SC manager checks the individual stages of the external material flow and adjusts them to the requirements of the internal material flows. The importance of the SC manager is comparable to that of a conductor of an orchestra. A successful masterpiece can only be achieved through a clearly defined sequence of a conglomerate of individual actors in harmony with the conductors if the conductor exerts specific influence through leading and controlling actions.

What could be improved at your department immediately without any expenses?

- Introduction of a supply chain director who takes over the role of GM/VP/ president and can use his detailed knowledge to make better decisions for the benefit of the company.

Below are some ideas about the tasks the new supply chain director has and how he can master them.

Supplier Management

Procurement as part of the supply chain has increasing importance in generating competitive advantages in recent years. Supplier management is a process-oriented, systematic approach to continuously optimizing the performance of suppliers and can be broken down into strategic and operational supplier management. As a result of reduced performance levels and global procurement markets, the task in supplier management has changed fundamentally. It is to be understood as the optimization of all buyer–supplier relationships along the entire value chain across all processes. This applies to direct and indirect procurement. Risk analysis is also an important part of supplier management because the latter must also deal with the recording of strategic and operational risks due to the increasing complexity and dynamics.

Before the suppliers are analyzed and evaluated, the materials should be clustered according to their value, i.e., procurement volume and supply risk. This results in a portfolio of goods to be procured. Such a classification can also be made for suppliers, whereby a portfolio of procurement sources is derived. Risk factors such as product substitution options, the technical complexity of the product, and the number of potential suppliers must be taken into account.

Particular attention should be paid to the procurement source "Strategic Material/ Strategic Supplier." It is particularly worthwhile to develop a supplier toward a strategic, partnership-based cooperation. The close cooperation with suppliers should be emphasized, particularly when it comes to important components so as to react flexibly at short notice. Supply chain management should promote cooperation with strategically important suppliers, also with a view to the joint development of components into systems. Complete solutions frequently offer the customer many advantages. When assembling entire systems instead of many individual components, a lot of time can be saved. It facilitates a more flexible response to customer requests and assembly costs can be saved.

Uniform criteria should be defined and the results communicated to the supplier, particularly when evaluating suppliers. Communication and collaboration can improve results on both sides. It is important that all departments are included in the assessment of the supplier. For example, a sheet with various criteria can be presented to those responsible from purchasing, logistics, etc., who are then assessed with a point system. The task of the supply chain manager is to ensure these evaluations, to schedule a meeting with all the people involved, and to bring about a joint evaluation.

The following graphic illustrates an evaluation as an example. The procedure is also called a gap analysis.

Customer Management

If the market demand forecast is poor, an article would not be produced in accordance with actual customer requirements. The article ordered by the customer is not available due to the poor forecast and the customer can only be partially supplied or not at all. This results in poor delivery service because the customer could not be satisfied. This pushes the importance of this key figure "delivery service" into the foreground and makes the connection to other processes and key figures clear. Flexible control of the production locations enables the delivery service to be ensured even in the event of deviations from the forecast, for example, through flexible use of production capacities due to largely homogeneous products or flexible expansion of production capacities. It is up to the supply chain manager to see these connections and to assess the consequences and effects of actions on adjacent areas. In a subsequent step, the supply chain manager takes suitable measures in cooperation with everyone involved in the process (Fig. 5.9).

Furthermore, customer behavior should be analyzed if there are strong fluctuations in ordering behavior. Knowledge of the customer's advertising measures is expedient and prevents the bullwhip effect. This describes the phenomenon that orders from the supplier tend to fluctuate more than sales to the customer and thus deviate from demand and that this deviation builds up in the upstream direction of the supply chain, i.e., the fluctuation increases toward the origin of the supply chain.

The problem is often that such information about the customer's advertising efforts is known to the sales department, but not to the demand manager. Effects on raw/auxiliary/operating materials, packaging, and transport are only recognized with a delay. Communication—both externally with customers and internally with other departments such as sales—has proven to be the key to increasing reliable and well-founded forecast accuracy, which is ensured by the supply chain manager.

In the automotive industry, delivery reliability is in the foreground through concepts such as just in time, and even more so through the delivery of several components precisely in time to production by just in sequence. Delays due to the availability of goods or delays in delivery are often associated with high contractual

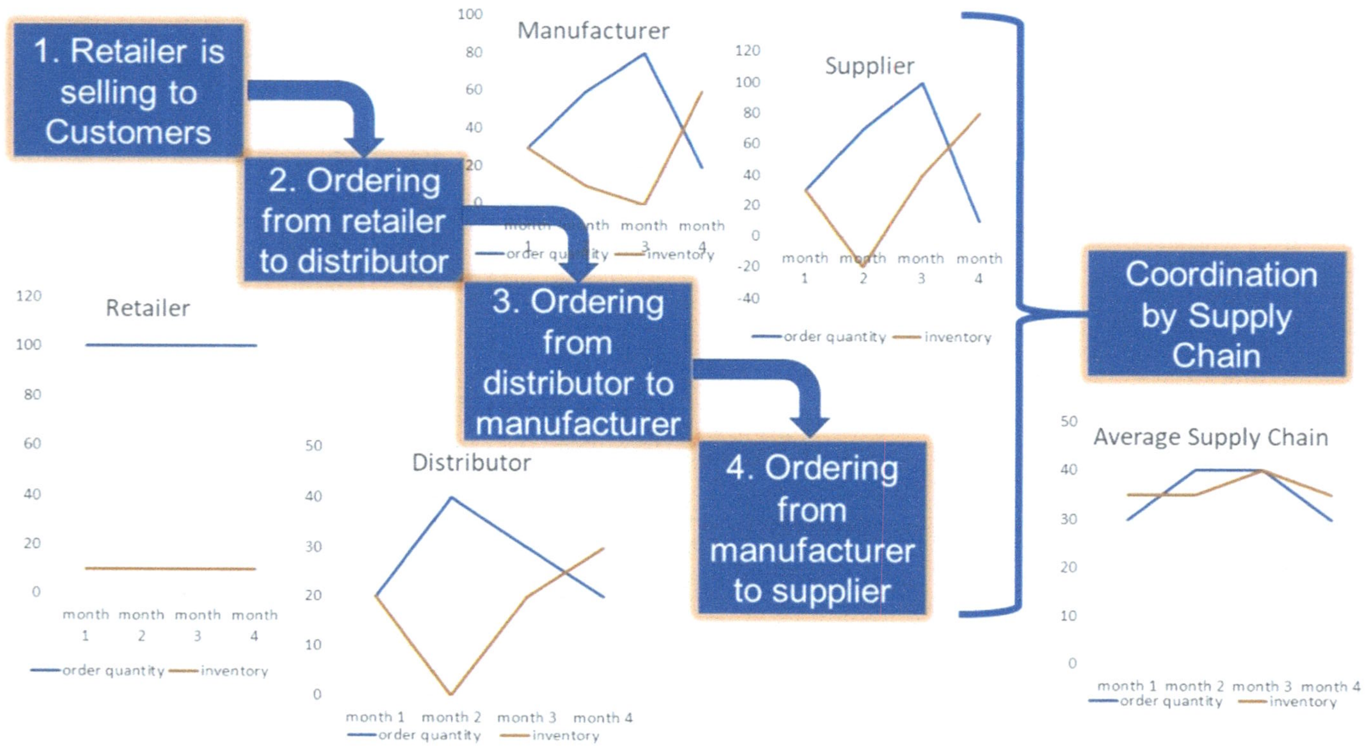

Fig. 5.9 Bullwhip-effect. Source: "Das Berufsbild des Supply Chain Managers", 1. edition, publisher "Bundesverbandes Materialwirtschaft, Einkauf und Logistik e.V. (BME)", page 42, 2013

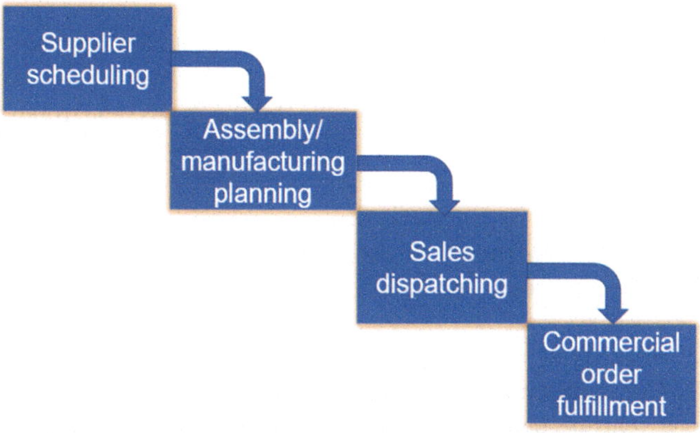

Fig. 5.10 Example of a cross-functional order-to-delivery process. Source: "Das Berufsbild des Supply Chain Managers", 1. edition, publisher "Bundesverbandes Materialwirtschaft, Einkauf und Logistik e.V. (BME)", page 44, 2013. Author Pascal Männche, Deutz AG

penalties. On time in full, i.e., 100% availability of goods and 100% adherence to delivery dates are important key performance indicators here.

The "Order-to-Delivery" Process

The order-to-delivery process is one of the core processes in supply chain management. It is about the holistic view from the order acceptance to the final delivery. Experience has shown that overall responsibility for the process should lie in one hand. Anyone who gives the customer promises regarding quantities and dates should at least have the planning opportunity to influence and fulfill them (see Fig. 5.10)

In companies that are organized strictly according to their functions, these subprocesses are assigned to different areas of responsibility; for example, the commercial order processing to the sales department, the assembly/manufacturing planning of the production, or the material disposition to the purchasing department. Only the management has overall responsibility for this process. We often hear sayings such as "The production doesn't produce what the customer has ordered," "The customer doesn't call up what we have produced," and "The suppliers should always deliver at short notice what we never had in forecast."

Last but not least, the purchased parts make up more than 60% of the total product costs in our company. It is therefore important that supply chain management deals with the "total cost of ownership" approach. It is a matter of taking other detailed costs into account in addition to the unit costs:

- Logistics (transport, packaging, customs, insurance, port fees, repackaging costs), taxes, and opportunity costs (quality, failure risks, lost interest effects due to long delivery times, brokerage costs).
- Increased storage costs due to larger purchase quantities or inventory increase (capital tie-up costs, renting additional storage facilities)
- Costs for auditing of suppliers and quality assurance

- Costs for delayed delivery (contractual penalties, production stop)
- Airfreight costs to cover short-term fluctuations in customer demand.

The supply chain manager is responsible for costs, system robustness, and flexibility.

Project-Based Process Optimization

The supply chain manager should ensure the competitiveness of a company in the long term by reducing costs, increasing quality, and reducing throughput times (Fig. 5.11).

The issue of acceptance among employees and their motivation also plays a decisive role. Due to different interests, this can be a major challenge for the supply chain manager. On the one hand, he has to monitor the process, analyze it, and redesign it optimally, on the other hand, predict the future. A permanent competitive advantage cannot be guaranteed without regular review of the processes. Various methods and tools such as Kanban and lean management can have a supportive effect.

Process optimization should not be purely about financial optimization but also about increasing employee and customer satisfaction and ergonomics. Uniform and consistent signage for the warehouses enables, for example, visual guidance through the warehouse like at an airport. The signage in both German and English led to more structure, order, and better orientation but also to more well-being for the employees. Although this measure has no influence on productivity, it increases soft factors such as employee satisfaction.

What are the reasons, but if a process is not followed? Instead of living best practices, processes are changed or even circumvented. Possible triggers can be self-interest, ignorance, technological complexity, and vanity. If employees undermine

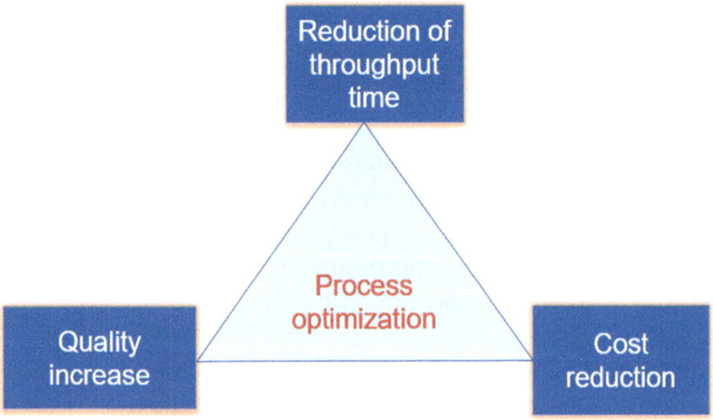

Fig. 5.11 How to ensure competitiveness. Source: "Das Berufsbild des Supply Chain Managers", 1. edition, publisher "Bundesverbandes Materialwirtschaft, Einkauf und Logistik e.V. (BME)", page 46, 2013. Author Gunnar Gburek

or disrupt a project or process, that employee must be transferred or, as a last resort, terminated. If there is no discipline, written rules are not followed.

However, responsibilities must be clearly defined. These definitions should be checked regularly to ensure that they are up to date and meaningful and, if necessary, adapted to the current processes in order to prevent responsibilities from becoming independent.

The trend is that companies have to react flexibly and quickly to orders. Many processes are described in a manual, but the processes are not lived accordingly. Processes should be shown in writing, but lived according to the 80/20 rule. Eighty percent consists of strict adherence to the processes specified in the manual, coupled with 20% in flexible design so as to react to changes and requirements accordingly, so that the company does not lose its competitiveness.

Furthermore, the company must learn to be quick in order processing. A company should not be driven by actions, but by processes. In addition to increasing customer orientation, processes should be optimized for cost reasons alone. It should be borne in mind that processes are gradual, accepted by everyone, and have to be driven by management over the long term.

In the case of new products and complaints, it is necessary to define and determine successes across departments (purchasing together with laboratory or incoming goods) and thus together with all departments involved in the process. Subsequent to this coordination, the entire process is shown as a flowchart and underlaid with a time window, RASICS, and job descriptions are put in place.

In order to promote the success of the projects or the taking of initiatives, a top-down approach can be expedient. The managing director or the CIP manager initiates processes or issue guidelines.

Initiated and implemented projects can also be given an additional bonus. During the "introductory/test phase," the bonus should not exceed a certain percentage. The bonus can increase with increasing experience and transparent exchange between all project managers.

Consultants can be brought in at the strategic level for concept development in order to receive input from outside. This decision can ensure that the concept is easily accepted in the company, as it was not thought up by the superior and communicated top-down but was introduced by a neutral person.

Pilot projects are carried out in selected locations. First of all, locations are selected in which the management has a very positive attitude toward the project. As a lighthouse location, further locations are to be won for the project. Communication is important. All employees will be involved in the projects. The current process understanding and ideas for improvement are collected on flip charts, blackboards, or only in PDCA lists. A new standardized process is then jointly defined from the results of all teams.

Dealing with employees and motivating them are therefore more important than simply looking at the technical competence that can be imparted with relative ease through training. The project stands and falls with the management style.

Regular meetings of all managers serve to exchange information about implemented initiatives, the status of projects in the process, and the discussion of the further strategy. In the long term, these results can be transparently viewed by all teams in order to promote the exchange of ideas for improvement, potentials, best practices, and approaches.

5.3 Checklist for Best-in-Class Buyers

Following please find best-in-class evaluation at purchasing/supply chain department, based on following activities. Please mark and follow up your progress according to PDCA steps.

Best-in-class activities	Not done yet	Partially done	Realized
Purchasing assumes responsibility for more than 90% of the total procurement volume			
Indirect purchasing is responsible for, e.g., travel, consulting, or marketing services			
Strategies are jointly defined for almost all procurement categories as to how costs can be reduced			
The hybrid form of organization (local buyers and global lead buyers) in connection with project purchasing and commodity group management is established			
The automation of the ordering and billing process in connection with the standardization of requirements is realized			
Our number of articles and suppliers is also only half as high as the average. This enables us to reduce costs by 30–50%			
We regularly carry out supplier evaluations. In recent years, this has enabled the supplier base to be optimized			
We operate on the principle of "one article–one supplier" and manage the risk through a good supplier relationship			
We regularly take part in analyses and statistical market evaluations and thus gain a clear lead over the competition			
Purchasing costs in % of the purchasing volume. Best KPI: 0.65–0.90			
Number of purchase orders per buyer. Best KPI: 2258			
Number of FTEs that procure material and services per I billion USD revenue. Best KPI: 14.8 staff			
Introduction of a few sensible KPIs and the comparison of the services with selected partners			
Restructuring for future challenges in procurement management and supply chain			
Increased value due to the assumption of all operational and strategic activities in the context of the procurement of materials, goods, operating resources, and services			

(continued)

Best-in-class activities	Not done yet	Partially done	Realized
The task of procurement is to work with the supplier to ensure the availability and required properties of the procurement objects for the company, with execution and planning being closely interwoven			
Regular subject-specific training and workshops to share experiences			
Procurement management and supply chain management			
Abolition of maverick buying and concentration of all important purchasing activities in purchasing			
Installation of strategic, value-added-oriented purchasing in DM and IM (including logistics)			
Purchasing is viewed as a success factor with a focus on strategic activities			
There is also a rethinking toward process orientation, which is supported by the creation of lean and digital processes			
Differentiation of project and series purchasing through differentiated JD, which increases the qualification in purchasing and ensures more reputation and importance in value creation			
Establishment of a hybrid purchasing organization with dotted line to BU buyers and lead buyers and transparency of names and RASICs			
Investigation and development of modular sourcing with strategic partners, which must be developed in order to avoid loss of know-how and high dependency			
Procurement market research can also be used to investigate which parts or modules could be purchased cheaply in neighboring countries around China, starting as a bottleneck supplier			
Discussions with the VP, R & D, sales director, and other internal customers are combined into a purchasing strategy and designed flexibly for adjustments over time. All articles are grouped based on common characteristics, which show a benefit for purchasing			
Classification of all purchased goods into the areas important/difficult to buy. From this, four different commodity group strategies are developed in cooperation with the suppliers			
Procurement is handed over to a service provider, who fills up the office materials, fasteners, and supplies on the shop floor independently			
Objective evaluation of all suppliers with a predefined question–answer matrix (similar to an audit) before the conclusion of a contract is absolutely necessary			
Elaboration of schedules for the negotiation of framework supply contracts and RASICs.			

(continued)

Best-in-class activities	Not done yet	Partially done	Realized
Elaboration of a step-by-step plan with specifications and measures for each important supplier			
Elaboration and tracking of improvements in purchasing itself, not in finance			
Introduction of risk management in purchasing through checklists and calculation of probabilities and the amount of damage			
Introduction of a supply chain director who takes over the role of VP and can use his detailed knowledge to make better decisions for the benefit of the company			
Do you have strategies for suppliers and material to reduce risks, and if yes, do you use SWOT analysis?			
Do you have a SWOT result of strength and weaknesses of purchasing department?			
Do you have a SWOT result of strength and weaknesses of regions and suppliers?			
Did you build a supply risk management by evaluation of risks at delivery, processes, sourcing, and enterprises?			
Do you have a digitalization and automation concept for Purchasing 4.0? For example, IT solution to reduce time and expenses for suppliers and PUR, purchase-to-pay, business analytic tool?			

5.4 The Best Websites for Buyers

5.4.1 Websites with Asian Products

Most purchaser would not buy raw material from China, but products instead.

For the importation of industrial products to European Union or other countries, safety regulations are necessary. You also need to know all the quality regulations, the national regulations, and all the documentation that is required for most industrial and/or customized products.

Some examples:

- CE mark on the product unit, its packaging, and user manual
- Mechanical and electrical regulations as required for each type of product.
- Declarations of conformity and technical documentation. Design and drawings, materials, risk assessment.
- ISO regulations

It is very important to check the warranty terms before purchasing products to avoid disappointment. That is why it is highly recommended to have purchasing agents for industrial products in China with experience, like www.gtec.asia or others. Being able to store spare parts in your location is often a good strategy to avoid delivery charges and shipping costs for damaged parts or products back to China.

When a customer wants to manufacture in and import industrial products from China, quality inspections are one of the most important steps. These must also be accompanied by the quality requirements for shipping. Carrying out quality controls comparing Chinese products with products produced in the importing country is crucial for any company wanting to import.

Quality controls will not only offer the greatest guarantee of the final product but also avoid significant financial loss should it be necessary to return a product to the country of origin. This is the best-case scenario providing the Chinese Custom Authorities to allow the return of the products.[17]

Importing or manufacturing products in China requires rigorous planning. Identifying trusted suppliers or manufacturers must also be done on-site and at the start of any production project to ensure success. It is not enough to know the supplier, instead knowing and identifying the whole process from beginning to end, is important as well.

Other important points to consider when importing industrial products from China are, for example:

- Negotiation of services and deals in the Chinese language
- Reviewing documentation and contracts
- Controlling of international documentation
- Importation licenses[18]

5.4.2 China

Most common Chinese shopping websites *that ship to the USA and Europe are for industry*[19]:

www.alibaba.com: As the world's largest b2b sourcing portal, usually it is the first website people turn to when searching for products in China. The range of suppliers and products is very comprehensive. Be careful, the website has counterfeits. Other issues include dodgy supplier verifications and scams.

---

[17] Source: https://www.groups3.com/importing-industrial-products-from-china/, published 2019, author S^3 Strategic Sourcing Solutions Group, Barcelona (Spain), access date 25.2.2021.

[18] Source: https://www.groups3.com/about-us, published 2019, author S^3 Strategic Sourcing Solutions Group, Barcelona (Spain), access date 25.2.2021.

[19] Source: https://www.chinacheckup.com/blogs/articles/china-sourcing-websites, author Matt Slater, published September 13, 2017, access date 25.2.2021.

globalsources.com: Their regular Hong Kong trade shows are very popular and help facilitate international companies to do sourcing in China face to face with trusted Chinese suppliers.

made-in-china.com: This website is a third-party platform for connecting buyers with Chinese suppliers and features a clean layout, which is easy to navigate. Similar to Alibaba.com, Chinese suppliers can create their own homepage on Made-in-China, which includes their company profile, introduction, and product listings.

en.china.cn: This website is owned by state-owned information office and connects global buyers and China suppliers. It is a useful website featuring many Chinese suppliers and products.

en.ofweek.com: This industrial b2b marketplace is specialized in high-tech and electronics, and Shenzhen-based OFweek is a well-designed website featuring many Chinese suppliers.

hktdc.com: Operated by the Hong Kong Trade Development Council, this website helped Hong Kong companies to establish relationships with buyers from around the world. Hong Kong companies operate factories in Mainland China and this is a good gateway to sourcing their products.

diytrade.com: It is a clean and easy-to-use global b2b trading platform, featuring over five million products across a wide range of industries from underwear to ball bearings.

ecvv.com: It is a bridge builder that empowers merchants to easily connect and do business. It is recommended by the Shenzhen Government and American International Business Council.

ec21.com: This Korea-based global b2b marketplace is one of the leading websites for Chinese manufacturers looking for international buyers.

ecplaza.net: Another South Korea-based platform features a large number of Chinese suppliers on their easy to navigate website.

globalmarket.com: This platform heavily promotes its GMC (Global Manufacturer Certificate) with reputable Chinese suppliers, which claim to be genuine manufacturers, definitely worth to have a look.

tradekey.com: Although a global sourcing website with headquarters in Saudi Arabia and offices in Guangzhou, Shanghai, and Beijing, tradekey has a strong Chinese presence. Website with both ISO 9001 and ISO 27001 certifications contains a hive of China sourcing information.

asianproducts.com: This website focuses on suppliers from Taiwan and China and has useful source of information with plenty of companies listed.

manufacturers.com.tw: This platform contains Taiwanese and Chinese manufacturers and focuses on industrial equipment.

yiwugo.com: The world's largest small commodity wholesale market—Yiwu International Trade Market, offers their physical stores an online presence, worth to have a look if you are planning a visit Yiwu.

taiwantrade.com: Many factories in China are operated by Taiwanese companies. Using this platform can be a great way of locating them. It is useful for finding made-in-Taiwan products, too.

Follow Chinese shopping sites are great for cheap electronics, basic clothing, and items for around the home:

AliExpress: Unlike Amazon, AliExpress does not sell any products itself. Instead, it is an e-commerce platform; it connects you with third-party sellers. It is widely used for companies looking to buy with low MOQs. Many vendors offer free shipping, but deliveries will take longer to arrive. You can also use DHL, UPS, FedEx, and other international couriers, depending on the seller.

Banggood: It is the best sites for buying cheap electronics. Although electronics are the site's main focus, you will also find sports equipment, fashion accessories, jewellery, and health products. Free deliveries abroad can take months, not weeks.

Gearbest: The site has close ties with Chinese smartphone manufacturer Xiaomi and offers much better deals on the company's products than you would be able to find in a domestic store. Other categories that the site covers include Baby and Kids, Home and Garden, Appliances, and Electrical and Tools. The price of the fastest option—expedited—is calculated by weight. It takes 3–7 days.

DHgate: It is primarily a fashion site. If you are looking for cheap shoes, wedding outfits, watches, hair and grooming products, or bags, DHgate should be your first port of call. DHL should get your order to you within a week. Some of the lesser-known carriers such as China Post Air and Singapore Post can take more than a month.

YesStyle: YesStyle sells menswear, womenswear, childrenswear, and lifestyle products. You will find everything from maternity clothes to cosplay outfits. They are predominantly Japanese and Korean labels. People who have a particular fondness for fashion in Japan and Korea will like the site; it has sections dedicated to the latest looks in each country.

LightInTheBox: It sells products across three core categories: clothing, small gadgets, and home and garden. The company has gone from strength to strength. In 2013, it is even listed on the New York Stock Exchange. You can choose from several shipping options, all of which will be charged by weight. As a courier, LightInTheBox offers DHL, UPS, FedEx, and TNT.

Shein: It specializes in women's fashion, though there are also some menswear and children's products available. Standard shipping costs $3.99 per order. If your order exceeds $49, shipping is free. Express shipping costs $12.90 but is free on orders above $99.

Geekbuying: As an electronics store, you will find Android phones, streaming boxes, wearables, smart security systems, tablets, and more. Like Gearbest, it offers exclusive rates on Xiaomi smartphones. The site also has some "fun" electronics. For example, there is a section dedicated to remote control cars and another dedicated to electric scooters. Shipping is free if you use standard delivery. DHL and TNT are also available.

RCMoment: This website has a very specific focus on remote-controlled devices. You will find gadgets like drones, cars, boats, planes, and robots.

DealeXtreme: Almost all the products are electronic. The breadth of products is impressive; you will find everything from glucose monitors to tattoo guns. The site also sells a lot of branded products. There are devices from SanDisk, Lenovo, Sony,

Asus, and more. This website offers free worldwide shipping on all its items, but you can ship express with couriers for an added fee.[20]

Other online shopping stores you will find at http://www.shops-in-china.com/

5.4.3 Asia

www.china.org.cn (reporting on events in China, e.g., economy)
www.tradebig.com (Chinese supplier directory and bulletin board)
www.chinawuliu.com.cn (China Federation of Logistics and Purchasing, China Logistics Society)
www.indo-german.com (https://indien.ahk.de, German-Indian Chamber of Commerce)

5.4.4 East Europe

www.materialcost.com (system manufacturer with production facilities in Austria, Bosnia, and Slovakia)

5.4.5 Global

www.alibaba.com (trade board for placing a worldwide supplier application. Enter an email address for feedback)[21]
https://www.practicalecommerce.com/15-Marketplaces-for-Handmade-Goods (online auction marketplace for craft orders. The placing of orders is free of charge, and the contractor pays a commission, depending on the order value).
www.payscale.com (salary data and career research center)
www.linkedin.com (with three million users the largest business network on the Internet)
https://spotcargohub.com/en/ (spot price management for industry and freight forwarders. Exchange transport enquiries and offers quickly, easily, and transparently online)
www.kartonagen.de (manufacturer and dealer)
www.blumenbecker.com (webshop for industrial technology, tools, and welding technology)
www.hug-technik.com (wholesale of maintenance products, material tables, and conversion factors)

[20] Source: https://www.makeuseof.com/tag/chinese-shopping-sites-ship-us/, author Dan Price, published March 17, 2020, access date 26.2.2021.

[21] Source: "Einkaufsmanager"/October 2005, page 3–12, Fachverlag für Einkaufswissen, Verlag der Deutschen Wirtschaft AG.

www.industrystock.com (network for sale of machines, industrial machinery, and industrial goods)
https://icm-chemnitz.de/netzwerke/ (e.g., interest group of companies to form purchasing pools for C positions)
www.strauss-advisor.de (purchasing service provider; fee only if successful)
https://www.plasticsnews.com/ (manufacturing processes, prices, directory)
http://metalprices.com (https://www.argusmedia.com/en/metals; products, methodology)
https://psytech.com/ (assessment products and solutions to maximize your workplace performance)

5.5 Useful Cost Reduction Tracking Templates

Check your available templates for the SC manager's work (Purchasing PUR + Logistic LOG + Supplier Quality SQ + Supplier Development SD + Quality Control QC):

1. A template for signing quality gates I and 2 by ECOCUT power user/experts, managers, and calculators
2. A template for generating useful figures for calculations and knowledge domain, e.g., the costs of die casting, the smelting process, the die casting scrap rate, and the tooling maintenance for die casting
3. A template for determining which country is the best in labor cost, energy cost, etc., such as which country has the highest/lowest labor cost, and energy costs.
4. A template for negotiations in different situations and countries (supplier questions/comments; buyer answers, e.g., killer arguments/stupid phrases and buyer response)
5. A template for a flip chart explanation of cost structure analysis, e.g., how to calculate the machine's hourly rate and manufacturing overhead costs
6. A part calculation template for recording in Excel (rough, detailed)
7. A template for preselection of suppliers, proposal project allocation template, benchmark supplier survey, and project allocation (ask PT Malaysia for details)
8. ABC product table (Excel)
9. Acetone contract (Word)
10. Benchmark table (Excel)
11. Buyer competence list (Excel)
12. Company chop procedure (Word)
13. Cost breakdown template (Excel)
14. Forecast of products (Excel)
15. Historic list of quality issues and solutions (Excel)
16. Monthly reporting (Excel or PowerPoint)
17. Monthly and quarterly meetings (Excel)
18. Newsletter/purchasing homepage
19. OT application form (Excel)

20. PPV funnel tracking for BOM and non-BOM (Excel)
21. Price tracking (Excel)
22. Review agenda (Word or Excel)
23. Saving Tracking (Excel)
24. SC action list (Excel)
25. SC audit for QM (Word or Excel)
26. SC employee interview evaluation sheet (Excel)
27. SC employee list
28. SC employee suggestion (Word or Excel)
29. Scrap metal contract (Word)
30. Security contract (Word)
31. Shipping plan (Excel)
32. Stationary application (Excel)
33. Supplier evaluation sheet (Excel)
34. Supplier claims ranking (Excel, PPT)
35. Supplier OTD list
36. Supplier scorecard sheet
37. Supplier WIP
38. WCP (warranty claim payment)
39. WPM (weak point management) action plan level 1

5.6 Personnel Development Plan for Supply Chain Staff

According to your personal job description, you will be part of a qualification matrix, where you see yourself which kind of knowledge you need to fulfill your job performance, which your bosses expect from you.

Ask your boss to get a list of trainings that are part of this qualification matrix. Do you have questions about your current tasks? Are you looking for solutions to problems or further information on a specific topic?

In the following, we have compiled some frequently used checklists for your department. The information you obtain will help you in increasing your performance and job satisfaction!

NPM (Nonproduction Material)

1. NPM basics training English/Chinese (company procedures and attachments, cost-saving template)
2. Negotiation basics for NPM (workflow, training plan, template price comparison/benchmark)
3. Personal and company KPIs, status reports
4. ERP input and statistics
5. Templates
6. NPM processes and documents
7. Networking

Purchasing and Logistical Efficiency for the Project Buyer and Series Buyer
We must all be aware of the following items so that we can work together and achieve our goals. These points are arranged alphabetically but could also be set according to your priorities.

1. *Centralization of procurement*: As a strategy for more efficiency in purchasing
2. *Creating a purchasing manual*: Communication of the purchasing strategy to the employees
3. *Early involvement of the awarding or procuring body*: For purchasing efficiency
4. *Formation of cross-functional teams*: Gathering know-how in the project team
5. *Impact and sensitivity analyses*: Elasticity of indicators
6. *Internal communication in the procurement process*: Involvement of internal stakeholders in the process
7. *Product group management Product group dossier*: Information for beginners for the introduction of product group management
8. *Purchasing strategy*: For innovative procurement
   (a) *Amortization calculation/break-even analysis*: When does my investment pay off?
   (b) Benchmarking: Learning from the best
   (c) *Creating a supplier pyramid by ABC analysis*: For example, to classify suppliers
   (d) *Evaluation and scoring procedures*: For example, as a decision-making aid for supplier selection
9. *Reference process purchasing*: The overview of core, strategy, and support processes
10. *SWOT analysis*: Strengths and weaknesses, opportunities, and risks

Supplier Quality Engineer (SQE)
Following you will find the basic requirements in knowledge for solving supplier quality tasks, for example:

1. Supplier evaluation: ensuring a uniform approach to comparability
2. APQP
3. Project management phases 0–4
4. VDA 6.3/VDA2 2020
5. IATF/ISO TS 16949
6. ISO 9001: 2015
7. Potential failure mode and effect analysis (PFMEA)
8. Production part approval process (PPAP)
9. Statistical process control SPC
10. Quality manual/supplier quality manual
11. IMDS

Supplier Development (SD)

The following lists the basic requirements for dealing with supplier tasks. For example:

1. The fundamentals of cost structure analysis
2. Eight wastes of the company's profit
3. Root cause analysis with five why for effective problem-solving
4. MES manufacturing execution system
5. Special manufacturing process: molds/plastic injection
6. Special manufacturing process: casting/die casting
7. Special manufacturing process: MIM
8. Special manufacturing process: machining
9. Special manufacturing process: stamping/deep drawing
10. Special manufacturing process: coating
11. Special manufacturing process: heat treatment
12. Special manufacturing process: plating
13. Special manufacturing process: soldering
14. Special manufacturing process: welding
15. Special manufacturing process: PCBA
16. Special manufacturing process: LED
17. Special manufacturing process: recycling
18. Supplier management process guideline
19. Electric battery systems
20. Electric vehicles
21. Die and mold tooling
22. Lean manufacturing and Six Sigma
23. Toyota production system TPS

5.7 Introduction of Digitalization at Purchasing in Asia

How to implement E-purchasing solutions, to reduce manual workload, and to reduce admin work? Target is to reduce time and costs for transactions, to be compliant and transparent of suppliers, market development and risks at the same time. A digitalization roadmap at PUR is needed, starting with standardization and automation of processes, as well as transparent networking with suppliers. This could be done by following actions, for example:

- Electronic/digital RFQs, E-auctions, robotic process automation
- workflow systems like Procure2Pay (e.g., www.kissflow.com/procurement/, www.sgh-asia.vn/purchase-to-pay-p2p/), Source2Settle, digital supply and contract management, knowledge management/databases, and cognitive procurement. Cognitive procurement provides the insights at the right time giving

enough time to take corrective action. The solution proactively flags incidents or mavericks based on some odd spend behavior.[22]
- Electronic catalog management, E-sourcing, common cooperative platforms, source-to-pay processes, and connection of e-tools to ERP system.

No doubt, there are already a lot of possibilities to optimize a commodity group by digitalization. Another solution is to structure and to use information by database and by a ticket tool system (like IT dealing with customers).

How to come from current process of missing digitalization to optimized integrated digitalization by this ticket tool system?

From current status to future of integrated digitalization (see Fig. 5.12).

[22] Source: https://digitate.com/ignio-cognitive-procurement/, issued 2021 by Tata Consultancy Services Limited, 2021 Santa Clara, CA 95054 USA. Access date 30.5.2021.

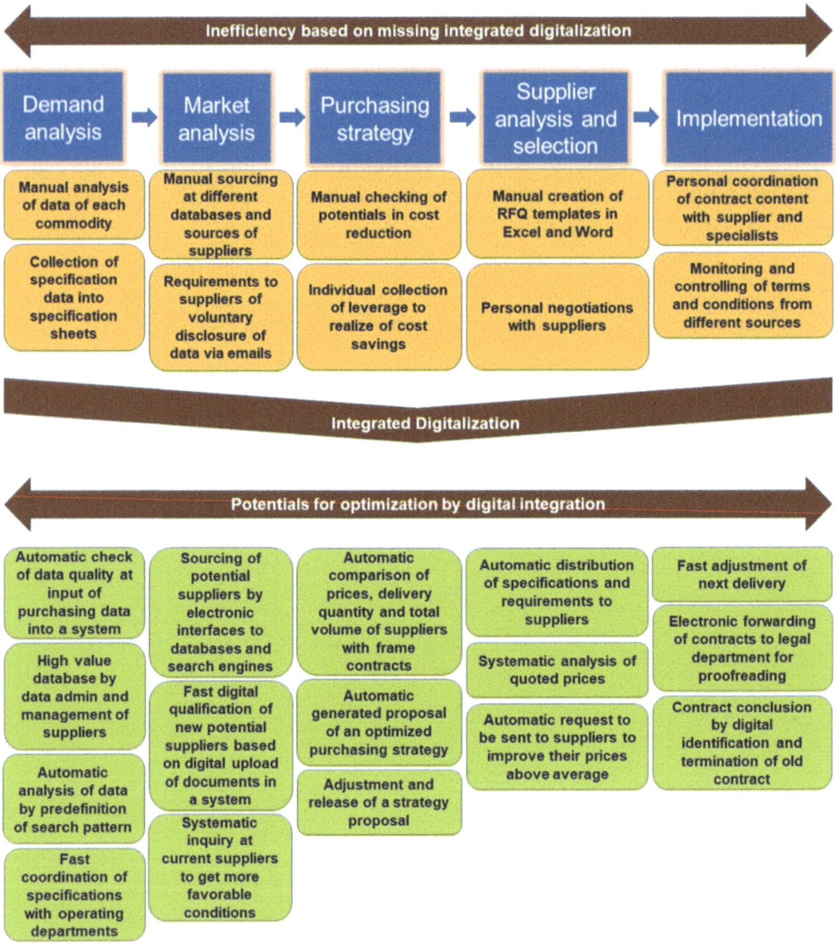

Fig. 5.12 Future of purchasing processes with integrated digitalization (Source: magazine "Beschaffung aktuell", page 26 to 32, issued June 2017 by Konradin publisher, Germany. Author Hoeveler Holzmann Consulting). Just to transfer manual processes to IT systems, which will lead significantly to lower process costs and to increasing speed to serve company internal customers

6 Cost Break Down and Cost Structure Analysis

We work with following calculation scheme of industry:

Material processed further during production	Raw material	Material costs	Own production costs	Total Selling Price (Net Sales Price)
raw material				
Raw material markup	Overhead			
Materials incorporated into the product unchanged	Purchased parts			
Semi-finished parts				
Storage and Inventory Interest for components dependent on material value:	Markup, Overhead			
Sub-Tier Transportation				
Storage—Material				
Sub-Tier Packaging				
Import duties				
Insurance while in transit				
Receiving department costs				
Purchasing department costs				
In-Plant Transportation				
Base Wage for Direct Labor	Labor rate	Mfg costs		
Fringe Benefits & Other Costs				
labor rate × manufacturing time per part (base time + handling time)	Overall Direct Labor Costs			

(continued)

K. Zuerl, *Effective Cost Cutting in Asia*, Management for Professionals,
https://doi.org/10.1007/978-3-030-82782-3_6

machine rate per minute (MMR) × cycle time/parts per cycle	Machine costs			
– Based on overall labor costs	Miscellaneous Plant Overhead			
– Based on machine costs				
Sales & Administrative Costs	Sales, General, & Administrative Overhead (SG&A)	Markups	Markups, Packaging Costs, Logistics, Amortization	
General Costs (e.g., Patent Fees)				
Scrap on Raw Material, Purchased Parts, Manufacturing				
Expendable Packaging &		Packaging Costs		
Rack Investment amortization				
Sequencing & Logistics to own Plants		Logistics		
Amortization—Tooling & Fixtures				
Development project management		In terms of design and research input. Engineering evaluation is based on cost-center based charges.	Own Development costs	
Design CAD (Concept, model validation, 2D/3D drawings and documentation, producing the individual/assembling/part drawing, DMU, packaging)				
Calculation, simulation (FEM, durability/crash)				
Research/trial and testing (static and dynamic)				
Prototype parts for supplier research (adjusted to reflect re-use)				
PT parts price according to purchased parts method, with QG				
			Supplier's development costs	
			Terms of Payment	
			Terms of Delivery	
			Profit on Raw Material & Manufacturing Costs	

6.1 Overview Cost Calculation (detailed)

Net Sales Price = Material Cost + Manufacturing Cost +Surcharges.

6.1.1 Net Sales Price

1. Net sales price
   1. Material costs
   2. Manufacturing costs
   3. Surcharges
      1. Surcharges on Product Costs (COGS)
         1. SGA
         2. R&D
         3. Warranty
      2. Product specific costs
      3. Profit
         1. Profit on material
         2. Profit on purchased parts
         3. Profit on added value
4. Terms of payment
   Interest rate by duration of payment terms
5. Terms of delivery (Transport costs/Transport insurance/Duty)

6.1.2 Material Costs

1. Net sales price
   1. Material costs
      1. Direct material
         1. Raw material cost
            1. Material usage
            2. Material waste
         2. Costs for subcomponents
         3. Costs for purchased manufacturing steps
         4. Reusage of rejects
      2. Material Overhead costs
      3. Interest on material in income storage
         1. Average duration of material in income storages
         2. Material value in income storage
         3. Interest rate
      4. Cost of Interest on finished products in warehouse

6.1.3 Manufacturing Costs

1. Material costs
2. Manufacturing costs

1. Manufacturing step costs
    1. Cost of the working system per time unit
    2. Cost direct labour per time unit
    3. Tool allocation per part
    4. Out put
    5. Residual manufacturing overhead costs
2. Cost for rejects, manufacturing

3. Interest cost on WiP (work in progress)

6.1.4 Manufacturing Step Costs

1. Net sales price
    1. Material costs
    2. Manufacturing costs
        1. Manufacturing step costs
            1. Cost of the working system per time unit
                1. Fix cost working system
                2. Variable cost working system
            2. Cost direct labour per time unit
                1. Utilization
                2. Qualification level
                3. Hourly wages
            3. Tool allocation per part
                1. Tool invest
                2. Lifetime, tool
                3. Type of allocation, tool investment
            4. Out put
                1. Cycle time
                    1. Duration machine movement
                    1. Technology
                    2. Machine power
                    2. Material process duration
                    1. Technology
                    2. Material features
                    3. Experience
2. Parts per cycle
    - Definition Tool size/Machine size
3. Machine utilization
    - Machine progress
    - Duration of machine down time
4. Scrap rate
5. Residual manufacturing overhead costs

- Cost for indirect labour
- Cost for equipment
- Cost for supplies (indirect)
- Cost for auxiliary space

6.1.5 Cost of the Working System

1. Net sales price
    1. Material costs
    2. Manufacturing costs
        1. Manufacturing step costs
            1. Cost of the working system per time unit
                1. Fix cost working system
                    1. depreciation
                    2. Interest cost of investment
                    3. Costs for space
                2. Variable cost working system
                    1. Energy consumption
                    1. Max. machine power
                    2. Average energy consumption
                    3. Energy price
                    2. Maintenance
                    3. Supplies

6.2 Material Costs

This is the process of how to calculate material costs (Fig. 6.1):

6.2.1 Raw Materials

These costs are calculated as a function of the technology used.

They are generally calculated using:

- Operating weight
- Net weight (Part weight)
- Raw material price
- Price for waste

The difference between operating weight and net weight:

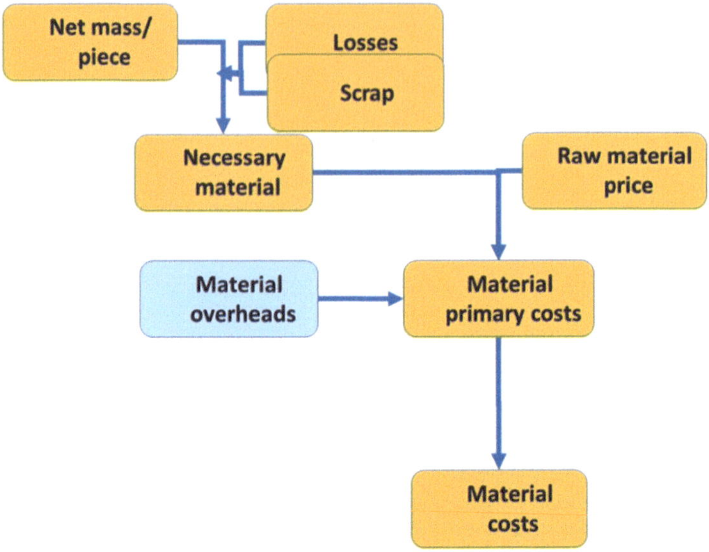

Fig. 6.1 Material cost structure. *Source*: General Motors Europe, 2004

- Machining: Weight of chips and first and last cut weight
- Injection moulding: Weight of gating system (eliminated by using a hot runner system)
- Casting: Dross weight and irretrievable losses (e.g. burn-off losses, slag)

Waste may be traded on the market. If no revenue is drawn from the waste, the cost of disposal has to be determined and added to the raw material cost.

We assume you work in a company which produces homogeneous parts. The material overheads will only be overheads for the calculated parts. The primary material cost is the result of multiplying the raw material price by the necessary material which is needed to produce the part. To obtain the necessary material you have to reduce incoming net mass by losses and scrap.

Losses depend on the production process (start-ups, stoppages), die design (sprue, burrs, cut-outs, etc.), and ulterior manipulations (machining). Losses are different for plastics and rubber injection/extrusion/compression, metal stamping, fabric punching, and treatment equipment.

When these losses can be re-used, the material cost has to be discounted again.

Scrap covers all parts with defects and all parts which are out of specifications or drawing dimensions. The scrap rate is different in each process, because it depends on the material and equipment quality, material-machine-relationship, and the process technology level.

For raw material prices see www.plasticnews.com or http://metalprices.com. A complex material cost calculation includes, for example, painted colours used for

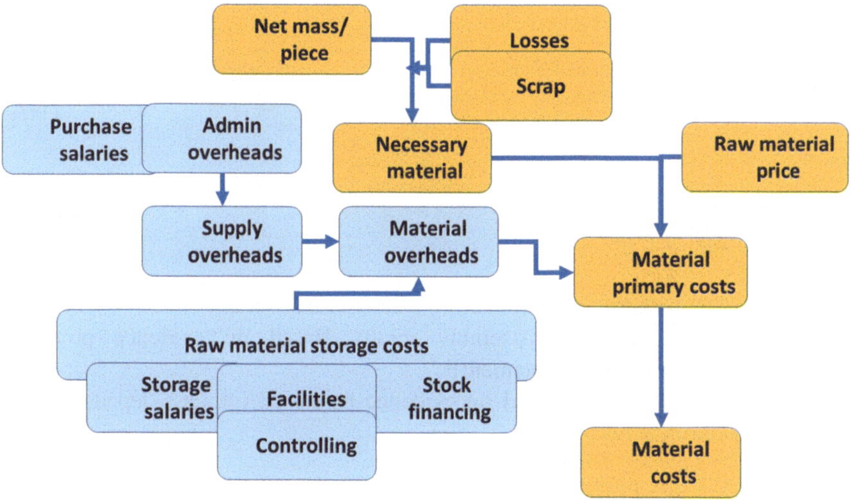

Fig. 6.2 Elaborated Material cost structure. *Source*: General Motors Europe, 2004

plastic bumpers. 24 of the 35 colours have a different price/kg. For painting colours there is a scrap of 4% for unicolour and metallized paints.

Supply overheads are salaries and management overhead within purchasing department. Raw material storage overheads include:

- Direct manpower in stores, storekeepers, truck unloading, agents
- Investments needed (e.g. installations) in the goods receiving stores
- Receiving control to verify quality and the quantity
- Stock financing overheads

To include elaborated material overhead costs, see the following charts (Fig. 6.2):

For example, material overheads make up a total of 5% at an enterprise with 300 employees:

Raw material storage	0.5%
Semi-manufactured product storage	0.5%
Raw material stock financing	0.35%
Semi-manufactured stock financing	0.35%
Store staff	1.00%
Purchasing staff	1.30%
Purchasing Management	1.00%
Second example, material overheads at a total of 5% at a company manufacturing plastic parts:	
Raw material storage	0.5%
Semi-manufactured auxiliary storage (if a previous stock is necessary for a later handling, e.g. assembly)	0.5%

(continued)

Raw material stock financing	0.75%
Material movements	1.00%
Material previous drying´	1.25%
Material dying process	1.00%

6.2.2 Scrap

(1) Scrap—raw materials (manufacturing and assembly scrap).
(2) Scrap—purchased parts (assembly scrap). Based on evidence produced (process-dependent/O.A statement)!
(3) Scrap—manufacturing. Based on evidence produced (process-dependent/O.A statement)!

No profit or overhead surcharges are allowed on scrap.

6.2.3 Purchasing of Raw Materials

It is well known that price developments depend mainly on industrial demand. If the world economy grows, material prices are likely to rise. Strong declines in inventories are also driving prices higher. China alone, with its need to invest in infrastructure, needs huge quantities of industrial metals (Figs. 6.3 and 6.4).

My recommendation: Price weaknesses and corrections can be used for hedging, Spot purchases and longer-term contracts. You need to observe the market and trends at least on weekly basis and understand the reasons behind.

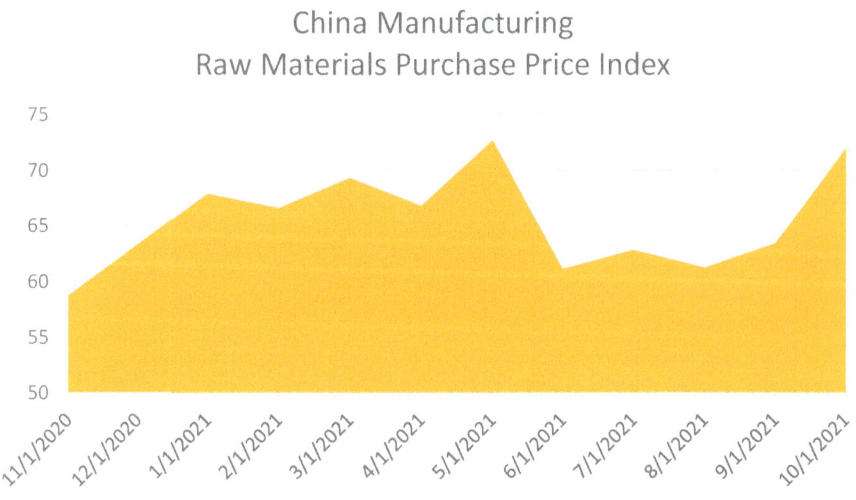

Fig. 6.3 China Manufacturing Raw Materials Purchase Price Index (see https://ycharts.com/indicators/china_manufacturing_raw_materials_purchase_price_index). Source: YCHARTS.com, USA, access date 19.11.2021

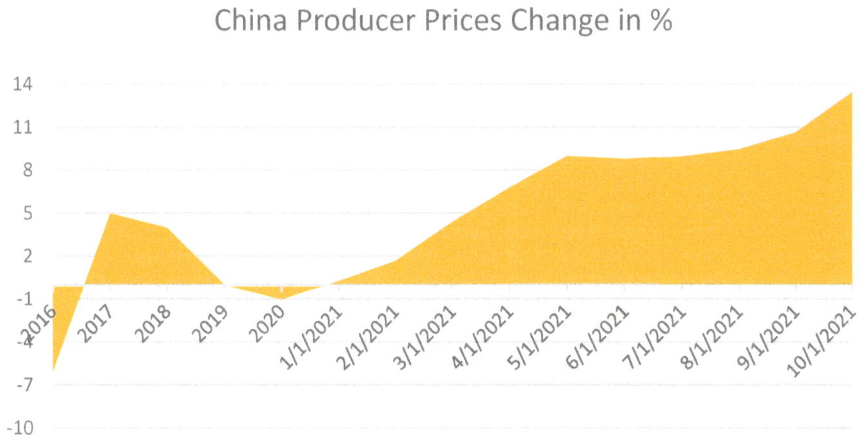

Fig. 6.4 China Producer Prices Change (see https://tradingeconomics.com/china/producer-prices-change). Source: tradingeconomics.com/ National Bureau of Statistics of China, access date 19.11.2021

Commodity markets outlook October 2020 (see http://pubdocs.worldbank.org/en/455451602618561458/CMO-October-2020-Executive-Summary.pdf).

China wants increased pricing power in the commodities markets it dominates, specifically when the country imports that ingredient. China no longer wants to be just a price taker, and also wants to bolster use of the yuan for transactions overseas. A long-term strategy to raise the profile and influence of the currency. At the same time, the government wants domestic companies to do more to hedge against volatility.

Economic stimulus measures announced at the China National People's Congress meeting in May 2020, amounted to around 7.5% of annual GDP. These measures boosted demand for steel from key sectors such as construction and manufacturing in 2021 (Figs. 6.5 and 6.6). In 2021 Q3, energy prices rose sharply, natural gas and coal prices soared due to high demand for electricity. Iron ore prices fell sharply from an all-time high as China reduced steel output, but overall base metal prices continue to rise. As well, crude oil prices are expected to rise before declining in 2023 as the recovery in demand is met by increased production. Looking ahead, commodity demand will be affected by a continued increase in urbanization.

However, 23 low-income countries are facing acute food insecurity, due to latest rally of coal and natural gas prices, which have sharply increased agricultural input costs and fertilizer costs. Elevated food prices combined with the recent spike in energy costs is pushing food price inflation up in these countries as well as higher-income EMDEs, including China. Increasing energy prices pose significant inflation risks in many EMDEs and could weigh on growth in 2022 among energy-importing countries. Natural gas and coal prices are expected to decline in 2022 and fall further

World Bank Commodities Price Data

Commodity	Unit	Annual Averages Jan-Dec 2018	Jan-Dec 2019	Jan-Dec 2020	Quarterly Averages July-Sept 2020	Oct-Dec 2020	January-March 2021	April-June 2021	July-Sep 2021	Monthly Averages August 2021	Sept. 2021	October 2021	Trends
Metals and Minerals													
Aluminum	$/mt	2.108	1.794	1.704	1.708	1.919	2.091	2.400	2.645	2.603	2.835	2.934	↗
Copper	$/mt	6.530	6.010	6.174	6.525	7.185	8.477	9.706	9.382	9.370	9.325	9.829	↗
Iron ore	$/dmt	69,8	93,8	108,9	117,8	133,2	167,2	200,7	166,9	162,2	124,5	122,9	↘
Lead	$/mt	2.240	1.997	1.825	1.876	1.904	2.014	2.128	2.333	2.414	2.248	2.345	→
Nickel	$/mt	13.114	13.914	13.787	14.266	15.957	17.618	17.359	19.112	19.141	19.377	19.362	↗
Tin	$/mt	20.145	18.661	17.125	17.690	18.810	25.099	31.026	34.644	35.024	34.887	37.723	↗
Zinc	$/mt	2.922	2.550	2.266	2.343	2.631	2.747	2.916	2.990	2.988	3.036	3.360	↗
Precious Metals													Trends
Gold	$/toz	1.269	1.392	1.770	1.912	1.875	1.798	1.815	1.789	1.785	1.775	1.777	→
Platinum	$/toz	880	864	883	904	939	1.160	1.182	1.023	1.009	973	1.017	→
Silver	$/toz	15,7	16,2	20,5	24,5	24,4	26,3	26,7	24,3	24,0	23,2	23,4	→
Energy													Trends
Coal, Australia	$/mt	107,0	77,9	60,8	52,1	68,6	89,5	109,7	169,1	169,6	185,7	236,9	↑
Coal, South Africa	$/mt	97,6	71,9	65,7	57,2	71,9	86,8	100,5	135,4	137,9	146,1	199,7	↑
Crude oil, average	$/bbl	68,3	61,4	41,3	42,0	43,6	59,3	67,1	71,7	68,9	72,8	82,1	↗
Crude oil, Brent	$/bbl	71,1	64,0	42,3	42,7	44,5	60,6	68,6	73,0	70,0	74,6	83,7	↗
Crude oil, Dubai	$/bbl	69,2	63,2	42,2	42,5	43,8	59,5	66,4	71,4	68,9	72,2	81,2	↗
Crude oil, WTI	$/bbl	64,8	57,0	39,3	40,9	42,6	57,8	66,1	70,6	67,7	71,6	81,3	↗
Natural gas, Index	2010 =100	82,1	61,1	45,5	42,3	59,2	78,7	83,2	140,3	129,8	178,4	222,5	↑
Natural gas, Europe	$/ mmbtu	7,68	4,80	3,24	2,87	5,19	6,52	8,79	16,93	15,43	22,84	31,05	↑
Natural gas, U.S.	$/ mmbtu	3,16	2,57	2,01	1,99	2,46	3,43	2,91	4,32	4,05	5,11	5,48	↑

Notes and Abbreviations:
$ = US dollar, dmt = dry metric ton, mt = metric ton, toz = troy oz, bbl = barrel, mmbtu = million British thermal units

Fig. 6.5 Commodity prices (see https://www.worldbank.org/en/research/commodity-markets). Sources: www.worldbank.org/commodities, published 2.11.2021. Access date 19.11.2021. Author of trend evaluation: GTEC, Schneckenlohe

in 2023, as demand growth eases (especially outside of Asia) and production and exports increase, driven by the United States.[1]

Copper

The price of copper is a reliable measure of economic health, as changes to copper prices can suggest global growth or an upcoming recession. With high volatility and strong liquidity, copper is attractive to traders. Copper spot price is affected by supply and demand. Detailed copper prices you can see at https://www.dailyfx.com/copper-prices.

USD 2000 per tonne had been paid between 2001 and 2004. LME copper prices increased, trading over $6500/mt in August 2020. Now, end of October 2020 we talk about 6714 USD per tonne, an increase of more than 200%. SHFE prices also

[1]This is an adaptation of an original work by The World Bank. Views and opinions expressed in the adaptation are the sole responsibility of the author or authors of the adaptation and are not endorsed by The World Bank.

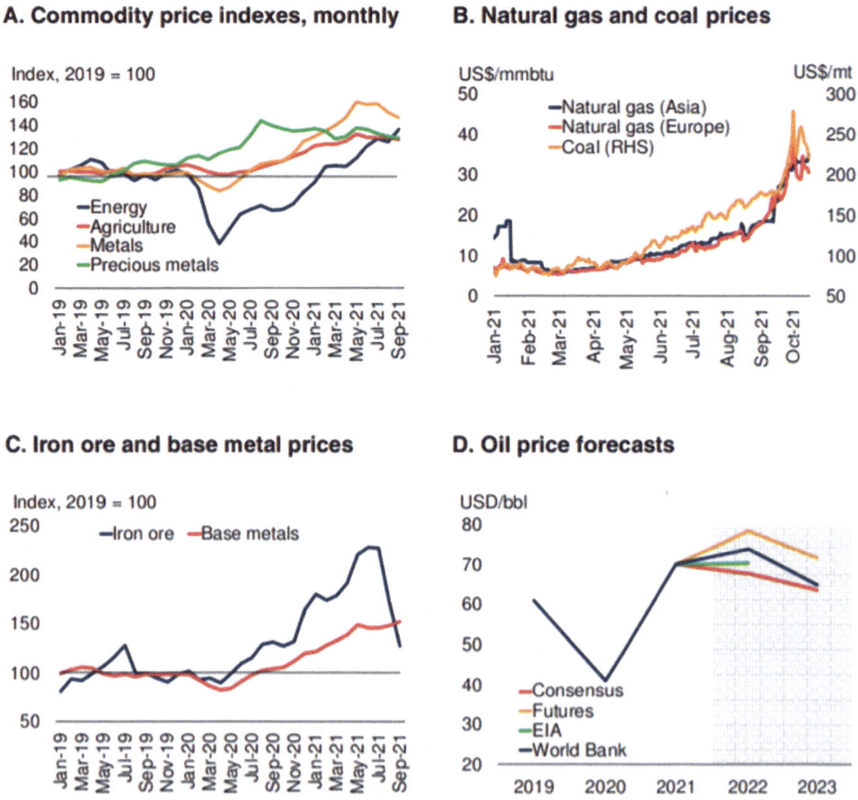

Fig. 6.6 Commodity market developments October 2021 (see https://openknowledge.worldbank.org/bitstream/handle/10986/36350/CMO-October-2021.pdf). Sources: Bloomberg; C40 Cities; EIA; IEA; OPEC; OurWorldinData; World Bank. Taken from pdf-file, page 2 of Commodity Markets Outlook: Urbanization and Commodity Demand, published October 2021. Author World Bank Group, Washington, DC. License: Creative Commons Attribution CC BY 3.0 IGO. Access date: 19.11.2021

increased during the same period, as local demand remained strong and refined production tightened. Copper prices continue to rise. The Copper monthly metal index MMI value increased in Asia in 2020 (in Japan, India, Korea and China). Therefore, here you find the five best practice metal sourcing strategies that will allow any buying organization to "buy well" consistently[2]:

[2] *Source*: https://agmetalminer.com/2020/09/15/copper-mmi-copper-prices-pick-up-aided-by-strong-Chinese-demand-supply-fears. Article "Copper MMI", author Maria Rosa Gobitz at Metalminer, issued SEPTEMBER 15, 2020. Access date 25.2.2021.

- Always buy by the weight, never the "each" and never by the square foot
- Always split out the value-add portion of your metal from the underlying raw material cost
- Always award contracts using some combination of TCO (total cost of ownership) or TLC (total landed cost). Never award based on piece price alone!
- Always have the absolute fewest number of suppliers necessary to serve your organization
- Never buy all of your metal using only one contracting mechanism—think portfolio!

The world's biggest copper consumer wants more sway over prices. In November 2020, overseas investors will be able to trade copper futures on the Shanghai International Energy Exchange. It is China's next move to open up its commodities markets. It's not the first such product. Since 2018, China has been allowing foreigners to trade oil and iron ore, along with rubber, low-sulfur fuel oil and purified terephthalic acid (PTA). Copper promises to be an even bigger advance. The metal is a key indicator for an economy that has recovered faster than the rest of the world from the coronavirus. The contract will exclude tax and customs duty, and will be delivered into bonded warehouses, helping it compete actively with the London Metal Exchange.[3]

Copper futures trend see https://www.dailyfx.com/copper-prices.

Zinc

As a result of stockpiling, the price fell from USD 1450 per tonne to USD 1200 per tonne in 2005. A high demand pushed the price up further. Now, end of October 2020 we talk about 2441 USD per tonne, an increase of more than 100%. However, Zinc price enters into a long term structural decline in 2021 (Fig. 6.7).

Government economic stimulus in China will continue to underpin a strong rebound in steel production and zinc demand (used in galvanizing steel) that will persist in 2021.[4] Fitch Solutions forecasts, Zinc prices will stabilize in 2022, but will remain elevated compared to pre-Covid levels. Until 2024, Fitch Solutions expects price will decline to 2200 USD/tonne.[5]

Tin

The unclear development of supply and planned capacity expansions by Peruvian and Asian manufacturers have caused the price curve to drop from USD 8500/tonne to USD 7100/tonne in 2005. Now, end of October 2020 we talk about 18,177 USD

[3] *Source*: https://www.bloomberg.com/opinion/articles/2020-11-15/china-copper-futures-have-timing-and-luck-to-succeed. Author Clara Ferreira Marques at Bloomberg, issued November 16, 2020. Access date 25.2.2021.

[4] *Source*: https://price.metal.com/, author SMM Information & Technology Co, Ltd., published 2021, Access date 25.2.2021.

[5] Source: https://www.mining.com/wp-content/uploads/2021/10/Fitch-Solutions-Zinc_-Prices-To-Weaken-In-2022-But-Remain-Elevated-Compared-To-Pre-Covid-Levels-07-Sep-2021.pdf.

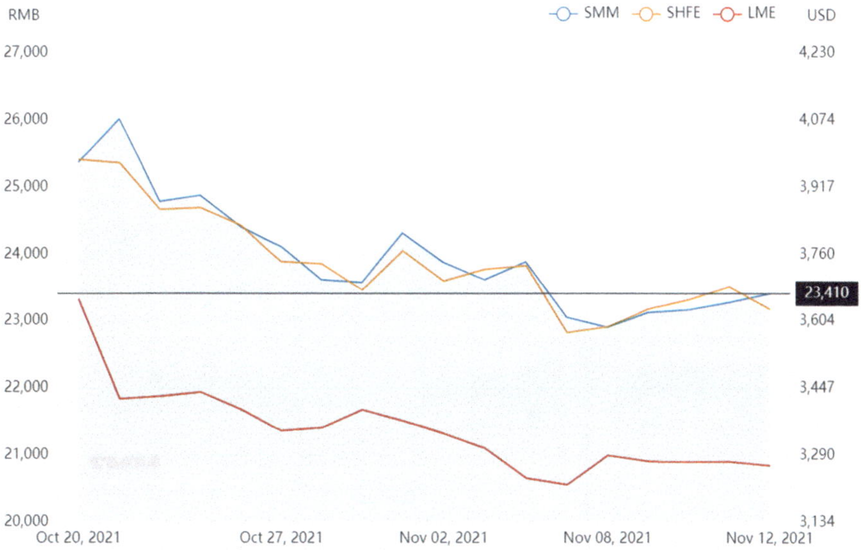

Fig. 6.7 Zinc price drop within one month. 13% VAT included, Guidance price, ex-works of GB/T 470-2008 Zinc ingots (Zinc content no less than 99.995%). Source: https://www.metal.com/Zinc/201102250173, Author: www.metal.com. Published Nov. 19, 2021. Access date: 20.11.2021

per tonne, an increase of more than 150%.[6] end of October 2021 about 38,925 USD per tonne (Fig. 6.8). Tin prices are expected to trend higher over the coming years due to a widening supply deficit as global demand growth outpaces production between 2017 and 2021, according to BMI Research.

Lead

The price of lead has dropped from 1000 USD to 900 USD/tonne. Stocks on the London Stock Exchange doubled to 55,000 tonnes. The price is therefore likely to fall further. But surprisingly, end of October 2020 we talk about 1776 USD per tonne, an increase of almost 100%. Even in October 2021, 2345 USD/mt (see Fig. 6.5). Lead Ingot & Concentrates in Chinese RMB from Tianjin, Henan and Guangdong from Shanghai Metals Market (SMM) see https://price.metal.com/Lead.

Nickel

Nickel is mainly used in the production of stainless steel and other alloys and can be found in food preparation equipment, mobile phones, medical equipment, transport, buildings, power generation. The tonne of nickel fell in 2004 and 2005 from USD 18000/tonne to USD 15000/tonne, after which USD 8000/tonne was still paid in 2001 to 2003. Since 2005 has been a rising industrial production, caused prices to

[6] *Source*: https://price.metal.com/Tin, author SMM Information & Technology Co, Ltd., published 2021, Access date 25.2.2021.

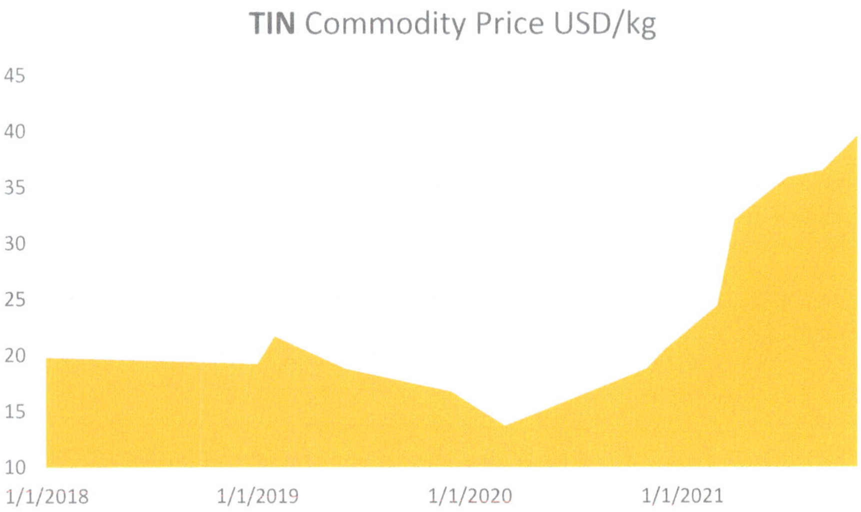

Fig. 6.8 Tin commodity price development (see https://markets.businessinsider.com/commodities/tin-price). Source: Business Insider, New York, published 18.11.2021. Access date 20.11.2021

rise again. Nickel futures have been rising steadily again since March 2020 to trade above $20171 per tonne in November 2021, due to increase supply of nickel ore to China's stainless steel sector, as the Chinese economy recovers from the coronavirus-hit (Figs. 6.9 and 6.10). The biggest producers of nickel are Philippines, Russia, Canada, New Caledonia, Australia, Indonesia, Brazil, Cuba and Colombia.

The nickel prices displayed in Trading Economics are based on over-the-counter (OTC) and contract for difference (CFD) financial instruments.

Aluminium

One tonne of aluminium fell in 2005 from 2000 USD/tonne to 1700 USD/tonne. Production capacity is expected to fall and demand to remain stable. However, the energy-intensive production of aluminium in Europe is becoming increasingly uneconomical due to rising environmental taxes and high energy prices. Inefficient aluminium plants will be closed worldwide. China has introduced a tax on aluminium exports and abolished tax incentives. An enormous price increase was therefore unavoidable. Later went back due to some crisis between, last was Corona in March 2020. Aluminum price continues to surge (Figs. 6.11, 6.12, 6.13).[7]

[7] *Source*: https://agmetalminer.com/2020/11/23/this-morning-in-metals-aluminum-price-continues-to-surge/, author Fouad Egbaria on NOVEMBER 23, 2020; access date 25.2.2021.

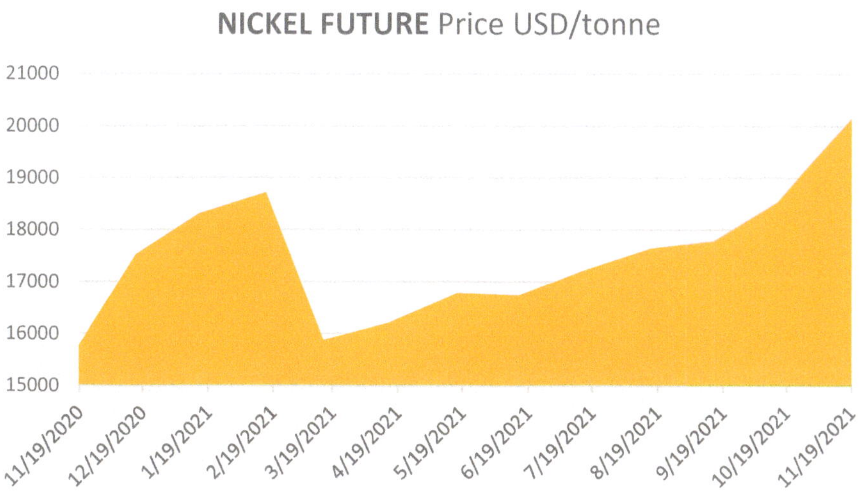

Fig. 6.9 Nickel Future Price Development at London Metal Exchange (LME) (see https://tradingeconomics.com/commodity/nickel). Source: Trading Economics, New York City, published 19.11.2021. Access date 20.11.2021

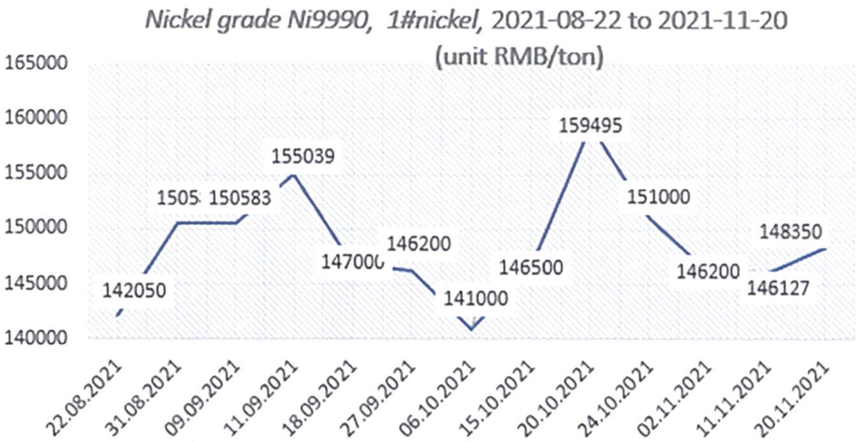

Fig. 6.10 Nickel China Spot Trading in 2021 from August 22 to November 20 in RMB/ton see http://www.sunsirs.com/uk/prodetail-432.html. Source: SunSirs–China Commodity Data Group, Hangzhou, published 20.11.2021. Access date 20.11.2021

Steel

The price of steel is determined by the shortage of volumes and rising demand. The Chinese economy has grown strongly in recent years, but steel imports have stopped. China has been exporting steel since the end of 2004. Thus, it is not China's hunger for steel that is a problem, but the global hunger for raw materials. The demand for

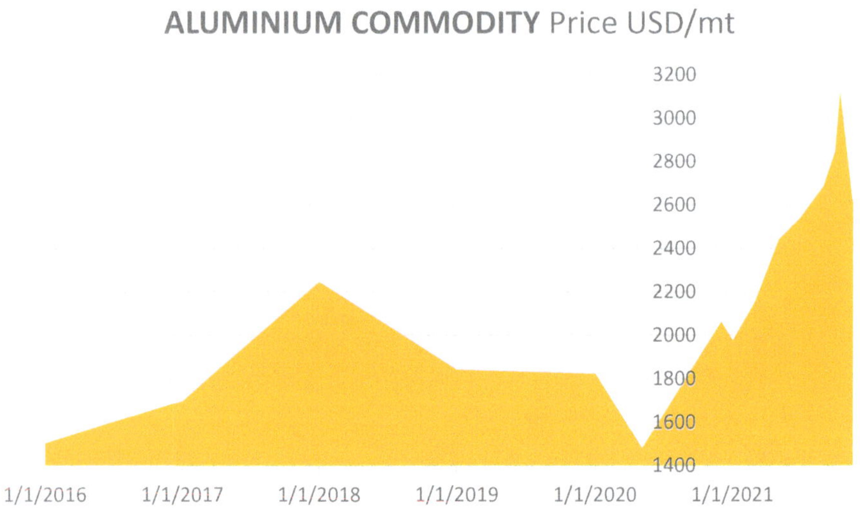

Fig. 6.11 ALUMINIUM Commodity price trend. 2676 USD/metric ton on Nov. 19, 2021 (see https://markets.businessinsider.com/commodities/aluminum-price). Source: Business Insider, New York, published 19.11.2021. Access date: 20.11.2021

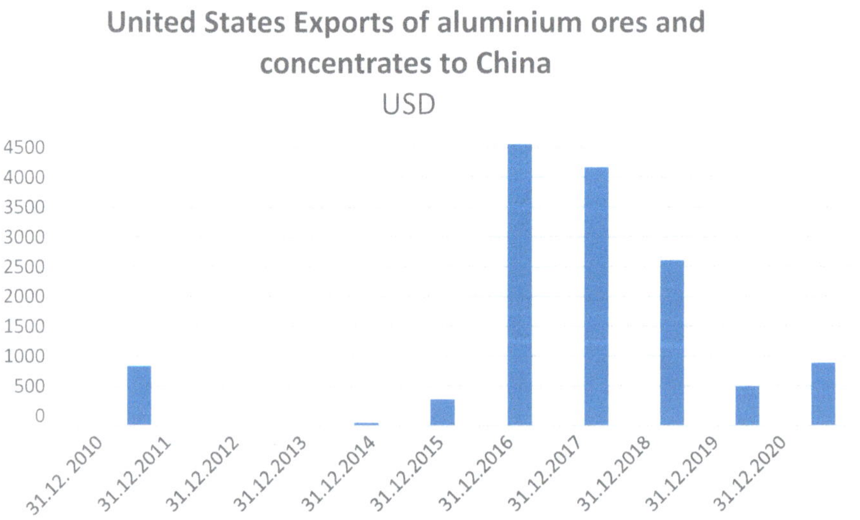

Fig. 6.12 United States exports of aluminium ores and concentrates to China was US$949 Thousand during 2020, according to the United Nations COMTRADE database on international trade. See https://tradingeconomics.com/united-states/exports/china/aluminum-ores-concentrates. Source: Trading Economics, New York City, updated November 2021. Access date 20.11.2021

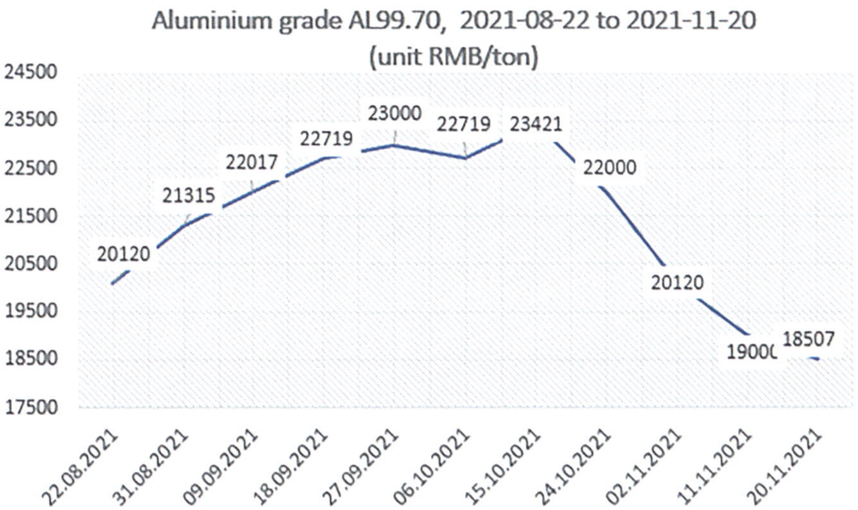

Fig. 6.13 China aluminum spot price in RMB/ton. See http://www.sunsirs.com/uk/prodetail-482.html. Source: SunSirs China Commodity Data Group, Hangzhou, published 20.11.2021. Access date 20.11.2021

all raw materials and industrial metals has increased extremely and will continue to increase. The markets remain tense, in terms of volumes and prices. In the future, prices will develop according to the product groups "flat products" and "long products". Flat products are produced on the basis of ore and coke and are closely linked to the raw materials market. Long products are produced on the basis of scrap prices (Figs. 6.14 and 6.15).

In US currency there was a record peak of $733 per tonne on July 14, 2008.[8] The data from China Iron and Steel Association reached an all-time high of 6333 RMB/Ton in 14 May 2021 and a record low of 2085 RMB/Ton ($231) in 18 Dec 2015.

Plastic

For decision making, please find trends in Internet of each kind of plastic material of each country you are dealing with. Following an overview, taken on Nov. 20, 2021 for Chinese market (Fig. 6.16). In comparison, you can find average monthly resin prices in Central Europe at https://www.plasticportal.eu/en/polymer-prices/lm/14/, which shows price development of different thermoplastics over the past 11 years (Fig. 6.17).

[8] http://steelbenchmarker.com/files/history.pdf, released February 24, 2021 by author SteelBenchmarker.com, access date 25.2.2021.

Fig. 6.14 Hot rolled angle steel 5#, ex works price in RMB/metric tonne, details see https://www.ceicdata.com/en/china/steel-price-index-weekly. Source: China Iron and Steel Association/ISI Emerging Markets Group Company (CEIC Data, EMIS Insights) Hong Kong (SAR), published 2021. Access date: 20.11.2021

Sector Steel
Compare Spot Prices from 2020 to 2021

	2021 Spot Price: Daily(Unit:RMB)			**2020 Spot Price: Daily**(Unit:RMB)		
Commodity	**Nov 18**	**Nov 19**	**Change**	**Nov 20**	**Nov 23**	**Change**
Mild steel plate	**4,988.00**	**4,988.00**	0.00%	3892,00	3884,00	-0,21%
Steel I bean	**4,620.00**	**4,620.00**	0.00%	3750,00	3750,00	0.00%
Rebar	**4,670.00**	**4,666.67**	-0.07%	4147,00	4164,00	0.41%
Stainless steel plate	**17,706.67**	**17,581.67**	-0.71%	12533,33	12583,33	0.40%
Galvanized sheet	**6,260.00**	**6,196.67**	-1.01%	5450,00	5472,00	0.40%
Hot rolled coil	**4,710.00**	**4,662.00**	-1.02%	4190,00	4170,00	-0,48%
Color coated sheet	**8,566.67**	**8,466.67**	-1.17%	7700,00	7716,67	0.22%
Cold rolled sheet	**5,586.67**	**5,490.00**	-1.73%	5222,5	5232,5	0.19%
Iron ore	614.44	587.33	-4.41%	**899,11**	**892,44**	-0,74%

Fig. 6.15 Spot price increases at all commodities (different steel metal types), except Iron ore. Details see http://www.sunsirs.com/uk/sectors-13.html. Source: SunSirs China Commodity Data Group, Hangzhou, published 19.11.2021. Access date: 20.11.2021

Sector Rubber & Plastics
Compare Spot Prices from 2020 to 2021

	2021 Spot Price: Daily(Unit:RMB)			2020 Spot Price: Daily(Unit:RMB)		
Commodity	**Nov 18**	**Nov 19**	**Change**	**Nov 20**	**Nov 23**	**Change**
Nutural Rubber	13,440.00	13,830.00	2.90%	13467,50	13750,00	2.1%
PVC	9,010.00	9,120.00	1.22%	7950,00	7950,00	0.00%
BR	16,080.00	16,080.00	0.00%	11060,00	11060,00	0.00%
LLDPE	9,040.00	9,040.00	0.00%	7750,00	8050,00	3.87%
PET	7,800.00	7,800.00	0.00%	4966,67	5033,33	1.34%
PA66	39,500.00	39,500.00	0.00%	29500,00	29500,00	0.00%
PC	24,950.00	24,950.00	0.00%	22500,00	22666,67	0.74%
PA6	16,100.00	16,100.00	0.00%	12400,00	12366,67	-0,27%
LDPE	12,462.50	12,462.50	0.00%	11300,00	11600,00	2.65%
HDPE	8,833.33	8,833.33	0.00%	8433,33	8533,33	1.19%
SBR	13,675.00	13,675.00	0.00%	11700,00	11700,00	0.00%
PP	8,390.00	8,370.00	-0.24%	8716,67	8883,33	1.91%

Fig. 6.16 China rubber and plastic spot prices in RMB/ton. Spot price increases at all commodities (different rubber and plastic types), except PP. Details see http://www.sunsirs.com/uk/sectors-15.html. Source: SunSirs China Commodity Data Group, Hangzhou, published 19.11.2021. Access date: 20.11.2021

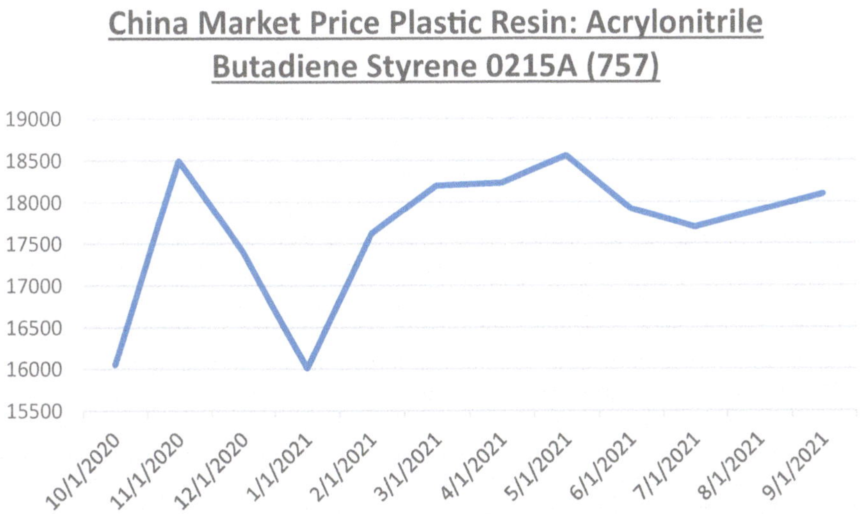

Fig. 6.17 China market price development of Acrylonitrile Butadiene Styrene Resin 0215A (see https://www.ceicdata.com/en/china/china-petroleum%2D%2Dchemical-industry-association-petrochemical-price-plastic-resin). The data reached an all-time high of 18,900 RMB/Ton in Nov 2010 and a record low of 8380 RMB/Ton in Feb 2002. Source: China Petroleum and Chemical Industry Federation/ISI Emerging Markets Group Company (CEICDATA.com, EMIS Insights) Hong Kong (SAR), published 2021. Access date: 21.11.2021

6.3 Asian Price Barometer Compared to the Previous Years

Following I provide a general overview of the (industrial) producer price index (PPI), sometimes also called output price index, as it is calculated and used at the level of all countries. The industrial producer price index measures the gross monthly change in the trading price of industrial products. There are also producer price indices for construction and for services.

The PPI measures price changes from the point of view of the producers/ manufacturers of a product. For producer prices on the non-domestic market, the prices are calculated at national frontiers, FOB (free on board); this means that the seller pays for transportation of the goods to the port of shipment, plus loading costs, and the buyer pays freight, insurance, unloading costs and transportation from the port of destination to his factory. All characteristics that determine the price of the products have to be taken into account. This includes quantity of units sold, transport provided, rebates, service conditions, guarantee conditions and destination.

In 2020 industrial producer prices dropped rapidly during the Covid-19 crisis. The size of the reduction was however smaller than during the financial crisis.[9,10]

In Germany, taken from Federal Statistical Office, Wiesbaden, for example you see price differences from 2018 to 2019 for producer prices of industrial products. Only for electronic components you will find producer price reductions, all others went up, partially significant.

What about the effect of US-China trade war? QIMA's data on production inspection and supplier audit demand confirms that neither the United States nor China are among the winners of the US-China trade war. While many US buyers moved their sourcing away from China, they were not in a hurry to bring the manufacturing back home, instead dividing the diverted business between near-shoring regions and China's neighbors in Asia, with Vietnam, Taiwan and Myanmar among the top winners, with Bangladesh enjoying renewed popularity. Meanwhile China, as a manufacturing hub, saw overall inspections and audits volumes decrease with the escape of North American, Australian and, to a lesser extent, European customers.[11]

China sourcing is bouncing back strongly but is yet to return to pre-Covid levels, while alternative sourcing regions such as Vietnam, India and Turkey are experiencing sustained levels of growth. But as global sourcing seeks a quick recovery, compliance violations are on the rise, with brands turning to digital technology solutions to better manage ethical risks and solve ongoing supplier communication and product quality challenges.

---

[9] *Source*: https://ec.europa.eu/eurostat/statistics-explained/pdfscache/ 1297.pdf, page 1–2, updated 3.2.2021, author Eurostat, access date 25.2.2021.

[10] *Source*: https://ec.europa.eu/eurostat/statistics-explained/index.php/Industrial_producer_price_index_overview, last modified on 3 February 2021, author European Union, access date 25.2.2021.

[11] *Source*: https://www.qima.com/qima-news/2020-q1-barometer-2019-in-review, author Courtney Terrey from QIMA, article "QIMA 2020 Q1 Barometer", accessed date 25.2.2021.

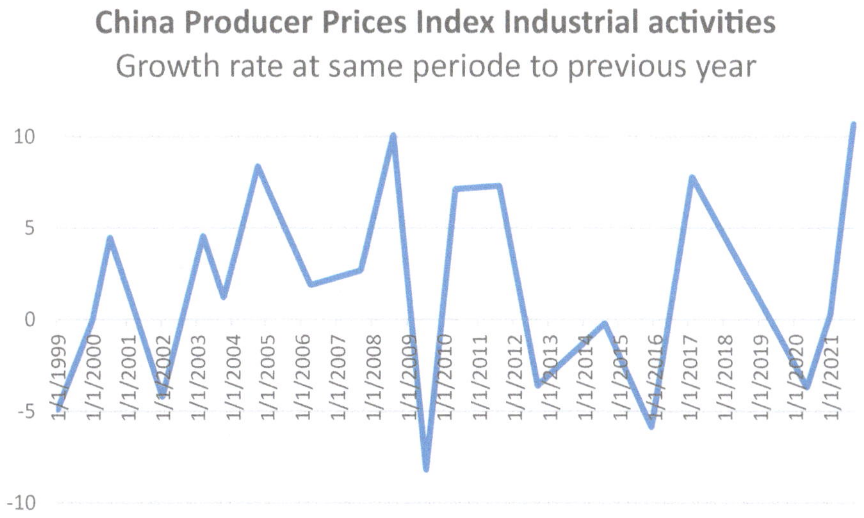

Fig. 6.18 Producer Prices Index China for Industrial activities from 1999 to Nov. 12, 2021. Source: Organization for Economic Co-operation and Development. Retrieved from FRED, Federal Reserve Bank of St. Louis; https://fred.stlouisfed.org/series/CHNPIEATI01GYM, November 20, 2021. Access date: 21.11.2021

China's rebound remains strong. Except digitalization products, growth struggles to reach pre-pandemic levels. Even though China continues to emerge strong in the post-pandemic period, the long-term diversification trends in global supply chain are continuing to chip away at its dominance. The Textile and Apparel sector is a vivid example of this trend: while textiles inspection demand in China rose, it still represented a – 20% drop compared to Q1 2019. By contrast, China's competitors in textiles and apparel, such as Vietnam, India and Bangladesh, recorded double-digit growth in demand for inspections compared to Q1 2019 (Figs. 6.18, 6.19, 6.20).

After a tough 2020, India now poised for a comeback, is being eyed by multiple sectors for sourcing. Following a year battered by pandemic-related lockdowns and massive order cancellations due to collapsed demand in the West, India has returned to the forefront as a sourcing destination of choice for many buyers. Notably, despite being traditionally viewed as a Textile hub, India as a buying market was regarded just as highly for Promotional Products, Footwear, and Eyewear, Jewellery and Accessories. However, this rebound for the moment appears dependent on how effectively India manages its ongoing battle against COVID-19 as case numbers dramatically rise in April and renewed pandemic-control measures are put in place.

Vietnam enjoys sustained popularity, dominating among China's regional competition in 2020 and 2021. A traditional first choice for buyers diversifying away from China, Vietnam saw its popularity among Western buyers grow by leaps and bounds over the past few years—a trend that has remained in effect so far in 2021. Vietnam represents a third consecutive quarter of growth that had initially begun as a

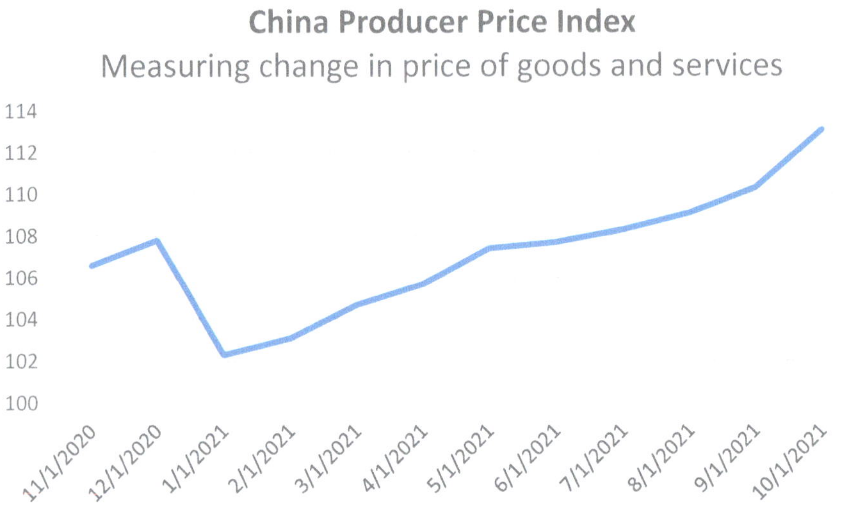

Fig. 6.19 Producer Prices in China increased to 113.10 points in October 2021 (see https://tradingeconomics.com/china/producer-prices). Data retrieved from National Bureau of Statistics of China. In China, the Producer Price Index measures the average change in price of goods and services sold by manufacturers and producers in the wholesale market during a given period. Source: Trading Economics, New York City, updated November 2021. Access date: 21.11.2021

Item	2018	2019	2020	Trend
Means of Production	104,6	99,2	97,3	↘
Mining and Quarrying Industry	108,8	102,4	94,8	↘
Raw Material Industry	106,3	97,4	94,4	↘
Processing Industry	103,5	99,7	98,7	↘
Consumer Goods	100,5	100,9	100,5	→
Food	100,5	102,7	102,9	↗
Clothing	100,8	101,1	99	↘
Articles for daily use	101	100,4	99,7	↘
Durable consumer goods	99,8	98,8	98,2	↘

Fig. 6.20 China producer price indices for Industrial products by category (5.13), see http://www.stats.gov.cn/tjsj/ndsj/2021/indexeh.htm. Source: National Bureau of Statistics of China, Beijing. Taken from China Statistical Yearbook 2021, updated 2021. Access date: 21.11.2021. Author of trend evaluation: GTEC, Schneckenlohe

post-lockdown rebound in mid-2020. It is worth noting that this growth is more than just a return to pre-pandemic levels. Furthermore, the appetite for Vietnam sourcing is far from satisfied and is poised to redefine the sourcing landscape in 2021. Around one-third of buyers globally and 38% of US-based buyers name it among countries from where they plan to buy more in 2021. That said, Vietnam is not the only country in the region to benefit from expanded business volumes. Southeast Asia shows double-digit growth across the board, fuelled by the renewed interest from American and European brands alike.[12]

Worldwide and Asian producer prices, see

- https://tradingeconomics.com/country-list/producer-prices
- https://tradingeconomics.com/country-list/producer-prices?continent=asia

To see different industrial sectors:

In comparison to Germany, please have a look at Federal Statistical Office, Wiesbaden for producer prices of industrial products), see https://www.destatis.de/EN/Press/2020/11/PE20_462_61241.html

6.3.1 Manufacturing Costs

Following please find the process for calculating manufacturing cost (Fig. 6.3):

The manufacturing (primary) cost will be calculated by adding machine (manufacturing) time rate and part production cycle time. Machine time rate includes installation cost (machine cost), manpower cost and manufacturing overheads. We obtain the total manufacturing cost by adding manufacturing primary cost and inspection costs.

Social burdens are fringe benefits and other costs:

- Social Security
- Unemployment Insurance
- Worker Accident Compensation
- Savings Plan Contribution
- Absenteeism
- Fringe Benefits =
  (a) Vacation
  (b) Holiday Pay
  (c) Pensions—Company
  (d) Vacation/Holiday Bonus
  (e) Health Insurance
  (f) Recreation
- Shift Premium
- Performance Bonus
- Overtime
- Set -up Costs (1)

[12] *Source*: https://www.qima.com/qima-news/2021-q2-barometer%2D%2Ddiversification-continues. Author Courtney Terrey from QIMA; published April 16, 2021. Access date 1.5.2021.

(a) Set-up costs will be put in the Direct Labour category when it is the operator's responsibility for set-up
(b) Setup costs will be put in Misc. Plant Overhead when it is done by a set-up crew

6.3.2 Cost of Working System

One or more machines represent a working system.

The cost of the work system is calculated as follows:

- Machine hourly rate (productive)
- Machine hourly rate (not productive)
- Set up costs

What types of work systems do we know?

- Standard machine (possible to produce different components)
- Dedicated special machine (impossible to produce different components)
- Standard machine with adjustable allocation to different components

The type of the work system decides whether productive periods must be calculated into the cost of the work system or not.

Machine Costs = machine rate per hour (MHR) × cycle time/parts per cycle.

Machine Hourly Rate

Machine Hour Rate (MHR) Components are:

- Fix cost of machine (purchasing costs and installation costs)
- Cost of Depreciation of Machinery
- Amortization of Equipment
- Utilities
- Maintenance & Repair
- Interest Expense of Investment
- Floor space Allocation (space, which is covered by the machine/working system (floor occupation, see Fig. 6.21a, b)
- Taxes.
- Purchased Services
- Insurance Expense—Liability
- Leases.

Procedure for Calculating Machine Hour Rate

- For new capital assets: full hourly cost rates
- For old and already depreciated machines:

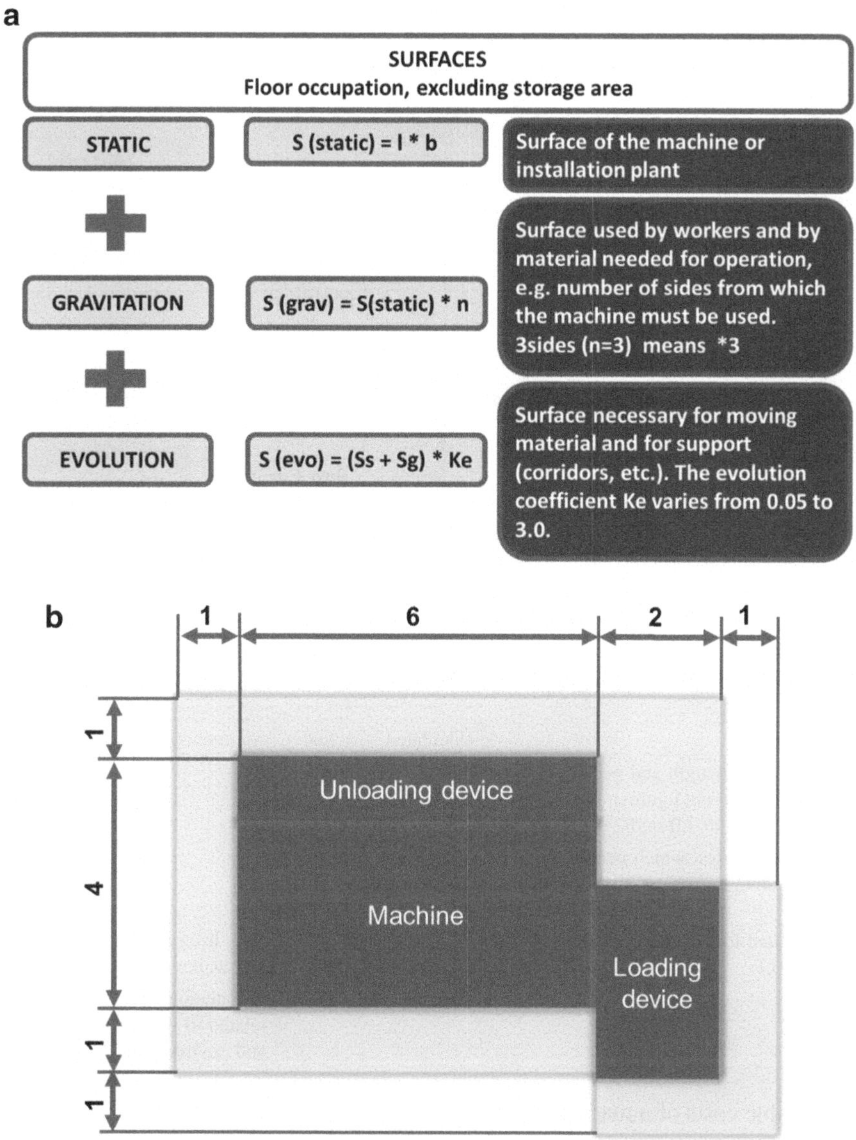

Fig. 6.21 Floor space allocation for surface cost calculation. Ss = S(static), Sg = S(gravitation) [*Source*: General Motors Europe, 2003] and an example of machine layout

Use of:

- Floor space allocation
- variable costs (energy...)
- maintenance costs (fixed and variable) (Fig. 6.22)

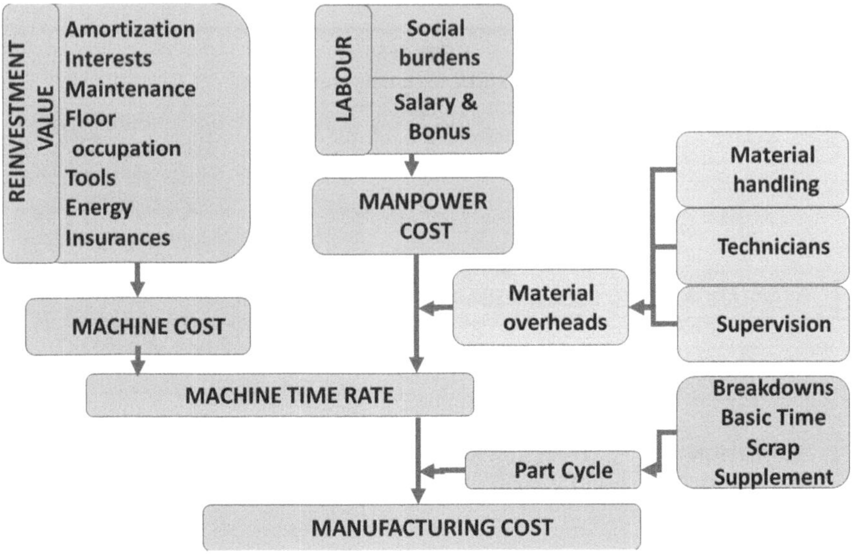

Fig. 6.22 Manufacturing cost structure. *Source*: General Motors Europe, 2004

Following there is an example, how to calculate floor occupation of a machine.

	calculated	actual	comments
Static machine length and width (according to layout figures): l1 = 6.0 m, b1 = 4.0 m; l2 = 3.0 m, b2 = 2.0 m	30 m2	30 m2	
+ number of sides, which need to be used (loading, unloading, maintenance): 2	60 m2	40 m2	
+ coefficient for moving material by forklift: 0.1	12 m2	0 m2	Fork lifter is using gangway and walkway
total	102 m2	70 m2	Calculation result varies, related to type of machines and environment.

Variable costs of a machine are:

- Costs for energy of machine
- Costs for supplies of machine
- Costs for maintenance of machine

Output (Application Rate)

It is calculated from:

- Cycle time
- Parts per cycle

- Utilization ratio of machine
- Scrap rate

Attention: There are three kind of outputs:

- Theoretical output ratio
- Available capacity in pieces
- Output of good parts

Latent is a risk to include data twice, e.g. the utilization rate of the machine, because this is already included in the calculation of machine hour rate.

Data must therefore be considered and checked, what is the correct value of the parameter for the calculation.

Exercise for 3 shifts (theoretical 7200 hours/year):

Cycle time 1 hour

Parts per cycle 100 parts

Utilization rate of machine 50%

Scrap rate 10%

Questions:

- Theoretical application rate in parts/year?
- Available Capacity in pieces/year?
- Output of good parts/year?

Solutions:

- Theoretical application rate: 7200 h/year × 100 parts/h = 720,000 parts/year
- Available Capacity in pieces: 720.000 parts/2 = 360.000 pieces/year
- Output good parts: 360.000 pieces × 0.9 = 324.000 pieces/year

Cycle Time

Is calculated with:

- Process time
- Down time

Process Time vs. Down Time

Manufacturing costs are strongly dependent on the value of the machines and the number of shifts. What about the time rate costs of an injection die machine with 4 employees and 50 parts/hour? How to calculate the effective shift? (Fig. 6.23)

The amortization cost is dependent on the kind of machines and their usage at the plant; this means we have to divide the value of the machines into number of years of depreciation and usage hours/year.

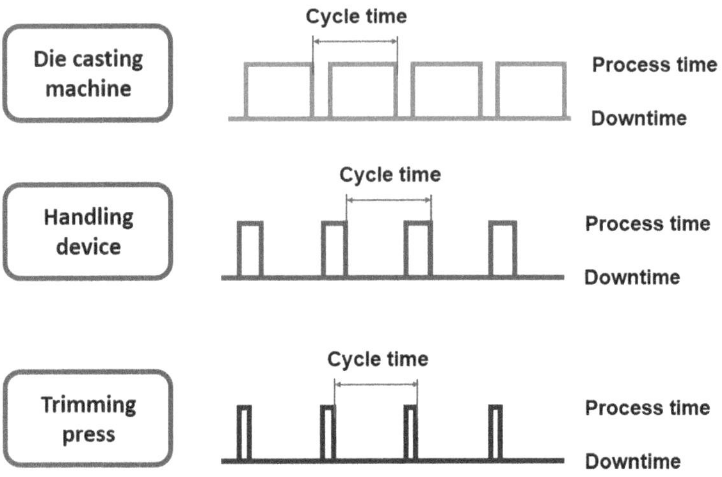

Fig. 6.23 Process time is working time. Down time is idle time. *Source:* Tsetinis & Partner, 2012

Table 6.1 List of minimum annual leave by country. Details see: https://en.wikipedia.org/wiki/List_of_minimum_annual_leave_by_country. Source: Wikimedia Foundation, Inc., London, Author: Wikipedia, Nov. 11, 2021. Access date: Nov. 26, 2021

	Paid vacation days (5 days work/week)	Paid public holidays	Total paid leave (5 days work/week)
China	5/10/15	11	16/21/26
Germany	20	10	30
USA	0	0	0
UK	20	8	28
India	12	15	27

How to Calculate Hours/Years?

In China, the duration of the annual leave entitlement is: (a) 5 days for employees who have accumulatively worked for 1–10 years; (b) 10 days for employees who have accumulatively worked for 10–20 years; and (c) 15 days for employees who have accumulatively worked for more than 20 years. Employers who offer more vacation time are legally obligated to grant it. Every worker is also entitled to 11 paid public holidays, which includes two semi-annual one-week holidays known as the Golden Weeks.[13] See Table 6.1.

In 2020, China has 251 working days, Germany, India and UK 254, Japan 247 and USA 252. Public holidays are already considered. As a standard you can

[13] *Source*: https://en.wikipedia.org/wiki/List_of_minimum_annual_leave_ by_country, last edited 7 February 2021, access date 26.2.2021

use this figures in workshops, assuming if staff goes on vacation, there is always one who can take over your job and continue operate machines.[14]

In our experience, in these countries 1500 hours for one shift, 3000 for 2-shift and 4500 hours/year at 3 shifts is a good figure. 250 days/year × 24 hours/day is the goal, but 25% stoppage of machines (standard e.g. of injection machines) gives you a practical figure of 4500 hours/year.

However in US in 2020 there are 262 working days with 1764 hours/year from an American source,[15] in Germany there are only 1371 hours/year available. For our cost calculation purpose, we ignore these sources.[16]

There is no correct number for person year—the best you can do is keep your channel of communication open with the company, consider all possible factors, and combine all your knowledge and expertise of workplaces to come up with an estimate that might work for cost calculation.[17]

Interest Rate of Machines

Current interest rates of machines are low, and investment loans for industrial purposes in Germany are at 1.8% and in China at 3.8% (see Figs. 6.24 and 6.25).

Assuming the same interest rates over a year of depreciation, investment costs will be calculated =

current purchase price/2

× type of annual interest rate/100

× 1/no of hours/year.

Details you will find at Chap. 5.

Maintenance Costs

What about checking the maintenance costs? The Opel Zaragoza Plant has 8000 employees with 100 doing maintenance. Check how many workers are working for this particular machine. Check the layout according to QS 9000 certification (PPAP). Industrial floor rent prices in Europe are 43–98 €/m^2 in Frankfurt, 26.4–87 €/m^2 in Vienna, 49–94 €/m^2 in Budapest, 61–79 €/m^2 in Prague.

Tooling costs belong to the process and are a part of the cost of the machine, e.g. belts, forge dies. Cost/h = total cost/Year divided into number of hours/years.

Industrial Electricity (Fig. 6.26)

Energy costs will be received out of the catalogue of machines. Refer to EUROSTAT or others on the internet, which gives you the figures in €/kwh.

---

[14] *Source*: https://china.workingdays.org/EN/workingdays_holidays_2020.htm, access date 26.2.2021

[15] *Source*: https://hr.uiowa.edu/pay/payroll-services/payroll-calendars/working-day-payroll-calendar-2020, author IOWA HR University Services Building (USB), published 2020, access date 26.2.2021

[16] *Source*: https://clockify.me/working-hours#:~:text=Working%20hours%20in%20Germany,than%20most%20other%20OECD%20countries. Author COING Inc., Palo Alto, USA, published 2021, access date 26.2.2021

[17] *Source*: https://www.publicspendforum.net/user/psfeditorial/. Author Public Spend Forum, published 2021, access date 26.2.2021

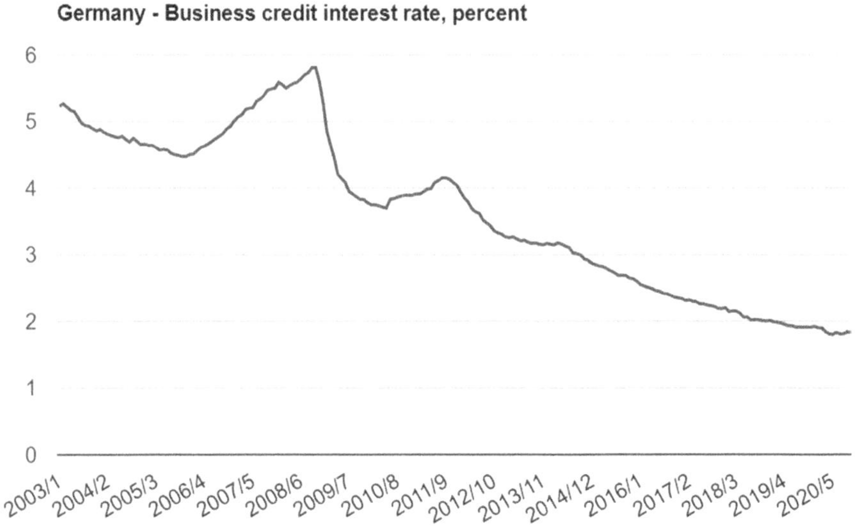

Fig. 6.24 Is the bottom reached? *Source: Deutsche Bundesbank. Source*: https://www.theglobaleconomy.com/ Germany/business_credit_interest_rate/. The globaleconomy.com, published 2021, access date 26.2.2021

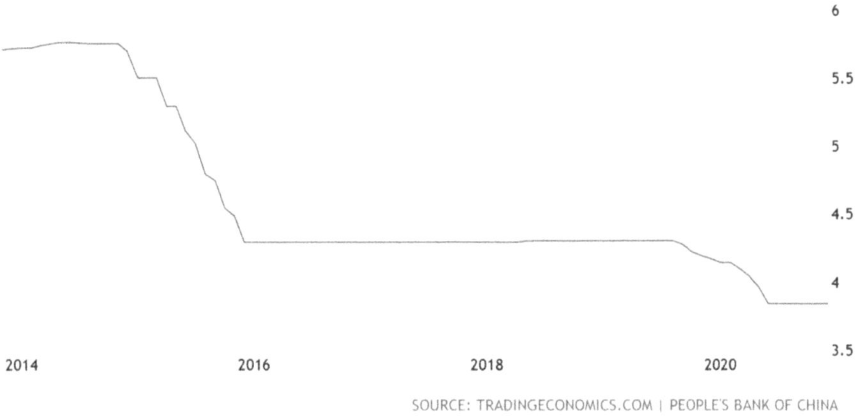

Fig. 6.25 China's loan prime rate. *Source:* People's Bank of China. *Source*: https://tradingeconomics.com/china/interest-rate; Author TRADING ECONOMICS, published 2020. Access date 26.2.2021

Electricity in Germany is generated from nuclear energy, lignite (brown coal), hard coal (stone coal), natural gas, water, wind and the sun. One MWh cost 20 euros in 2002, 35.8 in 2005, 48.25 euros in 2010, from 86–149.9 in 2018, from 90.4 to 155.7 in 2019. Only four companies share the market: Vattenfall, EON, EnBW and RWE. Energy-intensive industries are affected. Additional competitive

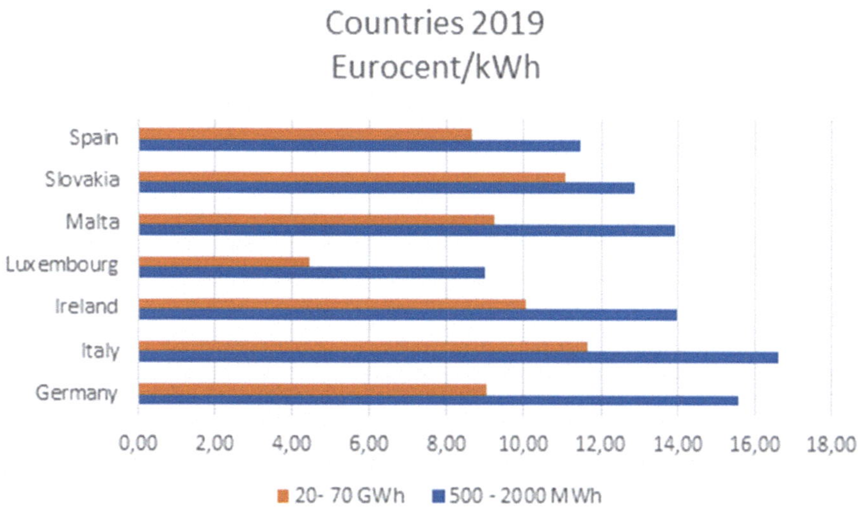

Fig. 6.26 The price industrial consumers pay for electricity varies depending on their annual power consumption. In 2018, industrial end-users in Germany with an annual consumption of 500 to 2000 megawatt-hours (blue bars) paid 14.99 Eurocents per kilowatt-hour of electricity, which was the highest in Europe. 2019, Italy was the highest with 16.61, followed by Germany with 15.57 Eurocents per kilowatt-hour. Source: https://www.statista.com/statistics/1046605/industry-electricity-prices-european-union-country/. Author Statista.com. Published Oct 2, 2020. Access date 26.2.2021

disadvantages are: network costs, special political burdens and CO2 emissions trading.

Germany:

In 2019, Electricity prices for industries with an annual consumption of 20,000 to 70,000 MWh (black bars) were highest in Cyprus at 15.28 euro cents per kilowatt hour. This was followed by the United Kingdom, where the average price was slightly less at 13.24 euro cents per kilowatt hour. Luxembourg had the lowest electricity price for industries, at 4.46 euro cents per kilowatt hour.[18]

In 2020 and following years, there is no secret, prices will increase again (Table 6.2).

For households, Germany has the highest electricity prices worldwide. In March 2020, German households were charged around 0.38 U.S. dollars per kilowatt hour plus value added tax. By comparison, in neighboring Poland, residents paid half as much, while households in the United States were charged even less. China average

[18] *Source*: https://www.statista.com/statistics/1046605/industry-electricity-prices-european-union-country/. Author N. Sönnichsen at Statista, published Oct 2, 2020. Access date 26.2.2021

Table 6.2 Table for development of industrial power prices in Germany. Average prices in ct/kwh depending on consumption. 2022 figures are estimated by GTEC. Sources: https://www.cleanenergywire.org/industrial-power-prices-and-energiewende. Author: Clean Energy Wire CLEW, Berlin. Published 4.12.2019, access date: 17.10.2021. Source: https://www.statista.com/statistics/595803/electricity-industry-price-germany. Access date: 17.10.2021. Source: https://www.mdpi.com/1996-1073/14/15/4484/htm. Access date: 17.10.2021

Development of industrial power prices in Germany								
	2008	2010	2012	2014	2016	2018	2020	2022
500–2000 MWh	11	12	14	15	15	15.08	17.81	20
2–20 GWh	10	11	12	13	12.5	12.5	14	16
20–70 GWh	9	10	11	11	10	8.7	12.06	14
70–150 Gwh	8.6	10	10	10	8	9		12
150 Gwh				4.8				8

is with 0.08 USD/kW about 20% of Germany prices. In Qatar, the average household pays only 0.03 U.S. dollars per kilowatt hour.[19]

China:

March 2020: The average price of electricity is 0.083 U.S. Dollar per kWh for households (0.545 RMB, in Shanghai 0.57 RMB, Suzhou 0.59 RMB, Zhaotong 0.67 RMB) and 0.102 U.S. Dollar (0.670 RMB) for businesses which includes all components of the electricity bill such as the cost of power, distribution and taxes.[20,21]

At December 2020, the average industrial power rate in China is around US$0.084/kWh—somewhere in the middle when compared to the rest of the world.

However, China's industrial power rates vary from region to region and are based on different voltage levels and transformer capacities. Understanding the power costs in China is therefore a challenging but necessary consideration at the pre-investment stage for foreign investors.

In terms of price fixing, China's electricity rates are highly regulated by the National Development and Reform Commission (NDRC), but actual prices in the provinces are determined by distribution network operators. This is why power rates vary across different regions in the country.

China charges electricity fees according to four types of electricity usage, namely residential electricity, agriculture production electricity, general commercial and industrial electricity.

Industrial electricity consumption has two categories—the general commercial and industrial electricity category and the large-scale industrial electricity category.

[19] *Source*: https://www.statista.com/statistics/263492/electricity-prices-in-selected-countries/. Author N. Sönnichsen at Statista, published Nov. 11, 2020. Access date 26.2.2021

[20] *Source*: https://www.globalpetrolprices.com/China/electricity_prices/. Author GlobalPetrolPrices.com, published 2021. Access date 26.2.2021

[21] *Source*: https://www.costtotravel.com/cost/electricity-in-suzhou. Author CostToTravel, published 2019. Access date 26.2.2021

General commercial and industrial electricity primarily involves small and medium-sized enterprises (SMEs) with a total transformer capacity of no more than 315 kVA,and are charged only according to the cost per unit based on three voltage levels—1kv, 10kv, and 35kv.

Shanghai: <1kv = 0.79 RMB/kWh, 10kv = 0.77 RMB/kWh, 35kv = 0.75 RMB/kWh (Status April 2019).

Large-scale industry users have a total transformer capacity of above 315 kVA. The cost of consumption in this category is broken down into two parts:

Cost per unit based on four voltage levels—10kv, 35kv, 110kv, and 220kv, and the fixed charge is based on maximum demand or transformer capacity.[22]

6.3.3 Exercise MHR Calculation

Formula MHR (Machine hourly rate) excluding supervisor/foreman:

1) depreciation/hour = investment / useful life in years/ (working hours/year * Utilization ratio)
+
2) maintenance, repair costs/hour = % of investment/ (working hours/year * machine utilization ratio)
+
3) imputed interests for invested capital = (investment/2 /interest rate)/ ((Working Hours/Year) x Utilization Ratio)
+
4) occupancy costs/hour = work space (qm) * rent/qm/month * 12 / (yearly performance (h) * utilization operating time rate)
+
5) energy costs/hour = electricity rate (kwh) * correction coefficient of machine power * rated power EUR/kwh * operating time rate
+
6) maintenance, repair costs/hour = % of investment/ (working hours/year * machine utilization ratio)

Working hours/year = production hours/shift* shifts/week * production weeks/year.

investment = acquisition value = machine purchasing price + installation costs (e.g. floor foundation).

[22] *Source*: https://www.china-briefing.com/news/china-electricity-prices-industrial-consumers/, published April 23, 2019 by Zoey Ye Zhang at China Briefing. Access date 26.2.2021

operating time rate = machine utilization ratio.

$$\text{Costs of Space/Hour} = \frac{\text{Costs of Space/Year}}{\text{(Working Hours/Year)} \times \text{Operating Time Rate}}$$

$$\text{Maintenance Costs/Hour} = \frac{\text{Maintenance Costs/Year}}{\text{(Working Hours/Year)} \times \text{Operating Time Rate}}$$

Exercise 1) Calculation of MHR (Machine hourly rate) of Chinese supplier in EUR/hour.

Total costs (MHR) = Fixed costs + variable costs.

Fixed costs	Variable costs
• Investment: 1 Mio EUR. • Depreciation: 10 years (useful life time). • Interest rate for taken loan at bank: 3.8%. • cost for space: 32 RMB/m2/month = 4 EUR/m2/month, • net space machine: 4 m × 5 m, • gross/covered space machine: 1 m distance space in length & width, • Shift: 3; • working days per week: 5, • working week per year: 50,	• Maintenance, repair: 2.5%/year. • Expenditure, supplies: 1%/year. • utilization ratio: 50%, • energy cost = 0.11 EUR/kWh, • max. Power of machine = 50 kW, • correction coefficient of machine power = 50%.

Result:

(1) Depreciation = investment 1 Mio Euro/useful life 10 years (= 100,000 Euro/year), divided by 6000 h* utilization ratio 50% = 33.33 Euro/hour.
+
(2) Maintenance, repair cost/hour = 2.5%/year of investment 1 Mio Euro (50,000 Euro/year), divided by 6000 h * utilization ratio 50% = 8.33 Euro/hour.
+
(3) Imputed interests = 1 Mio Euro investment/2, divided by performance (6000 h* utilization ratio 50%) × 3.8% interest rate = 6.33 Euro/hour.
+
(4) Occupancy costs = work space (30 qm) * 4 Euro rent/qm, divided by monthly performance of 500 h * utilization ratio 50% = 0.48 Euro/hour.
+
(5) Energy costs = 50 kwh * corrective coefficient 50% * 0.11 EUR/kwh * utilization ratio 50% = 1.38 Euro/hour.

+

(6) Expenditure, supplies costs/hour = 1%/year of investment 1 Mio Euro (10,000 Euro/year, divided by 6000 h/year * utilization ratio 50% = 3.33 Euro/hour.

Solution:

Total = 33.33 + 8.33 + 6.33 + 0.48 + 1.38 + 3.33 = 53.19 Euro/hour.

6.4 Improvements at Shopfloor and Toolshop

6.4.1 How to Improve Total Productive Maintenance (TPM) and Overall Equipment Efficiency (OEE) at the Shop Floor?

Intelligent manufacturing under Industry 4.0 has become the new trend. More and more manufacturing equipment tends to be highly automated and intelligent. Today's equipment is more intelligent, more sustainable, requiring reliable operation, and the overall equipment effectiveness (OEE) must be reduced after breakdown maintenance. You need to arrange a workshop at your supplier sites, depending on the supplier development program.

Workshop benefits:

- Grasp specific and feasible management technologies to enhance the comprehensive productivity of equipment and personnel
- Understand how to improve the maximum use of existing equipment and create excellent production management system
- Realize the benign interaction between humans and equipment for the normal operating level of equipment
- Develop the potential of equipment and establish a dynamic equipment maintenance system
- Effectively reduce sudden equipment failure, maintaining a stable production process while improving production efficiency and product quality

Workshop outline:

(1) To understand the overall equipment effectiveness (OEE).
  (a) Case study: Why is equipment so inefficient?
  (b) Six losses caused by equipment and the time waterfall of loss
  (c) OEE's origin and development
  (d) OEE case study for separate equipment and streamlined equipment
  (e) TPM under an OEE framework and system
  (f) Tool list and Application effect of TPM
  (g) Equipment efficiency index system: OEE, TEEP, SMED, MTBF, MTTR

(2) Equipment fault analysis and zero fault strategy
   (a) Zero-fault strategy for equipment
   (b) Equipment deterioration trend and potential failure modes
   (c) Fast Analysis of faults and improvement of judgment ability
   (d) Creating equipment failure mode and effect analysis (EFMEA)
   (e) Rapid fault analysis and rapid maintenance countermeasures
   (f) Application of equipment fault diagnostic technology
   (g) 3A management model for spare parts
(3) Analysis and improvement for shortening production preparation time
   (a) Quick Changeover
   (b) What is Quick Changeover?
   (c) Time analysis method for internal and external changing
   (d) Principle and technology for single-minute exchange of die
   (e) SMED case study from a Japanese company
   (f) Application exercise for improving the analysis table of SMED.
   (g) Implementation steps for SMED
(4) Establishment of a dynamic equipment maintenance system
   (a) Strategy, On-site information, Organizing and Normalizing system for equipment maintenance
   (b) Diagnosis technology for equipment deterioration
   (c) Professional maintenance activities for the equipment department
   (d) Methods and steps for carrying out professional maintenance activities
   (e) How to carry out self-maintenance activities for equipment
   (f) Develop predictive maintenance activities for equipment
(5) Maintenance activities based on product quality
   (a) The effect of equipment-performance reduction on quality
   (b) Common equipment performance deterioration and maintenance countermeasures
   (c) Periodic precision adjustment and functional verification
   (d) Cmk (Machine Capability Index) analysis in equipment maintenance
   (e) Equipment maintenance plan based on product quality data
   (f) Development of equipment and error-proofing measures
(6) Methods for staff productivity development
   (a) Influence of small faults leading to equipment shutdown on production efficiency
   (b) How to control the state of equipment at any time using the five-sense-method spot checking
   (c) Carrying out source search activities to stimulate employees' enthusiasm for participation
   (d) Graphical preparation of maintenance standards
   (e) Setting up training courses for autonomous maintenance
   (f) TPM Weekly report/single point teaching method

(7) Implementation steps for TPM based on OEE
    (a) Misunderstandings and methods for promoting TPM
    (b) Investigation on the present situation of equipment management and establishment of equipment archives
    (c) Equipment fault data collection and fault mode analysis
    (d) Improving employees' self-maintenance capabilities
    (e) Preventive and predictive maintenance plan
    (f) Visual management and organizational activities of TPM
    (g) Building an effective index and a continuous evaluation system for TPM[23]

6.4.2 Toolshops Cost-Check in Low Cost Country: China

Toolshops

Effective supplier management consists in the early search and development of a "second source". This means, in coordination with the "Group" or with Headquarters, looking for a new supplier, evaluating it and developing it according to your wishes. The disadvantage is needing to buy new tools (die & moulds), at best from the tool shop of the new second supplier. However, very few suppliers have a good tool shop on hand, but the quality of the parts and the total cost will nonetheless stand or fall with the tools.

In the sense of the "total cost" concept, the tool costs from low cost countries (LCC) consist of

- 10–20% support expenses (tool specification, design support, patent protection, development work),
- 10% rework costs (repair expenditure),
- 10–20% lower shot performance,
- 10–15% transport costs,
- 5% adjustment costs for "ramp-up"
- and 55–30% tool costs.

Buying die & moulds in China seemingly has high cost advantages based on the toolmaker's offer. But there will also be high risks, which are often underestimated:

(1) Distance (travel times, transport routes)
(2) In China, for example, toolmakers work closely with Chinese parts suppliers or are parts suppliers themselves (risk: know-how transfer)
(3) Cultural differences, e.g. investment behaviour in China:

[23] http://www.kingo-biz.com/en/index.html, published 2011. Author Kingo-biz.com, Shanghai, China. Access date 25.2.2021

   (a) Few trial runs, quick decisions (leading to bad quality of parts)
   (b) The most modern equipment (fresh financial support from banks, relatives or other investors)
   (c) Willingness to accept too many orders (too many projects running in parallel)
   (d) Trend towards automation, manufacturing cell management, in combination with measuring machines (quality assurance)
(4) Little experience, for example, of Chinese toolmakers with high-volume production tools, e.g. incorrect hardness, dimensional deviations
(5) Acceptance and practical implementation of "Payment Terms"
(6) Economic efficiency of tools (cycle times, tool life, modifications, support costs, purchase of suitable steel from abroad)
(7) Prices for high-quality tools are often just as high as in Germany (e.g. complexity, shot performance guarantee)
(8) Tools are often designed for manual assembly processes, leading to higher requirements for automatic assembly lines.
(9) Do not allow any changes to parts after tool kick-off (agree to a "Design Freeze" date)
(10) Own controlling of tools and material resources on site is necessary
(11) No universal tool construction available, high degree of specialization at tool shop is required
(12) The Chinese market for toolmaking and purchasing of parts is too complex and too dynamic to be treated and executed from Germany HQ
   (a) Application of milling strategies (target: time saving)
   (b) Manufacturing of complex 3D geometries
   (c) Milling and grinding in one clamping session, milling of highest surface qualities
   (d) Cost reduction in operations is not the main focus, e.g. no analysis of temperature critical areas leads to high cycle times
   (e) Technology of machines from the West is not exploited (often only used for prestige & as status symbols)
   (f) Modern machinery says nothing about the efficiency of the tool shop or company
   (g) Shortage of skilled workers leads to automation (quality assurance instead of cost savings)
   (h) High staff turnover and false certificates make incoming inspection necessary
   (i) Transfer of "lessons learned" is often difficult, because the next design will be done by another person
   (j) Most toolmakers are semi-skilled and have only a basic school education

Furthermore, what is different, for example, in a Chinese tool shop compared to a German one?

In production, there is often no possibility of multi-sided machining (manual re-clamping and setup is necessary). Skills by hand are rarely available (e.g. die spotting), and there is often no jig- and profile-grinding machine. In plastics processing, the tools are often not designed for an optimized injection moulding process of the part. If errors occur, there is no experience in the analysis of complex processes. The parts are visually optimized because there is often no understanding of the relationship between process and material properties.

From my point of view, the following also have a negative impact:

- Frequent changes of skilled personnel and managers
- Severely restricted communication in English
- The deburring of parts is cheaper (60–90 Euro/month incl. Accommodation, food) than having professional staff improve the tools (200–400 Euro)

From the entrepreneur's point of view, however, the following working conditions are positive:

- 300 days/year working in tool shops, 3-shift operation is possible
- Modern machinery, good CAD/CAM equipment (high investment)
- Sometimes still a low utilization of capacities (short delivery times)

The often enormous price difference to German toolmakers results from the current grants in aid given by Asian states, the favourable low labour costs, the cheaper materials used (shorter tool life), often no HSC (high speed cutting) milling, no tool coating (thus leading to shorter tool life), the self-built standard parts with accompanying low level of standardization (repair of the tooling in the West is therefore very expensive), and the design of the tool according to LCC methods for the manufacturing of the part (e.g. for manual assembly instead of automatic assembly).

It is therefore clear that tool sourcing, and thus projects for purchasing parts, are tedious. For cost reasons, a long-term partnership must be established (not just a single project). Right from the start, clearly defined specifications must be created, effective project control should take place every week, if possible, preferably with a project manager based on site, who also takes care of supplier development (for simple tools = at least need 1 year, for complex tools = at least takes 4 years). Tool sampling inspection and measurement needs to take place on site. In addition, know-how transfer to subsequent projects is required.

In the plastic injection molding business, hot runner technology and the manufacture of thin-walled plastic parts are still in the development stage. CAE, CAM, CNC and EDM are still not an issue in many places due to the inexpensive workforce. For sure, the time pressure of changes and the required process reliability will accelerate the application of these tools in the near future.

Therefore, no Western company is telling anyone about any reliable toolmakers they may have found in LCCs, since they have probably only been able to develop these after significant efforts. Each company tries to qualify its own selected suppliers in the hope of achieving ROI as soon as possible.

My buyers and SQA employees had the following experiences and recommend the following actions as part of any quality check:

(1) Specifying the tooling as precisely as possible (design, separations, steel, surfaces, etc.)
(2) Checking the design in the construction phase
(3) Sampling of the tool using original materials under production conditions
(4) Working step by step (mostly two steps forward, one backwards)
(5) Quality assurance:
   (a) Checking the obvious and basic things through regular supervision
   (b) Continuous checking of measurement results on measuring machines
   (c) The measured parts have to be delivered with other parts for documentation
(6) Drafting of contracts:
   (a) Personal relationships are more important than contracts
   (b) Rules for scope of delivery, shipping and payment terms need to be described in as much detail as possible
   (c) Realistic assessment of the granting of guarantees
(7) Mould making:
   (a) Adoption of German standards
   (b) Always using same CAD/CAM platform
   (c) Alignment of the machinery to your requirements, e.g.
      i. Always creating the same surface structure with die-sinking machines (EDM)
      ii. Comparable injection moulding machines used with equipment
   (d) Exchange of information and training in your own workshops
   (e) Toolmaker needs intensive support during projects (including regular project reviews)
   (f) Entrance in toolshop-development with several learning cycles, e.g. first ask for replicas, repairs, then order first tooling including design
   (g) Use acceptance tests in China/Far East with 16 hour trial runs and same approval criteria as in Europe
(8) Create innovations:
   (a) Cycle time reduction through reduction of wall thicknesses and non-productive times/downtimes, e.g.

i. thin-walled plastic parts
ii. high-speed handling
iii. automatic part disposal in trays
   (9) Permanent benchmarking with "Best in Class"'.
   (10) Reduction of components (types and parts)
   (11) Data exchange without interfaces to all people involved in the process
   (12) Close cooperation between development and production departments
   (13) Design to Cost (reduce, standardize, automate)

Cultural differences result in tips and tricks that have proven successful in the past implementation of LCC projects:

(1) Creating time buffers in each project phase
(2) Always using a second source
(3) Support from Germany (understanding of parts, tool requirements)
(4) Exact definition of requirements and functional specifications
(5) Limit contact people to a maximum of two (1 project manager, 1 technician)
(6) Define an unambiguous release process, including terms of payment (e.g. 30% for released parts)
(7) Use of international standards
(8) Start with simpler tools from China/Asia for Europe (C-supplier),
    (a) first let suppliers design and build B-tools
    (b) then let suppliers manufacture A-tools with permanent supervision)
(9) Market investigation with the help of external consultants, then starting your own visits to potential suppliers
(10) Selection of suppliers with similar variety of parts (complexity, output)
(11) Procure tools from China/Asia for Europe only in case of high cost saving potentials
(12) Standardization of tool release process, control of manufacturing steps, tool testing and correction
(13) Start with reproduction of tools by delivery of key parts from Germany (e.g. cutting parts/inserts)
(14) Relationship building instead of advance payments
(15) Produce drawings for manufacturing in China/Asia, otherwise you will get an incorrect interpretation of the dimensions/function of the part
(16) Raw tooling should be produced in China/Asia with fine-tuning and finishing machining in Germany

6.4.3 Tooling and Fixtures

Tooling is defined as forming and re-forming tools in accordance with DIN 8580 (Manufacturing processes—Terms and definitions, division), and as severing tools in accordance with DIN 8588 (Manufacturing processes severing—Classification, subdivision, terms and definitions).

6.4.4 Tooling Costs (Direct Payment)

Tooling cost subsidy and spare parts: Up to 80% of the tooling costs to be paid in advance.

Tooling cost supplier: 100% lumpsum payment to the supplier.

Costs for tooling changes: 100% lumpsum payment to the supplier.

Tooling costs include additional costs, tryout/audits. The costs for maintenance are included in the piece price. Amortization is included in the piece price as well. Fixtures, gages and machines are amortized in piece price, for example: buying or production costs, interest, and maintenance.

6.4.5 Die Casting and Plastic Injection Moulds

The cost calculation for the production of an injection mould is composed by:

- Design
- programming
- Tool structure (mechanical rough machining)
- Mechanical machining of inserts and sliders
- Hardening (through-hardening or nitriding)
- Mechanical finishing of inserts and slides
- Adjustment at the injection moulding machine
- Quality acceptance (FMEA, APQP)
- EMPB (Initial sample test report)

How to Reduce Costs for the Production of an Injection Mould?
First, the economic rationality of the design is very important to the cost control of the mold. Therefore, managers should strengthen the training of designers to enhance their ability and designing level.

Second, effective control of the factory's processing, improve workers efficiency and quality of work, hold morning meetings to arrange their work reasonably.

Third, material cost accounts for 30% in mold production. Therefore, injection mold materials should be selected correctly, and the planned material should be coordinated with the requirements of mold life.

Fourth, the control of mold cost is proportional to the quality and delivery date. If the mold quality is in place at one time, the delivery time will be shortened with less modification, so that the manufacturing cost will be reduced accordingly (Fig. 6.27).

In detail, the following parts for the tool must be manufactured and calculated (example for plastic injection):

- Clamping plate
- Ejector package
- Mould plate
- Intermediate mould plate
- Guide columns
- Guide bushings
- Guide pins
- Hot runner manifold block
- Hydraulic cylinder
- Ledge
- Heat protection plate

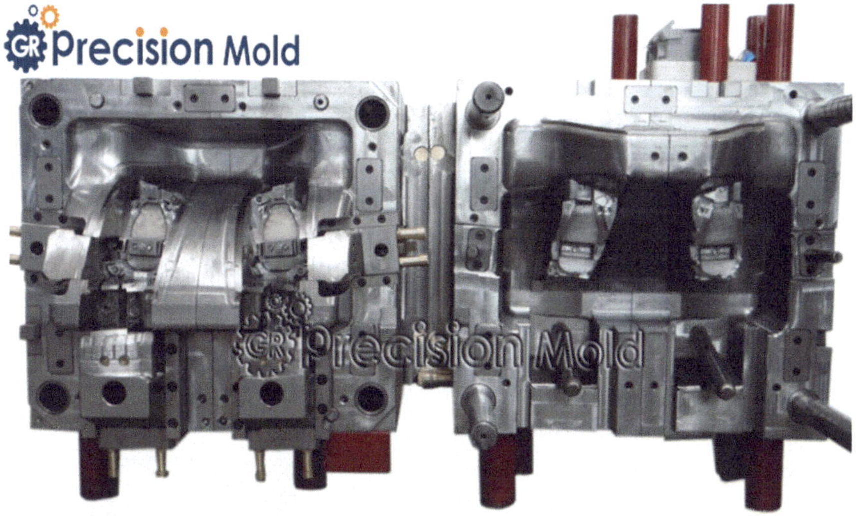

Fig. 6.27 Plastic Injection mold. Source: GRPrecisionMold, grprecisionmold.com, QingXi Town, DongGuan, China. Published 2021

How These Parts for the Tool Must Be Manufactured and Calculated?
First, for the mold inserts to define manufacturing procedure, you need to calculate the processing time required for each process of mold insert, and make a process plan schedule.

Second, improve production and manufacturing execution, improve the execution of manufacturing orders and solve low efficiency problems, then put the production schedule in place.

Third, prepare an Asaichi board of the manufacturing work arrangement in the workshop, and arrange tasks reasonably every day.

Fourth, check whether the materials (bill of materials) has been arranged to be in place in time. If raw material does not arrive on time, communicate effectively with the supplier, and ensure that the materials can arrive according to your updated time schedule, to deliver to your customer in time.

Fifth, hold a production meeting once a week to review and summarize last week's mold production situation, arrange this week's mold production schedule, and adjust urgent tasks.

Sixth, make a test plan of molds for the relevant departments according to the product drawing and other specifications and information provided by customer.

Seventh, after mold testing, the project engineer should make a final conclusion based on the test results of the sample, and arrange sending samples and documentation to client accordingly (Fig. 6.28)

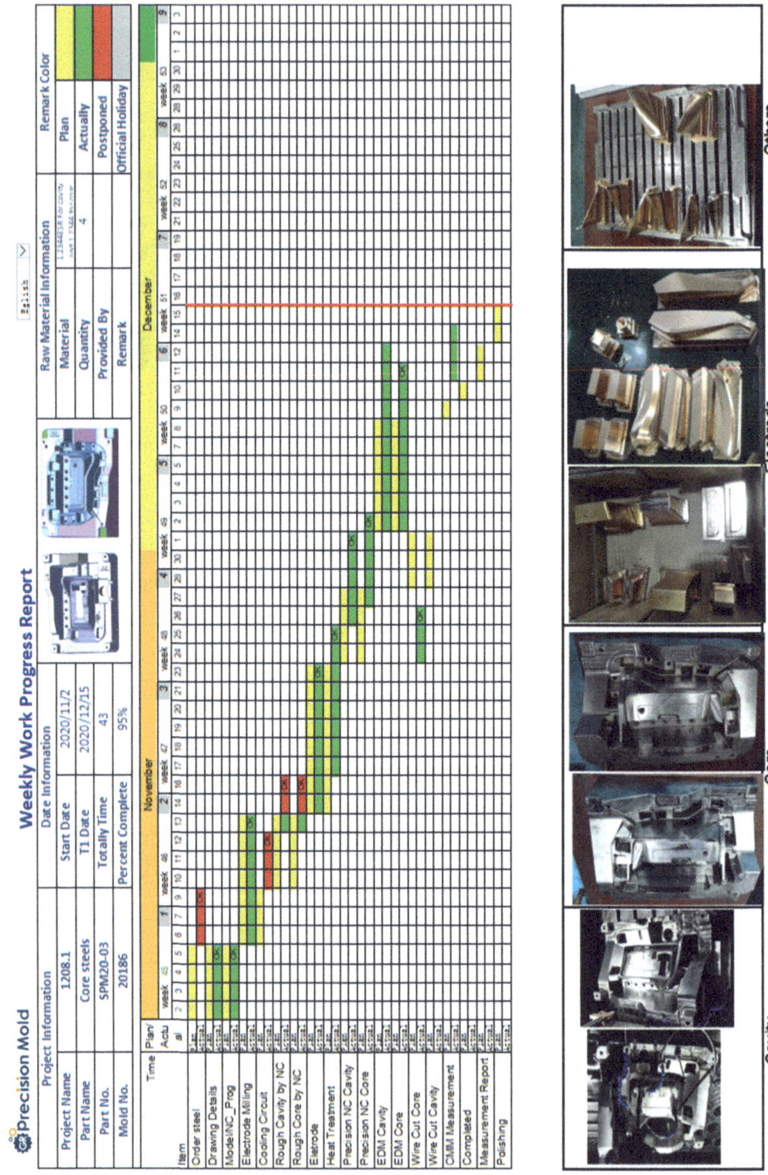

Fig. 6.28 Weekly Work Progress Report. *Source:* GRPrecisionMold, grprecisionmold.com, QingXi Town, DongGuan, China, published 2021

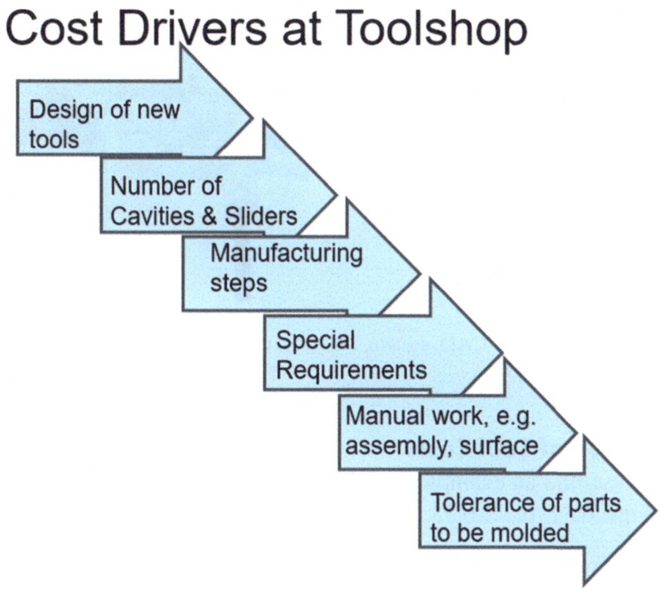

Fig. 6.29 Cost drivers at toolshops. *Source*: Adapted from Master Thesis of Rolf Meyer, page 59, 24.10.2002 at University of Applied Science, Offenburg

What Are the Cost Drivers at Toolshop?

You easily can lower your tool costs by design to costs and design to manufacturing. We call it frontloading by inviting experts from customer, toolshop, suppliers and manufacturing to discuss their requirements at beginning of R&D phase of part design (Fig. 6.29).

Influence of Design to Lifetime of Mold

How to lower your tool costs by design to costs and design to manufacturing?

First, the rational design of the product is a major factor for the cost of the mold. For example, in order to complete the under-cut structure of the product, the mold must be designed very complex, it will result in an increase in the cost of the mold.

Second, the general design scheme of the mold should be formulated reasonably and design concept should be correct, during the mold design process, the designer should consider more on future assembly, operation and deformation issues. This work can be done early to identify many of the assembly issues and interference issues in processing. These issues should be solved from the beginning of mold designing.

Third, the mold joint surfaces should be designed reasonably, this can reduce the processing workload and control the processing cost, which is improving the life and quality of the mould (Fig. 6.30).

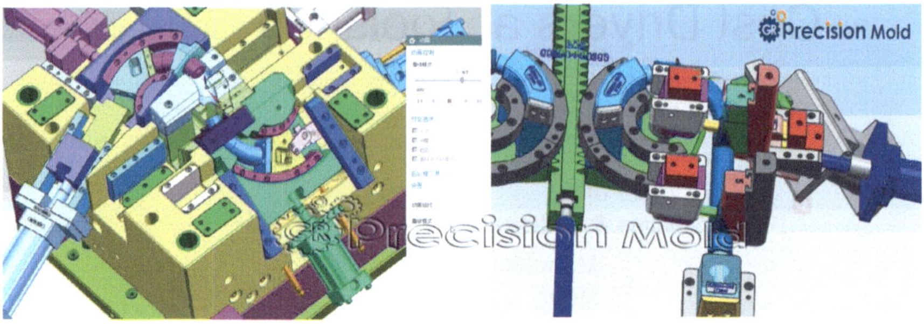

Fig. 6.30 Mold design with CAD system. *Source:* GRPrecisionMold, grprecisionmold.com, QingXi Town, DongGuan, China

Cost Calculation of Tool Costs

Following please find an example of cost calculation of a mould for housing, made of Zamak (Figs. 6.31, 6.32, 6.33, 6.34, 6.35, 6.36 and 6.37).

6.5 Overhead Costs

6.5.1 What About Material Overheads?

As explained in Sect. 3.4.1 and this chapter, material overhead are expenses for purchasing, inventory planning, warehouse entry storage, income inspection and product testing, and inhouse transporting. All needed resources to bring parts to the first working system (e.g., first machine) for further treatment.

Is material overhead dependent on parts size? Does this calculation have an impact on the price? If part size is large, is overheads up to 10% possible? In automotive industry, material overheads of 5% is standard. But actually, it is wrong, if you stick to details. High material share should have lower indirect material costs in %, to be reasonable.

Further details see Fig. 6.2, where you will find workflow of material overhead (OH) and payment terms, and this chapter, where you will get a summary of what could be added to MOC (material overhead costs) (Fig. 6.21).

Materials overhead (or materials handling costs) has a wide range of values of the price to the prime, which vary by company, stage of development (EMD or production), whether special handling is required, volume of the purchased materials, and so forth.[24] To reduce material overhead to become lean, following activities are recommended, with responsibility in Purchasing department:

[24] *Source*: https://www.rand.org/pubs/monograph_reports/MR1325.html, Cook, Cynthia R. and John C. Graser, Military Airframe Acquisition Costs: The Effects of Lean Manufacturing. Santa Monica, US, at RAND Corporation, published 2001. Access date 26.2.2021

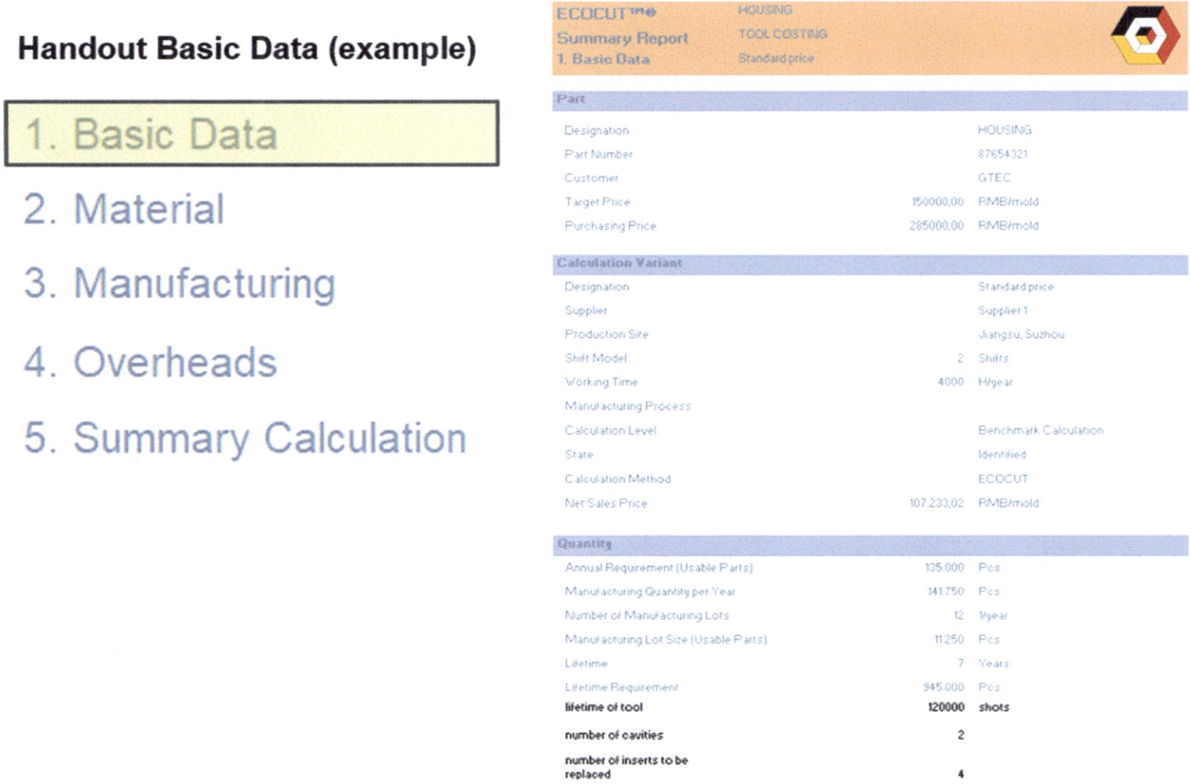

Fig. 6.31 *ECOCUT Handout Sheet no. 1 Basic data*

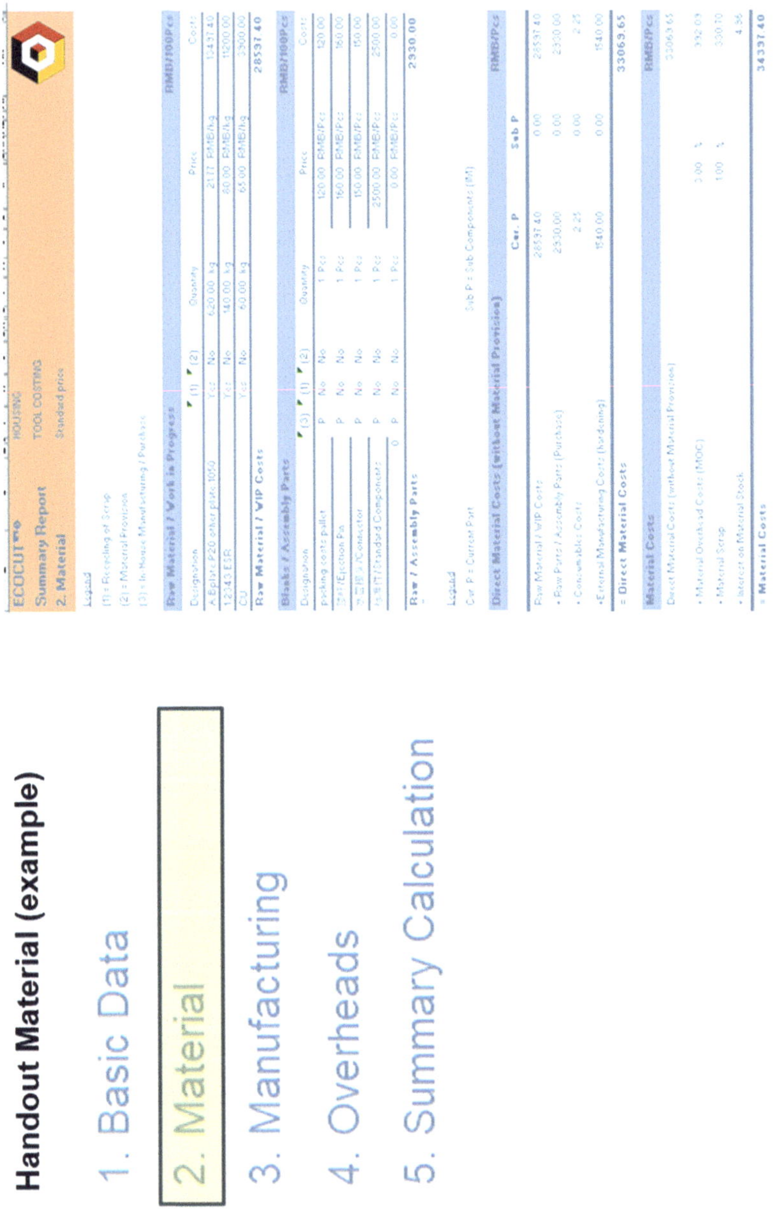

Fig. 6.32 *ECOCUT Handout Sheet no. 2 Material cost calculation*

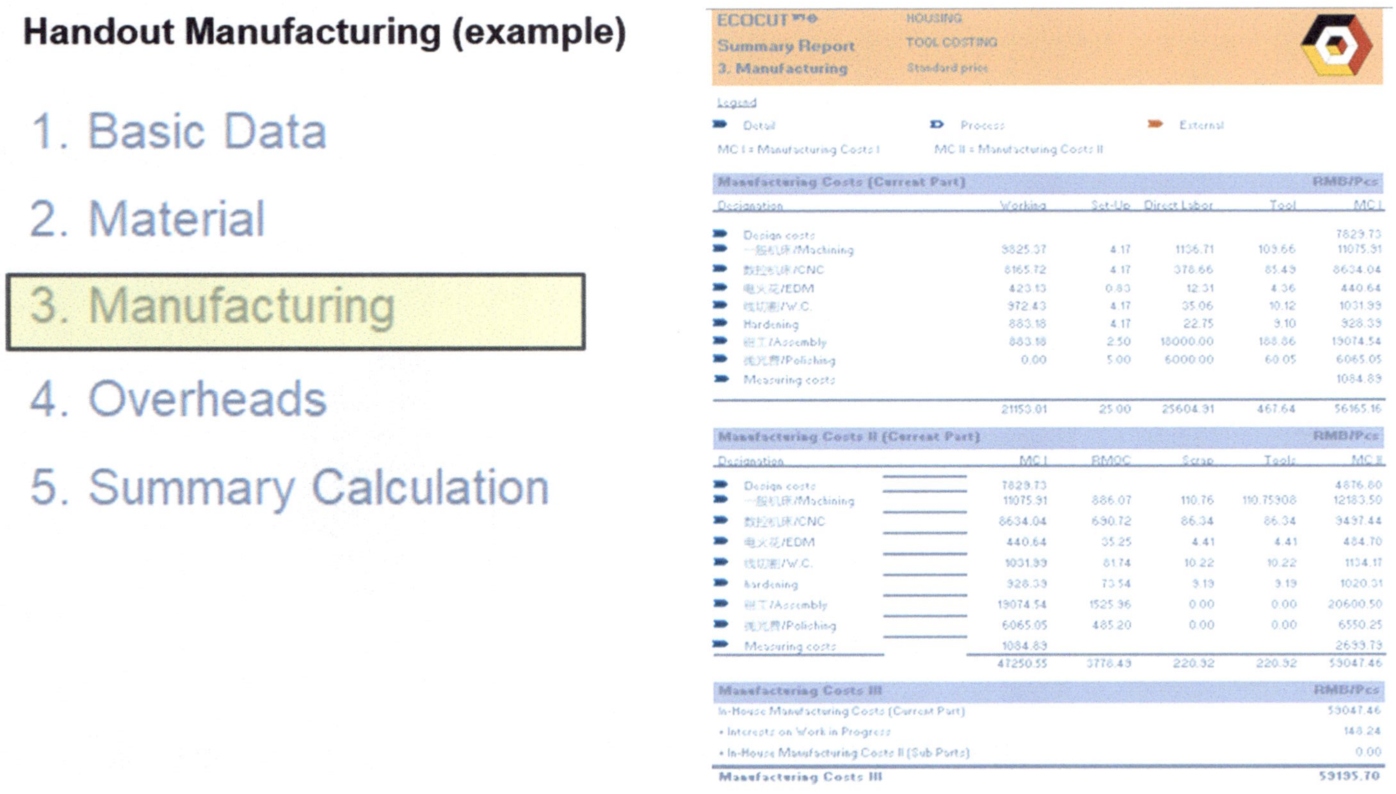

Manufacturing Costs (Current Part)					RMB/Pcs
Designation	Working	Set-Up	Direct Labor	Tool	MC I
Design costs					7829.73
一般机床/Machining	9825.37	4.17	1136.71	109.66	11075.91
数控机床/CNC	8165.72	4.17	378.66	85.49	8634.04
电火花/EDM	423.13	0.83	12.31	4.36	440.64
线切割/W.C.	972.43	4.17	35.06	10.12	1031.99
Hardening	883.18	4.17	22.75	9.10	928.39
钳工/Assembly	883.18	2.50	18000.00	188.86	19074.54
抛光费/Polishing	0.00	5.00	6000.00	60.05	6065.05
Measuring costs					1084.89
	21153.01	25.00	25604.91	467.64	56165.16

Manufacturing Costs II (Current Part)					RMB/Pcs
Designation	MC I	RMOC	Scrap	Tools	MC II
Design costs	7829.73				4876.80
一般机床/Machining	11075.91	886.07	110.76	110.75908	12183.50
数控机床/CNC	8634.04	690.72	86.34	86.34	9497.44
电火花/EDM	440.64	35.25	4.41	4.41	484.70
线切割/W.C.	1031.99	81.74	10.22	10.22	1134.17
hardening	928.39	73.54	9.19	9.19	1020.31
钳工/Assembly	19074.54	1525.96	0.00	0.00	20600.50
抛光费/Polishing	6065.05	485.20	0.00	0.00	6550.25
Measuring costs	1084.89				2699.79
	47250.55	3778.49	220.92	220.92	59047.46

Manufacturing Costs III	RMB/Pcs
In-House Manufacturing Costs (Current Part)	59047.46
+ Interests on Work in Progress	148.24
+ In-House Manufacturing Costs II (Sub Parts)	0.00
Manufacturing Costs III	59195.70

Fig. 6.33 *ECOCUT Handout Sheet no. 3 Manufacturing process step cost calculation*

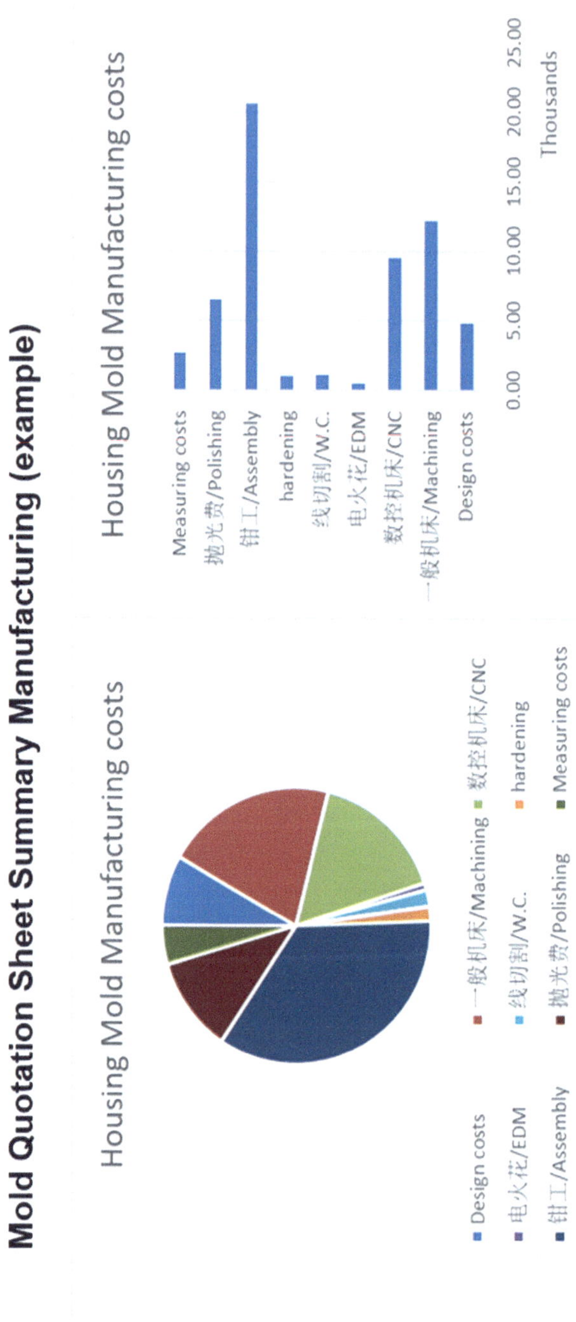

Fig. 6.34 *ECOCUT Handout Sheet no. 3 Manufacturing process step cost presentations*

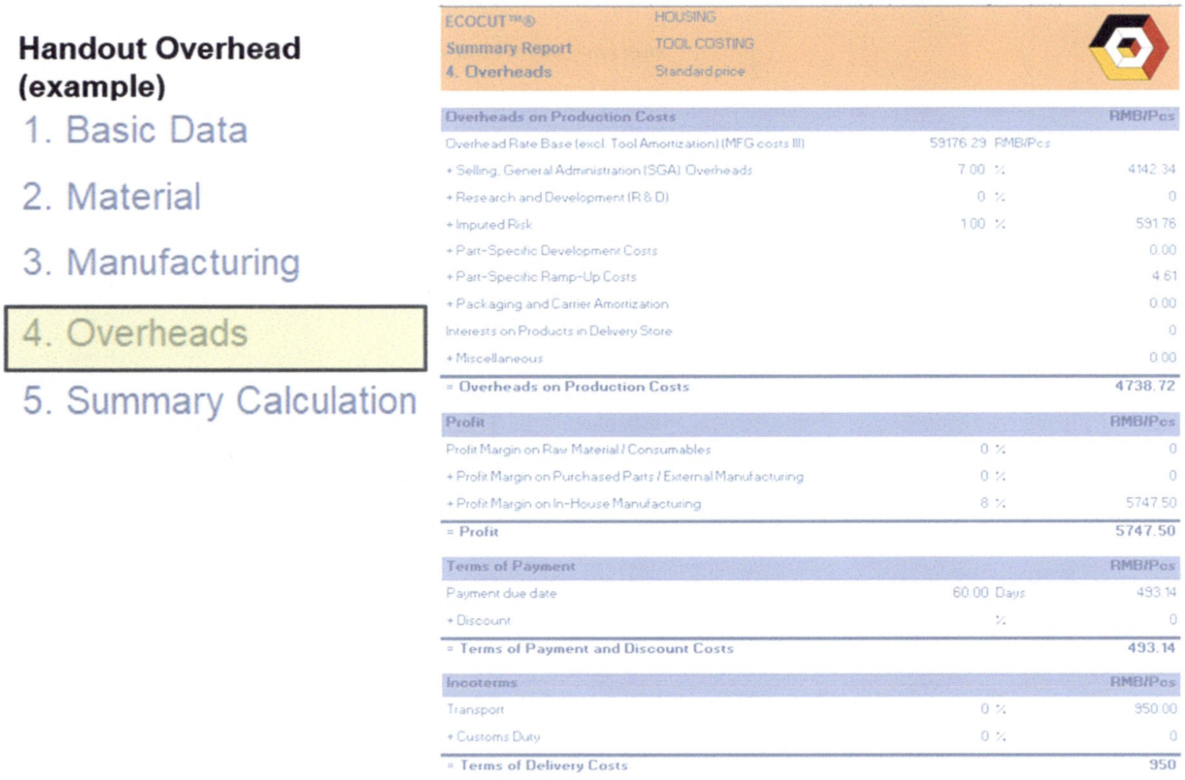

Fig. 6.35 *ECOCUT Handout Sheet no. 4 Overheads cost calculation*

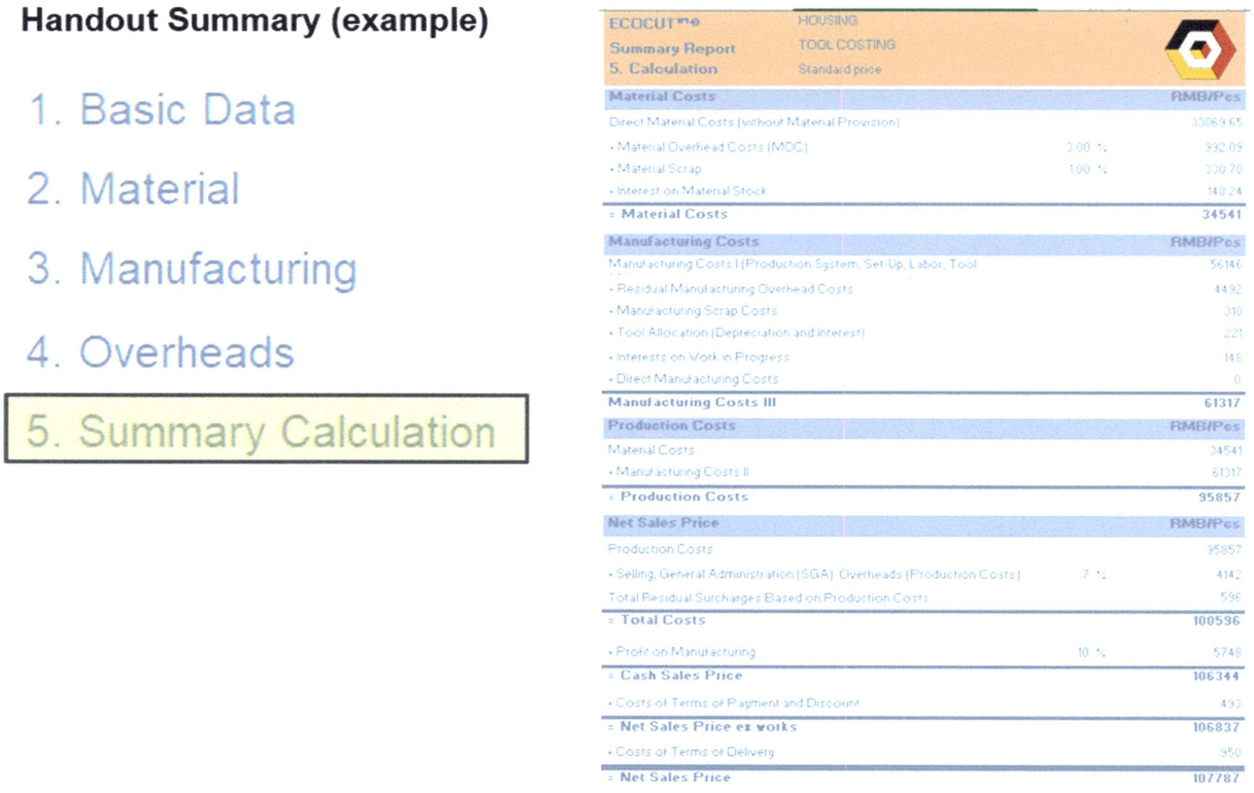

Fig. 6.36 *ECOCUT Handout Sheet no. 5 Summary of all sheets to get net sales price*

Mold Quotation Sheet Summary Net Sales Price (example)

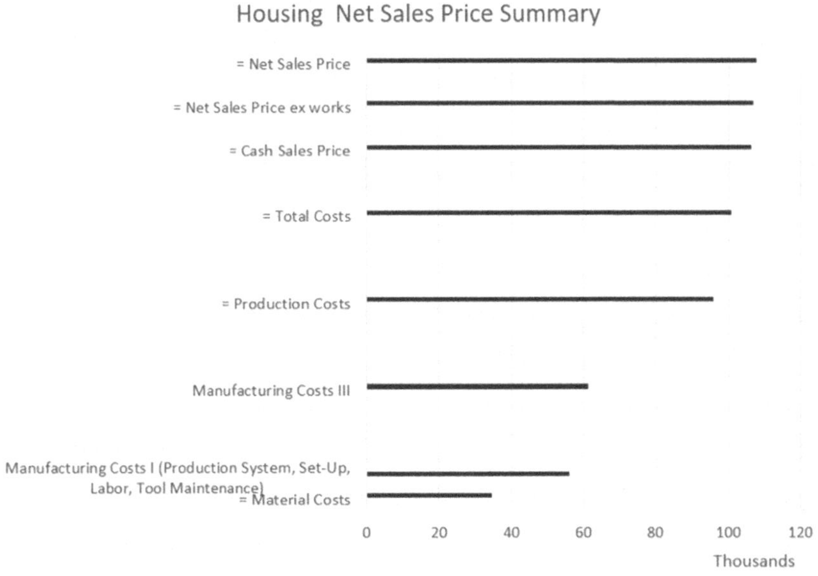

Fig. 6.37 *ECOCUT Net sales price presentation*

- Reduce the materials overhead costs at the prime and major subcontractors.
- A top-tier purchasing teams is well trained and will therefore sustain great core practices and move forward with employing disruptive procurement strategies, bringing entrepreneurship and innovation to supply markets and supply chains. You don't need many of them. Check your number of staff at purchasing department and keep it lean.
- Participate in every morning Asaichi meeting and plant tour to see ideas for improvements, especially at warehouse entry storage planning and checking incoming material turnover and flow.
- Write your ideas for improvements on boards, find commitments of responsible people and follow up accordingly.
- If supplier is telling you, he has high percentage of IMC, let it break down and work together with them to find the root cause, and improve within a given time frame (Tables 6.3 and 6.4).

6.5.2 Manufacturing Overheads MOHC?

Manufacturing overhead includes other costs **in manufacturing** that are neither direct materials costs nor direct labor costs. Therefore, sometimes it is calles Residual MOHC. Manufacturing overheads (also called in US factory burden, work or factory overhead FO) will be calculated as a percentage of primary costs,

Table 6.3 Calculation of IMC. Solution based on Fig. 6.42. Source: GTEC, 2020

Total costs	100%	100%
Material costs	55%	25%
IMC (Indirect Material Costs)	5%	5%
Manufacturing costs (incl. OH)	30%	60%
SG&A	10%	10%
Material costs/ production costs	60/90 = 67%	30/90 = 33%
IMC	about 3%	About 4.5%
Solution:	IMC too high	IMC too high.

Table 6.4 Shows a solution for cause justified allocation of indirect material costs. Figure 3.14 shows the corresponding graph. Source: Tsetinis & Partners, 2010

Material costs/ production costs	IMC (indirect material costs)
10%	5%
20%	4.5%
30%	4.5%
40%	4%
50%	4%
60%	3.5%
70%	3.0%
80%	2.5%
90%	2.0%

which includes all the indirect factory-related expenses incurred in manufacturing a product[25]:

- Wages of employees in the factory who for example work on record keeping and inspection of materials, e.g. costs of quality staff, administrative staff, cost of doctors, etc.
- Costs of internal transportation and material handling like forklifts
- Electricity for the equipment and lighting
- Cleaning costs of equipment, Janitorial Service
- Maintenance and repair of the equipment,
- Computing the operation of the process of manufacturing the product
- Safety and quality cost
- Plant Repairs
- Part Approval
- Purchased Services

[25] *Source*: https://en.wikipedia.org/wiki/MOH_cost; article "MOH cost", last edited on 11 February 2018; access date 26.2.2021

- Quality Control, Material Control
- Pre-production & Start-up
- Staff overhead and other overheads for indirect labour, Indirect Labour Wages, Plant Staff—Fixed

Which means, including production floor costs which are the wages paid to all indirect labours, like forklift drivers, material handlers, product inspectors, quality-control inspectors, and equipment repair and maintenance personnel.

Setup-crew: Set-up costs will put in the Direct Labour category when it is the operator's responsibility for set-up and in Misc. Plant Overhead when it is done by a set-up crew.

But also need to be considered other production-related costs[26]:

- Equipment, like gantry crane, telephone costs, miscellaneous plant equipment
- Operating supplies expenses, Lubricants, Fuel, Small Tools
- Heat and Light, Power, Water
- Auxiliary spaces, which are not covered by machines, e.g. canteen, buffer warehouse
- Defective work, spoilage, repairs
- Employee Fringe Benefits, Workers' Compensation Insurance
- Overtime Premium
- Plant Security
- All other Indirect Materials
- Telephone/Fax
- The lease/rental cost of a building used in manufacturing
- Taxes, property tax
- depreciation on factory
- Insurance expenses
- Storage—WIP (Work-in-Process)
- Storage—Finished Goods
- Utilities
- Equipment Overhead
- Interest Expense
- Depreciation of Bldg & Misc. Equipment
- Other Manufacturing Expenses (OME)

The collection of these expenses will be done via cost centres and their cost distribution sheets (operational accounting sheet):

[26] *Source*: https://smallbusiness.chron.com/determine-factory-overhead-budget-74673.html; By Karen Rogers, updated April 10, 2019, access date 26.2.2021

Guidance for Manufacturing Overheads

Technical Staff	0.84%
Production Staff	14.47%
Quality Staff	6.75%
Administration Staff	4.04%
Material Handling	4.04%
Other Overheads (doctors, etc.)	3.86%

Guidance for Maintenance Overheads (Processes)

	Printing	Treatments	Plastics	Rubbers	Textiles	Glasses	Foundry
Small Machines	5%						
Big machines	10%						
Painting		10%					
Electrolytic Covering		15%					
Compression			15%	18%			
Injection-Extrusion			20%	25%			
Punching					20%		
Spinning					30%		
Average						30%	25%

For example, say your direct materials, manufacturing and labor costs are $50,000, your factory overhead costs (manufacturing, maintenance, cleaning, etc.) are $20,000 and you produce 50,000 units. Divide $70,000 by 50,000 to get the $1.40 per-unit cost. Your selling price must at least exceed $1.40 to make a profit on each sale.

In this case, you ignored your SG&A, which is, for example, 10% of $70,000. If you do. Sales price must be above $1.54 to make a profit.

You can adjust your profit margin by increasing the sales price per unit while decreasing your production costs.[27]

Gross Salary Costs for Company

The gross cost of employees is salary + social + taxes.

In China (as large as Europe), salaries range widely. Even in the same area, the salary is different across industries, and different companies are also quite different. In the Shanghai area, an operator's salary is about 400 Euro/month. But outside Shanghai, it becomes 180 Euro/months. In the west and north of China, salaries can go down to 80 Euro/months (Fig. 6.38).

[27] *Source*: https://smallbusiness.chron.com/determine-factory-overhead-budget-74673.html, by Author Karen Rogers, updated April 10, 2019, access date 26.2.2021

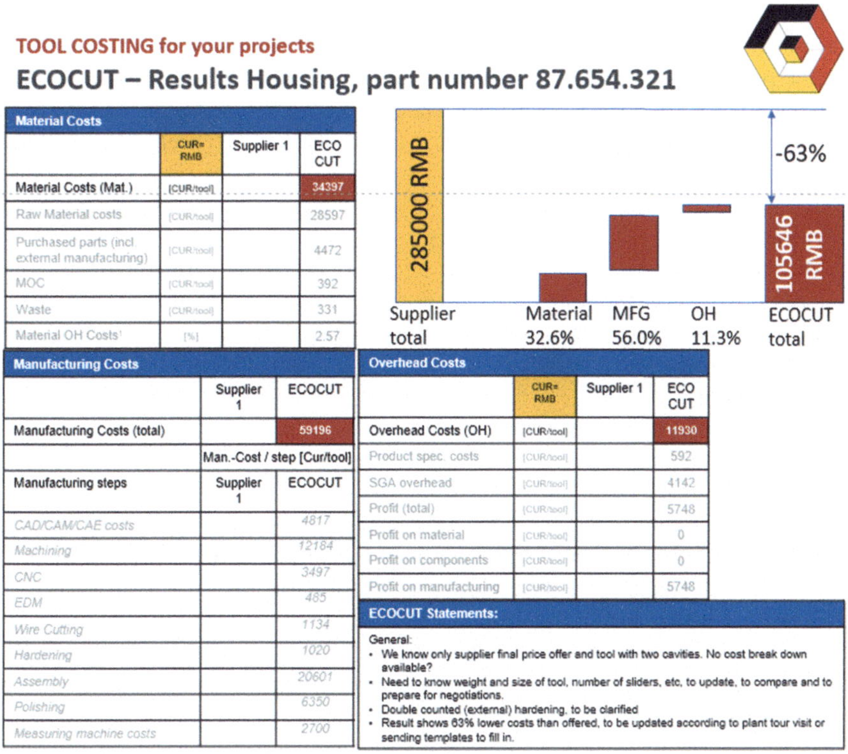

Material Costs	CUR= RMB	Supplier 1	ECO CUT
Material Costs (Mat.)	[CUR/tool]		34397
Raw Material costs	[CUR/tool]		28597
Purchased parts (incl. external manufacturing)	[CUR/tool]		4472
MOC	[CUR/tool]		392
Waste	[CUR/tool]		331
Material OH Costs¹	[%]		2.57

Manufacturing Costs	Supplier 1	ECOCUT
Manufacturing Costs (total)		59196
	Man.-Cost / step [Cur/tool]	
Manufacturing steps	Supplier 1	ECOCUT
CAD/CAM/CAE costs		4817
Machining		12184
CNC		3497
EDM		485
Wire Cutting		1134
Hardening		1020
Assembly		20601
Polishing		6350
Measuring machine costs		2700

Overhead Costs	CUR= RMB	Supplier 1	ECO CUT
Overhead Costs (OH)	[CUR/tool]		11930
Product spec. costs	[CUR/tool]		592
SGA overhead	[CUR/tool]		4142
Profit (total)	[CUR/tool]		5748
Profit on material	[CUR/tool]		0
Profit on components	[CUR/tool]		0
Profit on manufacturing	[CUR/tool]		5748

ECOCUT Statements:

General:

- We know only supplier final price offer and tool with two cavities. No cost break down available?
- Need to know weight and size of tool, number of sliders, etc. to update, to compare and to prepare for negotiations.
- Double counted (external) hardening, to be clarified
- Result shows 63% lower costs than offered, to be updated according to plant tour visit or sending templates to fill in.

Fig. 6.38 ECOCUT Handout of cost calculation comparison between Supplier and ECOCUT software. Source: Schaeffler AG, 2013

Minimum salaries in China is announced and published by Ministry of Human Resources and Social Security. It will be adjusted and increased every year with a certain percentage. Details can be find written at http://english.www.gov.cn/services. Each province, city or other administrative units sets its own minimum wage according to its local economic conditions. The minimum wage is divided into two kinds: monthly minimum wage applies to full-time workers and hourly minimum wage applies to part-time workers. For example, in Shanghai minimum salary is 2480 RMB/month in 2019 and 2020. Other provinces are even divided into several districts A to D with different minimum wages, where big cities of each province have the highest wages. Heilongjiang District D has the lowest minimum salary with 1030 RMB/months and hourly minimum wage of 10 RMB.[28]

To compare minimum salary with other countries, please visit https://tradingeconomics.com/country-list/minimum-wages

and/or

[28] *Source*: https://en.wikipedia.org/wiki/Minimum_wage_in_China, last edited on 2 November 2020;, access date 27.2.2021

https://en.wikipedia.org/wiki/Minimum_wage_in_China (in category Minimum wage in Asia).

Companies has to pay minimum required social costs and taxes to their employees, but will pay additional social insurances and other allowances, e.g. transportation, clothes, meals, etc., to attract and to keep Chinese staff motivated.

- Pension
- Medical Insurance
- Unemployment Insurance
- Work-Related Injury Insurance
- Maternity Insurance
- Housing Fund
- Commercial/Supplemental Health Insurance
- Supplemental Housing Fund (Fig. 6.39)

However, the contribution rates for social insurance and housing fund are updated every year and change according to city jurisdiction. So, some cities like Beijing, Shanghai, and Guangzhou have different contribution rates for employers and employees (Chinese and foreigners). For example Shanghai: (Fig. 6.40).

For engineers, they generally earn 1.5 to 2 times more than operators. For managers, no fixed standard is given. You need to prepare a database for each country, provinces and cities where your suppliers are located. During supplier visits you will ask how many people are working in which department and can calculate the direct and indirect manpower costs.

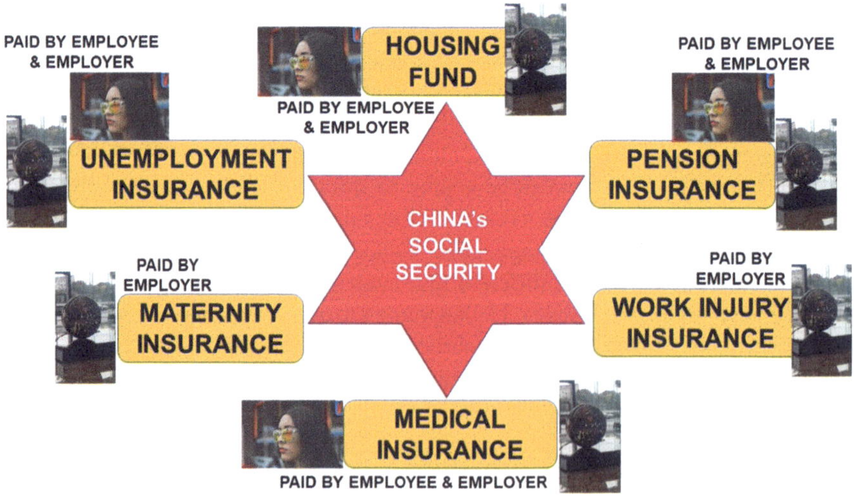

Fig. 6.39 China social security law. Source: https://www.hrone.com/guide-chinas-social-security-system-pays/. By HROne updated March 29, 2018, access date 27.2.2021

TOOL COSTING for your projects

ECOCUT – Results Housing, part number 87.654.321

Material Costs			
	CUR= RMB	Supplier 1	ECO CUT
Material Costs (Mat.)	[CUR/tool]		34397
Raw Material costs	[CUR/tool]		28597
Purchased parts (incl. external manufacturing)	[CUR/tool]		4472
MOC	[CUR/tool]		392
Waste	[CUR/tool]		331
Material OH Costs[1]	[%]		2.57

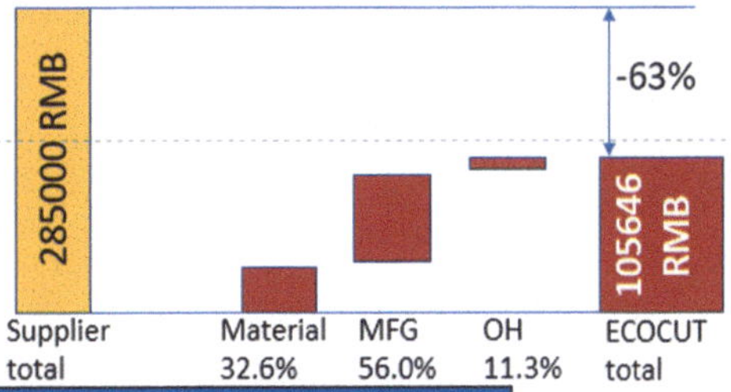

Manufacturing Costs		
	Supplier 1	ECOCUT
Manufacturing Costs (total)		59196
	Man.-Cost / step [Cur/tool]	
Manufacturing steps	Supplier 1	ECOCUT
CAD/CAM/CAE costs		4817
Machining		12184
CNC		3497
EDM		485
Wire Cutting		1134
Hardening		1020
Assembly		20601
Polishing		6350
Measuring machine costs		2700

Overhead Costs			
	CUR= RMB	Supplier 1	ECO CUT
Overhead Costs (OH)	[CUR/tool]		11930
Product spec. costs	[CUR/tool]		592
SGA overhead	[CUR/tool]		4142
Profit (total)	[CUR/tool]		5748
Profit on material	[CUR/tool]		0
Profit on components	[CUR/tool]		0
Profit on manufacturing	[CUR/tool]		5748

ECOCUT Statements:

General:

- We know only supplier final price offer and tool with two cavities. No cost break down available?
- Need to know weight and size of tool, number of sliders, etc, to update, to compare and to prepare for negotiations.
- Double counted (external) hardening, to be clarified
- Result shows 63% lower costs than offered, to be updated according to plant tour visit or sending templates to fill in.

Fig. 6.40 For Shanghai, employer need to add minimum 38.16% on top of salary. *Source*: https://www.hrone.com/guide-chinas-social-security-system-pays/ By HROne updated March 29, 2018, access date 27.2.2021

Details may be available on the websites of local government institutes in each provincial capital city, e.g. China Statistical Yearbook http://www.stats.gov.cn/tjsj/ndsj/2019/indexeh.htm, file 4–16, where you can find salaries at Chinese provinces and sectors. Alternatively see private companies websites like www.glassdoor.com for engineers.

6.5.3 Selling, General and Administration Expenses SG&A

SG&A includes all non-production costs. While SG&A typically doesn't absorb as much revenue as cost of goods sold, it is still usually anywhere from 15 to 25 percent of revenue.

Selling costs can include advertising, sales commissions, and promotional costs. General expenses would be things such as office rent, utilities, office supplies, and insurance. Finally, administrative costs encompass

- Salaries for administrative staff and executives, as well as fees or salaries for professional services such as IT, accounting, or attorneys
- Printing and stationery, other office supplies
- Office rent & lease rates, insurance expenses, depreciation of office building and other assets
- Legal expenses, audit fees, bank charges etc.
- Purchased Services
- Supplies Expense
- Taxes
- Correspondence Expense
- Travel Expenses
- Entertainment Expense
- Advertising Expense
- Interest Expense
- Utilities

Administrative overheads are to be analysed into two—one for production activities and other for sales and distribution activities.

Administrative overheads relating to production activities are to be apportioned to different production cost centres on the basis conversion costs of production cost centres.

The apportioned overheads are absorbed to products on the basis of the normal capacity or actual capacity, whichever is higher. In case of under-absorption or over-absorption of administrative overheads relating to production, the same shall also be adjusted with Costing Profit & Loss Account.

Apportionment and absorption of Selling overheads and Distribution overheads:

- The selling overheads and distribution overheads are collected under different cost centers such as: (a) Selling Overheads (b) Sales Employees cost (c) Rent (d) Traveling expenses (e) Warranty claim (f) Brokerage & Commission (f) Advertisement relating to sales and sales promotion (g) Sales incentive (h) Bad debt etc.
- Distribution Overheads are collected under: (a) Secondary Packaging (b) Freight & forwarding (c) Warehousing & storage (d) Insurance etc.[29]

High SG&A expenses in relation to revenue can be problematic for almost any business. Management often attempts to keep SG&A expenses limited to a certain percentage of revenue, though that figure may vary significantly depending on sector

[29] *Source*: https://icmai.in/CASB/casb-about.php; by The Institute of Cost Accountants of India, CAS3 revised 2015, access date 27.2.2021

Table 6.5 Shows a solution for cause justified allocation of Indirect Admin Cost IAC & Indirect Sales & Marketing Costs ISC. Figure 3.15 shows the corresponding graph. Source: Tsetinis & Partners, 2010

Portion of material costs in production costs	IAC & ISC
90%	1.8%
80%	3.6%
70%	5.4%
50%	9.0%
40%	10%
30%	11%

Table 6.6 Shows calculation of sales, general and administration overhead SG&A. Solution based on Fig. 6.45. graph. Source: GTEC, 2020

Total costs	100%	100%
Material costs (incl. OH)	60%	30%
Manufacturing costs (incl. OH)	30%	60%
Overhead SG&A costs	10%	10%
Material/ production costs	60/90 = 67%	30/90 = 33%
IAC & ISC	about 5.4%	About 11%
Solution:	SG&A too high	SG&A too low.

and industry, as well as from company to company, as different firms target their own operational models.[30]

How to calculate the total cost rate of sales and administration overheads? How many people are necessary for SG&A? Please check the number of customers and their turnover in relation to the amount of parts you are buying from your supplier.

SG&A overhead is based on production costs (material and manufacturing). High production costs is not cause justified. If there is a high cost of raw material, there must be a high refund of overhead costs.

Table 6.5 shows a solution for cause justified allocation of Indirect Admin Cost IAC & Indirect Sales& Marketing Costs ISC. Figure 3.15 shows the corresponding graph.

The administrative and marketing overheads are tiered as a function of the production depth. If their share of turnover is particularly high, the plausibility of the administrative costs and, in particular, the marketing costs is to be inspected. If there is no correlation, the administrative, sales and marketing overheads must be attributed to their causes (process cost analysis) (Table 6.6).

[30] *Source*: https://www.thebalance.com/selling-general-and-administrative-expenses-sga-357595, by Joshua Kennon, updated March 24, 2020. Access date 27.2.2021

6.5.4 Other Overheads

Basic Development Costs
are incurred as a result of innovative, ongoing development work unrelated to any firm customer order and in respect of technology and processes (not development costs specific to any particular part).

Generally speaking, basic development costs are incurred by system suppliers. Plausibility check of basic development work can be carried out using the following benchmarks:

- Manpower numbers and costs per employee for customer's basic development work
- Proportionate investment in customer's basic development work
- Number of units over life cycle

Basic development cost components:

- Process development/optimization
- Research
- Preliminary development

Supplier Engineering Development Costs
Supplier development costs cover engineering services, testing parts, and testing/ prototype tools for suppliers providing development services and series inputs. Supplier development costs must be shown separately in cost break downs.

Engineering services are comprised of services that occur in the product creation process for project management, design, calculation, simulation, and testing. However be aware suppliers' "Project realization costs", "project structure costs", or "project team costs" are already included in the materials overheads, residual overheads, or the administration and sales overheads.

Experimental parts cover all prototype parts, A, B, C, and D samples, as well as test samples and pre-production series parts. The hardware costs for the experimental parts of supplier should be refunded directly by customer.

Experimental tools include all mechanisms needed to create experimental parts. The term also covers all auxiliary and prototype tools and pre-production series tools. The development costs for experimental tools are refunded directly by customers by separate invoice, independent from product costing in series production.

6.5.5 Change Management

Change management (design changes, concept changes, new contents) is not included in the cost evaluation process. Normally suppliers are asked for

Reason for change / workflow	Caused by company	Supplier's written change notification	Caused by company and supplier		Caused by supplier
Change caused by	company	tbd	Company	supplier	supplier
communication	Company's written change notification	Supplier's written change notification		Supplier's written change notification	
agreement	Settlement like to current communication version	tbd	Settlement like to current communication version	No payment	No payment

Fig. 6.41 Supplier will be paid if changes caused by customer. Validation in all cases based on root cause based allocated costs. *Source*: Daimler Chrysler

modification of their offer and hand-in a new offer with cost-break down to purchasing department of their customers (Fig. 6.41).

6.5.6 Profit Margin

Gross profit margin = gross profit ÷ total revenue

For this exercise, assume your industry sector has a gross margin of 30%.

Take the numbers from your company's income statement and plug them into the gross profit margin formula:

TRMB162,084 gross profit ÷ TRMB 405,209 total revenue = 0.40, or 40%.

40% reveals that your company's business is much more efficient in the production and distribution of its product than most of your competitors.[31]

Operating (profit) margin = Operating Income/Sales.

To calculate the operating margin, divide your operating income result from above by total revenue.

Total revenue = total sales.

Operating Income/Sales = Operating Margin.

Gross Profit—Operating Expenses = Operating Income.

(Gross Profit—Operating Expenses) /Sales = Operating Margin.

Whether the percentage result qualifies as a good operating margin depends on the industry.[32]

[31] *Source*: https://www.thebalance.com/calculating-gross-profit-margin-357577, by Joshua Kennon, updated February 3, 2020. Access date 27.2.2021

[32] *Source*: https://www.thebalance.com/operating-income-and-operating-profit-margin-357587, by Joshua Kennon, updated October 26, 2020. Access date 27.2.2021

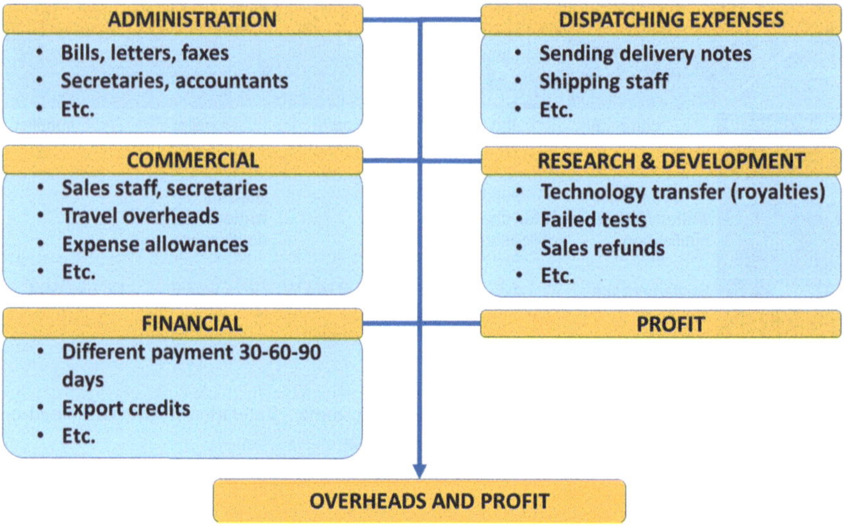

Fig. 6.42 Summary of SG&A. *Source:* General Motors Europe, 2004

6.5.7 Overheads and Profit

Example: Small Stamping Company (Fig. 6.42).

Administration Overhead:	2,55%
Commercial Overheads:	1,86%
Financial Overheads:	1,56%
Dispatching Overheads:	1,90%

6.6 Profit

Generally, a % rate calculated as profit on COGS (cost of goods sold). But in detail, there is

- Profit on material
- Profit on subcomponents and purchased manufacturing steps
- Profit on added value (inhouse manufacturing)

The profit on material and purchased parts is already included in the markup and is taken out of customer's piece price calculation. Suppliers will argue about it, as their cost break down is different. Normally, purchasing department doesn't like that suppliers become dealers, buying and selling material & parts, only assembly inhouse, as purchasing price is higher than buying at a supplier with high inhouse production depth.

In the automotive industry, profit has now become established to differentiate as well in the same way. Bases for profit is the market. As many suppliers in a competition, the profit margin here is rather low.

"From 300% profit on, crime will start"(Lenin).

6.7 Terms of Payment

Businesses that go bankrupt usually do not do so because they are not profitable. Rather, they go bankrupt because their cash reserves run dry, and they are unable to meet current payment obligations. An otherwise profitable company may also run out of cash because their capital requirements continue to increase in order to support additional investment in inventories and accounts receivable as they grow.

To avoid this pitfall, you need to take care of your working capital ratio, your cash flow and payment terms.

The working capital ratio is commonly used to assess a company's financial performance. Low working capital ratio values, near one or lower, can indicate serious financial problems within a company. The working capital ratio reveals whether the company has enough short-term assets to pay off its short-term debt.

Most major projects require an investment in working capital, which reduces cash flow. Cash flow will also be reduced if money is collected too slowly, or if sales volumes are decreasing, which will lead to a fall in accounts receivable. Suppliers that are using working capital inefficiently often try to boost cash flow by squeezing their customers.

The working capital ratio measures a company's efficiency and the health of its short-term finances. The formula to determine working capital is the company's current assets minus its current liabilities.

For example, if a company has $800,000 of current assets and $400,000 of current liabilities, its working capital is $400,000. If a company has $800,000 of current assets and $800,000 of current liabilities, it has no working capital.

Changes to either assets or liabilities will cause a change in net working capital.

For example, if a business owner invests an additional $10,000 in his company, assets increase by $10,000, but current liabilities do not increase. Thus, working capital increases by $10,000. If that same company were to borrow $10,000 and agree to pay it back in less than one year, the working capital has not increased, because both assets and liabilities increased by $10,000.

Low Working Capital

If a company's working capital ratio value is below zero, it has a negative cash flow, meaning its current assets are less than its liabilities. The company cannot cover its debts with its current working capital. In this situation, a company is likely to have difficulty paying back its creditors. If a company continues to have low working capital, or if it continues to decline over a period of time, it may have serious financial trouble. The cause of the decrease in working capital could be a result of several different factors, including decreasing sales revenues, mismanagement of inventory, or problems with accounts receivable.[33]

High Working Capital

An excessively high working capital is not necessarily a good thing either, since it can indicate the company is allowing excess cash flow to sit idle rather than effectively reinvesting it in company growth. Most analysts consider the ideal working capital ratio to be between 1.2 and 2. As with other performance metrics, it is important to compare a company's ratio to those of similar companies within the industry.

To sign contracts with suppliers, you need to have carefully evaluated your risks. For example, if suppliers need to be paid within 30 or 60 days, but your sales person signed a contract with a customer for 90 days, you will run into cash flow problems.

Terms of Payment, to be calculated out of the following two items:

- Period of interest
- Interest rate

Payment terms usually show the option of a long payment period without deduction, and payment terms with a shorter period and a cash discount.

To calculate payment terms, interest is calculated for the payment terms with the general interest rate. If a cash discount is also granted, this must be added separately.

a 60 days, net

Period of interest:	60 days
Interest rate:	e.g. 4,3%

b 3% discount within 10 days

Period of interest:	10 Tage
Interest rate:	e.g. 4,3%
Discount:	3%

For example: 3% discount for 10 days, or 60 days net.

6.8 Taxes

Any taxes are not part of your cost calculation, but need to be considered as part of your company business.

Value-Added Tax VAT

Value added tax VAT is always on top and vary from country to country and from commodity to commodity. You will get exact VAT figures from your chamber of commerce and finance department. As of 2018, 166 of the 193 countries with full UN membership employ a VAT, including all OECD members except the United States, where many states use a sales tax system instead. There are two main

[33] *Source*: Accounts Receivable (AR) Definition (investopedia.com), last updated Feb 24, 2021, by Adam Hayes at Ivestopedia.com. Access date 27.2.2021.

methods of calculating VAT: the credit-invoice or invoice-based method, and the subtraction or accounts-based method. Using the credit-invoice method, sales transactions are taxed. The credit-invoice method is used by all national VATs except for Japan, who is using the subtraction method.[34]

VAT Taxes Around the World

The seller charges VAT to the buyer, and the seller pays this VAT to the government. If the purchasers are not the end users, but the goods or services purchased are costs to their business, the tax they have paid for such purchases can be deducted from the tax they charge to their customers. The government receives only the difference; in other words, it is paid tax on the gross margin of each transaction, by each participant in the sales chain.

To fix this problem for import and export, nearly all countries that use VAT use special rules for imported and exported goods:

- All imported goods are charged VAT for their full price when they are sold for the first time
- All exported goods are exempted from any VAT payments

For example, in India VAT is 5.5% (0% in 2 of India's 28 states), Indonesia 10%, Japan 10% (with 8% at groceries), Philippines 12% (with 6% on petroleum products, and electricity and water services), Singapore 9%, South Korea 10%, Taiwan 5%, Thailand 10% (7%), Vietnam 10% (5% or 0%).[35]

Taxes in China

There are 14 kinds of taxes currently applicable to the enterprises with foreign investment, foreign enterprises and/or foreigners, namely: Value Added Tax VAT, Consumption Tax, Business Tax, Income Tax on Enterprises with Foreign Investment and Foreign Enterprises CIT, Individual Income Tax IIT, Resource Tax, Land Appreciation Tax, Urban Real Estate Tax, Vehicle and Vessel Usage License Plate Tax, Stamp Tax, Deed Tax, Slaughter Tax, Agriculture Tax, and Customs Duties.[36]

For Chinese companies, enterprise income tax CIT is levied at the rate of 25%. With regard to the income of a non-resident enterprise, like foreign-invested enterprises FIEs, the applicable tax rate is 20%.[37]

The standard rate of VAT in China is 13%. There is a reduced rate of 9% that applies to products such as books and types of oils, and 6% for services except for PPE lease.

[34] *Source*: https://en.wikipedia.org/wiki/Value-added_tax#China, last updated 15 February 2021. Access date 27.2.2021.

[35] *Source*: https://en.wikipedia.org/wiki/Value-added_tax#Comparison_with_sales_tax (item 7), last updated 15 February 2021. Access date 27.2.2021.

[36] *Source*: https://en.wikipedia.org/wiki/Taxation_in_China, last edited on 17 January 2021, access date 27.2.2021.

[37] *Source*: https://en.wikisource.org/wiki/Enterprise_Income_Tax_Law_of_the_People%27s_Republic_of_China/ last edited on 23 March 2020, access date 27.2.2021.

Fig. 6.43 Monthly tax formula: (taxable income * tax rate)—quick deduction = tax. *Source*: https://en.wikipedia.org/wiki/Income_tax_in_China#:~:text=The%20Individual%20Income%20Tax%20in,days%20on%20worldwide%20earned%20income. Article "Income tax in China", last edited on 23 February 2021; access date 1.3.2021

Taxable income (monthly)			
from [RMB]	to [RMB]	tax rate	Quick deduction
1	2,999	3%	0
3,000	11,999	10%	210
12,000	24,999	20%	1,410
25,000	34,999	25%	2,660
35,000	54,999	30%	4,410
55,000	79,999	35%	7,160
80,000	over	45%	15,160

What is interesting for companies, especially in China, is where you pay your taxes, as they vary from each location. For example, if you do benchmark for relocation of your complete plant, you will consider tax reduction payment as well.

In development zone in PINGHU, close to Shanghai, the local portion of Corporate Income Tax CIT (32%) will be 100% returned for the first 2 years and 50% returned for the next 2 years. The local portion of VAT (20%) will be 100% returned for the first 2 years and 50% returned for the next 2 years.

In comparison, the development zone JIAXING port, as well close to Shanghai: Local portion of IIT: 32%. Local portion of VAT is 40%. Local portion of CIT: 32%. Offer of local government: The local portion of individual income tax will be 100% returned for the first 3 years and 50% refunded for the next 2 years. The local portion of VAT will be 100% returned for the first 3 years and 50% returned for the next 2 years, the local portion of CIT will be 100% returned for the first 3 years and 50% returned for the next 2 years (Fig. 6.43).

China IIT

This individual income tax need to be paid by employee. Finance Accounting will direct transfer.

6.9 Delivery Terms

For shipping from supplier to customer, there are following costs to be considered:

(1) Warehouse management and Inventory costs
(2) Logistics (Transportation costs incl. Transport insurance etc.)
(3) Customs clearance costs, Customs duties
(4) Embargo, Trade barriers (Fig. 6.44)

Incoterms	Export Customs Declaration	Carriage to port of export	Unloading of truck at port of export	Loading charges at port of export	Carriage to port of import	Unloading charges at port of import	Loading on truck at port of import	Carriage to place of destiantion	Insurances	Import Customs Clearance	Import Taxes
EXW	Buyer	Buyer	Buyer	Buyer	Buyer	Buyer	Buyer	Buyer	Buyer	Buyer	Buyer
FCA	Seller	Seller	Buyer	Buyer	Buyer	Buyer	Buyer	Buyer	Buyer	Buyer	Buyer
FAS	Seller	Seller	Seller	Buyer	Buyer	Buyer	Buyer	Buyer	Buyer	Buyer	Buyer
FOB	Seller	Seller	Seller	Seller	Buyer	Buyer	Buyer	Buyer	Buyer	Buyer	Buyer
CFR	Seller	Seller	Seller	Seller	Seller	Seller	Buyer	Buyer	Buyer	Buyer	Buyer
CIF	Seller	Seller	Seller	Seller	Seller	Seller	Seller	Buyer	Seller	Buyer	Buyer
CPT	Seller	Seller	Seller	Seller	Seller	Seller	Seller	Seller	Buyer	Buyer	Buyer
CIP	Seller	Seller	Seller	Seller	Seller	Seller	Seller	Seller	Seller	Buyer	Buyer
DAT	Seller	Seller	Seller	Seller	Seller	Seller	Seller	Seller	Seller	Buyer	Buyer
DAP	Seller	Seller	Seller	Seller	Seller	Seller	Seller	Seller	Seller	Buyer	Buyer
DDP	Seller	Seller	Seller	Seller	Seller	Seller	Seller	Seller	Seller	Seller	Seller

Fig. 6.44 Duties of the seller according to Incoterms. Who carries the duties? *Source:* Incoterms 2010

6.10 Warehouse and Inventory Costs

Sometimes, customers tell you they want to reduce risks in delivery by having a consignment stock close to their plants. They request you to keep stock between a minimum and maximum value and will pay you only if they need to take goods out of your stock. You are able to charge your consignment costs to their part price, but you need to make every cost transparent.

How much is your consignment stock in RMB?

How much is your inventory in RMB?

Are you below your maximum level? Do you measure monthly/yearly?

By the same principle, you can negotiate or dictate to your suppliers. Then you can prepare a regular overview:

How many suppliers do you have in total?

How many of them deliver to a consignment warehouse? How much value in RMB is present in each warehouse type? Please prepare a pie chart to get visualized.

You should mark in red those warehouses or consignments which are owned by your company.

How many of them are defined by customers?

With how many of them have you already negotiated yearly prices?

For example, usually suppliers from Asia do not have any consignment experience abroad. You need to ask your HQ to push and persuade your suppliers to accept consignment close to your plants. If they can accept, you can easily reduce high inventory costs of incoming goods by about 20%.

However in China, there are many warehouse and consignment stock operators and their prices (status 2020) varies a lot. For example for automotive parts, in Northern China between 18 and 42 RMB/m2/month, distribution rate between 0.75 and 7%. China Post Express logistic and few other companies has no charges for warehouse, but distribution rate is between 3.2 and 5.5%.

6.11 How to Improve Warehouse Management KPIs of Suppliers

An overall Lean warehousing strategy depends on measuring the right Key Performance Indicators. Following learn about each **warehouse KPI**, how it is measured, and how it helps drive savings in their distribution centres.[38]

[38] *Source*: https://legacyscs.com/warehouse-kpis-to-measure/, author LEGACY Supply Chain Services; access date 1.3.2021

6.11.1 Carrying Cost of Inventory

Every warehouse manager knows the inventory in their warehouse is costing them. Quantifying these specific carrying costs—including capital costs, inventory risk, inventory service costs and obsolescence—help a warehouse manager make smarter buying and forecasting decisions, leading to higher inventory turnover.

Inventory Carrying Rate × *Average Inventory Value*
= *Carrying Cost of Inventory*

6.11.2 Inventory Turnover

Your supplier already know that high inventory turnover is good. But looking at their inventory rate also helps gauge your buying practices and product demand. Your Warehouse Management System (WMS) provides visibility and enables forecasting to keep goods moving.

Inventory turnover measures how many times per year their distribution centre is able to go through its entire inventory. Compare this rate against industry averages for a clear picture of their distribution centre performance:

Cost of Goods Sold/Average Inventory
= *Inventory Turnover*

6.11.3 Order Picking Accuracy

In addition to tracking shipment and delivery status, you should also measure order picking accuracy. An inaccurate order by customer can result in inventory being put back on shelves, increasing shipping time per average order, rate of return, etc. Lean distribution center practices eliminate waste and streamline order-picking processes—and help maintain a high order accuracy rate. Industry Best-in-Class: > = 99.9%; Median: 99.4%*.

Total Number of Orders/Perfect Order Rate
= Order Picking Accuracy

6.11.4 Inventory to Sales Ratio

The Inventory to Sales Ratio is affected by economic conditions, as well as by a company's ability to weather unpredicted disruptions. It helps warehouse managers predict early cash flow problems by identifying increasing inventory levels against dropping sales rates. Conversely, it can help prevent back orders by identifying sales influxes and potential for an increase in buying to help satisfy a spike in demand.

Inventory to Sales Ratio in a successful warehouse distribution centre will reflect a streamlined order fulfillment process. Warehouse managers of suppliers should frequently monitor this KPI and use it as a tool in forecasting and predicting inventory needs.

End-of-Month Inventory Balance/Sales for Same Month
= Inventory to Sales Ratio

6.11.5 Units Per Transaction UPI

The Units per Transaction (UPI) metric is a metric common to many businesses. Depending on your industry, this number may or may not be realistically expected to increase. Compare suppliers warehouse distribution centre UPI with that of historical averages and trends within your industry for the most useful analysis.

Number of Units Sold/Number of Transactions
= Units per Transaction

6.11.6 Rate of Return

This is an incredibly useful KPI in a distribution centre, especially when segmented by cause for return. Identifying causes for return—damage, late delivery, inaccurate product description, wrong item shipped, etc.—helps warehouse managers address underlying issues, and make necessary improvements.

Number of Units Returned/Number of Units Sold
= Rate of Return

6.11.7 Inventory Accuracy

The accuracy of your physical inventory should match that listed in your database, but realistically there's often a disparity in any large distribution centre. A high rate of inaccuracy in inventories can lead to unexpected backorders, customer dissatisfaction and, ultimately, higher overall costs. Visibility is key to a high-performing warehouse.[39]

Inventory Accuracy can be improved by performing regular checks against your database, using **cycle counting** as a way to continually validate your database records. Inventory Count Accuracy by Currency/Units. Best-in-Class: > = 99.9%; Median: 99.2%.

Database Inventory Count/Physical Inventory Count
= Inventory Accuracy

[39] *Source*: https://legacyscs.com/supply-chain-data-visualization/#:~:text=Contextual%20Data%20Visualization%20Helps%20You,helps%20you%20make%20informed%20decisions.&text=Compiling%20and%20tracking%20supply%20chain,making%20decisions%20about%20your%20business. Article "Supply Chain Optimization"; access date 1.3.2021

6.11.8 Back Order Rate

A warehouse's Back Order Rate is a telling indicator of success in forecasting purchases and inventory supplies. A sudden spike in demand will understandably result in a temporarily high back order rate for any given item, but a consistently high or increasing back order rate indicates poor planning and lack of responsiveness.

You can decrease your Back Order Rate with more accurate order forecasting and vigilant monitoring of your warehouse's Inventory to Sales Ratio. A high Inventory Accuracy rate will also improve this KPI. Industry Best-in-Class: <0.14%; Median: 2%*.

Orders Unfilled at Time of Purchase/Total Orders Placed
= Back Order Rate

6.11.9 Perfect Order Rate

This KPI measures how many orders your supplier's warehouse successfully delivers without incident: the correct item, shipped on time and received in good condition by the customer who ordered it. Lean practices help identify errors or inaccuracies before orders leave the warehouse.

A Perfect Order Rate can be improved by strict adherence to warehouse and distribution center best practices. By identifying potential problems as they arise and treating them at the source, imperfect orders can be caught before they ship to the customer. Industry Best-in-Class: > = 99.3%; Median: 96%.

Orders Completed Without Incident/Total Orders Placed
= Perfect Order Rate

Defining and improving these KPIs will put supplier's warehouse on track to increase performance and drive cost savings at every level. Working with an experienced supply chain engineer will help you identify additional performance metrics for warehouses or distribution centres.

6.12 Inhouse Transportation with Forklifts in China

The target should be to bundle purchasing price within your company for each plant. Which brand has already been negotiated by HQ? If you need to buy new fork lifters due to environmental protection regulations in China, you need to react quickly. In the following links, you can find (incomplete) lists of where to find forklift prices and companies to get in contact with.

https://hechaforklift.en.made-in-china.com/

https://www.made-in-china.com/multi-search/forklift/F1%2D%2DPP_electric%2Bforklift/1.html

- Heli HELI (Anhui Forklift Group Co., Ltd.)
- Hangcha HANGCHA (Hangzhou Fork Group Co., Ltd.)

- Linde Linde (Linde (China) Forklift Co., Ltd.)
- Longgong (China Longgong Holdings Co., Ltd.)
- Liu Gong LiuGong (Guangxi Liugong Machinery Co., Ltd.)
- TOYOTA Toyota Forklift (Toyota Industrial Vehicles (Shanghai) Co., Ltd.)
- Dalian Forklift (Dalian Forklift Co., Ltd.)
- Hyster Hyster (Shanghai Hyster Forklift Manufacturing Co., Ltd.)
- Nuoli NOBLIFT (Zhejiang Nuoli Machinery Co., Ltd.)
- Xiamen XGMA (Xiamen Xiagong Machinery Co., Ltd.)

Pricelist

You can prepare a template like the following and add your collected information and prices.

Prices need to be calculated in Euro or USD for international comparison, therefore you see a mostly common exchange rate for 2020 to convert RMB into Euro. In China, you need to sort out your diesel driven forklifts. Sooner or later, your local government will stop running. If you need to buy, please consider leasing or renting as an alternative solution.

These different purchasing prices in RMB are an indication for reference only, as these are mostly related to age, and need to be negotiated with the sales department of these companies by benchmarking with your technical requirements. Repair and maintenance costs are important to know. If these costs are higher than your yearly depreciation costs, you immediately need to buy or lease a new one to lower your costs (Fig. 6.45).

6.13 Benchmarking Transportation Costs China

First get a standard overview of the transportation costs for a manufacturing company in China. For example:

(1) Inbound Sea freight/Air freight/Railway to other countries
(2) Outbound Sea freight/Air freight/Railway to other countries
(3) Inbound domestic transportation within China
(4) Outbound domestic transportation within China

Then break down and benchmark all items step by step, and prepare an overview of your results. You can compare your current forwarders with other current ones, or compare them with new fresh forwarders. Please consider that at the end, you need to reduce the number of forwarders rather than increasing them, due to the fact that your handling and admin costs will increase as well. Some managers set tough targets: to have only one international forwarder for sea, air and railway, and only one for the whole domestic China business.

For templates and collected prices of domestic and international forwarders, see attachments.

Recommended template for company internal forklifter vehicle pool of all your plants worldwide. For example Plant CHINA, EUR/RMB exchange rate: 7,21 (Nov. 26, 2021), see https://www.x-rates.com/table/?from=CNY&amount=1									
No.	Brand	Model	Type*	Fuel type (battery, gas, or diesel)	purchased or leased	purchased price/ leasing rate per vehicle	final date of leasing contract/ date of scrapping or re-selling	details on repair & maintenance contract	details on spare parts management
1									
2									
3									
* The most popular forklift types on the market today are: Warehouse Forklift, Side Loader, Counterbalance Forklift, Telehandler, Industrial Forklift, Rough Terrain Forklift, Pallet Jack, Walkie Stacker, Order Picker, Reach Fork Truck.									

Fig. 6.45 Template for collected information and prices of forklift equipment. Details see https://www.bigrentz.com/blog/forklift-types, published Sept. 10, 2018. Access date: Nov. 26, 2021. *Source*: GTEC, 2021

If you collect the prices, and carry out a comparison to choose the cheapest forwarder and calculate your savings, it will not work:

Forwarder (import)	Seafreight	Railfreigth	Airfreight
Domestic			
International			

To be successful, you instead need to go into the details; for example, when calculating airfreight imports, differentiate between airfreight charges, origin charges and destination charges. Furthermore, airfreight charges for different weights. For example, transportation from Europe to China (Figs. 6.46 and 6.47).

6.13.1 How to Calculate Savings by Benchmarking?

At Fig. 6.49, please find an Excel sheet template as screen shot for information for calculating imports into Shanghai. There are a number of challenges:

- Following benchmarking, a forwarder wins the competition for the most important and most frequently used five air transportation routes in 2020, but has only done the job for 3 pickup places in 2019
- The benchmark covers 88%. The other 12% has to be calculated separately or ignored, depends on expected savings (Fig. 6.48)

In this example, out of the three pickups there are 10.7% savings, with a cost reduction from 18.2 to 16.1 RMB/kg.

Expected expenses in 2020 for 100% transportation is 17.1 RMB/kg, whereas in 2019 it was 22.1 RMB/kg, representing savings of 5 RMB/kg from this forwarder. You need to benchmark this price reduction with other forwarders.

	Description	Currency EUROPE	Currency America	UOM	Remarks
Origin Charge	AWB/ENS FEE	EUR	USD	PER SHIPMENT/ PER HAWB	
	AIRPort TERMINAL HANDLING/security fee	EUR	USD	per shipment	
	Anti Terror Compliance/ Securing		USD	per shipment	
	Transfer Fee, Handling			per kg	
	Export customs clearance	EUR	USD	PER SHIPMENT	
	Export customs documentation				
	Linehaul charges	EUR	USD	Per kg	
	Export Handling charge (Admin), Forklift	EUR	USD	Per bill	
	Export Declaration/ Origin Handling	EUR	USD	Per shipment	Incl. 2 HS Code
	THC Terminal Handling Charge/Terminal Fee	EUR	USD	Per kg	
	PNS/X-Ray	EUR	USD	Per kg	
	AMS filing	EUR	USD	per AWB	
	AMS			per shipment	
	Pick-up	EUR	USD	Per kg	<100kgs
		EUR	USD	Per kg	+100kgs
		EUR	USD	Per kg	+300kgs
		EUR	USD	Per kg	+500kgs
		EUR	USD	Per kg	+1000kgs
		EUR	USD	Per kg	+1500kgs
		EUR	USD	Per kg	+2000kgs

Fig. 6.46 Template pattern for Origin Charge Airfreights. *Source*: GTEC, 2018

Destination Charges	Terminal & Handling Charge (Include D/O, handling, import custom clearance) 海关报关费	CNY	Per kg	
	Handling Charge (applicable to MAWB cut to TSN)	CNY	Per kg	
	出入库费 Entry and exit charges	CNY	Per kg	
	装卸费 Handling charges	CNY	Per kg	
	短驳费 extra movement charge	CNY	Per kg	
	理货费 Tally fee	CNY	Per kg	
	Storage fee	CNY	Per kg/day	
	Storage free	days		
	Customs Handling & Inspection, CIQ Packaging Inspection Fee (paper carton) 国检包装检查费（纸箱）	CNY	piece	
	(wooden case)国检包装检查费（木箱）	CNY	piece	
	Admin, customs documentation, D/O Exchange Fee换单费; Not applicable if Brokerage is handled by CEVA	CNY	per shipment	
	检验检疫、验货代理费 Inspection and quarantine, inspection agency fee (if any), CIQ clearance	CNY	Per shipment/ entry	
	Trucking fee to YANTAI HUF (non-bonded truck LTL service only)	CNY	Per kg	<100kg
				+100kg
				+300kg
				+500kg
				+1000kg
				+3000kg
	Transit time			
	Frequency			

Fig. 6.47 Template pattern for Destination Charges China. *Source*: GTEC, 2018

	A	B	C	D	E	F	G	H	I	J	K	L	M	N	O	P	Q	R	S	T	U	V
1		QUOTATION FOR AIR SHIPMENT									Forwarder 2020					Forwarder 2019						
2		Supplier's name and address	Country	Package	Gross Weight	average KG	Delivery frequency	Transport Way	Delivery Terms	volume in kg	origin charge	airfreight charge	destination charge	Quotation/ transport	Quotation in RMB/Year	origin charge	airfreight charge	destination charge	Quotation/ transport	Quotation in RMB/Year	Savings	%
3	1	A	Germany	Pallet 1.5m3-2m3	600-800KG	700KG via FFM	every two weeks =26 transports/year	By Air	EXW	18200	3945	5286	1688	10920	283908	4797	5523	2090	12410	322663	38755	12%
4	2	B	Germany	Pallet 4m3-8m3	700-1200KG	950KG via DUS	every one weeks =52transports/year	By Air	EXW	49400	4750	7282	2287	14320	744626	6276	7496	2515	16287	846924	102298	12%
5	3	C	Spain	Pallet Carton	1-70KG	45KG	every two weeks =26 transports/year	By Air	EXW	1170	1341	955	103	2399	62383				0	0		
6	4	D	Portugal	Carton	1-70KG	45KG	every one month =12 transports/year	By Air	EXW	540	2367	781	103	3251	39018				0	0		
7	5	E	Mexico	Carton	30-50KG	45KG	every one month =12 transports/year	By Air	EXW	540	4086	1378	103	5567	66805	4568	1378	103	6049	72593	5788	8%
8										68140					1095340					1242180		10.7%
9								Savings	2.2	16.1	RMB/kg									18.2	RMB/kg	11.8%
10									benchmark	69850					1196740						146840	11.8%
11									2019=2020	79113			expected expenses in 2020		1355443	17.13 RMB/kg					146840.1	
12								Air transportation Shanghai import	2018 (kg)	119898			expenses in 2018 (RMB)		2647088	22.08 RMB/kg						
13										79113			expenses in 2018		1746644	22.08						
14														savings in 2020	391200	4.94 savings RMB/kg						

Fig. 6.48 Template pattern for Airfreight Price comparison & reduction from 2019 to 2020. *Source:* GTEC, 2018

6.13.2 Sea Freight China

Using the same principle for comparison as with air freight, you need to go into the details. As you can see, forwarder 1 charges for fewer items with higher and lower costs. So who is actually cheaper? How important is the enormous lead time difference of 9 days, to select the right forwarder? (Fig. 6.49)

For sea freight benchmarking, you need to select the most important transportation routes, with realistic volumes and delivery frequency. Then send an RFQ to your well-known international forwarders. Attached please find a list of them.

6.13.3 Railway Service China

Rail freight forwarding is the most cost-effective friendly solution for transporting bulky and heavy items across long distances.[40]

Rail freight significantly reduces CO2 emissions in comparison to air freight.

If we talk about price and time, for example, sino-shipping.com charges 50% less by rail than air freight and shorten transportation time by rail via sea freight by 50%. Following container types can be used: 20'GP, 20'HQ, 40'GP, 40'HQ, 45'GP, 45′ reefer container, garment hanging container, open container OT. Freight train service includes door-to-door deliveries, FCL and LCL, classic and dangerous goods.

If customers need to deliver to final destination as fast as possible at reasonable price, rail transportation is the best choice. Trains are typically used for transporting raw products such as coal or steel., but this mode of transport is also the best for high-value industrial products such as vehicles, electronic and computer equipment, but also for promotional and seasonal products.

This train routes from China to Europe are getting more and more attractive for its economic and logistical advantages. Started on January 3, 2016 in Yiwu, 44 containers began a 12,000-kilometer journey to Europe. In 2020, about 1700 freight trains made the trip to Europe, and vice versa.

There are two routes which frequently used. China Europe Block Train from Yiwu to Madrid (Spain), which arrives in Moscow (Russia) in 12 days, Warsaw (Poland) 12 days, Hamburg (Germany) 14 days, Brussels (Belgium) in 12–14 days, Lyon (France) 14–17 days, London (UK) in 18–20 days. Another freight train goes directly from Moscow to Beijing. On this Eurasian Land Bridge with both trains also other cities in Russia, Kazakhstan and Mongolia can be delivered or loaded.[41]

In April 2021, a new container shipping line opened between Chinese Jiangsu Taicang Port and Russia's Far Eastern Port of Vladivostok. One-way trip takes four days. What this news has to do with railway service? Currently on weekly basis, Chinese cargoes can be sent to the inland cities in Russia, as well to other European

[40] *Source*: https://www.eurosender.com/en/s/services/rail-freight; Author Eurosender.com, published June 15th, 2020. Access date 2.3.2021

[41] *Source*: https://www.sino-shipping.com/rail-freight-china. Access date 5.4.2021

	Example Sea Import from LE HAVRE-SHANGHAI	1. Exclusive of VAT 2. Rates is not applicable for Hazardous, high value goods, dutiable goods, density, reefer, live stock, perishable, personal effects, oversized/overweight and/or over-length cargo 3. Offer based on 1pallet, 1cbm 1ton							
	Description	**Currency**	**UOM**	**forwarder 1**		forwarder 2 (Le Havre -Shanghai)			
				20"	**40"**	20" STD	40" STD	40" HC	**LCL**
Origin Charges	Ocean Freight	USD	Per container	650 USD	800USD	620	850	880	10
	Leadtime	days		35	35	26	26	26	26
	International maritim organization IMO surcharge	USD				70	140	140	/
	Pick Up, trucking charge from supplier location in FRANCE	EUR	Per Container	350	350	420	450	450	200
	FORWARDING HANDLING	EUR	Per B/L			60	60	60	60
	Wharfage charge, Fuel charge	EUR	Per B/L			85	90	90	45
	Automated Manifest System AMS	EUR	Per B/L			35	35	35	
	BL Fee, Documentation, Admin	EUR	Per B/L	100	100	75	75	75	55
	SOLAS Charge, VGM - Administration, Security	EUR	Per Container			20	30	30	10
	port filing BHT/ZAPP		per shipment						
	SECURITY FEE, CFS Charge	EUR	Per B/L			Ocean Line	Ocean Line	Ocean Line	
	OTHC (Terminal Handling Charge)	EUR	Per Container	200	200				
	EXPORT Customs Clearance	EUR	Per Container			65	65	65	65
	Export customs charge	EUR	Per B/L	40	40				
	Verfied Gross Mass Fee	EUR	Per B/L			9.5	9.5	9.5	25
	Carrier Security Fee	EUR	Per B/L			20	20	20	35
	LHALL	EUR	Per W/M			/	/	/	
	Stuffing	EUR	P W/M			/	/	/	
	Transfer Fee	EUR	P W/M			/	/	/	
	SOLAS Fee	EUR	Per Shipment			/	/	/	
Destination Charges	Documentation Turnover Fee, Admin	CNY	Per BL	400	400	400	400	400	500.00
	Inspection costs (customs)			500	500				
	Port Charge (agent)	CNY	Per container	600	800	1250	1650	1650	200.00
	Terminal Handling Charge (THC):	CNY	Per container	850	1,250	850	1250	1250	/
	Customs Clearance (Yangshan)	CNY	Per BL				600		600.00
	Delivery Order Handling Charge:	CNY	Per BL				200		/
	CIQ Handling Charge (Agent)	CNY	Per Set				200		/
	Warehouse in/out fee	CNY	Per Cbm				/		260.00
	Delivery: to Shanghai	CNY	Per container	1,600	1,800	1600	2200	2200	100.00

Fig. 6.49 Template pattern for Sea freight Price comparison & reduction between two forwarders. *Source*: GTEC, 2018

countries via sea-land multimodal transportation. The average transport cost can be reduced by 30 percent from pure overland transport and the average transport time by 50% from pure sea transport.[42]

6.13.4 Parcel Express Service China

For benchmarking parcel services in China, Fedex and TNT are both under the same roof, but they still have two different price lists in 2020. Please ask for updated price lists, available in English and Chinese. Refer also to the template at next page to see that there is a slow express service (IE) and a fast express service (IP). Also Import and Export prices from and to the same destination are different.[43]

The packages are separated, and range from envelopes to 1000 kg packages. To reduce your costs, you should eliminate fast express service (3 days), since slow express service (5 to 7 days) is acceptable in most cases. Therefore, a little bit of planning in advance is necessary to receive the goods in time.

If you like to go on with DHL Express, please check website for price and timing. For shipping medical equipment to Europe, Shipper in China must submit export clearance documents via www.5idhl.com. DHL will review and approve submitted documents which could take up to 3 days.[44]

According to my investigation and benchmark between these three companies, I calculated expected yearly savings of 260,697 RMB in 2020 (assuming 2020 will have similar volumes as 2019), for import (inbound) and export (outbound), by using only IE service.

6.13.5 Domestic Transportation

There are thousands of local Chinese transportation companies available. But some automotive OEMs request that only wing trucks, which are expensive, for easy loading and unloading by forklift, can enter their plants. Therefore, you need to integrate one additional column in your Excel spread sheet to get a detailed overview by benchmarking.

If benchmarking for customer delivery is carried out, you can use this result for a new forwarder contract. Therefore, some columns are added to show details of responsibility and work content.

Vertically, you need to have a destination of each customer plant and sum this up with the total costs, given by forwarders (Fig. 6.50).

[42] *Source*: Weixin ID isuzhou365, published 13.4.2021, access date 20.4.2021.

[43] *Source*: https://www.fedex.com/en-cn/home.html#, author fedex.com, published 2021. Access date 2.3.2021

[44] *Source*: https://mydhlplus.dhl.com/cn/en/shipment.html#/rate-and-quote#address-details. Author Deutsche Post AG, published 2021. Access date 2.3.2021

CHINA CUSTOMER Daily Work Information

				Supplier address—customer address (R: FORWARDER)									Forwarder	Driver (R: FORWARDER)		
Sn.	CUSTOMER Delivery Address	JIS/ JIT	Customer Part No.	Packing Structure	Monthly Delivery	Pallet	cbm	Gross weight (kg)	pallet size (mm)	wing trucks (Y/N)	Delivery Frequency Monthly	Distance (one way)	Name	Proposed Working Time	Work Content	Operating Details

Fig. 6.50 Template pattern for comparing domestic transportation between several forwarders. In this case, from supplier plant to OEMs in China. *Source*: GTEC, 2018

Domestic Transportation Costs in China

After benchmarking, you can choose the best-in-class forwarder company. Comparison of delivery from Shanghai to different locations by this company shows different prices, due to their internal strategies, from "Milkrun" to bundling delivery, to the same or close by locations for other customers of this forwarder. All trucks need to be wing trucks, in line with receivers' (automotive OEMs) requirements. Prices always include transportation and truck loading areas as a mixed calculation. This leads to RMB/km or RMB/kg (if using 重泡货heavy cargo), as well as other units (Figs. 6.51 and 6.52).

6.13.6 Distributors or Direct Purchasing From Manufacturers?

You already know, for every decision you make, that there are disadvantages and advantages. You may pass on your stock risks to distributors and don't want to handle small order volumes. But you may get much better prices by bundling volume within your company, instead of buying from each plant separately. Here comes an example of how to calculate cost savings by direct buying (Fig. 6.53).

6.13.7 Why Not Ask Your Operators at Your Chinese Warehouse?

As you need to find ideas for improvement, why not interview all your operators at the warehouse and the logistics department face to face? You will have better success by interviewing without supervisors being present.

If you are afraid of sharing their answers, after a few interviews, you need to organize several interviewers at the same time. Please involve management and company work council in advance, to avoid any potential trouble. They will probably not try to block this great idea, but they like to be informed of what is going on.

Here are some ideas for questions. The answers will be summarized after the interview. Best ideas should be awarded with incentives or prices.

- What tasks are you responsible for during your daily work? 你在日常工作中负责什么工作?
- What kind of challenges do you currently have at this work? 你目前在这项工作中面临什么样的挑战?
- Why did this happen? What could be the root cause? 为什么会这样?根本原因是什么?
- What ideas do you have to improve this situation? 你有什么想法可以改善这种情况?
- If you were the company owner, what would you change and improve?
- Do you see any waste (transportation, space, movement, storage, etc.)? 你看到任何废物(运输、空间、移动、储存等)吗?

delivery city (destination)	Distance km from Shanghai to destination	RMB/ delivery	RMB/ km	RMB/ kg	RMB/ cbm
Changchun	**2019**	558	0,3	0,9	296
Yantai	**908**	163	0,2		362
Wuhan	**840**	559	0,7	0,7	163
Guangzhou	**1440**	1628	1,1		173
Chongqing	**1674**	271	0,2	1,4	310
Shenzhen	**1480**	262	0,2		256
Changsha	**1081**	492	0,5		169
Nanchang	**717**	362	0,5		131
Beijing	**1207**	115	0,1		
Hefei	**471**	145	0,3		291
Wuhu	**351**	189	0,5		271
Haikou	**2021**	125	0,1		
Jinzhong	**1319**	504	0,4		168
Da Jiangdong	**1008**	1373	1,4		92
Hangzhou	**177**	267	1,5		128
Nanjing	**307**	23	0,1	0,3	110
Anting	**33**	335	13,4	1,0	40
Ningbo	**217**	221	1,0	4,8	110

包车 Chartered Wing Trucks (9.6m)					
delivery city (destination)	Distance km from Shanghai to destination	RMB/ delivery	RMB/ km	RMB/ kg	RMB/ cbm
Changshu	**103**	1600	15,5		52
Taicang	**52**	1100	21,2		37
Shanghai	**30**	875	29,2		238
Yantai	**908**	8000	8,8		
Shenyang	**1735**	16300	9,4		
Changshu	**103**	1100	10,7		1375
Jinzhong	**1319**	7000	5,3		700
Nanjing	**307**	2100	6,8		1511
Zhengzhou	**963**	7000	7,3		1169
Ningde	**682**	7000	10,3		
Da Jiangdong	**1008**	2400	2,4		96

Fig. 6.51 Best in Class Prices in 2021, made only for reference. *Source*: GTEC, 2021

	Length	Width	Height
Truck	12,00 m	2,50 m	2,50 m
Europalet	1200 mm	1200 mm	1200 mm
Europalet/Truck	40		
RMB/km	0,75		

	Length	Width	Height
Part dimensions (mm)	300 mm	300 mm	300 mm
Distance (km)	300 Km		
Empty return (Y/N)	Y		

Parts/Truck	2304	
Total Cost per Truck	450	RMB
Total Cost per Part	**0,195**	**RMB/Part**

Fig. 6.52 Quick estimation of transportation costs. Yellow and blue figures are given, white is calculated. *Source*: GTEC, 2021

- What do you think could be changed to reduce costs at the warehouse? 你认为可以改变什么来降低仓库的成本?
- What do you think could be changed to reduce costs related to transportation with forwarders? 你认为可以改变什么来降低货运代理的运输成本?

If you would like to add any other comments, please do so. Please prepare a timetable with names and available times for interviewing.

6.14 How to Build Databases

If you want to serve a customer inquiry quickly or calculate your own internal costs, it is essential to set up your own database of personnel costs, materials, machines, process manufacturing and tools. I recommend that the data be updated in your database immediately after each calculation. This method will save time for your next calculations. Even if you store links or sources instead of data, it will help you to save time.

6.14.1 The Personnel-Cost Database

- Part number and part designation
- Manufacturing site
- Country

The direct gross wage for manufacturing of a part is calculated (as the sum total):

manufacturer price in 2020		Distributor Price(USD) in 2020			manufacturer EXW + company own logistics		savings		
USD piece price	inco-term	USD piece price	inco-term	convert to CNY Price	Logistis cost of pick up goods from manufacturer (CNY)	CNY Price pick up total	saving	%	sum up saving
$0,993	EXW	$1,074	DDP	¥8,5922	**¥0,1075**	¥8,0515	**¥-0,54**	-6,3%	**¥-486.702,36**
$1,990	EXW	$2,071	DDP	¥16,5664	**¥0,1075**	¥16,0275	**¥-0,54**	-3,3%	**¥-646.740,00**

current exchange rate	8,00

2021 purchasing volume	LOGISTICS & SAVINGS	
	company + distributor stock	2021 cost saving/ month
900.000	1.200	¥-161.477
1.200.000	8.000	¥-98.987

Fig. 6.53 Distributor or direct purchasing from manufacturer? In these two cases above, direct purchasing creates big savings. *Source*: GTEC, 2020

- Hourly rate for planner; quantity
- Hourly rate for quality assurance; quantity
- Hourly rate for foreman; quantity
- Hourly rate for setup of machine; quantity
- Hourly rate for skilled workers; quantity
- Hourly rate for auxiliary staff; quantity
- Hourly rate for cleaning personnel; quantity

Internal setup (relevant for machine downtime)

- Hourly rate for setup; quantity, setup time
- Hourly rate for skilled workers; quantity, setup time
- Hourly rate for auxiliary staff; quantity, setup time

External setup

- Tool construction; quantity, setup time
- Hourly rate for skilled workers; quantity, setup time
- Hourly rate for auxiliary staff; quantity, setup time

6.14.2 The Material Database

The material database contains information about the following values:
Basic data:

- Planned quantities
- Annual requirement
- Lifetime
- Lifetime requirements (Lifetime × annual requirements)
- Material form (e.g., granulate)
- Basic material, e.g.:
  - Steel materials
  - Cast materials.
  - Plastics.
  - Nonferrous metal materials
  - Sintered metals
- Material type (for example, PBT)
- Part number
- Manufacturer's designation
- Tensile strength
- Filler (e.g., glass fibre)
- Color.
- Purchase price per kg

Gross mass:

- Net mass per part (g)
- Density of the material (g/cm^3)
- Surcharge for sprue (%)

Disposal:

- Scrap yield (euros/kg)
- Scrap disposal (euros/kg)
- Recycling rate sprue (%)

Material price:

- Material base price (euros/kg)
- Average price (euros/kg)

6.14.3 The Machine Database

All default values are preconfigured in the machine database. The machine cost calculation is used to determine the default values.

How do we calculate the machine costs? Which information is useful and which data is used to calculate the machine-hour rate?

The following list is used first:

Machine data:

- Machine type
- Machine designation
- Manufacturer
- Machine size (length × width) in meters
- Number of necessary machines
- Total investment in machinery
- Replacement value in euros/piece
- Age of the existing machine in years
- Required area (incl. Ancillary areas)
- Power consumption in kilowatts (kW) and operating time in %. Both kW and % calculate the energy costs in euros per year and per hour

Depreciation:

- Imputed depreciation (depreciation) per year and per hour
- Calculated interest in % (standard: 6%, calculated with yield/2 on replacement value) per year and per hour

Maintenance of replacement value per year (%)

- This results in maintenance costs in euros per year and per hour

  Other consumables in % of replacement value in euros per year and per hour
  Setup data:

- Machine downtimes in minutes (longest, shortest)
- Number of setups of the machine per production lot
- Setup time for internal setup (total personnel) in min
- Equivalent internal setup wage in euros/hour
- Setup time for external setup (total personnel) in min
- Equivalent external setup wage in euros/hour
- Sum of the setup scrap in units

  This is used to calculate the setup costs:

- Set-up costs of the machine per production lot in euros/hour
- Tool set-up costs per production lot in euros/hour
- Total setup time per production lot in min
- Power consumption costs per production lot in euros

  Machine-related consumables:

- Compressed air (consumption/h, costs, hourly rate)
- Gas (consumption/h, costs, hourly rate)
- Waste water (consumption/h, costs, hourly rate)
- Cooling/lubricant (consumption/h, costs, hourly rate)
- Water supply (consumption/h, costs, hourly rate)

  The calculated machine-hour rate is given in euros/hour.

6.14.4 The Process Database

To calculate in-house production costs and production overhead costs, it is essential to list the following information:

Process manufacturing step:

- Part name
- Part number
- Creation date
- Manufacturing site
- Process manufacturing step number
- process manufacturing step name
- Percentage of production lot
- Cost-center number

Parameters of the working system (machine):

- Number of working days per week and year.
- Number of shifts per working day
- Number of weeks per year
- Number of working hours per year
- Lot size (in pieces)
- Stock quantity before the work system (in pieces)
- Lead time through the work system (in hours)
- Annual requirements (in pieces)
- Capacity of the working system (pieces/year)
- Utilization of the work system (%)
- Required starting quantity (pieces)
- Interest costs on current assets (in euros/unit)

Process data:

- Cycle time (seconds)
- Parts per cycle
- Utilization rate of the working system, exclusive setups
- Share of rejects (%)
- Capacity of the working system (pieces/hour)
- Output of the working system (pieces/hour)
- Available working time per part (seconds)
- Reject costs in euros/item
- Unit and quantity of the process variable
- Specific costs (euro/unit)
- Residual manufacturing overhead (RMOC) in % and euro/unit
- In-house manufacturing costs (IMC), incl. RMOC in % and euros/piece
- Material and overhead surcharges for external production
- External manufacturing costs (EMC), incl. Surcharges in % and euros/piece

Wage costs:

- Labor costs for direct labor (LC).
- Surcharge factor for wage.
- Gross wage excl. Ancillary wage costs in euros/hour
- Number of employees per working system
- Wage costs, incl. Ancillary wage costs (ALC) in euros

For example, plastics can be injection molded, extruded, dried, conditioned, deep drawn or blown. Different machines are available with different clamping forces and sizes (clamping surface in width, height and opening width).

Example of necessary data for the **cycle-time calculation** for plastic injection molding:

Data for the first component

- Material of the first component.
- Density
- Filler content
- Maximum wall thickness

Data for second to nth components

- Material of the second to nth components.
- Density.
- Filler content
- Maximum wall thickness

Further information:

- Projected area
- Component shape
- Narrow tolerances (yes/no)
- Thimble shape (height, diameter, ratio)
- Foil type
- Flame retardant (yes/no)
- Number of cavities
- Number of cascade steps
- GID (internal gas injection molding) procedure (yes/no)
- Two-stage ejector (yes/no).
- Which multi-component technology?
- Which type of slider?
- Which type of unloading?
- Inner mold pressure (in bar)
- Correction factor
- Calculated machine press force (kN)
- Selected machine size (kN)
- Mold wall temperature
- Mold release temperature
- Thermal diffusion
- Melting temperature

The following cycle times for the 1 K, 2 K and nK-materials (in seconds) are calculated from the above, producing a total:

- Opening and closing
- Inlaying the insert
- Slider
- Filling in material (injection time)
- Cascade
- Foil
- Surcharge for narrow tolerances

- Surcharge for GID (internal gas injection molding), thimble
- Component injection molding (2 K, 3 K)
- Cooling time (incl. Holding pressure)
- Removing cast from robot
- Removing cast by hand
- Part downtime

6.14.5 The Tool Database

The following data is required for costing:
Tool assessment:

- Number of tools for the production of one part per year
- Costs per tool in euros
- Total investment per year in euros
- Number of parts per cycle (pieces)
  - Tool cost allocation (in euros/piece)
  - Tool output (good parts) of all cycles

Tool maintenance due to tool wear out:

- Maintenance in % of tool costs (%)
- Tool maintenance costs in euros/piece
- Tool maintenance costs in euros/tool

Circulation and safety stock:

- Additional tools in circulation (units)
- Average period of circulation (months)
- Supplier's share of tool costs (%)
- Imputed interest (according to country database or manual entry, e.g., assumption in Germany 6%)
- Outstanding stock and safety stock in euros/year and from this euro/item

The sum of tool costs is given in euros/piece.

6.14.6 ECOCUT Databases

Additional features include the databases in ECOCUT©, among other functions. Even though it is possible to create calculations without the extensive databases, GTEC uses country, material and machine databases for cost calculation.

Negotiations with Asian Suppliers 7

Let us explore the methods that professionals use in negotiations with suppliers.

We have a 3-year contract with our supplier A delivering biggest volume of ceramic goods for industry to us. However, this contract will run out soon and the turnover dropped down of 40% from last year.

After dinner and hotel arrangements, which the supplier paid, the next morning meeting started to negotiate their required price increase for the next contract period. Table in front of us is filled with fruits, water, and coffee. We went there with two purchasing guys, me as GM and the German company's owner, who visited China for that reason.

Yesterday evening, the owner of the supplying company said that in the previous week a Korean customer with two people visited him and they observed their drinking habits. However, we thought, for this important negotiation, we needed more people to stay at the same level so that we could cover travel costs instead. We have a 10% profit margin as a dealer, and our customers do not like price increases. So, we were caught between a rock and a hard place.

Our travel planning includes to visit competitors as well in this small city. As we know, supplier A's company driver would take care of our transportation during the visit. He would see which supplier we should visit and would report back to his boss. It was a backup arrangement that could increase the pressure in the event of failure early in the negotiation.

Opposite us sat the elderly owner of the company, which had 400 factory employees, a translator, and two saleswomen who processed paperwork.

We explained that within the next year we expected a high volume of orders from our Japanese customer, which would bring us back to last year's attractive turnover. Our first question was about how much of a price increase they required. Instead of giving a figure, the owner started to explain their cost increase based on the inflation rate, raw materials, environmental protection measures, safety protection, electricity, and labor. He said his company had dramatically improved quality for overseas clients in order to reduce the risk of defects. We had a severe quality issue the

K. Zuerl, *Effective Cost Cutting in Asia*, Management for Professionals,
https://doi.org/10.1007/978-3-030-82782-3_7

previous year, in which our customer found damaged parts that were coated in dust. He also said their staff had received 15% salary increases during the past 2 years.

It was a good opportunity for a discussion. Even we know the fact that it is hard for this company to gain good and young staff due to the heavy work at dirty environment, as nobody would like to do. Immediately, we argued that in China 15% had not been reasonable for a very long time, adding that our company increased 3% the previous year and that the next year would not be more than 3%. We also said any cost increase would have to be balanced against productivity improvements and reduced costs in order to maintain the current level of expense. Without process improvements, the company would eventually run into deficit and would have to close the plant.

The company's owner invited us for a plant tour to see how they produce our parts.

It was evident that they produced on a stock basis. It did not matter how much we ordered, because they were able to immediately deliver all kinds of part numbers.

We saw mostly elderly men and women filling bags, shipping goods, and manufacturing by hand instead of using automation. The replacement of workers with proper designed machines could shorten the cycle time and reduce mistakes. I asked for the reason to continue that way, although I knew their personnel costs were rising year by year. They did not have their own engineering department that could deal with automation and never gave order for invention to outside companies due to high investments and time-consuming testing.

We saw, throughout the working process, half of the workers standing and observing, while the other half did the work. Apparently, their capacity planning was not accurate. Idle time among workers is a kind of waste that must be avoided.

Thus, there was room for improvement and we offered our support in the event some help was needed. There was one reason for that: We were sitting in the same boat. If the supplier was going down, we would be forced to find another supplier, thus risking increased costs as well as diminished quality and timing.

Finally, the supplier requested an increase of 8% within the course of the year. We refused, because we could not afford it. We would immediately stop ordering because our purchasing price would run out of control. We asked for a solution for the next three or even 4 years, as our customers always require long-term contracts with us. We offered them a 4-year contract with yearly price increases of 2%, or approximately 8.2% by the fourth year. They refused, and consequently, we had a break for internal discussion on both sides.

Internally, we discussed the possibility of suggesting a price increase in relation to the volume reduction. For example, a lower volume could be paid with higher costs at the end of each year. However, the situation becomes complicated when sales want to get money back from the customer if the orders are insufficient.

Finally, to make a long story short, they came with 4–2–2% and we see that he needs to keep us as a customer. Therefore, we offered 3–2–2%. However, they did not want to continue in negotiation, but instead wanted to postpone to a new meeting within next months. We refused and asked to find a solution that morning. Otherwise, we would have to look somewhere else. Then, we met at 3.5–2–2% and signed a contract just before lunchtime. For us, the result was a success. At their canteen, supplier's staff were relaxed and we drank *baijiu* together, but their boss had another appointment. Over the following months and years, he did not feel like a looser, because our product quality did not decrease and they still delivered the parts on time.

Following three items need to be considered for successful preparation:

1. Negotiation process
2. Negotiation plan
3. Action plan

Negotiation Process
Successful negotiation, like good preparation, involves a series of important steps. Do not overlook any of them.

1. Set goals: What do you want to reach, and when do you want to reach it? Do you want to negotiate at the supply site or at your office?
2. Situation analysis: Is it the right time? What is the current financial and HR situation at the supplier and in that district/province?
3. Topics generation: What does your agenda look like? Who at the supply site you need at plant tour and on the table?
4. Priority sequence: What steps are required in order to move ahead?

Negotiation Plan
- Define the range for agreement: What arguments and counterarguments do you have? Which answers and questions may you supplier have?
- Assign roles/tasks in the negotiation: What strategy you will drive? Which role each of your team member should play?

Action Plan
The following steps will help you define an action plan:

- Review the guidelines.
- Be prepared and use internal brainstorming.
- Acknowledge the differences in perception.
- Anticipate an agreement based on the bottom line.
- Be creative and flexible.
- Ask questions and listen to the answers.
- Look for trade-offs (compromises).
- Suggest a deadline but avoid threats and ultimatums.
- Make a deal instead of seeking a victory for your ego.

7.1 Productive Negotiation Between the Buyer and the Supplier

Chinese proverb: One who can talk well is not as worth as one who listens attentively.

That is why: Before we argue and make our point clear, we first listen and then use keywords to ask the interviewer what we have understood:

- "Let's see if I understood you correctly . . ."
- "If I understood you correctly, you mean . . ."
- "It is particularly important to you that . . ."

Justify emotionally or rationally. Emotional reasons have their origin in your own experiences. At this point, talk about contrary experiences. Set a different good feeling against it.

Rational is often justified with principles and facts and expert judgments. Hold against and counter their arguments, which are likely to include questions such as "How far does the principle go," "Do you think of the interpretation possibilities," and "Doesn't the client frequently determine the experts and their results?"[1]

7.2 Strategies in Negotiation

7.2.1 Project Management with a Systematic Approach

Supplier project systematic approach with negotiations of cost structure after quality gate 2. You must prepare in advance (Figs. 7.1 and 7.2).

7.2.2 Stage 1 Out of 5: Analysis with a Benchmark Calculation

Tasks/Content

- Compile the available data on actual manufacturing processes (cost breakdown PQP, FMEA, value stream mapping, etc.).
- Use best practice processes and benchmarks from related calculations, i.e., from ECOCUT databases.
- Map all process and cost parameters in ECOCUT (generate a benchmark calculation).
- Analyze the benchmark calculation (cost breakdown, cost drivers, price indication vs. purchase price, parameters that must be validated, etc.).

[1]Text from "Einkaufsmanager"/September 2005, Fachverlag für Einkaufswissen, Verlag der Deutschen Wirtschaft AG.

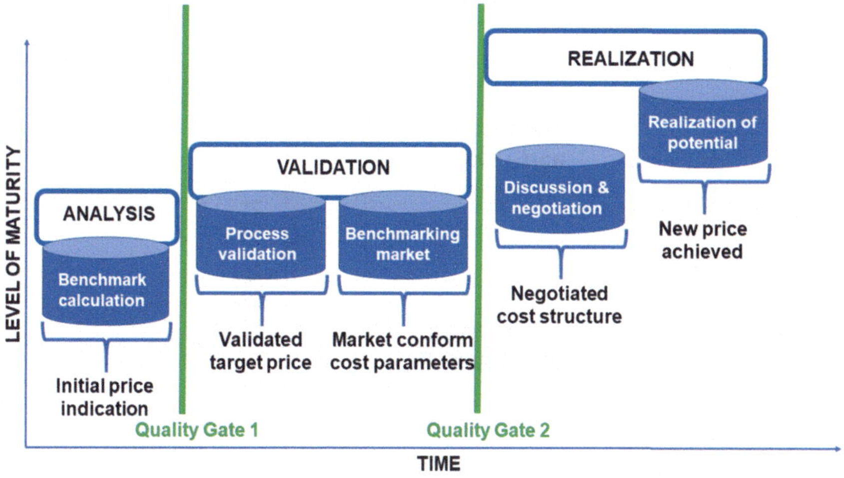

Fig. 7.1 Project management with discussion and negotiation. Source: Robert Bosch GmbH, 2010

- If necessary, create initial variable calculations based on alternative premises (process version, production site, etc.).

Result Price and potential indication.

Responsible Professional purchaser or project buyer.

7.2.3 Quality Gate 1

Tasks/Content
- First check to see whether initial reasons for decision for ECOCUT supplier project are still valid.
- Validation of benchmark calculation from stage 1 between professional purchaser or project buyer and person responsible for ECOCUT

Group Procedure
1. Presentation of case study
   (a) Summary of status
   (b) Initial buyer benchmark calculation (ECOCUT file)
2. Validation of benchmark calculation
   (a) Identify the cost drivers.
   (b) Cross-check the basic calculation premises/parameters.
   (c) Correct the errors (validation of benchmark calculation).
   (d) Create a list of parameters to be validated.

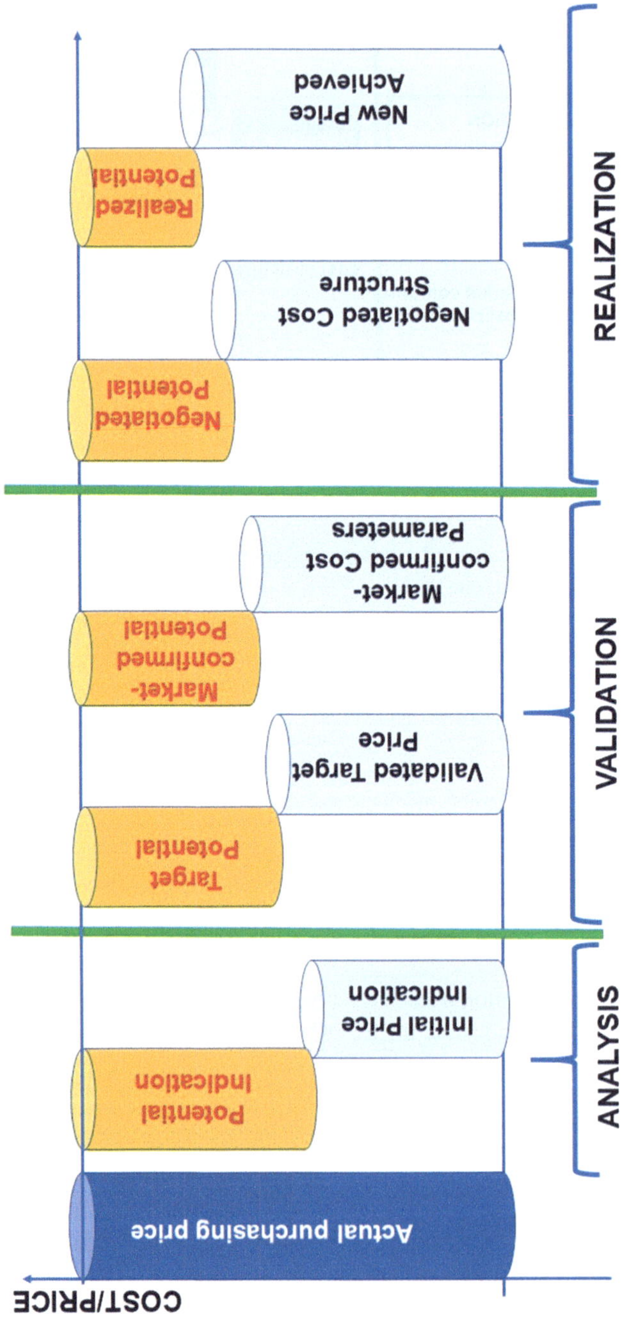

Fig. 7.2 Your calculated potentials would not be realized in negotiations. Source: Robert Bosch GmbH, 2010

3. Participants present the results of the group exercise
4. Discussion and questions
   (a) Initial cost–benefit ratio estimate (potential indication vs. implementation expenditure)

Result Go/no-go decision for start-up validation phase.

Responsible Professional purchaser or project buyer together with an ECOCUT expert.

7.2.4 Stage 2: Process Validation

Tasks/Content

- If necessary, (new) tour of the current supplier's production site (without using the name ECOCUT).
- Talk through process with internal experts (TEF, CR, PUQ, etc.), i.e., external experts (machine/tool manufacturers, etc.).
- Revise benchmark calculation from stage 1 based on validated process and cost parameters.
- If necessary, identify or determine optimization ideas and create respective variable calculation.
- Determine a "realistic" target price.

Result Validated target price and target potential.

Responsible Professional purchaser or project buyer together with support from ECOCUT expert.

7.2.5 Stage 3: Benchmarking Market

Tasks/Content

- Request information from alternative suppliers and acquire competitor quotations (cost breakdown, process, and cost parameters)
- Cross-comparison between validated benchmark calculation and quotation information acquired
- If necessary, discuss alternative manufacturing concepts, i.e., process versions with alternative suppliers
- If necessary, carry out a cost evaluation of alternative concepts, i.e., processes using the corresponding variable calculations

Result Market conform cost parameters and realization potential.

Responsible Professional purchaser or project buyer together with case-by-case support from ECOCUT expert.

7.2.6 Quality Gate 2

Tasks/Content

- Evaluate the results and the "quality of work" from the validation phase (process knowledge, "quality of the calculation," etc.).
- Evaluation of whether the basis for argumentation is sufficient for a successful ECOCUT discussion
- Estimate new cost–benefit ratio based on current state of knowledge

The benefits must outweigh the cost/expenditure in order to initialize/continue the ECOCUT *project.*

Check again to see whether initial reasons for decision for ECOCUT supplier project are still valid (Figs. 7.3 and 7.4).

Group procedure to estimate cost–benefit ratio:

1. Set the benefit and cost criteria, placing them in the order of importance.
2. What criteria are can be quantified (monetarily); which should be evaluated from a qualitative perspective?
3. Evaluate individual quantity, i.e., quality criteria (document in writing).
4. Weigh the total of the expected cost against the total of the expected benefit and reach a decision for or against the ECOCUT project.
5. Briefly explain the decision and derive core project goals (quantitative and qualitative) from it.
6. Present the results of the training group.

Result Go/no-go decision regarding the entry into the realization phase and ECOCUT supplier info.

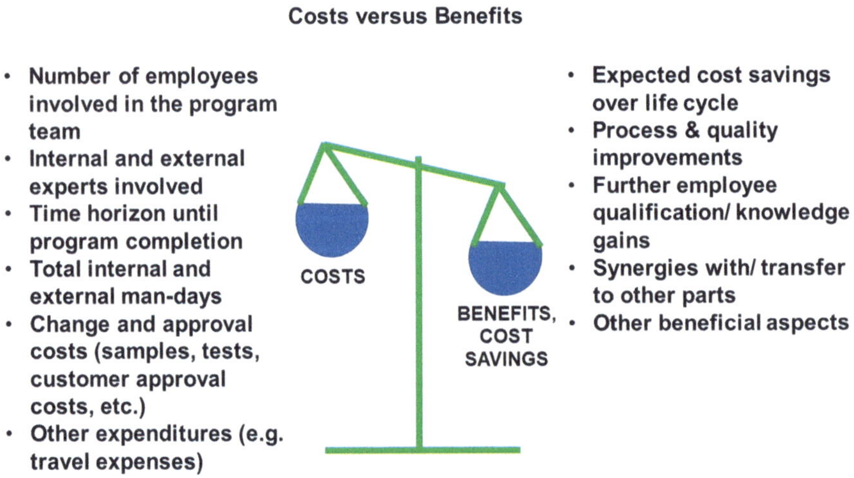

Fig. 7.3 Costs versus benefits. Source: Robert Bosch GmbH, 2010

Step	Dos	Don'ts
Evaluate cost and benefit aspects	Qualified estimates	"Seemingly accurate" calculation
Make a decision for/against ECOCUT program	Entrepreneurial decision	Applying an inflexible scoring model
Set realistic goals	Consider opportunities & risks in a balanced manner	Falling victim to adequate optimism/ being immoderate modest

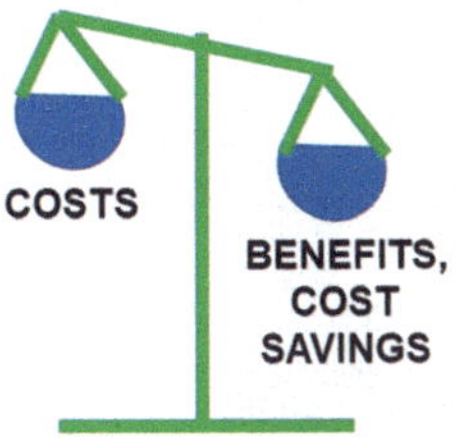

Hint:
If estimations vary within the program team, differentiate considering best and worst case scenarios!

Fig. 7.4 Attention to dos and don'ts at Step 2. Source: Robert Bosch GmbH, 2010

Responsible Professional purchaser or project buyer together with an ECOCUT expert.

7.2.7 Stage 4: Discussion and Negotiation

Tasks/Content

- Provide initial information to the supplier about the objective, content, and procedure of the ECOCUT project.
- Organize and prepare content for ECOCUT discussions.
- Launch the process and collect data at the supplier's site, doing so with PPC-supported calculation comparison together with the supplier.
- Coordinate cost potentials, negotiate price targets, and work together with the supplier to create a realization plan.

For details, see supplier project checklist/guideline.

Result Negotiated cost structure/potential.

Responsible The negotiation team organized and led by the purchasing professional or project buyer.

See sequence diagram in 12 steps (Fig. 7.5).

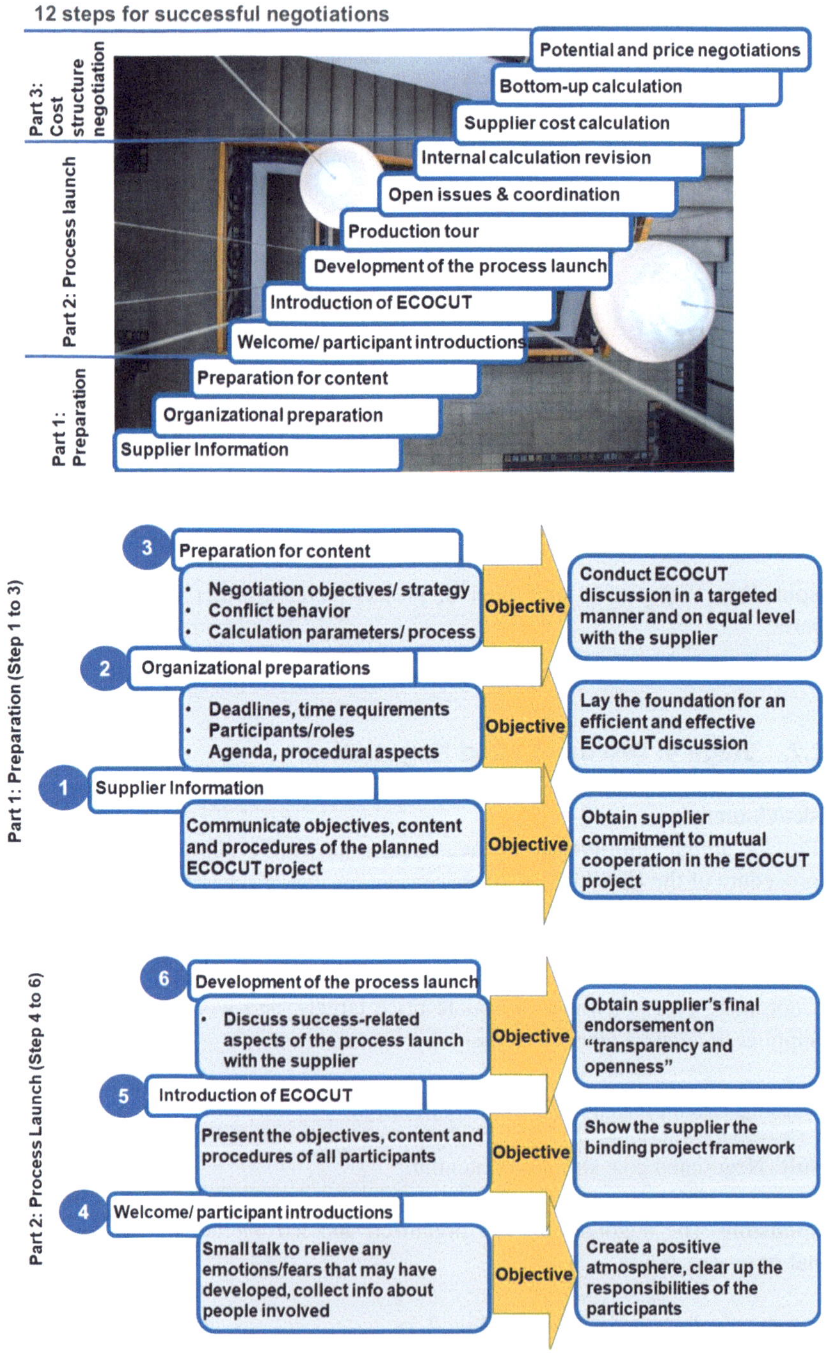

Fig. 7.5 12 steps for successful negotiations. Source: Robert Bosch GmbH, 2010

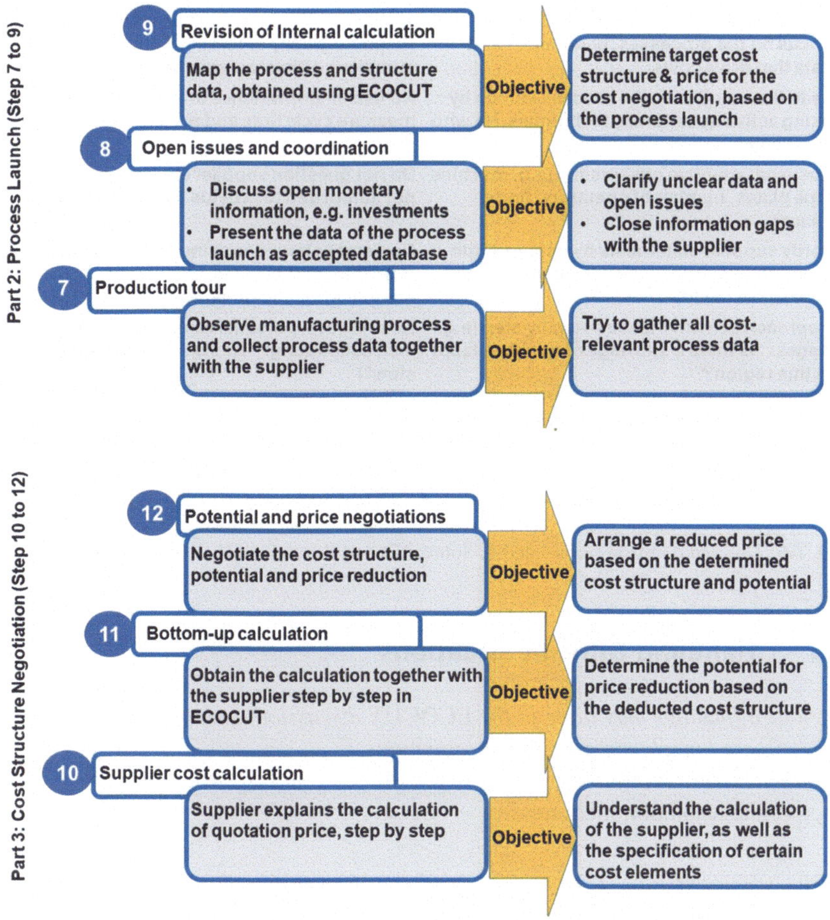

Fig. 7.5 (continued)

7.2.8 Stage 5: Realization of Potentials

Tasks/Content

- Supplier carries out agreed measures (along with the RB project team if required)
- Determine date/terms of contract conclusion with the supplier
- Project documentation and knowledge transfer in ECOCUT knowledge databases (according to ECOCUT network guidelines)
- In the event of significant deviations, i.e., technical ratio potentials, initiate a follow-up project (SDT, PUQ)

Result Newly negotiated price, achieved potential.

Responsible Professional purchaser or project buyer.

Basis behavior rules (do's and don'ts) at the time of process launch (Fig. 7.6).

Dos	Don'ts
Focus on the processes, parameters and data that drive costs	No photography or filming without the supplier's official agreement
Lead the way during the process launch by using active questioning techniques. He who asks leads.	No use of stopwatches or wristwatches to measure cycle time and process times
Focused, attentive observation (e.g. machine type plates, number of operators, floor space)	Do not question supplier employees who are not authorized to provide information
Verify supplier statements by using a logic cross comparison (e.g. cycle time vs. quantity per shift)	No demonstrative copying facts and figures from info boards of manufacturing equipment, scrap rates, etc.
Approach sensitive issues step by step (e.g. wages: "is there a shortage of qualified labor in this region?"	No critiques, personal evaluations or instructions (e.g. "This machine is really slow")
Stick to these rules will increase success for the process launch, e.g. data collection at the suppliers' site!	Not obeying these rules can put the supplier in a bad mood and let him "shut down" and close conversation, relationship and business

Fig. 7.6 Dos and don'ts at steps 4 and 5. Source: Robert Bosch GmbH, 2010

7.3 Handling Difficult Situations

Various difficulties may arise in the ECOCUT *discussion during supplier information/process launch/cost structure* negotiations:

Actively observe the supplier, identify difficult situations early on, and apply appropriate resolution measures.

A Supplier emotions, mistrust and fears regarding ECOCUT (e.g., damaged pride, everything being out in the open, loss of profit)

B Killer arguments made by the supplier regarding methodology, ECOCUT tool, etc. (e.g., "Your approach is theoretical and superficial!")

C "Fake" cooperation/covering up" defensive behavior (e.g., the supplier intentionally provides incorrect information)

D Categorical rejection of ECOCUT (absolutely unwilling to cooperate)

7.3.1 Important Behavior Principles

- Discuss/negotiate professionally: Treat the person and the matter at hand separately (being "soft" when it comes to the person but "resolved" when it comes to the matter at hand).

- Active listening: Be focused. Put yourself in the suppliers' shoes, be attentive (such as by nodding), and repeat important statements
- Acknowledge the suppliers' fears and emotions. Talk about them openly and show that you understand, and control your emotions.
- Use "I messages" and "meta-communication" with respect to your own feelings and emotions. Create a calm atmosphere for discussion and establish trust.
- Involve the supplier in the decision-making process and allow him to participate (ensure acceptance on the part of the supplier)

7.3.2 Emotions, Mistrust, and Fears Regarding ECOCUT

Practical Examples

- Associating ECOCUT with price pressure and profit maximization
- Damaged pride ("So now the purchasing manager wants to show us what we're doing wrong!")
- Mistrust that ECOCUT would not be applied fairly
- Concerns regarding knowledge transfer and confidential information
- Fear of "losing face" in cases where information provided on costs, etc., was incorrect

Solution Approaches (Selected)

Clear communication: "What does ECOCUT mean for the supplier, what does it not mean?"

- Clear up supplier objections during the introduction to ECOCUT.
- Use "I messages" and "meta-communication" with respect to your own feelings and emotions. Create a calm discussion atmosphere and establish trust.
- Create a set of "ECOCUT game rules" together with the supplier (dos and don'ts).

7.3.3 Killer Arguments Against ECOCUT

Practical Examples

- "We have already aligned our processes and costs!"
- "The ECOCUT methodology is too theoretical; it can't be applied in practice!"
- "ECOCUT is an impermissible attack on our entrepreneurial freedom!"
- "The ECOCUT software calculates completely differently from the way we calculate; that's why you can't compare the results with each other at all!"

Solution Approaches

1. Do not evaluate the killer argument; do not take a direct position in opposition to the argument
2. Ask the supplier to clarify his statement ("What exactly do you mean by . . .? ")
3. Ask about the basis for experience ("How often have you used this method before?")

4. Ask for reasoning and evidence ("Let's look at the project and determine to what degree your point of view applies for this part, all right?")

7.3.4 False Cooperation on the Part of the Supplier

A Typical Situation from the Field

- The supplier acts friendly, open, and cooperative.
- But the suppliers' behavior leads you to believe that he does not want to provide you with insight into critical areas (e.g., during the production tour).
- Or certain information the supplier provides does not seem plausible, or you suspect that the information has been faked or exaggerated.

Solution Approaches (Selection)

- Set clear game rules in advance and, if necessary, set limits on the amount and type of information revealed to each other (acts as a precautionary measure with respect to "concealing" information and provides you with legitimate grounds for objection)
- Carry out a "logic cross-comparison" with the supplier using existing information (avoid a loss of face on the part of the supplier).
- Use "I messages" to convey your own feelings to the supplier openly and professionally (avoid using judgmental "you" messages)

7.3.5 Categorical Rejection of ECOCUT

A Typical Situation from the Field

- The supplier has unique selling points when it comes to the part in question; competition through other suppliers is low.
- The supplier refuses to disclose his processes and cost parameters.
- Moreover, the supplier makes reference to his low delivery price (and the possibility of customer acquiring the part from a less expensive supplier).

Solution Approaches (Selection)

- Work out and initiate a supplier-specific escalation strategy.
- Communicate specific sanctions (e.g., not being considered when requests are submitted or new projects are awarded).

7.3.6 Discussions in Difficult Situations

- *Buyer*: Here, we have a software called ECOCUT, and we have calculated the cost of this part.
- *Supplier*: We have a different way to calculate the price, and there is a distinct difference in the result. We do not trust your software.

How to understand the supplier's method quickly and explain the method behind ECOCUT so as to convince the supplier.

- *Buyer*: We have just given you our *Preferred Supplier* title. However, you have not made a cost down for us. Some parts even have prices that are 50% higher than our European suppliers.
- *Supplier*: Our volume has decreased because your orders have not reached our goal for these years. We still guarantee that your parts will be delivered on time despite the fact that we have more customers waiting.
- *Buyer*: We have calculated the part cost according to your quotation, and the calculated price is 50% cheaper than yours. Please explain it to us. If you have no reasonable excuse, then please make cost reduction for us.
- *Supplier*: We have not given that detailed information in our quotation. Moreover, we are not clear with some specific figures. So, your calculations are based on various assumptions. Please show us how you arrived at this price.
- *Supplier*: So, we have agreed to use your software to calculate the part price. However, why is it much higher (lower) than our offered price? Please give me a good explanation.
- *Supplier*: The *scrap rate* is calculated differently in comparison with your software. You have to change your software to do this.
- *Supplier*: About your request for *overhead* information, we do not have a detailed figure. What was your assumption in that regard?
- *Supplier*: For parts that have been produced over years, your European suppliers already have a very low price with *depreciated* machines. However, for us with brand-new machines, it is very difficult to achieve the savings you are requesting.
- *Supplier*: We are the only one in AP who can achieve your requirement. We do not want to discuss the price anymore.

7.4 Win-Win Negotiation

7.4.1 Goals and Basic Principles

道 *Truth*
术 *Strategy*
法 *Technique*
器 *Tool*
用 *Application*

1. Reach win-win solution
2. Achieve reasonable benefits
3. Discover opportunities for business growth

4. Develop long-term win-win relationships with partners
5. Right time for negotiation:
   (a) The other party has sincerity, right conditions, and authority to make decision.
   (b) You want to make the deal, but the other party still has some disagreements.
   (c) You have still space in which to maneuver.
   (d) You have or you can get the authority to make decision.

7.4.2 Negotiation Strategies and Countermeasures

In negotiations *you can drive following strategies*:

- Good guy/bad guy
- Insufficient rights
- Ultimatum/final deadline
- Piecemeal encroachment
- Make a deceptive show of strength (bravado)
- Showing a tendency to be conciliatory
- Look one way and row another
- Cherry picking

7.4.3 Good Guy/Bad Guy Characteristics

- The *bad guy* is aggressive, tough, and sometimes unreasonable.
- The *good guy* is normally reasonable, friendly, calm, and professional.
- The counterpart may easily make concession to the *good guy*.
- Sometimes the *bad guy* can be an unreasonable condition or terms.

Recommended Countermeasures for Suppliers

- Hold your bottom line and focus on *interests*.
- Do not be overawed by the bad guy (sometimes an unreasonable or one-sided agreement).
- Do not use the bad guy's condition to judge the good guy.
- Keep asking questions, listen, and respond without delay.

7.4.4 Insufficient Rights Characteristics

- The counterparts excuse that they do not have the authority to make the final decision, so they can only make a referendum contract or an agreement with several restrictions.
- The persons who may make the final decision include boss, legal department, finance department, and technical experts.

Recommended Countermeasures for Suppliers

- Realize that normally the decision maker would not appear in the negotiation. This leaves more space for maneuvering.
- Invite the person who has the full authority to make the decision.
- Show respect to the counterparts. They may not be able to make the decision. However, they can definitely ruin the whole business.
- Ask more questions, listen more for your counterparts, and get more information from side door/other channels.

7.4.5 Ultimatum/Final Deadline Characteristic

- The counterpart suggests/indicates that it is the last offer or quotation to force you to yield.

Recommended Countermeasures for Suppliers

- Do not feel intimidated.
- Stay calm and look for other tactics.
- Introduce new alternatives or other possible solutions.
- Consider stopping the negotiation but keep the good relationship with the counterparts.

7.4.6 Piecemeal Encroachment Characteristic

- The counterpart asks for more and more benefits or concessions such as a discount, longer guarantee, and free maintenance.

Recommended Countermeasures for Suppliers

- Be good prepared in advance and clearly know your own bottom line for negotiation.
- Use stalling tactics such as ask for permission from boss.
- In the unavoidable case, make fewer valuable concessions.
- If it is common that you have to give the counterparts discounts, incorporate the cost into the total cost in advance.

7.4.7 Make a Deceptive Show of Strength/Bravado Characteristic

- Defiant or swaggering behavior in the negotiation, such as claiming that you have to give them better price than other suppliers to get the contract.

Recommended Countermeasures for Suppliers

- Determine the real reason for the current situation.
- Try to hold your own position.
- Do not be too eager to concede.

7.4.8 "Showing a Tendency to Be Conciliatory" Characteristic

- The counterparts pretended to be at a loss/perplexed, helpless, or unconversant with the negotiation status and hope to receive your sympathy.

Recommended Countermeasures for Suppliers
- Express sympathy but do not make any concession.
- Be aware that the counterparts may be cunning.
- Do not carelessly breach any information that the counterparts should not have.

7.4.9 "Look One Way and Row Another" Characteristic

- The counterparts emphasize some unimportant issues and make some concessions in order to continue the exchange in more significant respects.

Recommended Countermeasures for Suppliers
- Prepare thoroughly and find out the real interests of the counterpart as more as possible.
- Ask different questions.
- Use informal discussions to discover the counterpart's actual interest.
- The vital issue is that you must stick to principles.
- If you realize there is a lack of frankness or fair play in the negotiation, simply express your opinion.

7.4.10 A Characteristic of Cherry Picking

- Sourcing from different suppliers

Recommended Countermeasures for Suppliers
- Have a better idea of your quotation system and strategy.
- Notice that buyers normally do not distribute orders to many suppliers.
- Establish a good mutual relationship with the counterpart.

Negotiation Process for Cherry Picking
- Plan and preparation: Shop around to get a good buy. Calculate carefully and budget strictly.
- Build the base of cost breakdowns with good purchases from different sources.
- Overcome disagreements and arguments from suppliers.
- Restart the negotiation.
- Bargain and then make a decision.

7.5 Negotiating in Critical Situations

The type of negotiation is influenced by an individual's personality structure, attitudes, assumptions, beliefs, experiences, and expectations.

There are several basic styles of negotiations (Fig. 7.7).

What are the opportunities and risks of the *tough/soft style* of negotiation?

- *Short term* (i.e., during the negotiation)
- *Long term* (i.e., during the course of cooperation)

Communication Guideline Rules

- Repeat what you hear or learn, using your own words.
- Repeat it in context (e.g., not more than..., not less than...).
- Repeat correctly (without interpretations or manipulation).

Objection Is Not Always Objection

An objection is not always what it seems. An objection is often disguised as an excuse.

- *Excuse*

  An excuse is used to avoid having to give the real reason for rejection, e.g., to cover up the real situation, to avoid further discussion, to put off the salesperson or avoid having to place an order now. Excuses are basically used when the other side is not ready to be frank.

  Examples

  No time

  No interest

  No budget

  Strategy

"Soft"	"Tough"
• Harmony	• Force
• Passive	• Active
• Co-operative	• Competitive
• Offer concessions to improve relationships	• Concessions are a precondition to business
• Trust the other side	• Distrust of the other side
• Willingness to consider other positions	• Insistence on own position
• Make proposals	• Make demands
• Open strategy	• Hidden strategy
• Avoid power struggle (initially)	• Win power struggle
• Yield in the face of resistance (initially)	• Fight in the face of resistance

Fig. 7.7 Soft vs. tough (Source: Robert Bosch GmbH, 2010)

Act as though you did not hear what was said. Instead, focus on redirecting attention back to the subject under discussion and finding an aspect which attracts your partner's interest.

N.B.: Differentiate between *objective and subjective* excuses.

- *Objective*
  An objective excuse has to do with the actual subject under discussion. It is a *statement of fact.*
  Examples
  Low turnover
  Another supplier
  Price is too high
  Strategy
  Take the objection seriously. Show professionalism by discussing it openly and viewing it from another perspective in relation to the whole package.
- *Subjective*
  A subjective objection is an *indication of one's feelings*. The reasons for such objections have to do with a person's attitude, beliefs, assumptions, prejudices, preferences, etc.
  Examples
  No benefit
  No use
  Too complicated
  Strategy
  Express your understanding of your partner's perspective. Show respect for their feelings. Endeavor to learn more about the situation before explaining your point of view.

7.5.1 Dealing with Objections

Aims

- By accepting an objection for what it is, you appear to be taking the same side as your partner. You demonstrate that you understand their viewpoint.
- You show respect for your partner's feelings. Your partners' sense of self-esteem is reinforced, rather than being questioned or doubted.
- The real reasons why a decision is blocked can be revealed.
- Rational information can be presented with a greater chance of being accepted by your partner.

Whenever an objection is repeated, it means that the real reason, the missing piece of information or the true feeling behind the objection hasn't been identified, nor can it be resolved.

Useful Phrases Which Express Understanding

I understand that...
I can follow your point of view...
I realize that...

It's clear to me that...
What you say makes a lot of sense...
I can put myself in your situation...
I can understand what that must be like...
I know how you feel...
I understand how you feel...
I'm surprised to hear that...
I would feel the same way...

7.5.2 The Model for Dealing with Objections

Objections can be dealt with in five steps:

1. *Rephrase (partial repetition)*
   By repeating the objection in part or in full, literally, or context, you demonstrate to the other person that you take them seriously and you have been listening carefully. It also gives you more time to think.
2. *Show understanding*
   By confirming that your partner has a right to think the way he or she does, you create a positive relationship with that individual but without actually agreeing with what has been said. It buys you some time in which to think.
3. *Acknowledge (show acceptance)*
   At this point, you verbally confirm to your partner that you have seriously noted his objection. Either of the following will be true:
   (a) The objection is new, unexpected, or surprising to you.
   (b) The objection is already known. It is expected and will have to be handled anyway.
   You then inform your partner that you would like to have the opportunity to discuss the objection with him.
4. *Statement (expressing one's viewpoint)*
   Aspects related to the objection are then discussed in general terms. Your partner should also agree that the aspects you choose to talk about are indeed relevant to the subject.
   Examples of relevant aspects could be:
   (a) Time
   (b) Costs
   (c) Benefits
   (d) Persons
   (e) Activities
5. *Probe (forward movement)*
   Listen for how your partner has taken what you have said. Ask your partner a positive, forward-looking question which reveals more about his preferences, situation, conditions, attitude, aims, intentions, or plans.
   Depending on the situation and people involved, these five steps can either be applied in full or in part, as required.

7.6 Dealing with New Projects

ECOCUT: Discussion of Structured Preparation for a General Approach to New Projects

- Supplier's attitude to ECOCUT
  - It is easier to start ECOCUT discussions with suppliers before *sourcing meeting*, because they are *more cooperative*.
  - In this process suppliers normally have their *own cost breakdowns* along with their quotations. However, some *detailed figures* are sometimes *missing*.
  - Some suppliers may *doubt* the ECOCUT software. However, they still want to get the project. So, it is possible to spend time to *introduce* the software and *convince* them to use/accept ECOCUT for cost calculation.
- The role of ECOCUT™
  - For a new project, PUR normally use ECOCUT to do benchmark calculation according to quotations to estimate supplier's *gross profit rate*.
  - Before the framework agreement signed with suppliers, ECOCUT calculations are used as *reference* for the price negotiations.
  - For suppliers who have *good relationship* with your company or are willing to *trust* you, it is possible to show ECOCUT to them and discuss the detail.
- Sufficient understanding of ECOCUT and cost structure
  - Sufficient understanding of cost calculation is a criterion for ECOCUT discussion
  - Buyers should quickly understand the supplier's way of cost calculation and find out the main differences to ECOCUT
  - Buyers should know how to convert the supplier's information into the form that ECOCUT needs for calculation.
  - Find an effective interface between supplier and ECOCUT calculation data sheets. One proposal is to use flipcharts to explain your calculations, e.g., how you calculate machine hourly rates and overhead calculations.
- Difficult situations for ECOCUT
  - Supplier-dominated market
  - Urgent delivery time
  - Too low purchasing volume
  - Killer arguments
  - Fake cooperation

7.6.1 New Project Concept for ECOCUT Discussion in AP

Summary of Your Questions

- There is always a difference between our calculation template and the suppliers, and how to find a bridge that connect our calculation and that of the suppliers?
- Do you calculate the cost before negotiating with suppliers for new projects?
- It is fairly important to build a good relationship with the supplier management. How do you start up the relationship with the supplier?

- Is there any other difference for new projects in China in comparison with Europe? For example, is there a difference in terms of suppliers and markets?

7.6.2 New Approaches

Check of Cycle Time

- Review and check the cycle time when the project has already begun.
- Review and check the unverified quotations.
- See the process, measure the time, calculate the cost, consult the experts, and propose the improvements in yearly reviews.

Win-Win Solution

- Use ECOCUT to find from which direction or process the supplier can control and manage, and how many people should take care of this process.
- Discuss proposal and possibilities with the supplier for improvements in yearly reviews.

Inquiry of Cost Breakdown

- Export ECOCUT report sheets. Send them to the supplier one by one, from *summary* to *detail*.

Calculation Before Discussion

- Based on the parts and the supplier's proposal
- Calculate supplier's information and proposed process (e.g., machines, cycle time)
- Analysis by using ECOCUT to see how the cost gives the supplier enough profit
- Decide final price for negotiation.

Buyers in the Supplier's Eye

- A difficult customer
- Too many visits paid, but few projects offered

7.6.3 EU Versus AP

Relationship with Suppliers

EU	AP
Long-term partnership with suppliers	Cooperate in one or two projects and shift the third to other business units
Suppliers come on knees to ask for business	Ask suppliers for delivery
	Consolidate the relationship with the supplier because of financial situations and lack of qualified suppliers

Market Difference

EU	AP
An enormous supplier base	A small supplier base, particularly for high-tolerance, highly sophisticated machines
Developed manufacturing, process, overhead, and personnel management	Less controlled, no detailed process information to provide

7.7 General Approach to Yearly Negotiations

One supplier might deliver large numbers of parts to your company for one or several business units.

The yearly negotiation focuses on the strategic level with supplier.

A *stable relationship* with the supplier has been established.

The negotiation would not strictly focus on single parts that are carefully calculated with ECOCUT. Instead, the parties will discuss several parts.

Summary of Questions

- Why do suppliers want a price increase in yearly reviews?
- Why do buyers want price decreases?
- Before discussion, do you go to the supplier's side to check the figures?
- When suppliers cannot offer satisfactory information, how can you find a win-win solution that guarantees contract signature?
- Why suppliers want a price increase in yearly reviews?
  - Raw material price increase
  - Exchange rate increase
  - Volume decrease (a set price for a set volume)
  - Limited supplier resources (market-dominated)

  *Under these circumstances, the buyer has to accept in order to ensure delivery.
- Why do buyers want price decreases?
  - Old products
  - Available EU suppliers (European suppliers have depreciated the manufacturing equipment over a period of years)
  - Product localization
- Before discussion, do you go to the supplier's side to check the figures?
  - Review and check the cycle time when the project has already begun.
  - Review and check the unverified quotations.
  - See the process, measure the time, calculate the cost, consult the experts, and propose the improvements in yearly reviews.
- When suppliers cannot offer satisfactory information, how do you find a win-win solution that guarantees contract signature?
  - Use ECOCUT to identify the direction or process from which the supplier can control and manage, and then determine how many people should take care of the process.

– Discuss a proposal and possibilities with the supplier for improvements in yearly reviews.

7.8 36 Stratagems for Negotiation

These tricks are useful to know in negotiations by purchasing staff with suppliers and by salespeople in negotiation with customers.

7.8.1 Winning Stratagems 1–6

Stratagem 1: Cross the Sea Under Camouflage

Explanation It is often the case that people are often blind to the things that they are most familiar with and get relaxed when dealing with them. If one learns this and hides plot in the common phenomenon, he can have a great chance to reach his aim, which means to mask your real goals, by using a fake goal, until the real goal is achieved. For example, tactically, in front of everyone, you point westwards, when your goal is actually in the east.[2]

Negotiation Skill: Pretend to Withdraw Pretend that you are not satisfied with the negotiations and leave the process, but actually you are controlling behind the scenes.

Stratagem 2: Besiege Wei to Save Zhao

Explanation When the flood (enemy) came in a full force, you should avoid facing it. Rather, you should divide them into small streams. When your enemy is weak, you should take the chance to destroy them, like building the dike to contain the water.

Negotiation Skill: Delay Time to Mitigate Tension The aim is to create a cooling period to relax tension and through depth thinking to gain time and more materials and, alternatively, to identify and attack the weakness of the strong enemy and attack it while avoiding a head-on battle.[3]

[2] Source: https://br.pinterest.com/zhoulei0865/chinese-culture/; Author Pinterest.com, San Francisco, published 2021. Access date 2.3.2021.

[3] Source: https://www.google.com/books/edition/Thirty_Six_Stratagems/1i3gDwAAQBAJ?hl=en&gbpv=1&dq=cross+the+sea+under+camouflage&pg=PT12&printsec=frontcover. Author Kathy Wu, China Publishing House Ltd. Singapore. Article "Stratagem 2," published 2015. access date 2.3.2021.

Stratagem 3: Borrow Others' Hands to Kill

Explanation When you are sure of your enemy and unsure of you ally, you should trick your ally to attack your enemy so that you can spare your force and benefit from the defeat of either, for example, to bribe some top officials on one's side to take certain provocative actions against the other.

Negotiation Skill: Competition In negotiation strategy, it is mainly to borrow the third force or to use or create conflict inside enemy to achieve one's goal. For example, provoke the relationship among different competitors, in order to consolidate our position.

Stratagem 4: Await the Exhausted Enemy at Your Ease

Explanation The aim should be to control the development of situations by taking initiative. It will be a matter of time when the enemy will be weakened by one of his adventures. Then, we will have the breathing space to overcome any of enemy's weaknesses to do battle with him in future. It is about choosing the appropriate time for fighting against the enemy and about waiting for the enemy to get exhausted by its predicaments.

Negotiation Skill: Prepare Fully to Cause Psychological Stress The art of negotiation lies in leading others instead of being led by others. If we are well prepared, you can make use of this strategy to give the psychological pressure to the opposing party, so that they can accept our request.

Stratagem 5: Loot a Burning House

Explanation This stratagem describes how to capitalize on the enemy's chaos. When the enemy is in difficulties and danger, it is a good time for us to attack. The intervention of a power must end in the resignation of the weak. It is a good time to conquer the enemy's territory when the enemy is beset with internal conflicts.

Negotiation Skill: A Threat Strategy We can openly express the threat to the opposing party. When a company is beset by internal conflicts, when disease, ravage, fire, explosion, etc., happened, when corruption and crime are rampant, then supplier will be unable to deal with an outside threat. This is the time to attack and demand lower prices.[4]

Stratagem 6: Make a Noise in the East While Attacking in the West

Explanation It is to make a false impression to cheat the enemy into making wrong decisions. To make the leader of the enemy confused, flexible methods must be applied. Pretend to attack a place you did not be seen through by your enemy.

---

[4] Source: http://allempires.com/article/index.php?q=thrity_six_strategies; Authors at http://en.wikipedia.org/wiki/Thirty-Six_Strategies, http://afpc.asso.fr/wengu/wg/wengu.php?l=36ji; registered at 10 February 2002, access date 2.3.2021.

Negotiation Skill: Gain the Upper Hand Through Hard Weave Even when face to face with a supplier in negotiation, surprise can still be employed by attacking where he least expects it. To do this, you must create an expectation in the supplier's mind through the use of a feint. For example, if we want to order accessories and suppliers seem disinterested, we can start the negotiation for the main components of the equipment to attract the interest of the supplier. Then, negotiations for the auxiliary components tend to receive better results.[5]

7.8.2 Enemy Dealing Stratagems 7–12

Stratagem 7: Create Something Out of Nothing

Explanation Create an illusion to show that you have what you really do not or that you do not have what you really do. If creating illusions can take time, then you need to start thinking about these ahead of time. That is deceit. However, deceit should not last too long in case it should be seen through by the opponent. Thus, it is not feasible to remain false for too long a time.

Negotiation Skill: Pretend to Be Angry The important part of using illusions is that the other side believes them. A way this is done by paying attention to the details. For example, make use of an angry expression to frighten the opponents, so that the opponents feel that the situation is extremely serious.[6]

Stratagem 8: Advance Secretly by an Unknown Path

Explanation Attack the enemy with two convergent forces. The first is the direct attack, one that is obvious and for which the enemy prepares his defense. The second is the indirect attack, that the enemy does not expect and which causes him to divide his forces at the last minute, leading to confusion and disaster.

Negotiation Skill: Good Preparation Pretend to care about an issue and later give it up to get what you really want. Before the negotiation is officially launched, we can provide wide amount of information to the opposite party in order to make them feel safe. Observe the relationship of your suppliers with others and give the right information to achieve your goal.[7]

[5] Source: http://allempires.com/article/index.php?q=thrity_six_strategies Authors at http://en.wikipedia.org/wiki/Thirty-Six_Strategies, http://afpc.asso.fr/wengu/wg/wengu.php?l=36ji; registered at 10 February 2002, access date 2.3.2021.

[6] Source: http://changingminds.org/disciplines/warfare/36_strategems/36_stratagems_7.htm; Author "Changing Works," updated 2002–2021, access date 2.3.2021.

[7] Source: https://imperialcombatarts.com/thirty-six-stratagems.html; Author "Imperial Combat Arts," updated 2009–2020, access date 2.3.2021.

Stratagem 9: Watch a Fire from the Other Side of the River

Explanation Monitor the situation and delay entering the field of negotiation/battle until all the other players have become exhausted fighting among themselves. Then, go in full strength and pick up the pieces. It means you should keep calm to observe the changes.

Negotiation Skill: Make the Supplier Compete During the negotiation, we can have the introduction of other competitors, increasing competition among them, in order to get the best results. If you are the "small player," never join the fight of "market leaders." Wait until your competitors have exhausted themselves. For example, if another supplier gives a better price below production costs to customer than you, simply observe how long he can survive.[8]

Stratagem 10: Hide a Dagger in a Smile

Explanation It is a strategy to have the opponents be off their guard. This strategy is characterized by its outward kindness and inward malevolent intent.

Negotiation Skill: Establish a Friendship Charm your competitors to gain their trust. Through building trust, we get the most suitable deal out of the friendship. Never appear price competitive, but project an image friendliness., and strike when a favorable opportunity presents itself. For example, before you will take over competitors, give them aid and even sent consultants to train their staff. You will learn about and gain control of the company, and eventually index acquisition costs.[9]

Stratagem 11: Palm Off a Substitute for the Real Thing

Explanation The development of the situation will undoubtedly cost a price. Remember to sacrifice partial profit for the whole advantage or victory.

Negotiation Skill: Learn How to Bluff Pretend our leader who is granted power to make decision is not satisfied with the price. Then, we persuade the opposing party to lower the price to make the negotiation successful. Be ready to accept a small loss to achieve a better gain. For example, to accept losing money in the introductory stage of a product, with the hope that when the product takes off, the profits will be greater than the initial losses.[10]

---

[8] Source: https://readingraphics.com/36-business-stratagems/; article "Watch the fires burning across rivers"; author Readingraphics, updated 2021, access date 2.3.2021.

[9] Source: https://readingraphics.com/36-business-stratagems/; article "Hide a knife behind a smile"; author Readingraphics; author Readingraphics, updated 2021. Access date 2.3.2021.

[10] Source: /http://docshare01.docshare.tips/files/23858/238585109.pdf; Stratagem 11, Page 61 to 65, author Lan Bercu at LAC International Press; published 2014. Access date 2.3.2021.

Stratagem 12: Take the Opportunity to Pilfer a Goat

Explanation Use the slight negligence or loophole of the enemy and try to create some advantage even it is the smallest. Take advantage of any opportunity, even small, and avail yourself of any small profit. Likewise, look for your competitor's mistakes and make them work for you. Look for niche markets that your competitor may have overlooked or neglected.

Negotiation Skill: Rediscuss the Matter We can rediscuss the matter, give up the previous position, or/and propose additional requirements.

7.8.3 Attacking Stratagems 13–18

Stratagem 13: Hit the Grass and Alert the Snake

Explanation To investigate suspicious situations again and again, and then take action after having complete information. Repeated survey is an important means to detect hidden competitors.

Negotiation Skill: Lure the Opposing Party Stir things up before beginning to negotiate for your true interests. Then, we can provide the most favorable examples in negotiations to support the opposing party's program and make them nod in agreement.

Sample Drawing price competitors secretly from other channels and expose the info when negotiating consciously, which helps us to put pressure on the supplier to get a more competitive price.

Strategy We get a fake agreement with a low price from competitors and show it to our supplier. The supplier will offer a lower price to get a contract.

Stratagem 14: Revive in a New Guise

Explanation Revive a dead proposal by presenting it again or in a new way. It means revive something from the past by giving it a new purpose or to reinterpret and bring to life old ideas, customs, and traditions. Revive old ideas by infusing them with a new purpose.

Negotiation Skill: Anti—Its Meaning and Use It During the negotiation, we can use the reverse thinking to negotiate the usual, easy to be neglected fields, in order to avoid large differences. Here are some ideas for the preparation of a strategy: You can merge, acquire, buy in, or buy out when a business has the potential and is not too expensive to acquire. Liquidate or restructure a failing business or organization to reposition it in a new light. Test different names or purposes with the same content to see which one works best or how the market responds to it. Reinvent or rebrand by building on existing ideas. Adopt and adapt an idea to fit the market.[11]

Stratagem 15: Lure the Tiger Out of His Den

Explanation To attack the well-prepared enemy is very dangerous, while waiting for enemy's attack is beneficial to us. Therefore, never directly attack an opponent whose advantage is derived from its position. Instead, lure him away from his comfort zone, separating him from his source of strength, and then destroy him, which means influence others' decision making by drawing them away from their norms, routines.

Negotiation Skill: Focus on Inconspicuous Issues Try to focus on the issues that the opposing party is not very interested in, so that the opposing party may increase in satisfaction. Avoid competing head-on at what he is best at. Instead, reverse the situation and make him compete in what you are best at. When you do, critical thinking is weakened, leaving them vulnerable. Ideal solution: Find a market segment, product, service, where no tigers are operating.[12]

Stratagem 16: Let Off the Enemies in Order to Catch Them Afterward

Explanation It does not mean we do not chase them, but the key point is how we chase them. If you drive your enemies mad, they may give you a terrible counterattack. It is better to let them go for a while. You can wait until the enemies drop their guard and become less mindful. At this time, we can start our attack and wipe out the enemies. The most important thing is to understand the situation. Then, you can cooperate with your competition and achieve synergy. Learn to coexist with your competition so that you can break-free when you are sufficiently strong.

Negotiation Skill: Convince the Opponent If we negotiate in ways that are rational, beneficial, or incremental, we can be more convincing. Doing so will also help us understand the effort to reduce the price.

Sample We can pretend to ignore the supplier but evaluate the facts seriously before achieving preliminary targets during negotiation.

Strategy In sales negotiations, for example, do not try to sell. Build relationships instead. Do not push a product, you need to build a community around it. Do not sell

[11] Source: http://docshare01.docshare.tips/files/23858/238585109.pdf; Stratagem 14, Page 74 to 78, author Lan Bercu at LAC International Press; published 2014. Access date 2.3.2021.

[12] Source: https://en.wikisource.org/wiki/Thirty-Six_Strategies, Stratagem 15, last edited on January 13, 2013, access date 2.3.2021.

products on the basis of price. Instead, emphasize the added value. Do not start a sales pitch. Instead, ask questions and listen.[13]

Stratagem 17: Throw Away a Brick in Order to Get a Gem

Explanation Prepare a trap then lure your enemy into the trap by using bait. In war, the bait is the illusion of an opportunity for gain. In life, the bait is the illusion of wealth, power, and sex. Like fishing, we go fishing by using bait and giving benefit to them first in order to make them swallow the bait.

Negotiation Skill: Use Concession Value depends on what one plans to do with the item or resource in question. The key to success in negotiations is in identifying the individual's values and creating an opportunity for exchange. For example, concede something that is less important to you but more important to your counterpart. Do not treat your product or service as a commodity, instead add value and turn it into a consultative sale at a premium price. Define, create, and add your value by yourself and promote it in negotiations.[14]

Stratagem 18: Capture the Ringleader First in Order to Capture All His Followers

Explanation Destroy the main force and capture the chief commander of the enemy, the fighting power of it will quickly collapse. If the commander falls, the rest of the army will disperse or come over to your side.

Negotiation Skill: Identify the Principal Negotiator When the negotiation starts, we should try to learn who is the principal negotiator of the opposing party, and then we focus on him/her. Convince the leader and the rest will follow.

Sample We should focus our energy on the supplier's top negotiators who have the absolute decision-making power. In this way, we can save our time and achieve our target.

Strategy To incapacitate your competitor's organization, destroy the glue that holds it together. For example, to impair your competitor, recruit its executives.

---

[13] Source: http://docshare01.docshare.tips/files/23858/238585109.pdf. Stratagem 16, Page 83 to 87, author Lan Bercu at LAC International Press; published 2014. Access date 2.3.2021.

[14] Source: http://docshare01.docshare.tips/files/23858/238585109.pdf. Stratagem 17, Page 88 to 90, author Lan Bercu at LAC International Press; published 2014. Access date 2.3.2021.

7.8.4 Chaos Stratagems 19–24

Stratagem 19: Take Away the Firewood from Under the Cauldron
Explanation When the enemy is too powerful for you to defeat directly, you can fight it by destroying its imposing state. The essence of this stratagem is to attack the tough in a mild way. For example, to eliminate the source of their strength.

Negotiation Skill: Looking for Breakthrough Through Multiple Information. Example 1 Because we occasionally buy products in small quantities, we need to ask agents to complete them. We can master the price of products from manufacturer in advance, and then estimate the price of agents, in order to avoid confusion by agents' rhetoric words.

Negotiation Skill: Strengths by Own Developments. Example 2 Identify and develop your own strengths/niche market/competitive edge, or "firewood," which could make your enemy's strength and power irrelevant in negotiations.

Negotiation Skill: Prevent Strengths of Your Competition. Example 3 Find out what makes your competition strong and then prevent them from drawing on that resource. You can acquire it, destroy it, or disable it.[15]

Stratagem 20: Fish in Troubled Waters
Explanation A distracted enemy is more vulnerable. Take advantage of the inner struggle happening inside the enemy. Make full use of the situation when the enemy has relatively less power and in a state of disunity.

Negotiation Skill: Make Use of Our Strengths to Win People are sympathetic, even if our suppliers have the purpose to maximize profits. Do something unusual, strange, and unexpected as this will arouse the enemy's suspicion and disrupt his thinking. For example, bundle your products or services to create a perception in your favor. Or confuse customers with details that distract them from their main concerns.

Stratagem 21: Slip Out of a Predicament Like a Cicada Shedding Its Skin
Explanation When you are in trouble, secretly escape. Carefully and secretly transfer the main forces so as to avoid the danger while the enemy is not aware that anything out of the ordinary may be happening. In fact, it is a way of separating the skin and the body, for example, keeping the appearance while transferring the main content.

[15] Source: http://docshare01.docshare.tips/files/23858/238585109.pdf. Stratagem 18 + 19, Page 91 to 97, author Lan Bercu at LAC International Press; published 2014. Access date 2.3.2021.

Negotiation Skill: Pretend to Have No Power. Example 1 When we find that we are forced to make many more concessions than we can accept, we will declare that we lack the authority to make such an agreement.

Negotiation Skill: Good Cop, Bad Cop. Example 2 In negotiation, use the "good cop, bad cop" stratagem to confuse your counterpart. One acts as a lure, the other as a striking force.

Stratagem 22: Catch the Thief by Closing His Escape Route

Explanation This stratagem is especially designed for coping with the enemy's scheme of luring you into the deep. For example, offer significant added value to keep your customers engaged. Captivate your customers by catering to their needs and solving their problems. Engage customers by continually being interesting and reinventing yourself and your brand.

Negotiation Skill: Making the Opposing Party Responsible for Their Own Mistakes During the process of negotiations, the opposing party may not realize their own mistakes. Then, we can be based on their mistakes and ask for lower prices.[16]

Stratagem 23: Associate with the Distant States and Attack the Neighboring Ones

Explanation If you are confined by the geographic positions and situations, it will be beneficial to you to attack the enemy nearby and harmful to attack the distant enemy first. When you are the strongest in one field, your greatest threat is from the second strongest in your field, not the strongest from another field.

Negotiation Skill: Destroy One by One. Example 1 If we are negotiating with a group of opponents, we can try to convince one of them to accept our proposal. Then, this person may help us convince other opponents.

Negotiation Skill: Seek for Alliances. Example 2 Identify the right competitor and partner with him to achieve a specific goal. Seek to disrupt alliances that threaten you, while creating partnerships that offer you power. Joint ventures, licensing, or franchising can be a cost-effective starter to distant places.

Negotiation Skill: Seek Niche Markets. Example 3 To bring your negotiations in a pole position by push technologies like Internet, social media, e-commerce, and

[16] Source: http://docshare01.docsharc.tips/files/23858/238585109.pdf. Stratagem 20–22, Page 98 to 109, author Lan Bercu at LAC International Press; published 2014. Access date 2.3.2021

cloud computing to gain a global presence. Avoid overcrowded markets and intense competition by operating in underserved segments (niches).[17]

Stratagem 24: Borrow a Road to Invade Guo

Explanation For a small country between the enemy and ourselves, we can provide it with aid while in fact infiltrating our power into it when it is threatened by the enemy force. Temporarily join forces with a friend against a common enemy.

Negotiation Skill: Find Potential Supplier in Advance. Example 1 Identify our second-best option in case you cannot reach agreement with your primary supplier or customer.

Negotiation Skill: First Learn from Others. Example 2 Take an apprenticeship to learn the tricks of the trade. Alternatively, accept a minor, inferior role to get a foot in the door. Using your ally as a "borrowed road," find an agreement. Later you can further your own goals without relying on the longevity of the relationship.[18]

7.8.5 Proximate Stratagems 25–30

Stratagem 25: Steal the Beams and Change the Pillars

Explanation This stratagem suggests replacing something real with a fake. For example, pretend to attack so that the enemy is compelled to shift its battle array and defeat it as soon as its weak points show up. This tactic can be very effective due to its ability to make the enemy move. Another example is to sabotage, incapacitate, or destroy them by removing their key support.[19]

Negotiation Skill: A Deliberate Distortion. Example 1 Intentionally distort the opposing party's meaning and behavior, such as by misinterpreting or manipulating the facts.

Negotiation Skill: Think Critically. Example 2 In Sales, produce fake products at lower quality and sell them to a lower price to customers. Vice versa, as a purchaser, do not assume that people have the same ethical and moral standard as yours and be skeptical of anything that seems too good or too cheap to be true. Use your critical thinking to avoid falling into the deception trap.

---

[17] Source: http://docshare01.docshare.tips/files/23858/238585109.pdf. Stratagem 23, Page 110 to 113, author Lan Bercu at LAC International Press; published 2014. Access date 2.3.2021.

[18] Source: http://docshare01.docshare.tips/files/23858/238585109.pdf. Stratagem 24, Page 114 to 117, author Lan Bercu at LAC International Press; published 2014. Access date 2.3.2021.

[19] Source: https://www2.hawaii.edu/~barkai/HO/36.doc; article THE 36 CHINESE STRATEGIES APPLIED TO NEGOTIATION, authors John Barkai, Cultural Dimension Interests, the Dance of Negotiation, and Weather Forecasting; published 2008. access date 2.3.2021.

Stratagem 26: Scold the Locust While Pointing at the Mulberry

Explanation If the strong wants to control the weak, it is advisable to take a tough-minded attitude to warn them. Being appropriately tough can win support, while handling matters in a decisive manner can gain respect from others.

Negotiation Skill: Point Out the Weakness. Example 1 In sales, point out the inadequacies and weakness of our competitors (without mentioning names) in order to allure customers to accept our request. In negotiations with suppliers, show other suppliers' weaknesses (without mentioning names). We choose to complain about others weaknesses to allure the opposing party to follow our plan, but convey our intentions and opinions indirectly.

Negotiation Skill: Direct vs. Indirect Cultures. Example 2 In sales, focus on the details of your product or service that solve the customer's pain and problems, while comparing these with what your competition cannot provide. Do not use names, so you cannot be accused. Use intermediaries, third parties, and others. As a Westerner, always be aware that indirectness is a popular conflict resolution style in Asia. Always be mindful of "face." Keep face, give face, and save face. As an Easterner, when dealing with direct cultures, you need to remember: Be mindful of problem-solving assumptions. Separate relationship from the problem. Learn to openly express opinions and points of view. You cannot rely on nonverbal, intuitive understanding, instead express with evidence, facts, and figures. Make a well-planned proposal. Be prepared for up-front challenge, accept criticism, counterproposals, and suggestions. Limit your use of silence since it can be taken for incompetence and inefficiency. Ask more effective questions.

Stratagem 27: Feign Madness Without Being Insane

Explanation Pretend to be a pig in order to eat the tiger. Pretend to know nothing, but actually have a keen sight into matters, pretend to have no high ideals, but indeed the reason is that it is better to do nothing, if a great achievement is on the way. Play dumb and then surprise them. Let them underestimate you. This stratagem advises you to avoid appearing to be a threat. When you appear nonthreatening, your adversary will discount you and your efforts. When enemies put their guard down, you will come in and attack.

Negotiation Skill: Make Two Parties Enter into a Collaboration. Example 1 After hard negotiation, the collaboration between two parties may not be entered. Then, we can see from some minor aspects to look for opportunities in order to surprise attack.

Negotiation Skill: Play "Columbo." Example 2 Rather than talk, listen actively and ask effective questions so that you can gain information and exploit any slip of the tongue. Leverage your strong position to renegotiate or change the rules of the game. Prepare, prepare, and then prepare some more. Be disciplined and mentally focused. Use the "Columbo technique" to tie unrelated details together.

Stratagem 28: Remove the Ladder After the Enemy Has Climbed Up

Explanation Lead enemy into a trap, and then cut off their escape and supply routes. Pretend to show one's weak points to cajole the enemy into coming and cut off his reinforcement afterward. Then, your enemy will be in a hopeless situation.

Negotiation Skill: Sales Tactics. Example 1 Install loyalty programs, bonus cards, points, customer cards, freebies, and other gimmicks. Use up-selling, cross-selling, peer pressure, or an installment plan to attract customers.

Negotiation Skill: A Large Amount of Information. Example 2 Before a large scale of negotiation has not been officially launched, we can provide a wide coverage of information to the opposing party, in order to reach target before the furious negotiation, because the opposing party may take long time to understand the whole information.

Stratagem 29: Put Artificial Flowers on Trees

Explanation Reframe deceitfully. Expand the pie with objects of little value. If some situation or means to form favorable disposition, a weak troop can appear to be comparatively stronger. False appearance and traps can help to achieve a deceptive show of power, which succumb or even defeat your enemy. For example, those who deck a "bare tree" with false blossoms and using splendid materials to embellish a wretched reality are Ponzi or pyramid schemes.

Negotiation Skill: Our Advantage Is the Other Consideration If the opposing party does not know us clearly, we can try to show our advantages, which may receive very good results. Or we can form alliances, organize associations, or join existing associations to create a strong, consolidated front and network. Attract partners, alliances, and contributors to form a strong force. After we appear strong for others, we try to make opposing party to consider long-term cooperation with us, and then make use this advantage to demand price cuts (in negotiation with suppliers), or price increase (in negotiation with customers).

Stratagem 30: Turn from a Guest into a Host

Explanation The stratagem advises accepting an inferior position so that you do not appear as a threat—getting a foot in the door and then extending your influence beyond the immediate arena when your rival is not watching. Try you best to exploit an advantage and occupy the chief position. When the time comes, take the control over others. By offering help, they secured their position in their allies, and then took the possession step by step.

Negotiation Skill: Seize the Initiate. Example 1 Decide what to concede if necessary to reach agreements and try control the process of the negotiation.

Negotiation Skill: Seize the Initiate. Example 2 Develop trust and credibility. In negotiation, offer a joint venture to learn, and then take over, buy out, or establish on your own. Make them (competition or customer or partner) dependent on you. Take charge of needed resources; gradually assume control over desired access to people and things. Become an expert, the "go-to" person. If you are indispensable, people must come to you for advice and knowledge.

7.8.6 Desperate Stratagems 31–36

Stratagem 31: Sexual Pleasure Trap

Explanation When dealing with a resourceful leader of the enemy, try to take down his morale. To conserve your strength, take advantage of your enemy's weakness. To attack powerful troops, you would better make use of the shortcomings of their generals; to deal with smart generals, you would better try your best to ruin their wills. Once their generals are frustrated and the soldiers are dejected, the troops would never be aggressive again.

Negotiation Skill: Show Off Achievements First identify what your counterpart needs and wants, and then identify your levers and how you can move them to achieve your end goal. Before going into negotiations, polish the appearance and build a favorable image of your company, and sharpen communication skills of negotiators to your advantage. For better odds of success, form a complete package of pleasant attitude, and high performance. However, if the opposing party questions your past experience to contempt you, we should pretend shock and quote our best achievements of the past to them.

Stratagem 32: The Empty City

Explanation When the enemies have doubts in their mind, they would hesitate to take actions. They are afraid of being trapped and wonder whether there is ambush in the city. The deliberate display of some weakness can conceal your vulnerability and prevent an attack.

Negotiation Skill: Pretend to Be Well Prepared. Example 1 Threatening to use another supplier, but in fact we have only this potential supplier.

Negotiation Skill: Display Weaknesses and Emerge. Example 2 Create mystery with a deliberate display of your weaknesses. Your audience is most engaged and connected when they hear about your struggles, failures, and setbacks and how you emerge and rise. This means let get people involved in building trust and relationships with you because, psychologically, people want to be a part of some important cause.

Stratagem 33: Sow Discord Among One's Enemies (The Double-Agent Ploy)

Explanation Provide inaccurate information to mislead them, particularly through informal channels. The deception should be skillfully made as true. Only in this way, the enemy will be fooled and make wrong judgments and then take wrong actions.

Negotiation Skill: Internally Decompose. Example 1 We can try to convince the member of opposing party to know and accept our ideas. Then, he/she may influence other members.

Negotiation Skill: Use Agents as Spies. Example 2 Before you go into negotiations, use the enemy's spies to spy for you, and you would not lose the battle. For example, find old connections, classmates, or friends who work for your opponent. Recruit people from your competitor. Look for those who have resentments or are demotivated, pushed aside, or under difficult circumstances. Train and send your own agent to your competitor. Instruct him to plant false information and report back to you.[20]

Stratagem 34: Deceive the Enemy by Torturing One's Own Man

Explanation Feign weakness while arming yourself. No one would like to be hurt and if he is hurt by others, it must be true. Therefore, if false is taken for true, it is certain that your enemy would have no doubt and the strategy would take its effect.

Negotiation Skill: A Defensive Weakness. Example 1 When we are in a weak position, we can pretend us to be weak and make the opposing party feel they are large. Using this strategy, to get sympathy from the opposing party, we can get lower price.

Negotiation Skill: "Self-injury" Scheme. Example 2 Offer a heavy discount to attract customers and promote sales. Lower the price to gain market share; then, raise the price to make profit later.

Stratagem 35: Make Use of a Series of Tactics

Explanation Devise a set of interlocking stratagems to defeat enemies. It refers to using several tactics, one after another, with the one to restrict the enemy and the other to attack them. No enemy could resist so many tactics. The reason is never rely on one stratagem for success, instead use linking stratagems to generate new ones. By using interlocking stratagems, your strategy is unpredictable by competitors, customers, and suppliers.

---

[20] Source: http://docshare01.docshare.tips/files/23858/238585109.pdf. Stratagem 25–33, Page 118 to 156, author Lan Bercu at LAC International Press; published 2014. Access date 2.3.2021.

Negotiation Skill: A Series of Preparation Firstly, review notes from previous negotiations, courses, etc., in order to get tips for success. Secondly, create an agenda for the negotiation and practice. Finally, start the negotiation confidently.

Stratagem 36: Retreat

Explanation If all else fails, run away, because a smart man does not fight a losing battle. When troops are in the inferior situation, it is wiser for them to retreat. The sayings going like this, "when there is life, there is hope." Active retreat can also lure the enemy, and have them move troops here and there, thus creating good opportunities for this side.

Negotiation Skill: Give Up If a negotiation is not in accordance with the direction of your plan, we should prepare to leave. Never negotiate under circumstances without any chance, because you will always be in disadvantage. Withdrawing from an industry or market where you are no longer competitive is a smart move. Never fall in love with a deal, instead be decisive in cutting your losses.

8 Cultural Diversity in Asia-Pacific

Cultural diversity commitment is a strategic business advantage, one that leads for companies to better hires, reduced employee turnover, higher employee engagement, greater insight into customers, and more. Companies, who ensure that the needs of all employees are reflected in and protected by their policies, will get them behind vision and missions.

Following, please find basics of how to use the knowledge of diversity in negotiating successful in some selected Asian countries (Source: Robert Bosch GmbH).

8.1 Common Attributes in Asia-Pacific

- Hierarchy
- Harmony
- Face
- Interpersonal relationship
- Indirect communication (Fig. 8.1)

Hierarchy

- Seniority and age always rules.
- If in difficult situations, focus on the people higher in the hierarchy.
- The functionaries and managers are the key to solve the problems. Do not let them feel neglected. Respect them!

Harmony

- Harmony means to achieve a balance in which extremes and opposites are reconciled. In short, to avoid a direct "No."
- Focus more on the person himself and his network of human relationships and less on the objective level of fact.

K. Zuerl, *Effective Cost Cutting in Asia*, Management for Professionals,
https://doi.org/10.1007/978-3-030-82782-3_8

Attribute / Country	Hierarchy	Harmony	Keep Face	Guanxi	Indirect Communication
China	√	√	√	√	√
Japan	√	√	√	√	√
Korea	√	√	√	√	√
Malaysia	√	√	√	√	√
Vietnam	√	√	√	√	√

Fig. 8.1 Common attributes in Asian countries (Source: GTEC)

- Resolve critical situations politely rather than at the expense of harmony. In fact, harmony is more important than honesty.

Face

- "Face" stands for dignity, honor, (self-)respect, prestige, influence, recognition, fairness, and acknowledgment.
- Loss of face must be avoided at all costs. You must ensure that no other person loses face on account of your actions.
- To keep face, never raise your voice or become discourteous in difficult situations.

Interpersonal Relationship

- Interpersonal relationship is one of the most important foundations for business contacts.
- Even formal agreements are not as effective as having the right personal contacts.
- The most solid foundation for a business relationship lies in personal trust.
- The interpersonal relationship is associated with mutual expectations and obligations, interests, and benefits.

Indirect Communication

- Indirect communication means at first a great deal of information related to the problem is conveyed, which may be considered to be "irrelevant." The speaker will only "come to the point" after he receives a positive signal from the listener.
- The form of a statement is sometimes more important than its contents. In fact, the form is to a certain extent itself content as it conveys important information (Fig. 8.2).

The right tone, respect for traditions, and commitment to doing the work it takes to learn about a culture can help open doors, build trust, and, most importantly, help a business thrive.[1]

[1] Source: https://www.wolterskluwer.com/en/expert-insights/business-etiquette-tips-asia-pacific-region; Author Wolters Kluver, published April 07, 2020; access date 2.3.2021.

Fig. 8.2 Direct vs. indirect communication (Source: GTEC)

8.2 Negotiation Tips for Main Countries in AP

Excellent cross-cultural negotiators proceed slowly, testing their assumptions about what strategy will be effective with the other party. While they are not willing to compromise on their goals, they are willing to adjust their strategy to achieve them.[2]

8.2.1 China

- Common solution should be found without any participants losing face. Always come back to the common ground in difficult situation.

[2]Source: http://knowledge.essec.edu/en/strategy/5-tips-negotiating-business-deal-asia.html; By Sarah Brown, based on research by Ta Wei Chao. Published 25.04.2016, access date 2.3.2021.

- Main message always comes at the end. Important points are repeated many times and gain weight in the process.
- Due to a lack of political stability, a guarantee of short-term profit is an important criterion for lasting business association.
- Interpersonal relationship is the key to survive Chinese bureaucracy. Use the "key person" to filter out the organizational entity which has the authority over the required resources.
- Eating out together, looking for points of mutual agreement, and making compromises are advisable approaches.

Hierarchy and Respect for Elders

Hierarchy plays an important role in Chinese society. A person's prestige and age play an important role in determining the position of a person within the hierarchy. As a general rule, authorities and older people are shown respect and consideration. People holding official positions are often trusted sooner than anonymous institutions or laws. Older people are expected to be role models for the young. So, they are usually accepted as such. Additionally, older people are expected to care about the welfare of younger people.

The Chinese concept of hierarchy and its meaning for society becomes visible in seating arrangements forms of address and the significance of business cards.

Face and Loss of Face

The concept of "face," which is so important in Asian cultures, stands for dignity, honor, (self-)respect, prestige, influence, recognition, fairness, and acknowledgment. In China, loss of face must be avoided at all costs. However, the individual is not just responsible for keeping his own face but must also ensure that no other person loses face due to his actions.

A person can lose face, for example, if they insist on a confrontational approach, become angry, or lose their self-control. One behavioral rule that demands a certain degree of patience from people from Western cultures is to never raise your voice or become discourteous!

But a person can also lose face if you ask their colleague for advice instead of them.

Harmony, Avoidance of Conflict, and a Direct "No"

Harmony and reconciliation are central values in both Confucianism and Taoism. The aim is to achieve a balance in which extremes and opposites are reconciled. For that reason, Chinese avoid open conflict and a directly expressed "no." To guarantee harmony, the focus of perception is placed less on the objective level of fact and more on the person himself and his network of human relationships. In a harmonious relationship, "the parties give each other face."

Behavior that promotes harmony includes keeping silent and being reticent. An effort is made to resolve critical situations politely rather than at the expense of harmony. In fact, harmony is more important than honesty.

Body Language and Personal Space: Smiling and Its Significance

In China, a smile creates trust and signalizes willingness to cooperate. Someone who does not smile very often will be thought of as cold, dissatisfied, and threatening. Generally, a constant smile merely means that someone is listening. People also smile if they are at a loss or are insecure or have not understood a question.

Respect plays an important role in the body language of Chinese. This is expressed by avoiding eye contact. Direct eye contact might be read as a sign of aggression, whereas avoidance of direct eye contact indicates good manners.

Handshaking has come to be accepted and is now the norm, particularly among Chinese who have a lot of contact with Europeans and Americans.

Establishing Contacts

Positive business contacts are absolutely essential for business and are generally characterized by courtesy, respect, and a desire to achieve a consensus. However, such contacts take time to establish. Generally, relationships only work reliably in stable and mature structures. Considering that hierarchy plays a major role in business as well, a businessman must work his way through the hierarchy in a sequence of meetings before coming face to face with the real decision makers.

Guan Xi

A keyword for social relationships in China is "guanxi." This term denotes a specifically Chinese form of social networking and loyalties. The interpersonal relationship takes precedence here and is associated with mutual expectations and obligations, interests, and benefits. These are fundamental for a person's social status and influence. They are not based on an emotional tie but are for personal benefit. Guanxi requires an exchange of favors, also in material terms, such as presents and favors, which are viewed as a long-term investment.

If guanxi is entered into by someone, he will automatically be included in a much larger, existing network of relationships (*guanxi wang*). This network also functions as an information network.

Guanxi is one of the most important foundations for business contacts: Even formal agreements are not as effective as having the right personal contacts. The most solid foundation for a business relationship lies in personal trust.

Information Exchange

In China, meetings are for exchanging information. Controversial discussions are generally avoided. This means that hardly any decisions are made in a meeting and there are very few binding results. Rather, a meeting is just one step in a long process of agreement and reconciliation. Decisions are prepared, but no final decision is made.

Chinese like to sound out the interests of the other party in an informal discussion. That is why direct questioning is often compared to interrogation.

The beginning of a meeting usually consists of positive information or pleasantries. The really important points are left to the end. Closed, yes, or no questions are not suitable for identifying the attitudes of a Chinese business partner. Open questions give a partner the opportunity to answer in the indirect fashion he is used to.

Hierarchy

The hierarchical structure also plays a role in meetings. Employees will often only speak after being asked to by their superior. A superior is not normally contradicted because the hierarchy determines who can speak and who can participate in the decision-making process.

No Fixed Agenda

To people from some other cultures, Germans for instance, Chinese participants often seem to be little prepared. Chinese are often not punctual and behave passively during a meeting. It is normal that people come and go during a meeting. Generally, mobile phones are not switched off.

Direct criticisms should be avoided in the closing evaluations, as this can easily be counterproductive.

Chinese are normally unwilling to make written agreements during meetings.

Decision Making

Hierarchy plays an important role in the decision-making process. For that reason, it is wise to address someone higher up in the hierarchy if a negotiating partner is prevaricating.

Consensus Is the Objective

In the classical Chinese understanding, the aim of a discussion is not that the best arguments should prevail but that a common solution is found without any participants losing face. A discussion should seek consensus, reconcile different opinions, and incorporate these in the solution.

The position of the participants must be considered in a discussion. On the job, it is usually the boss who opens a discussion and finishes it by declaring a "solution": regardless of whether the issue has been completely cleared up or not.

Avoidance of Conflict

In China, conflicts are generally avoided at all cost. The relationship between the conflicting parties and the power structures involved is important for the outcome of a conflict. If conflict has already broken out into the open, it is usually too late to save the situation.

In Chinese culture, which is so concerned with harmony, it can be helpful to "overlook" a potential conflict. Negative points and problems are not usually focused on, they are tolerated instead. Common denominators are sought in an attempt to balance the various interests. If a foreigner finds himself in a conflict situation in China, it is not wise to try to push for clarification. A better option is to find a local in whom to confide and ask advice.

The manner in which Chinese people handle conflicts depends very much on their group affiliation. Within the group, any nonconforming behavior meets with strict sanctions and affiliation to the group becomes dogma: regardless of the issue under dispute.

In business negotiations, an attempt to solve a conflict diplomatically can be helpful. Eating out together, looking for points of mutual agreement, and making compromises are advisable approaches. Symbolic gestures can also help to restore harmony.

Bureaucracy

Guanxi is absolutely critical if one is to survive Chinese bureaucracy. It is good to know who has power and influence in a certain field so as to filter out that organizational entity that has the authority over the required resources from the confusing number of national, provincial, and local offices.

For details, please see https://www.drcomgroup.com/en/articles/chinese-digital-ecosystem

8.2.2 India[3]

- Face-to-face communication is preferred in India, do not negotiate online. Points that have already been agreed on should be written down to avoid a negotiation start all over again. It is better to say something pleasant than the truth.
- The bargaining stage of a negotiation can be extensive. Prices often move more than 40% between initial offers and final agreement. However, technical assistance, training, and other costs may also be important bargaining factors and Indians remain flexible throughout most of the bargaining. Leave yourself a lot of room for concessions at different stages. You need to explain your cost breakdown and limits in a friendly way.
- Although the primary negotiation style is somewhat competitive, Indians nevertheless value long-term relationships and look for win-win solutions. Long waiting time for official approval should also be counted in due to the bureaucracy. Be patient and make a good book for it.
- Avoid being confrontational. You need to show flexible attitude and should not be too insistent with your demands. Aggression of any kind or extremely direct communication is seen as a lack of respect. Should a dispute arise of a negotiation, you may be able to reach resolution through showing friendliness, respect, and willingness to compromise.

[3] Source: http://www.leadershipcrossroads.com/mat/cou/India.pdf; Article "Negotiating International Business – India". Author Lothar Katz, Published 2017, access date 2.3.2021.

- Show your commitment to the relationship, do not argue as this will only make matters worse. As long as you remain friendly, this likely opens new paths to obtaining agreement. The agreement should be a compromise in which a positive atmosphere and the personal relationship with the business partner play a role.
- Indians like to retain a certain degree of flexibility. Delays can happen at any time. Negotiation may drag on or proceed rapidly because Indians believe in "Lucky Days." Managers make every decision even trivial.
- Contracts and agreements represent the beginning of cooperation more than the end of the negotiations. If the relationship remains good, it becomes easier and easier for the Indian party to initiate business because they feel that trust is a product of a personal relationship (and not the product of a contract worded by a lawyer).
- Hierarchy between superiors and employees is usually quite marked. A superior is very rarely criticized. Criticism is usually not made directly but is wrapped carefully. The positive aspects of the relationship are emphasized first, then the criticism is made, and finally a positive encouraging statement closes the message.
- As many Indians work on multitasking, interruptions like phone calls and crosstalks could take part during negotiations.
- Written contracts should be clear and concise, without too many details. Signing the contract is important as a strong confirmation of your Indian partners' commitment.

8.2.3 Japan[4]

- The Japanese avoid formal negotiations, because for them, negotiations are a form of social conflict. Every Japanese has been taught at home and at school to avoid social conflicts. Instead, they prefer to develop an interpersonal relationship, as value for informal, frank discussions, where progress can be made on a pragmatic basis.
- Determine the size of the Japanese delegation in advance and do not send a single person to negotiation, better equally large group. Selected business partners should be decent and trustworthy people. Business deals should be the beginning of a long-term relationship.

[4]Source from book "Case Studies in Japanese Negotiating Behavior". Authors Michael Blaker, Paul Giarra, Ezra F. Vogel at US Institute of Peace Press, published 2002, access date 2.3.2021 at Google books, Page 4, Introduction page 1–11.

- The Japanese are very punctual and generally keep their appointments. In negotiations, the oldest person is shown the most respect, even if they possibly do not possess the most knowledge or the greatest ability. They are patient listeners, and this is also expected of foreigners.
- Japanese enter negotiations with very little room for maneuver, which largely excludes to use of trade-offs, bluffs, and unethical tactics. Anticipatory concessions mostly have already been made in advanced in-house, to reach a consensus. Thus, when confronted with demands for concessions, the Japanese may say "we already did that!."
- When you present a new proposal or raises new issues, the Japanese negotiating team cannot offer any response until a new in-house consensus has been forged. However, where negotiators feel that there is not a basically good relationship, they can become very stubborn.
- In conflict, the help of mediators and mentors (the person who introduced the parties to each other) is usually drawn on. The conflict is then addressed indirectly and possible solutions are outlined.
- Talks and discussions are based on the common ground. Once a mutual basis of agreement has been established, the topics and differences can then be discussed in more depth. Avoid using threatening gestures during negotiations. Pushy or highly emotional negotiating techniques would not lead to a positive result either.
- Silence (and this might last minutes), during negotiations, for example, is not unpleasant for the Japanese. Rather, it is a sign of deep thought. It is extremely impolite to interrupt someone who is speaking.
- An agreement or a contract is evidence of a good relationship but not a formal declaration of the fixed terms governing collaboration. A contract can always be renegotiated by either party if need be. The transfer of know-how follows a clear hierarchy: The supplier is situated beneath the customer in the hierarchy and is dependent on the customer.

8.2.4 South Korea[5]

[5]Source: https://instruction2.mtsac.edu/rjagodka/busm_51_project/Negotiating/SouthKorea.pdf; Article "Negotiating International Business—South Korea". Page 1–9, author Lothar Katz, published 2008, access date 2.3.2021.

- Korean negotiators are willing to spend considerable time gathering information and discussing various details before the bargaining stage of a negotiation can begin. At this point, they try to find the other side's weaknesses to gain bargaining advantages. Overall, negotiations will be protracted. Relationship building, information gathering, bargaining, and decision making take extensive time.
- In negotiations, both sides are expected to "take care of each other" because they are partners in a mutual dependency that is bound by their relationship. Negotiators may focus equally on near-term and long-term benefits.
- Koreans believe that tough negotiating may require extreme measures but that neither side should take anything personally. Even if Koreans can be very emotional, aggressive, or outwardly adversarial, foreigners are expected to remain more controlled. It is best to remain calm, friendly, patient, and persistent.
- Never allow issues during the negotiation process to create personal conflicts with your counterparts. Should a dispute arise at any stage of a negotiation, you might be able to reach resolution through emphasizing personal relationships and re-establishing trust.
- Sharing apparently confidential information or asking confidential IP questions, your Korean counterparts may just "test the waters." They may only be looking to learn more about your product or service, deciding that they prefer to build rather than to buy. Be prepared to protect your intellectual property throughout your negotiation, even if the other side requests early access.
- It may be effective to have side discussions on a one-to-one basis with the most influential person on the Korean side. In difficult situations, harmony takes the highest priority. To keep face, conflicts are not normally brought out into open. Remain cool and calm. Keep a smile. Keep the atmosphere during the negotiation as positive and pleasant as possible.
- Negotiations should be held between superiors of equal status on the respective sides. The supplier is expected to be represented by a higher management level. In Korea, decisions are usually made by the upper levels of the hierarchy, but it can take some time before managers at top level can be contacted and convinced.
- If your Korean counterparts stall and slow down the negotiation, carefully assess whether they are evaluating alternatives or that they are not interested in doing business with you. However, mostly this behavior indicates an attempt to create time pressure in order to obtain concessions.
- A contract often only forms the basis for further negotiation. The personal relationship with your partner is much more important than the contract. It is not unusual for them to reopen a discussion over items that had already been agreed upon. Negotiators from strongly monochronic cultures may find this style highly confusing and irritating.

8.2.5 Vietnam[6]

- It is important to note that the Vietnamese society is family-oriented, as well as community concerns, will almost always come before individual or business needs.
- Do not be late and always make appointments for meetings. Like in the USA, remember to reconfirm meetings a day before, particularly if it is set outside the company. Do not arrange meetings during Vietnamese New Year holidays. The dress code for business meetings in Vietnam is a dark-colored suit and tie for men in the north and white-colored suits and casual apparel in the south.
- You must invest in the relationship before you begin the negotiation. For Vietnamese, the creation of trust, comfort, and mutual respect come before business communication. As a result, negotiating in Vietnam is a bit slow due to the time it takes to build a relationship with a potential client. During a meeting, you should shake hands with all members in the room, starting with the oldest and highest ranked person. Vietnamese women offer their hands first. If they do not initiate the gesture, you can bow slightly as a sign of respect.
- One of the ways to build a relationship, by which you convey respect and appreciation for your Vietnamese business partner, is to exchange small gifts (alcoholic beverages, tea, fruits, or flowers). You should avoid sharp objects, such as scissors or knives, which symbolize the cutting of the relationship. Avoid black wrapping paper, which evokes misfortune and is frequently associated with funerals. However, the color red represents luck and wealth, while green is associated with rebirth and renewal.
- Additionally, Vietnamese place maximum value on harmony and therefore they avoid openly addressing conflict. Use casual, unofficial talks during coffee breaks or when eating together to determine what stage of agreement you have reached with your counterparts.
- In price negotiations, Vietnamese business partners are very much open to financial arguments. Cost structures, financial possibilities, and the need to ensure profits can all be brought into the discussion. There is no risk of losing face.

[6] Source: https://www.cekindo.vn/blog/business-culture-in-vietnam-negotiation-and-gifts-giving; article posted 8.03. 2019, last update on 19.02. 2021; author Cekindo. Access date 2.3.2021.

- The speaker in negotiation is not the decision maker. Negotiations with various departments are normally required. The decision-making process may take a very long time.
- Written agreements, minutes, or contracts may not be regarded as binding but will be seen as the basis for a business relationship and more detailed discussion. Therefore, be aware of the bureaucracy. The application of law is not often defined.
- As Vietnamese embraces reciprocation as part of their values, after being invited for a dinner, you are recommended to arrange a return dinner as well, with a location that is of the same quality and standard.

8.2.6 Malaysia and Singapore[7]

- Interpersonal relationship plays an important role in this region. It is the basis of a functioning long-term social relationship. Concepts of face, harmony, and Chinese negotiation tactics govern the large number of Chinese based in companies there. It is good to study Chinese stratagems and underlying strategy and the Chinese way of doing business first, before starting negotiations with them.
- Even there are Chinese, Malaysia, and Singapore are Moslem countries. All taboos and etiquettes regarding Moslem should be given great attention. Described as a minefield of multicultural sensitivities and as the most ethnically diverse region in the Asian Pacific, racial harmony has been given the highest priority in this region.

[7] Source: https://resources.sansan.com/blog/5-ways-to-negotiate-effectively-in-singapore-and-malaysia; article posted 30 APRIL 2020 by SANSAN; Access date 2.3.2021.

- Due to the special relationship between Malaysia and Singapore, making comparison between the two countries should be very careful, as Malaysia's attitudes to Singapore and vice versa are very ambivalent.
- Address people there with their last name. First name basis cannot be assumed, as in the west.
- Mutual gains are usually the goal in a business deal. Win-win is especially important in Singapore and Malaysia, where the concept of "saving face" is always a consideration. Try your best to ensure that everyone leaves the negotiating table with something positive, which will make future discussions much smoother.
- Often, people will say something like, "We'll think about it," which means "no." That means they are simply not interested. In this case, it is the best for you to move on to another point.
- It is useful to keep track of your discussions with each individual in the meeting room. That way you will be prepared the next time you meet them. Their hobbies and preferences can be extremely valuable as you build the relationship.
- Singaporeans and Malaysians are known to appreciate a good bargain. It is the same in the boardroom. Be prepared to work out how much concession your company can give, even before you sit down to work on a deal.
- Avoid informal handshakes. Any contract made between two parties in Malaysia falls under the Contract Act 1950. Contracts should be detailed and precise in order to avoid any ambiguity. Thus, a formal contract is always preferred over an informal agreement.
- Familiarity with negotiation tactics and knowledge with the contracts of local business environment will be instrumental in your success.

8.2.7 Indonesia[8]

- Indonesia is primarily a Muslim country. All taboos and etiquettes regarding Muslim should be given great attention.

[8]Source from book "Islam and Popular Culture in Indonesia and Malaysia", edited by Andrew N. Weintraub at Routledge; published 2011. Access date 2.3.2021.

- The flight is booked, meetings confirmed, and appointment with agenda is set. If you are unpunctual, you should be either very important or provide good reasons for your delay.
- Appointments with longer lead are often understood as tentative and nonbinding and thus may be changed on short notice. A better way is therefore to catch up with someone on short notice or even by just showing up at their office. If the person is not available, you might be asked to come again later or simply to wait until the person is free to meet you. So, always have a good book with you to overcome the time waiting for someone.
- However, dealing with time here is relaxed and flexible. There is serenity in speed. A fixed time agenda is rather more a framework. The advantage is it opens up good opportunities to extend an appointment if that seems helpful.
- In negotiation process, there is a lot of showing politeness, beating around the bush or endless small talk. For a business traveler having a tight schedule, this may be quite irritating.
- However, what in Indonesia counts is not the result, but the quality of the relationship between business partners. Negotiations are therefore lengthy and require several appointments until the desired result has been reached. Are some points simply ignored or not further discussed shows that they are either not important or it indicates rejection by your partner.
- Within your meetings, delegation you should discuss and define the roles (as negotiator, expert, arbitrator, observer, and mediator) well in advance and distribute tasks before the meeting takes place.
- It is recommended that your team shows up with the same number of participants as your Indonesian negotiation partners do.
- Hierarchy and seniority play a decisive role. Consensus decisions and the seniority principle are still the most common features of decision making. Small talk is certainly a goodway to get to know the other party and build trust as you establish a relationship.
- Silence can be used in Indonesian culture to communicate extremely different messages. Depending on the context and the situation, it can be interpreted as extreme rejection or extreme attentiveness. For example, pondering silence is a sign that a statement is considered carefully.
- If you would like to invite your counterparts, the hotel you choose will give a first impression of your status to your negotiation partner. Therefore, pay attention to the good reputation of your house. Very popular is to hold talks by a lunch, dinner, or brunch.
- Interruptions are not taboo, nor do they signal the collapse of negotiations. Instead, they give you a chance to continue the talks behind the scenes and solve ambiguities. Are negotiations getting stuck or conflicts arise, search for the support of an Indonesian expert or adviser.

Glossary

Amendment This is an addition to a completed written document, most commonly a proposed change or explanation (such as a list of goods to be included) in a contract, or a point that has been subject of negotiation after the contract was originally proposed by one party.

BP Business Development

CIP (Continuous Improvement Process) This is a series of actions taken to identify, analyze, and improve existing processes within an organization to meet new goals and objectives. These actions often follow a specific methodology or strategy to create successful results.

COGS Cost of goods sold

CRM Customer relationship management

CSR Corporate social responsibility

DDP "Delivered duty paid" means that the exporter completes the import clearance procedure at the destination specified by both the import and export parties, and then hands the goods over to the importer.

DFSS Design for Six Sigma

DMAIC Define–measure–analyze–improve–control refers to a data-driven improvement cycle used for improving, optimizing, and stabilizing business processes and designs.

DTD Door to door, pick-up to delivery to location decided by end customer.

ECOCUT Effective cost cutting, trademark of GTEC in China.

EOQ Economic order quantity

EHS Environment, health, and safety

FMEA Failure mode effect analysis

GTEC German Technology and Engineering Cooperation, support of Western companies with profit growth in Asia. www.gtec.asia

Kaizen strategies These are the methodologies and measures implemented to achieve the desired future state, according to the Lean vision.

KPIs (key performance indicators) KPIs are quantifiable measurements, agreed to beforehand, that reflect the critical success factors of an organization.

LCC Low-cost country

K. Zuerl, *Effective Cost Cutting in Asia*, Management for Professionals,
https://doi.org/10.1007/978-3-030-82782-3

Lean drivers These are the aspects of business for which the client is willing to pay because they are perceived as indicators of success.
LPTA Lowest price, technically acceptable
MFA Material flow analysis
MFG Manufacturing
MHR Machine hour rate
MIM Metal injection molding
MOCs Manufacturing overhead costs
MOHCs Manufacturing overhead costs
MOQ Minimum order quantity
NPM Nonproduction material
OEE Overall equipment efficiency
PDCA Plan–do–check–act
PM Purchasing manager
QM Quality management
R&D Research & Development
RCA Root cause analysis
RFQ Request for quotation
RMO Repair, maintenance, and operations
RMOCs Residual manufacturing overhead costs
SC Supply chain
SD leader This is the person responsible for managing the supplier development program, guiding the supplier through a series of kaizen strategies to achieve the desired future situation.
SG&A Sales, General & Admin Expenses
Shop floor This refers to the specific place where actions are taken place, meaning the working area, the warehouses, etc., depending on the information that wants to be obtained.
SIOP Sales Inventory and Operations Planning
SMED Single-minute exchange die
SPC Statistical process control
SPECTRA Supplier Process Evaluation and Cost Transparency: trademark of GTEC in China
SQE Supplier quality engineer
SQA Supplier quality assurance
SRM Supplier relationship management
TPM Total productive maintenance
TPS Toyota Production System
TQM Total quality management
TTP Throughput time (manufacturing cycle time)
VAVE Value analysis value engineering
VSA Value stream analysis
VSM Value stream mapping

Value stream design The representation of the future state desired according to the company's Lean vision

Value stream mapping/analysis The representation of the current state of the value stream serves to visualize waste and find opportunity areas to improve the value stream.

Value stream planning This is a tool for the holistic optimization of business and production processes. It simplifies the analysis and data gathering process in order to visualize existing value streams from supplier to production and at last to the final consumer. Special symbols are representing different activities, material movements, and information flows within this chain.

VSM team It is formed by the key personnel of the value stream, who knows it at its best. It includes logistics, production, quality, maintenance, and management leaders.

WFOE Wholly foreign enterprise

Index

A

ABC analysis, 24
Accounting, 92, 98, 104–108, 292
Aluminium, 238
ANDON, 120
ASAICHI, 25, 120, 144, 145, 156, 157, 277
Asia Pacific, 357–358
Automotive, xxv

B

Basic development costs, 286
BD, xxv
Benchmarking, 8, 23, 27, 46, 48, 49, 51, 54, 60, 61, 108, 109, 113, 114, 177, 221, 264, 298–309, 323
Best-in-class, 184–187
Bullwhip effect, 208

C

Certifications, 129
Chaku Chaku, 123
Change management, 286
Changeover time, 68, 148–150
Cherry picking, 334
China, viii, xi, xiii, xxv, xxvi, 6–8, 14, 17, 19–21, 44–54, 59–61, 70, 91, 101, 104, 119, 165, 167, 176, 178, 182, 214–218, 232, 233, 235, 236, 238, 239, 244, 252–257, 261–265, 280–283, 291, 292, 294, 297–309, 317, 318, 339, 341, 359–363
Cognitive procurement, 223
Communication, 176, 221, 335, 358
Consumables, 3, 53
Continuous improvement process (CIP), 120, 122, 144, 155, 156, 371
Contract2Pay, 222
Copper, 234–236
Cost analysis, 25
Cost breakdown (CBD), 114–118, 225–316
Cost calculation, 3, 6, 11, 16, 94, 96, 230, 249, 253, 266, 270, 272, 273, 275, 290, 312, 316, 338
Cost drivers, 8, 10, 113, 175, 269, 320, 321
Cost reduction, vii, 15, 17, 18, 20, 21, 23, 24, 37, 43, 54, 58–60, 70, 91, 94, 112, 123, 169, 171, 181, 299, 331
Cost savings, 11–15, 160, 230, 231, 250
Costs of goods sold (COGS), 102, 105, 227, 288
Cost structure analysis, 225–316
Critical situations, 335–337
C-TPAT, 131
Cultural diversity, 357
Customer management, 207–209
Customer relationship management (CRM), 166–169

D

Databases, 21–22, 178, 296, 309–316, 320, 327
Define–measure–analyze–improve–control (DMAIC), 34, 35
Delivered duty paid (DDP), 182
Delivery terms, 3, 292
Design changes, 286
Design for Six Sigma (DFSS), 121
Dies & moulds, 36, 51
Difficult situations, 328–334, 338
Digital RFQs, 222
Direct costing, 104–107
Distributors, 307
Downtime, 40, 149, 150

K. Zuerl, *Effective Cost Cutting in Asia*, Management for Professionals,
https://doi.org/10.1007/978-3-030-82782-3

E
E-auctions, 222
ECOCUT, vii, viii, xxvi, 2–4, 6–17, 20, 90, 139, 140, 165, 271–277, 316, 320, 321, 323–325, 327–331, 338–340
Economic order quantity (EOQ), 110, 111, 371
Electricity prices, 255
Electronic catalogue management, 223
Environment–Health–Safety (EHS), 54
E-sourcing, 223
Example, 44–54, 99, 100, 105, 117, 142, 143, 156, 158–160, 163, 182, 183, 230, 231, 250, 288, 314, 348–354
Exercise, 99, 100, 251, 257–259

F
Face, 357, 358, 360, 363
Failure mode effect analysis (FMEA), 124, 266, 320
First supplier development visit (FSDV), 135, 140, 142
5S, 67, 69, 125, 126
5 Ws, 124
Fixed costs, 140, 258
Forklifts, 46, 47, 278, 297–298

G
German Technology and Engineering Cooperation (GTEC), vii, viii, xiii, xxvi, 1–18, 32, 45, 52, 55, 57, 92, 94–97, 100, 158–160, 165, 230, 231, 250, 288, 300–302, 304, 306, 308, 316, 358, 359
Gross Salary Costs, 280–283

H
Harmony, 357, 360
Hierarchy, 357, 360, 362, 364, 370
Hoshin, 127

I
India, xxv, 176, 235, 252, 284, 291, 363–364
Indirect communication, 357
Indonesia, 238, 291, 369–370
Industrial electricity, 253–257
Integrated digitalization, 223, 224
Inventory, 25, 32, 124, 126, 147, 151, 157, 175, 176, 225, 292, 294–297

J
Japan, xxv, 217, 235, 252, 291, 364–365

K
Kaizen, 42–45, 67, 70, 120, 122, 123, 127, 371
Kanban, 67, 121, 123, 124
Key performance indicators (KPI), 15, 25–27, 117, 126, 132–135, 141, 142, 144, 151, 152, 155–158, 161, 162, 178, 294, 296, 297
Kingdee, 132
Knowledge management, 222

L
Lead, 22, 23, 25, 37, 137, 142, 143, 147, 157, 161, 162, 164, 192, 237, 314, 352
Lead buyers, 22, 23, 37
Lean office, 43
Lean production, 125
Lenovo, 217
Levelling, 123
Logistics, 28–31, 36, 46, 59, 112, 133, 134, 142, 144, 162, 173, 226, 292
Low cost countries (LCC), 182, 183, 261, 263, 264
Lowest price technically acceptable (LPTA), 108–109
Low-hanging fruit, 27–28, 31–42, 59–60

M
Machine hour rate (MHR), 248, 257–259
Machines, 47, 51–52, 94, 253, 280
Maintenance costs, 253
Maintenance overheads, 280
Malaysia, xxv, 368–369
Manufacturing costs, 3, 100–101, 226–228, 247–248
Manufacturing overhead costs (MOHCs), 277–283
Manufacturing overheads, 277–283
Manufacturing step, 100, 228–229
Material costs, 3, 98–100, 229–241
Material flow analysis (MFA), 122
Material overhead costs (MOC), 3, 98, 270
MFG, xxv, 123
Milk run, 123
Minimum order quantity (MOQ), 23, 129

Minimum salaries, 281
Mould, 266, 270
MUDA, 124

N
Negotiations, vii, xxv, 1, 2, 6, 8, 10, 11, 16, 21, 23, 47, 49, 51, 52, 54, 91, 94, 98, 103–105, 115, 118, 165, 169, 174, 179, 215, 220, 317, 319–328, 331–335, 338, 341–355, 359–370
Nickel, 237–238
Nonproduction material (NPM), xi, 37, 44–55, 220

O
Objections, 329, 336, 337
On-time delivery (OTD), 128, 135, 165
Operators, 60, 92, 119, 127, 137, 142, 143, 157, 162, 163, 256, 282, 294, 307–309
Overall equipment effectiveness (OEE), 68, 126, 127, 140, 142, 143, 148–150, 157, 161–164, 259–261
Overheads, 2, 3, 98, 102–103, 115, 118, 225–227, 248, 270–288

P
Parcel express, 305
Payment terms, 129
Plan–do–check–act (PDCA), 122, 156
Plastic, 2, 169, 222, 241
Poka yoke, 120, 124
Price Barometer, 244–259
Process evaluation, xxvi, 6, 90–96, 165
Procure2Pay, 222
Production capabilities and capacity, 130
Productivity, 24, 33, 40, 42, 63–118, 121, 126, 143, 149, 154, 164, 259, 260, 318
Profit, xxvi, 3, 102, 118, 226, 227, 284, 287–289
Profit margin, 287
Project management, 36, 43, 44, 53, 221, 320–322
Pull principle, 123
Pull system, 121
Purchasing controlling, 201
Purchasing manager (PM), 56
Purchasing performance, 184
Purchasing process, 194–212

Q
Quality gate, 321–325
Quality management (QM), xxv, 127

R
Railway service, 303–305
Raw materials, 3, 151, 226, 232–241
Rejected material, 99
Relationship, 170–172, 265, 339, 357, 358, 366
Repair, maintenance, and operations (RMO), 47
Request for quotation (RFQ), 6, 24, 139, 140, 303
Research and development (R&D), 16, 44, 50, 102, 115, 168, 174, 227, 269
Residual manufacturing overhead costs (RMOC), 3, 314
Risk costs, 96
Risk management, 202
Robotic process automation, 222
Root cause analysis (RCA), 124, 125

S
Sales, General & Admin Expenses (SG&A), 226, 278, 280, 283–285, 288
Sales inventory and operations planning (SIOP), 121
Savings, vii, viii, 15, 36–37, 56, 161, 226, 247
Scrap, 99, 141–143, 145, 148–151, 157, 161–163, 228, 230, 232, 251, 312
Sea freight, 303
Shainin, 124
Shop floor, 155, 372
Singapore, 128, 217, 291, 341, 368–369
Single-minute exchange of die (SMED), 69, 120, 260
Six Sigma, 34, 121, 222
Sourcing strategies, 192–194
Source-to-pay processes, 223
South Korea, 216, 291, 365–366
SPECTRA, xxvi, 6, 165, 166, 169
Standardization, 59, 265
Statistical process control (SPC), 124, 221
Steel, 239–241, 311
Stratagems, 341–355
Strategies, 122, 320–327, 332, 342, 343, 346
Supplier development (SD), 9, 15–17, 115, 119–172, 219, 222, 372
Supplier diagnosis, 67–90
Supplier engineering development costs, 286

Supplier ethical data exchange (SEDEX), 131
Supplier management, 199–201, 206–207, 222
Supplier pyramid, 24, 134
Supplier quality assurance (SQA), 125, 263
Supplier quality engineers (SQEs), 9, 15, 17, 127, 169, 219, 221
Supplier relationship management (SRM), 166–169
Supplies, 1, 30, 53–54, 59, 90, 119, 160, 161, 176, 220–222, 229–231, 250, 284, 294, 296
Supply chain (SC), xxv, 1, 9, 59, 60, 90, 119, 127, 160, 203, 205, 212, 219–222, 294, 296, 372
Supply-chain manager, 203–212
Surcharges, 102–103, 226, 227

T
Taxes, 248, 279, 284, 290–292
Teamwork, 59–60, 115, 166, 182
Teardown, 22–23
Terms of payment, 289–290
Ticket-tool-system, 223
Time—throughput (TTP), 68
Tin, 236–238
Tooling costs, 253, 265
Toolshops, 261–265
Total productive maintenance (TPM), xxv, 67, 69, 127, 259–261
Total quality management (TQM), 126
Toyota production system (TPS), xxv, 16, 63–66, 134, 222
Transportation, vii, 24, 46, 51, 59, 124, 127, 149, 182, 244, 278, 282, 297–309, 317

U
Useful phrases, 336

V
Value-stream, 123, 144–146, 373
Value stream analysis (VSA), 172
Value stream mapping (VSM), 134, 145, 373
Variable costs, 104–106, 249, 258
VA workshop, 113
Vietnam, xxv, 244, 291, 367–368

W
Warehouse, 99, 140, 292, 294, 295
Waste, 54, 98, 127, 230, 313
Websites, 212, 214–219, 283
Wholly foreign enterprise (WFOE), 19
Win-win, 331–334
Workflow systems, 222
Working standards, 125

Y
Yamazumi, 127
Yearly negotiations, 340–341

Z
Zinc, 236
Zoning, 125

The manufacturer's authorised representative in the EU is Springer
Nature Customer Service Centre GmbH, Europaplatz 3, 69115 Heidelberg,
Germany. If you have any concerns regarding our products, please
contact ProductSafety@springernature.com

Printed and bound by CPI Group (UK) Ltd, Croydon, CR0 4YY
30/09/2026
02225699-0013